MILITARY TRIALS OF WAR CRIMINALS IN THE NETHERLANDS EAST INDIES 1946–1949

Military Trials of War Criminals in the Netherlands East Indies 1946–1949

FRED L. BORCH

with best wishes,
and in friendship —

OXFORD
UNIVERSITY PRESS

OXFORD
UNIVERSITY PRESS

Great Clarendon Street, Oxford, OX2 6DP,
United Kingdom

Oxford University Press is a department of the University of Oxford.
It furthers the University's objective of excellence in research, scholarship,
and education by publishing worldwide. Oxford is a registered trade mark of
Oxford University Press in the UK and in certain other countries

First Edition published in 2017

Impression: 1

Published in the United States of America by Oxford University Press
198 Madison Avenue, New York, NY 10016, United States of America

British Library Cataloguing in Publication Data
Data available

Library of Congress Control Number: 2017945344

ISBN 978–0–19–877716–8

Printed and bound by
CPI Group (UK) Ltd, Croydon, CR0 4YY

Foreword

This book on the post-Second World War trials of war criminals in what was then called the Netherlands East Indies is as remarkable as it is shocking to read.

In the Netherlands today recent research by Remy Limpach, and other Dutch historians, has revealed that the Dutch armed forces committed war crimes against both Indonesian civilians and insurgents between 1946 and 1949. These war crimes arose out of Dutch attempts to reestablish colonial rule in the East Indies after 1945, which required defeating Indonesian insurgents who wanted freedom from Dutch colonial rule. The revelations of Limpach and others have provoked much controversy and soul-searching among the Dutch, and that is a good thing. But what is remarkable about Fred Borch's book is that it *complements* the history uncovered by Limpach and others, in that it shows that the inhabitants of the East Indies had already been victims of war crimes. Certainly, some members of the Dutch armed forces committed war crimes against Indonesians but the Dutch and other inhabitants of the colony had themselves been victims of war crimes at the hands of the Japanese occupier between 1942 and 1945. Based on primary archival material, chiefly the war crimes records of tribunal judgments involving more than 350 Japanese, Dutch, Chinese, and Indonesian defendants, Fred Borch uncovers the horrific nature of the war crimes committed by Japanese forces, assisted by thousands of Indonesian, and also a few Dutch collaborators.

As the first and only comprehensive English-language book about Dutch war crimes prosecutions in the Netherlands East Indies, Borch's critical analysis is truly groundbreaking, in that he unearthed and worked meticulously through many trial records and files. But Fred Borch also manages to place the history and the specific nature of these crimes in a broader context, in the sense that they should be considered a "manifestation of the race war," triggered by the "Asia for Asians" ideology and the "code of Bushido"—thus demonstrating an empirical link between the Japanese ideology and their conduct in war.

This book is not only about Dutch lawyers trying to do justice to their history. Those responsible for committing war crimes had not only murdered and tortured the Dutch, but they had also severely mistreated Eurasian, Chinese, Indian, Malay, and Indonesian citizens of the East Indies. Fred Borch argues that, rather than viewing these trials as late-colonial attempts to demonstrate the illegal character of the Japanese occupation, or to show how the Dutch came to liberate the Indies from the Japanese occupation, these war crimes prosecutions were part and parcel of an Allied plan to restore order and justice, and to show that in the new world order created by the United Nations, war crimes would no longer go unpunished. Millions of men, women, and children had died during the Second World War, and those who were responsible should be punished for any war crimes connected to these deaths.

Obviously, the history of the Dutch counterinsurgency campaigns and military offensive against the newly independent Republic of Indonesia has largely obfuscated the parallel legal history of the war crimes committed by the Japanese against the Dutch, Eurasians, and other citizens of the Indies. Still, history is not neat and tidy, and Fred Borch offers us this striking narrative of a Dutch way of dealing with vicious crimes committed against them by means of international law, while the Dutch were at the same time committing crimes that were similarly atrocious. How ironic, and how unfortunate.

Fred Borch is probably the only historian who could have written this book in this fashion. Having lived in the Netherlands as a child, speaking the language fluently, working as a military lawyer in the US Army for twenty-five years, he combines all the professional and inside knowledge necessary for assembling the material and writing it down in a sober yet compelling way.

The chapters are organized around the types of war crimes, including trials for violations of the terms of the armistice, criminal group responsibility (instead of adjudicating only single war criminals), and trials for mass murder and unlawful executions. Most striking is the chapter on forced prostitution. For the first time in legal history, perpetrators were being brought to justice who had engaged in a "large scale officially organized system of rape." Korean, Chinese, Filipina, and Dutch women and girls had been forced into prostitution in brothels licensed by the Japanese military. With this particularly sensitive topic, Fred Borch shows how the law dealt with this war crime, thus demonstrating that judicial action can be important in history—as exhausting and unnerving for the legal specialist and the victims as this may be.

Fred Borch does not shy away from controversial issues involving the law, legitimacy and efficiency. Did the organization of the trials enable the Dutch to obtain a good outcome? Was it a satisfactory form of retribution, given that so many defendants were put to trial and sentenced? The trials had far less of a pedagogical or educational impact than the Nuremberg trials had in post-Second World War Germany, if for no other reason than they occurred thousands of miles from Europe and were overshadowed by both Nuremberg and Tokyo. Certainly, these Dutch trials were not as extensively covered in the news media as have been the trials of Balkan war criminals since the 1990s. Yet what the Dutch authorities did in the Netherlands East Indies from 1946 to 1949 was a much more thorough endeavor than the Dutch managed to carry out with the special courts against Dutch collaborators and war criminals in the motherland, the Netherlands itself, after the defeat of Nazi Germany.

What this book does show is that the issues of retribution, purification, and adjudication after military conflicts can be both inevitable and ambivalent. Inevitable in that there will always be a desire to affix responsibility or attach blame to the losing party in a conflict. Ambivalent in that, despite the best intentions, a selected process may lead to ambivalent results. But this book also demonstrates how little those in power, in this instance the Dutch authorities in the Indies, were capable of learning from history in seeking justice and upholding law and order themselves. With this in mind, Fred Borch's study is a tragedy because it shows how a state may believe it is winning a struggle to restore a legal, and even moral order after a war is concluded, when it is actually losing the peace.

Professor Dr. Beatrice A. de Graaf
Professor of History of International Relations and Governance
University of Utrecht, Netherlands

Table of Contents

List of Illustrations

Maps

Photos

Tables

Introduction

The post-World War II trials of war criminals in the Netherlands East Indies (NEI) are not well known, and the chief goal of this book is to change that forever, if only because these prosecutions were unique in legal history.

Between September 1946 and December 1949, Dutch colonial authorities convicted 1,038 Japanese (and Koreans and Formosans) and a handful of Europeans, Eurasians, Chinese, and Indonesians for war-related offenses. NEI authorities convened nearly 450 "temporary courts-martial" in twelve locations in the archipelago known today as Indonesia; only U.S. authorities conducting war crimes trials in the Asiatic-Pacific Theater held more trials.

While these numbers alone make the NEI war crimes trials worth researching and writing about, their unusual features—some of which were unique legal history—make them even more deserving of study. For example, the Dutch took a radically different approach when they created the legal system for trying war crimes, in that they departed from their civil code tradition and instead used customary international law as the basis for war crimes prosecutions. The Dutch also tried war-related offenses that had not previously been prosecuted by any nation at any tribunal. Alone among the Allies conducting war crimes trials, the NEI authorities successfully prosecuted Japanese soldiers for the war crime of forced prostitution. The Dutch also were the only Allied nation successfully to prosecute Japanese soldiers for the war crime of violating the terms of the armistice after the cessation of hostilities in August 1945. Finally, NEI authorities were also unique in prosecuting "criminal groups" for war crimes. In these prosecutions, where the evidence showed that war crimes were committed within the framework of the activities of a group of persons, the group was tried and convicted. Individual members of the organization then were sentenced based on their level of involvement in the war crimes committed collectively by the organization. No other Allied war crimes tribunal took this approach to determining criminal liability. These and other unusual aspects of NEI war crimes trials are addressed in the chapters that follow this introduction.

With that as background, *Military Trials of War Criminals in the Netherlands East Indies (1946–1949)* is organized in the following manner. Chapter 1 sets the stage by providing a brief history of the Dutch in the East Indies from 1595, when sailors from Amsterdam first arrived in the islands, until the surrender of Dutch forces to the Japanese in 1942. Chapter 2 examines how Japan's "Asia for

Military Trials of War Criminals in the Netherlands East Indies 1946–1949, Fred L. Borch.

the Asians" philosophy and the code of "Bushido" are the key to understanding what happened during the Japanese occupation of the Indies from 1942 to 1946. Chapter 3 discusses how temporary courts-martial were created and organized in the NEI to prosecute war criminals after World War II, including how the colonial authorities determined the law and procedure for these trials. Chapter 4 looks at how evidence was gathered and cases selected for prosecution.

With these four chapters as background, the next seven chapters look at cases by categories of crimes. Chapter 5 examines trials for the mistreatment of civilians, prisoners of war, and civilian internees. Chapter 6 discuses prosecutions for mass murder and unlawful executions. Chapter 7 looks at trials for the war crime of forced prostitution. Chapter 8 examines group criminal responsibility and Chapter 9 discusses trials for violations of the terms of the armistice. Chapter 10 looks at cases where the defendants—all senior ranking officers—were prosecuted for war crimes based on a command responsibility theory of liability. Chapter 11 looks at prosecutions of Dutch nationals for collaboration with the Japanese enemy.

Chapter 12, the last chapter, tells the story of the abrupt end to the war crimes prosecutions in the NEI, and the repatriation of the Japanese war criminals in 1949. A brief "Conclusion" provides some observations on the importance of the Dutch war crimes prosecutions in legal history and their impact on the development of the law of armed conflict.

An important question is why this book is the first comprehensive treatment of NEI war crimes trials to be published in any language, and why it has taken more than sixty-five years for any detailed treatment of the topic to reach non-Dutch language readers. There seem to be at least three reasons for this lack of research and writing on the subject. First, professional historians—and members of the public in the Netherlands—were chiefly interested in the experiences of the Dutch under Nazi rule in World War II. Consequently, the focus of post-1945 war crimes scholarship has concentrated almost exclusively on the horrific acts committed by German troops in the Netherlands from 1940 to 1945, especially the brutal treatment of Dutch Jews.

Second, the failure of the Dutch to reestablish colonial authority in the NEI between 1946 and 1949 meant the end of a way of life in an area of the world that had been under Dutch rule for more than 300 years. The thousands and thousands of men, women, and children who now were unwelcome in the newly independent Indonesia, and left the archipelago for the Netherlands, hoped to find a more welcoming land. They soon discovered, however, that life in the Netherlands required them to forget the past, or at least keep their experiences to themselves. No one wanted to be reminded of Dutch failures—political and military—in the NEI. Moreover, the Dutch who had suffered under Nazi rule in World War II were in no mood to hear about any suffering these newcomers had experienced at the hands of the Japanese during the occupation of the NEI. As a result, those who had suffered in Japanese prisoner of war and internment camps were discouraged from talking about their experiences, and this inevitably meant that there was less interest in any study of war crimes committed by the Japanese, much less the war crimes trials that had been held between 1946 and 1949. Finally, once these NEI colonial transplants to the Netherlands began to age and then pass from the scene, interest in their life and times during the Japanese occupation diminished even more, if for no other reason than there were fewer and fewer victims of Japanese war crimes to tell their stories.

As an aside, this relative lack of interest in war crimes committed *during* the Japanese occupation does not apply to war crimes committed after 1945 by Dutch forces against Indonesian rebels during counterinsurgency operations, as evidenced by the recently published *Colonial Counterinsurgency and Mass Violence: The Dutch Empire in Indonesia* (2014) and the Dutch-language *De brandende kampongs van Generaal Spoor* (The burning *kampongs* [villages] of General Spoor) (2016).

While these two reasons probably best explain the dearth of research and writing on the topic, there is a third and more practical reason: The war crimes records of trial are written in Dutch, and only a few have been translated into English. This meant that, even if a historian was interested in studying the prosecution of war criminals in the NEI, that scholar had to be sufficiently fluent in Dutch to be able to read and understand these primary sources. Since non-native speakers of Dutch are few in number, and the language is difficult to learn unless one has family connections to the Netherlands or is resident there, this explains why English-language work on the topic has been limited.

A few notes about the sources. Chapters 1 and 2 rely heavily on *The Collapse of a Colonial Society* and *The Encyclopedia of Indonesia in the Pacific War*. The former is an English translation of a section of Louis de Jong's truly masterful multi-volume history of the Netherlands in World War II. It is a comprehensive, insightful, and nuanced look at the Japanese occupation of the NEI between 1942 and 1945. Any person who wants to understand the destruction of a 350-year-old colonial presence must read this book. As for the latter, it too is critical to understanding what happened in Indonesia during World War II and the encyclopedia contains a wealth of detail not found anywhere else.

The remaining chapters are based almost exclusively on my analysis of the original war crimes tribunal judgments (Dutch: *vonnissen*) involving more than 350 Japanese, Dutch, Chinese, and Indonesian defendants. These are in Dutch, are typed single-spaced (although one decision was handwritten!), and were authored by the three military judges in each case. In the rare situation where an official English translation of the Dutch decision exists, this is acknowledged in the endnotes accompanying the text. As I am fluent in Dutch, I was able to read these decisions in their original form and, unless otherwise noted, quotes from these decisions are my English translations from the Dutch. As for one of my themes in this book, that the large number of vicious and cruel war crimes committed by the Japanese in the NEI and the horrific nature of these crimes are the manifestation of the "Asia for the Asians" ideology and Code of *Bushido*, this is my own conclusion. This is not to say that others familiar with the history of the Dutch in the Indies have not reached the same conclusion; only that I arrived at this theme independently.

While my chapters rely heavily on the original Dutch temporary court-martial decisions, I would be remiss if I did not acknowledge Levinus F. de Groot's unique contribution to the topic. His privately published, two volume *Berechting Japanse Oorlogsmisdagers in Nederlands-Indië 1946–1949*, is the only comprehensive Dutch-language secondary source in existence. De Groot served as a judge on the military tribunal in Batavia from 1947 to 1949 and, consequently, when he discusses a particular war crimes trial, his first-hand knowledge of the proceedings provides a wealth of information on Japanese defendants and is a unique insight into this episode of military legal history. Unfortunately, de Groot's book is not particularly well written or well organized, and it focuses mostly on proceedings in which he participated as a judge. But that does not make it any less valuable, especially as the book contains two appendices that list all those defendants prosecuted in Batavia and all those sentenced to be shot by firing squad.

The credit for the maps belongs to the U.S. Army's Center of Military History in Washington, D.C. As for the photographs in the book, these were either in the archives of the Netherlands Institute for Military History in The Hague or the Netherlands Institute for War Documentation in Amsterdam. My thanks to all three institutions for providing these items, as they provide important context for the text.

A few notes about the text, too. The first time an individual is introduced to the reader, his or her surname is capitalized. This is chiefly because most English-language readers not only are unfamiliar with Japanese first names and surnames, but would be unable to distinguish a first name from a family name. Consequently, when first identified in the text, Army Captain Kenitji Sone is identified as Kenitji SONE. Additionally, while the Japanese would refer to this officer as Sone Kenitji (because the family name precedes a first name in Japanese), this book uses the Western style of naming when identifying Japanese defendants, so as to be consistent with Western style naming, i.e. first name followed by family name. For the sake of consistency, all last names are capitalized, even those of Europeans. Finally, the reader should also note that Indonesians (especially Javanese) in the colonial era generally did not have last (family) names. Consequently, Sukarno, the famous political and military leader, is identified simply as Sukarno.

Japanese nouns and phrases are italicized, such as *Kempeitai, Tokkeitai*, and *rōmusha*. As for Dutch words and phrases, where an English word or phrase is used, any accompanying Dutch word or phrase is italicized.

In the discussion of courts-martial, where words and phrases are in quotations (" . . . "), this indicates translated language from the court decision being discussed.

Many individuals made this book possible, but I would like to recognize a few. Mr. Piet Kamphuis, Prof. Dr. Petra Groen, and Prof. Dr. Jan Hoffenaar, all of the Netherlands Institute of Military History, sponsored my research as a Fulbright Scholar. Dr. Elly Touwen-Bouwsma and Jeroen Kemperman, both of the Nederlands Instituut voor Oorlogsdocumentatie (Netherlands Institute for War Documentation), were extraordinarily helpful in locating case files and other war crimes documentation.

Prof. Dr. Beatrice de Graaf, University of Utrecht, Prof. Suzannah Linton, Bangor University, and Prof. Gary D. Solis, U.S. Military Academy and Georgetown University, offered advice and assistance as I began to write. Professor Dr. de Graaf encouraged my initial interest in the topic and Professors Linton and Solis both read draft chapters; their comments and criticisms were extraordinarily helpful. Dr. Lisette Schouten's excellent scholarship on war crimes also helped me to better understand the topic. Finally, Prof. Bruce Vandervort, Virginia Military Institute, edited my original article on the subject before it was published in the *Journal of Military History*. The success of that article led directly to this book.

Lieutenant General (retired) Dana K. Chipman, then the Judge Advocate General of the Army, permitted me to take a leave of absence from my position as the Regimental Historian and Archivist for the Judge Advocate General's Corps in order to be a Fulbright Scholar in the Netherlands. Similarly, Colonel (retired) David Diner, then serving as the Dean of the Judge Advocate General's School, was unwavering in his support of my Fulbright Scholar application, and my research and teaching at the University of Leiden's Centre for Terrorism and Counterterrorism in the Netherlands. Professor Jack L. Goldsmith, Harvard Law School and Professor Alberto R. Coll, DePaul College of Law, were equally supportive of my Fulbright endeavor, and also deserve my thanks. Were it not for my Fulbright experience, I would not have been able to undertake the research for this book.

Finally, a brilliant Fulbright recipient and Belgian attorney, Ms. Cilia Mathieu spent hours helping me with the nuances of the Dutch language in the written decisions, as did her Fulbright colleague and Dutch lawyer, Mr. Raphael Donkersloot. Thanks to both, this is a better book.

As for my own interest in the subject of Dutch war crimes prosecutions in the Indies, my three years in the Netherlands as a child, and my knowledge of the Dutch language and culture, gave me a lasting interest in the history of the Low Countries. Many years later, my service as the first Chief Prosecutor for the Military Commissions at Guantanamo Bay, Cuba, meant a very personal involvement with war crimes. More than anything else, these two factors combined to make me want to research and write about Japanese war crimes committed in the East Indies, and the military tribunals that followed.

Finally, I owe a great debt of gratitude to my wife, Janet. No one is more deserving of accolades in making this book a reality. Janet's love of the Netherlands, its people, and its culture inspired me to become a Fulbright Scholar to the Netherlands and her steadfast support of my research and writing made this book possible.

While I have done my best to be fair and accurate in this book, there are certain to be errors in the text. These are my responsibility alone.

Fred L. Borch III
Charlottesville, Virginia U.S.A.
February 2017

1

Setting the Stage

The Dutch in the East Indies from 1595 to 1942

If the British considered India to be the "jewel in the crown," then the Netherlands East Indies (NEI) must be seen as almost the entire jeweled headdress that Queen Wilhelmina and her predecessors wore as sovereigns of the Netherlands.[1] After all, at 733,000 square miles, the NEI was almost fifty times larger than the 15,000 square mile Kingdom of the Netherlands. More importantly, the rich raw materials in the archipelago—oil, rubber, tin, bauxite, nickel, and manganese—made it a critical part of the Netherlands economy in the early decades of the 20th century. In oil production alone, the NEI ranked fifth in the world in 1940.[2]

This chapter provides a context for understanding the role of the Dutch in the Indies from 1595, when sailors from Amsterdam first arrived in the islands, to 1942, when the Japanese invaded the NEI and inflicted a devastating defeat upon the colony. This history of the Dutch in the Indonesian archipelago is critical to understanding the impact of the Japanese occupation after 1942, and the nature of the war crimes committed by the Japanese on the islands. This is because the ultimate goal of the Japanese occupiers, a goal that went beyond the immediate need to capture the NEI's rich oil fields in order to wage war successfully, was to eliminate all aspects of Dutch culture and influence in the East Indies, thereby destroying a colonial society that had existed for more than three centuries. Since war crimes were an inevitable result of this goal, exploring the development of the NEI's government, people, economy, and culture—and how they existed at the time of the March 1942 invasion—provides the background for better appreciating why Japanese war crimes were so pervasive and so horrific in the NEI, and why the war crimes trials conducted by colonial authorities between 1946 and 1949 were so different from trials conducted by the Allies elsewhere after World War II.

The chapter begins with an examination of the early Dutch settlement of the archipelago and development of a colonial economy. It then discusses the emerging role of the Dutch government in the islands, and the so-called "Ethical Policy," which sought to unify the islands under Dutch rule, while implementing

[1] Queen Wilhelmina (1880–1962) reigned from 1890 to 1948, longer than any other Dutch monarch. She abdicated in favor of her daughter, Juliana, in 1948.

[2] Muhammed Abdul Aziz, *Japan's Colonialism and Indonesia* (Martinus Nijhoff 1955) 99.

European ideas about civilization, culture, and prosperity. A look at the colony's social structure in the period prior to the Second World War follows, including the emergence of a conservative (rather than liberal or progressive) ideology for governing the NEI, along with an examination of the growth of Indonesian nationalism in the early 20th century. The chapter closes with a discussion of the colony's preparations for war with Japan, examines the Japanese invasion of the NEI that began in January 1942, and ends with the surrender of the Dutch in the East Indies in March 1942. A short postscript explains what occurred between August 1945, when the Japanese surrendered, and December 1949, when the NEI ceased to exist.

The Arrival of the Dutch

The Dutch first appeared in the Indonesian archipelago in 1595, when a small fleet of ships sailing from Amsterdam arrived on the islands. In making this dangerous sea voyage, the Dutch followed the route used by the Portuguese around the southern tip of Africa, and they very much hoped to engage in the same lucrative trade that the Portuguese were enjoying with Asia. While these first Dutchmen in the "Indies" suffered tremendous losses (only 87 of the original 247 men returned to the Netherlands in 1597), the expedition was a success: Profits from the sale of spices they brought back with them not only covered the cost of the voyage but, more importantly, demonstrated that there was money to be made from buying and selling Asian goods, especially spices like cloves, nutmeg, mace, and pepper.

In 1602, the eight Dutch companies involved in the Asian trade combined to form the United East Indies Company (Dutch: *Verenigde Oost-Indies Compagnie* (VOC)). The new company was a huge financial success, and quickly established a commercial network that extended from South Africa to Japan. The focus of the VOC's activities, however, was in the Indonesian archipelago. Perhaps most importantly, the company had military and naval assets to protect—and expand—its increasingly profitable trading empire. There were confrontations with both the Spanish and Portuguese, and the VOC ultimately ejected the latter from the Moluccas or "Spice Islands." Since these islands were the chief source of the spices that originally had attracted the Portuguese to the Indian Ocean, the Dutch traders had long coveted them.

By the end of the 1600s, the VOC was headquartered in a fort called Batavia on the island of Java, and the company had a monopoly on many products important to European consumers. The VOC also gradually expanded control over more and more islands in the Indonesian archipelago, including Java, Sumatra, the Moluccas, the island of Madura, and several locations on the Celebes. The indigenous rulers did not welcome this control, but were unable to prevent it.

All went well for the VOC until increasing competition with the English East India Company, and a war between the Netherlands and England, which started in 1780 and lasted until 1784, forced the VOC to declare bankruptcy in 1796.

The company was formally dissolved in 1800 and its territorial possessions, after a brief period of control by the British, were transferred to the newly established Kingdom of the Netherlands. In 1816, the Netherlands East Indies (NEI) was formally created when the new Dutch monarch, William I, appointed a governor-general for the colony.

Evolution of the Colony

In 1830, the Netherlands introduced an economic plan designed to obtain the greatest possible financial benefit from the colony. The so-called "Culture System" (Dutch: *cultuurstelsel*), implemented on Java, was based on the idea that the government owned all the land on the island and that it was entitled to receive rent from those cultivating the soil. Each village was required to use one-fifth (later one-third) of its land to grow crops for export, such as cinnamon, cloves, coffee, indigo, nutmeg, and sugar. This also meant that roughly two-thirds of Javanese farmers and their families were forced to work on these government-destined agricultural products, for more than two months out of every year. These export crops were collected by the government, which then sold them; the profits went to the Dutch treasury. While the indigenous farmers were paid for their labor with a "crop payment," so that it might appear that both the government and the people benefited from the Culture System, as a practical matter the system was a heavy burden on the local people. The export crops could not be eaten (and so growing them did not provide any food source), they depleted the land, and they used precious water.

But the Culture System was a phenomenal success, in that profits increased from 13 million guilders in 1830 to 74 million guilders in 1840 to 725 million guilders in 1870.[3] Moreover, as this money constituted almost one-third of the national revenue for the Kingdom of the Netherlands, the government was soon convinced that the country could not survive without its colony. The NEI itself, however, did not share directly in the largesse; only a small amount of the Culture System money remained in the colony. But the Culture System did increase international trade, especially after the opening of the Suez Canal in 1869, and it stimulated Javanese industry, and increased the prosperity of some Europeans, Eurasians, and other groups involved in the export of commodities.[4]

The success of the Culture System, and the government's monopoly on the economy of the NEI, naturally engendered jealousy—and opposition—from those who wanted to share in the profitable export trade. The result was that, by the end of the 1800s, the government's monopoly was dissolved and the economy

[3] According to the Royal Netherlands Academy of Arts and Sciences, one guilder in 1870 would have the purchasing power of 25 guilders (€11, US$ 12, GB£ 9.80) in 2015. International Institute of Social History http://www.iisg.nl/hpw/calculate2.php> (last accessed 20 October 2016).

[4] Louis de Jong (with an Introduction by Jeroen Kemperman), *The Collapse of a Colonial Society: The Dutch in Indonesia during the Second World War* (KILTV Press 2002) 8–9.

of the NEI was opened to private enterprise. The growing of tea and the mining of coal, gold, and tin ore emerged as new profitable enterprises, with oil and rubber soon joining the list of important colonial exports.

The economic progress of the colony was complemented by territorial expansion. At the beginning of the 19th century, there were some 300 independent or partly-independent kingdoms in the East Indies. By the end of the century, the Dutch colonial authorities had expanded beyond Java and Madura to other islands, including Bali, Ceram, Sumatra, Timor, Celebes, and parts of Borneo and New Guinea. This geographic expansion of the NEI was not always easy; witness the forty-year long war with the inhabitant of Aceh, a sultanate on Sumatra. The struggle to overcome resistance to Dutch rule ultimately cost 400 million guilders and cost the lives of some 30,000 European and Indonesian soldiers; between 60,000 and 70,000 Aceh men, women, and children died.

Economic progress—and private enterprise—also brought population changes to the NEI. The flourishing export market meant that increasing numbers of Chinese, Arabs, and Malaysians immigrated to the islands to take advantage of economic opportunities. By 1940, there were 1.25 million Chinese, 50,000 Arabs, and 25,000 Malaysians living on NEI soil. More importantly, the Dutch population in the colony rose quickly. Before 1870, there were never more than a few thousand Dutch nationals, many of whom were soldiers or colonial administrators. By 1940, however, there were 300,000 Europeans and Eurasians. About 100,000 came from the Netherlands and 200,000 had been born in the NEI. By way of comparison, there were *four times* as many Europeans living in the Indies as there were Europeans living in British India. This fact only underscores the importance of the NEI to the Dutch, both economically, culturally, and psychologically. The inhabitants of the Netherlands saw themselves as a major player on the world stage because they, like the British, had a colony like India.

At the turn of the 20th century, the Netherlands government decided that it was time to implement a new colonial policy in the NEI. As Prime Minister Dr. Abraham Kuyper explained in a speech in 1901, the Dutch now would take an active role in the development of colony and its peoples, and would implement an "Ethical Policy" (Dutch: *Ethische Politiek*) that had two prongs. First, there "would be home rule under Dutch guidance and according to a Western model (the idea of guardianship)." Second, there would be "unification of the entire archipelago under Dutch dominion."[5] The foundation of this new policy was the firm belief that the peoples of the archipelago would achieve progress and prosperity if they embraced Western ideas about civilization and culture. The colonial authorities hoped that the Indonesian people would willingly accept the tenets of the Ethical Policy, but acknowledged that force might be required to overcome resistance (as happened in Aceh).

Those implementing the Ethical Policy, however, did try to improve living standards in the islands by promoting education, agriculture and industry, and they

[5] ibid 10.

achieved some success. By 1940, some 2.3 million Indonesian children were in primary school, and probably 40 percent of children between the ages of six and fourteen had been exposed to reading and writing in some sort of school setting. But 70 percent of the adult Indonesian population remained illiterate, which meant that the indigenous peoples of the archipelago generally were not able to take advantage of economic opportunities in business or industry. As for agriculture, improvements in irrigation meant that Java, which had the largest population of all the islands, and which suffered periodically from famine, was now a rice-exporting island. Advancements in food-production, however, were undercut by ever increasing population growth. Between 1900 and 1940, for example, the population of Java grew from 28 million to 47 million; it had been 16 million in 1870. If population growth continued at this pace, there was no way that rice production could keep up.

Finally, the Great Depression of the 1930s severely undercut any government efforts to improve the lot of Indonesians; there was simply a lack of financial resources to do all that might have been done to bring economic benefits to more segments of NEI society.[6] While the Ethical Policy had mixed results, it was the official policy of the colonial regime from 1901 until the Japanese invasion of 1942, and consequently is important to understanding how life was in the Indies in the first four decades of the 20th century.

Emergence of Indonesian Nationalism

The Ethical Policy demonstrated that the Dutch had definite ideas about the direction that the NEI should take in its development, and the shape that the future should take. The problem for the Dutch, however, was that an increasing number of inhabitants of the islands were interested in self-determination. The Europeans (mostly Dutch) and Dutch Eurasians may have been satisfied with the trajectory envisaged by the Ethical Policy, but there were more than a few Indonesians (and even some Eurasians) who were not. Like their compatriots in India and the Philippines, these politically aware individuals were interested in self-determination and freedom from Dutch colonial rule. When one remembers that there were 68 million Indonesians (including 47 million on the islands of Java and Madura alone), Indonesian nationalism—once it was born—had a large population from which to draw both adherents and energy.While a number of Indonesian associations advocated changes to the status quo in the early 1900s, most were limited in their goals and visions of the future. Not until the late 1920s did more threatening (to the Dutch) politically aware Indonesians take center stage. Chief among them was the charismatic SUKARNO,[7] an architect by education who had been born on Java in 1901. Sukarno proclaimed that there must be one fatherland, and that this nation would be called Indonesia. All Indonesians would speak one language,

[6] ibid 9–11.

[7] During this period, the Javanese generally had only a single name; Sukarno (also spelled Soekarno) was no different. For more on Sukarno see Bob Hering, *Soekarno, Founding Father of Indonesia: A Biography, 1901–1945* (KITLVP 2002).

called Indonesian (Malay). The symbol of this single indivisible nation would be a flag of one horizontal red stripe and one horizontal white stripe. It inexorably followed that there was no place for Dutch rule in Indonesia; full independence required freedom from the Dutch.

Recognizing the danger posed by Sukarno and his adherents, the NEI government arrested him and three other nationalist leaders in 1929. They were prosecuted, convicted, imprisoned, and exiled. But this only harmed Indonesian nationalism in the short term, as when Sukarno was released in late 1931, he returned to Java as a hero. He joined the newly formed *Partai Indonesia* and began mobilizing the Indonesian people with his great oratorical gifts. The result was that, on the eve of the Japanese invasion, Sukarno was the most important nationalist leader in the NEI.

Instead of listening to Sukarno and the nationalists, or beginning some kind of dialogue with them about political reforms that might be possible in the future, the Dutch colonial authorities instead worked to repress Indonesian aspirations for even limited autonomy. As expressed by the Dutch aristocrat Esquire (Dutch: *jonkheer*) B.C. de JONGE, who was the NEI Governor-General in the mid-1930s, there was no place for Sukarno and his ideology in the archipelago: "I believe that now we have worked in the Indies for three hundred years, another three hundred years will be needed before the country will perhaps be ripe for a form of autonomy."[8]

While the next Governor General, Esquire Alidius W.L. TJARDA VAN STARKENBORGH STACHOUWER, who was appointed in 1936 and served until the Japanese occupation in 1942, was somewhat more enlightened in his views about Indonesian independence, his limited reforms were simply too little, and too late. Consequently, when Dutch colonial rule ceased abruptly in March 1942, Sukarno and thousands and thousands of Indonesians looked to the Japanese as liberators who would help them achieve independence—and freedom *from* the Dutch. The inexorable result was widespread collaboration between many Indonesians and the Japanese, especially since "the great mass of the Indonesian population was not unsympathetic to Japan" and its desire to liberate Asia from colonial control.[9]

Netherlands East Indies on the Eve of World War II

On the eve of the Japanese invasion, the NEI was an economic powerhouse, at least in terms of exporting raw materials. In 1940, almost 40 percent of world rubber exports (450,000 tons annually) came from the archipelago, which meant that the Indies ranked second in the world after British Malaya. The colony ranked third in the world in the production of tin, and there was also manganese (used in alloys, such as steel), bauxite (the principal ore of aluminum), and nickel. Finally, the Dutch oil fields were producing millions of barrels of oil every year.[10]

The vast majority of the 300,000 Dutch, other Europeans, and Eurasians living in the Indies were convinced that, regardless of what might happen in the

[8] See de Jong (n. 4) 23. [9] ibid 42.

[10] War History Office of the National Defense College of Japan, *The Invasion of the Dutch East Indies* (University Press 2015) 11–12.

short term, the colonial society in which they lived, worked, and loved would survive. Whether it would continue for three more centuries, as Governor General de Jonge had envisaged in 1936, might be an open question, but few men and women resident in the archipelago thought the NEI would cease to exist in the near future, if for no other reason than that the Dutch had been in the islands for so long and seemed omnipotent.

There were at least two other reasons that the Dutch in the Indies—and those in the Netherlands—were unwilling to acknowledge that life in the islands might change. First, the NEI economy provided employment for 100,000 Dutch citizens and was a significant part in the national income of the Netherlands. No one was interested in losing these golden eggs. A Dutch saying expressed it best: "With the Indies gone, calamity is born" (Dutch: *Indië verloren, rampspoed geboren*). Second, those Dutch living in the Indies "moved in their own circles, and social contacts with Indonesians were generally limited and superficial."[11] They assumed that everyone in the Indies was content and consequently did not desire much in the way of change. But, as *The Collapse of a Colonial Society* puts it, the Dutch and other Europeans resident in the NEI had no idea what was happening in Indonesian society, much less that the indigenous peoples of the islands had any desire for self-determination and freedom; there was a "deep gulf between Europeans and Indonesians."[12]

After the German attack on Poland in September 1939, and the defeat of Dutch forces and the occupation of the Netherlands in May 1940,[13] it was clear to the government authorities in the Indies that war might soon come to the colony. Given Japan's desire to become a great world power and its aggression in China, an attack by Japan on the colony was highly likely, if for no other reason than that Japan had been short of all raw materials "indispensable for the self-sufficiency" of the country, but especially petroleum; Japan could meet only one-tenth of its own needs. The NEI's oil would not only satisfy Japan's domestic consumption needs but also fuel its war machine.[14]

In June 1940, the Netherlands authorities (now a government in exile in London) rejected almost all Japanese demands (made in February 1940) that the NEI supply Japan with more oil and other minerals. Undeterred, Japan sent a delegation to Batavia in September 1940 to press its demands again, and added a few more: The East Indies must now permit facilities in the Indies for exploiting oil and minerals and the NEI would now have to join Japan's "Southern Resource Zone."

After the leader of the Dutch negotiating delegation, Lieutenant Governor-General Hubertus J. VAN MOOK, rejected these demands in June 1941 and the Japanese attacked Hawaii and the Philippines in December 1941, the only question was when an invasion of the NEI would come.

[11] See de Jong (n. 4) 26. [12] ibid.

[13] For a comprehensive look at the invasion of the Netherlands in World War II see Herman Amersfoort and Piet Kamphuis (eds.), *May 1940: The Battle for the Netherlands* (Brill 2010).

[14] See de Jong (n. 4) 12.

What could be done to strengthen the defenses in the colony? After the occupation of the Netherlands, the NEI could expect no help from The Hague. Moreover, with Great Britain facing a very dark and uncertain future, no help would come from the British Isles. Only the United States and Australia were able to provide some assistance. It was very limited, however, and only a small number of Australian and American troops were in the NEI by early 1942. This meant that the Japanese mostly faced the soldiers of the Royal Netherlands Indies Army (Dutch: *Koninklijk Nederlandsch Indisch Leger* (KNIL)). This was a multi-cultural, multi-ethnic, and multi-lingual army. Prior to World War II, the KNIL had numbered about 32,000. About 10,000 were Europeans (mostly Dutch, who served as officers and senior noncommissioned officers) and about 22,000 were Indonesians. Of the latter, more than half were Javanese (13,000), with the remaining troops consisting of Manadonese (5,000), Ambonese (4,000), Sundanese (2,000), and Timorese (1,000).

With war on the horizon, the KNIL had expanded rapidly after 1940, so that there were about 70,000 men in uniform when the Japanese invaded Java in March 1942. Fifty thousand were stationed on Java, the most important and most populous island of the NEI. The remaining 20,000 were positioned at various locations, including Borneo, Celebes, Sumatra, and Hollandia. While it would have been difficult for the KNIL to defend the 2,000 miles long NEI archipelago from an external attack under almost any circumstances, the chief problem for the KNIL was that it simply was no longer an effective fighting force, at least when compared to the well-equipped and well-trained Japanese Army. This is because the KNIL had evolved into a police force by the end of the 19th century, with its principal mission being to maintain law and order in the NEI.

With this policing mission, the KNIL had not been given the attention—money, equipment, or training—that would have prepared it for war. On the Outer Islands, for example, most of the troops were armed only with a rifle and a machete; there were few automatic weapons. Even on Java, there were shortages of artillery, mortars, anti-tank weapons and anti-aircraft guns. Insufficient numbers of the latter underscored an even more critical shortcoming: The Military Air Force (as the NEI air force was known), with its 350 old, if not obsolete aircraft, was never going to be able to counter Japanese air power. The Dutch in the East Indies, who had watched the German Luftwaffe's operations from afar, knew that an inability to control airspace above the NEI would ultimately bring defeat. Finally, while the NEI did have some naval assets, these also were no match for the Imperial Japanese Navy.

Japanese Invasion and Occupation

The beginning of the end for the Dutch in the East Indies began on the night of January 10–11, 1942, when 6,000 Japanese troops landed on Tarakan (an island off northeast Borneo) to seize oil installations there. This attack was followed by an assault on the Balikpapan (located on southeast Borneo), where the Japanese intended to seize more oil installations. Unfortunately for the Japanese, the defending KNIL troops destroyed the wells and set fire to the oil tanks on both Tarakan and Balikpapan. This sabotage, however, had dire consequences. The Japanese murdered the KNIL troops and civilians who had set fire to the Balikpapan oil installations; seventy-eight Europeans were killed. While it may or may not have been the first war crime committed by the Japanese on NEI soil, it was certainly the largest in terms of victims.

After Tarakan and Balikpapan, the Japanese took a different approach to the oil refinery at Palembang, which was especially important as it was the source of more than half the oil produced in the NEI. On February 14, 1942, the Japanese 1st Raiding Group dropped 600 paratroopers, who successfully seized the Palembang refinery and captured 1.8 million barrels of oil, as well as British and U.S. aircraft and other weapons and material.[15]

These attacks on Tarakan, Balikpapan, and Palembang were not a surprise to the Dutch. Tokyo calculated that a large-scale war with the United States, Great Britain, and the Netherlands would require 56.4 million barrels of oil a year. Since the Indies had produced 56.4 million barrels of oil in 1939, it made sense for the Japanese to seize the oil fields before making any other aggressive moves against the Indies.[16]

With the NEI oil fields in Japanese hands by mid-February 1942, an amphibious invasion of Java, Sumatra, and other islands was imminent. All that month, Japanese aircraft bombed and strafed Java, the strategic and operational center of gravity of the Indies.[17] The intent was to isolate the island before any amphibious invasion. In fact, the Japanese planned for landings on Java to occur on February 26 and two large invasion fleets sailed toward the NEI from the north. Allied naval authorities, deciding that they must stop at least one of these Japanese convoys, took action. On February 27, 1942, Dutch Rear Admiral Karel DOORMAN, leading five cruisers (two Dutch, one British, one American, and one Australian) and nine destroyers (four American, three British, and two Dutch), engaged a Japanese fleet escorting one of the invasion convoys. Unfortunately for Doorman and his ships, the Japanese guns and torpedoes had greater ranges, and the battle was a disaster. Doorman was killed (he went down with his cruiser, *De Ruyter*); the Allies ultimately lost all five cruisers and more than 1,000 sailors. Three Allied

[15] See War History Office of the National Defense College of Japan (n. 10) 332–3.

[16] See de Jong (n. 4) 29.

[17] In military parlance, a "center of gravity" is "that source of massed strength (physical or moral, or a source of leverage) whose serious degradation, dislocation, neutralization, or destruction would have the most decisive impact on the enemy's or one's own ability to accomplish a given military objective." See Milan N. Vego, *Operational Warfare* (Naval War College Press 2000) 634. In 1942, Java was the strategic center of gravity because the colony's central government was located there; the island was the operational strategic center of gravity because the greatest number of KNIL soldiers were located there.

destroyers also were sent to the bottom of the sea. In contrast, Japanese Navy losses were light: One destroyer damaged. The Battle of the Java Sea and the crushing defeat inflicted on the Allies meant that a large-scale invasion could no longer be prevented.

On the night of February 28 and March 1, 1942, there were major amphibious assaults at four locations on Java. The landings involved some 25,000 Japanese troops of the 16th Army. They quickly overwhelmed the Allied defenders and, in the fighting that lasted only a week, committed still more war crimes, including the immediate execution of about 80 British and Dutch soldiers who had surrendered at the airfield of Kalijati, on West Java.

On March 9, 1942, at this same airfield, Dutch Lieutenant General Hein ter POORTEN, Supreme Commander of the KNIL and all Allied Land Forces in the NEI, signed the surrender document prepared by General Hitoshi IMAMURA, the Commander of the Japanese 16th Army. For all practical purposes, the war in the Indies was over—although the last major NEI units (located on Sumatra and Aceh) did not capitulate until March 28, 1942, when they surrendered to the Japanese 25th Army.[18] The accompanying map shows the NEI in the Pacific, and the extent of Japanese control in March 1942.

When all the fighting was over, the Japanese had captured 42,200 European prisoners of war and another 38,000 indigenous KNIL personnel. The Europeans were immediately marched to prisoner of war camps; most of the captured KNIL soldiers were released after a short period of captivity but many were immediately pressed into service by the Japanese as *heihos* (auxiliary soldiers). Ultimately, there were nearly 50,000 Japanese Army and Navy *heihos*.

By the end of the war, the Japanese also had interned 100,000 civilians, all Europeans and some Eurasians. These numbers are important because, when compared with the number of the Americans in the Philippines, British in Malaya, Singapore, and Hong Kong, and French in Indo-China, the NEI was unique: In no other Western colony occupied by Japan during World War II did the Japanese have to deal with so many "enemy" aliens. For example, there were 20,000 British civilians interned in Malaya and 27,000 French civilians interned in French Indo-China.[19]

As the occupation began, the NEI was divided into three administrative areas. The 16th Army was tasked with administering Java, the most populous island in the NEI, and Madura, an important island adjacent to it. The 25th Army was in charge on Sumatra. The Imperial Japanese Navy was responsible for the administration of all the remaining islands, including Borneo, Celebes, the Moluccas, the Lesser Sunda Islands, and New Guinea.

[18] For an excellent English language account of the Japanese conquest of the NEI see Lionel Wigmore, *The Japanese Thrust* (*Australia in the War of 1939–1945*, Vol. IV) (Australian War Memorial 1957). For U.S. Army involvement in the defense of NEI, see U.S. Army Center of Military History, *U.S. Army Campaigns of World War II: East Indies* (Government Printing Office 1992).

[19] See de Jong (n. 4) 11.

Map 1 World War II in the Pacific May 1942; Limit of Japanese Advance.
Credit: U.S. Army Center of Military History, Washington, D.C.

A Postscript

While the purpose of this first chapter is to provide context for understanding the occupation that lasted from March 1942 until August 1945, a "postscript" about the aftermath of the occupation is appropriate.

Following Japan's capitulation, the vast majority of Dutch nationals, both in the Indies and in the Netherlands, assumed that life would return to normal in the colony, and that the Dutch would again rule from Batavia. Certainly, those in prisoner of war (POW) and internment camps must have assumed that the colonial authorities would be welcomed as liberators by everyone—Europeans, Eurasians, Chinese, Malays, Arabs, and Indonesians—who had endured the Japanese occupation. After all, as will be discussed in the next chapter, the Japanese had dismantled the existing government, placed virtually the entire white population in concentration camps, and done everything possible to destroy more than three centuries of Dutch civilization in the NEI. It also was true that virtually everyone, indigenous peoples included, had suffered from hunger and deprivation under the Japanese, and so one might have thought that re-establishing Dutch colonial authority would have gone fairly smoothly.

But everything had changed in the NEI during the occupation, and nothing was going to be the same again. While it was true that the Japanese initially had paid only lip-service to the idea of an independent Indonesia, they quickly understood that the desire of many Indonesians for freedom from Dutch colonial rule might be used as a way to obtain support for the war effort. Certainly, this explains why Sukarno, convinced that the Japanese would win the war in the Pacific and that it was time to ally with the eventual victors, began collaborating with them. If Japan was going to defeat the Allies in the Pacific, Sukarno and the nationalists reckoned that some form of cooperation with the Japanese was the smartest course of action—and that it might ultimately lead to independence.

Sukarno's instincts were good as, when the war in the Pacific began going badly for the Japanese, they showed a new interest in Indonesian nationalism. In December 1944, Japanese Prime Minister Kuniaki KOISO announced that the NEI would be "made independent in the future" and that, as a sign of Japan's goodwill, the nationalist anthem could be played in public and the red and white flag of Indonesia flown alongside the Japanese flag. There is no doubt that Koiso hoped that this concession to nationalists would mobilize them (and other Indonesians) to make a larger contribution to Japan's war effort.[20]

This hope did not materialize for the Japanese, but it did increase expectations among the nationalists and encouraged them to take action. As a result, on August 17, 1945, just two days after the Japanese surrender, Sukarno declared that Indonesia was a free and independent nation.

The Allies, including the Dutch, were completely unprepared for both the Japanese surrender and this declaration of independence. Complicating matters was that the British who, in the absence of the Dutch armed forces, had authority over the newly liberated NEI, were chiefly interested in evacuating POWs and internees, and disarming the Japanese. As for the new Indonesian Republic, the British took a wait-and-see attitude. They certainly had no intention of disarming the young Indonesian nationalists who had obtained a wide variety of Japanese weapons during the six weeks between the surrender and the arrival of the first Allied troops, and were now a formidable armed force. Moreover, given the tumultuous situation in the Indies, the British had little choice but to insist that the Japanese help them maintain law and order (albeit under British authority), and that the Japanese protect civilian internees, who had to remain in the camps for their own safety.

What followed was the so-called *Bersiap* (Indonesian for "Be Ready" or "Get Ready") period, a time of chaos and anarchy.[21] Despite the landing of British and Dutch soldiers at the end of September 1945, and an attempt to restore order,

[20] ibid 45.

[21] For eyewitness accounts by Dutch nationals on the chaos of the *Bersiap* period see Sheri G. Tromp (ed.), *Four Years Till Tomorrow: Despair and Hope in Wartime Dutch East Indies* (Vanderheide Publishing 1999); Jan A. Kracher (ed.), *The Defining Years of the Dutch East Indies, 1942–1949* (McFarland and Co., Inc. Publishers 2003). For the best scholarship in Dutch on the *Bersiap* period see Elly Touwen-Bouwsma and Petra M. H. Groen, *Tussen Banzai en Bersiap. De afwikkeling van de Tweede Wereldooorlog in Nederlands-Indie* (Sdu Uitgevers 1996). For the most recent scholarship in Dutch on the *Bersiap* period see Remy Limpach, *De brandende kampongs van Generaal Spoor* (Boom, 2016) 128–79.

violence steadily increased. On Java, British and British Indian, and Japanese troops, fought fierce street battles with groups of young Indonesian *pemudas*.[22] The last three months of 1945 saw thousands of bombings, kidnappings, and murders perpetrated by these radical Indonesian nationalists against civilians. Many of the victims were Chinese and Eurasian men, women, and children. But Dutch civilians, both those inside and outside the internment camps, were also attacked and murdered by *pemudas*. Probably about 5,500 Dutch and Eurasians were killed during the *Bersiap* period, although there could have been as many as 20,000 victims. But the *pemudas* suffered casualties as well; between 30,000 and 100,000 were killed on Java alone.[23]

By early 1946, the Dutch colonial authorities had managed to restore some law and order in the NEI, at least on Java. But the insurgency against the Dutch continued, and could not be defeated despite the fact that there eventually would be 100,000 Dutch troops on Java alone. In the midst of this turmoil, the NEI authorities began repatriating Japanese civilians and military personnel. By late June, only 20,000 of the original 300,000 Japanese nationals remained in the islands, of whom about 3,000 were being held as war criminals. The first war crimes tribunals began in Batavia in August 1946 and the trials continued in various locations until late December 1949 when, having failed to defeat Sukarno and the nationalists, the Netherlands acknowledged the independence of the Republic of Indonesia. Until that day, however, NEI authorities vigorously prosecuted those men and women who had committed war crimes during the occupation.

The import of this short postscript about the period from August 1945 to December 1949 is that military trials of Japanese war criminals (and those who collaborated with them) occurred in an increasingly unsettled, if not violent, environment. Gathering evidence, finding, and interviewing witnesses, and prosecuting cases was not easy in the midst of a revolution. Moreover, the transfer of sovereignty from the Netherlands to the new Republic of Indonesia not only meant the abrupt end to war crimes prosecutions, but an unraveling of more than a few tribunal decisions. As will be seen, this was very much an unsatisfactory end-state, at least as far as the Dutch were concerned.

[22] A *pemuda* (English: youth) was a young Indonesian political activist involved in the struggle for independence. While the *pemudas* saw themselves as freedom fighters, the NEI authorities considered them to be nothing more than young Indonesian thugs bent upon lawlessness and destruction. During the *Bersiap* period, *pemudas* were chiefly responsible for the violence against Dutch, Eurasians, Chinese, and those Indonesians (such as civil servants) whom they believed were supporting the colonial authorities. The word also is spelled *pemoeda*.

[23] Nederlands Institut voor Oorlogsdocumentatie (NIOD), *Indischekamparchieven.nl* (NIOD 2010) 6–7. See also https://www.indischekamparchieven.nl/en (last accessed October 25, 2016).

2

"Asia for the Asians," *Bushido*, and Japanese War Crimes in the Netherlands East Indies, 1942 to 1946

The 300,000 Europeans and Dutch Eurasians residing in the Netherlands East Indies (NEI) in March 1942 must have believed that their lives under Japanese rule would not be significantly different from life before the invasion. No doubt there would be some changes with the Japanese Army now running the government in Batavia and, along with the Navy, occupying Java, Sumatra, Borneo, and other islands in the Indies. Naturally, KNIL and Australian, British, and American soldiers who had been captured would be sent to prisoner of war (POW) camps. But certainly, day-to-day colonial life would continue as before, if for no other reason than maintaining a healthy economy would require the retention of European businessmen and technicians who could keep factories running and commercial enterprises operating and European bureaucrats and administrators who would keep the government running. This optimistic view was buttressed by widely held conviction that, while there was no doubt that the Dutch colony had suffered a crushing defeat at the hands of the Japanese invader, it would be only a matter of months, if not weeks, before the Allies returned to liberate the NEI and return life in the colony to the *status quo ante bellum*.[1]

At the same time, Sukarno and other politically aware Indonesians must have thought that the arrival of the Japanese heralded a new future, and that life in the islands soon would be very different. If the Japanese really believed that Asia was for the peoples of Asia, then there was every reason to think that self-determination and an independent and free Indonesia would soon be a reality.

[1] At the end of March 1942, the commander of the KNIL Air Force, Major General L. H. van OYEN, began making radio broadcasts to the NEI from Melbourne, Australia. When he ended his broadcast with the words "I hope to see you again soon," his listeners in the Indies believed that this meant that Allied landings on Java were imminent. Similarly, Dutch language broadcasts from Radio San Francisco advised listeners to "Keep your courage up! We'll be coming soon!" These proclamations fueled an unrealistic optimism about the future course of the war, and encouraged clandestine resistance activities that, as shown in Chapter 11, were ruthlessly crushed by the Japanese when discovered. See Louis de Jong (with an Introduction by Jeroen Kemperman), *The Collapse of a Colonial Society: The Dutch in Indonesia during the Second World War* (KILTV Press 2002) 89, 189, 221.

Military Trials of War Criminals in the Netherlands East Indies 1946–1949, Fred L. Borch.

Map 2 Netherlands East Indies 1942.
Credit: U.S. Army Center of Military History, Washington, D.C.

What actually occurred between March 1942 and August 1945 was a shock to the Dutch and other Europeans and largely a disappointment to the Indonesian nationalists. This is because, from the beginning, the Japanese occupiers implemented political, economic, and cultural policies designed to integrate the Dutch East Indies into the "Greater East Asian Co-Prosperity Sphere." The goal of this

"Japanization" was to transform all races living in the Indies into loyal subjects of the Emperor, with one important exception: "Asia for the Asians" meant that there was no place for the white race in the NEI, and this required the eradication of all Dutch civilization in the archipelago. As for the Indonesian nationalists, while Asia might be for the Asian peoples, the Japanese believed that, as they were racially and culturally superior to all other Asians and, alone among the peoples of the world, were blessed to have a deity ruling over them, they were best able to determine the destiny of Asians living in the NEI.

But, while the Japanese had no intention of granting independence to the Indonesians, much less permitting some degree of self-determination, Japan needed the support of the indigenous population if it were to defeat the Allies and create a new order. Consequently, the Japanese initially encouraged nationalist sentiment as a way of obtaining support for their war effort. But regardless of claims by the Japanese that they had an affinity for Indonesians as Asians, the Japanese could be just as ruthless in their treatment of Indonesians as they were in their handling of prisoners of war (POWs) and European civilians. Witness the brutal treatment of indigenous laborers (Japanese: *rōmusha*) recruited by the Japanese, which included using hundreds of them as human guinea pigs in an unsuccessful medical experiment (discussed in Chapter 5, *Trials for the Mistreatment of Civilians and Prisoners of War and Civilian Internees*), and the mass murders and unlawful executions of Indonesian men and women (discussed in Chapter 6, *Trials for Mass Murder and Unlawful Executions*).

As this chapter explains, eradicating more than three centuries of Dutch imperialism—and restructuring life and society in the islands from top to bottom—required a "hard" approach toward the recalcitrant Dutch (and their Eurasian and Indonesian allies), who naturally resisted any changes that would end their privileged status in the colony. It was this hard approach that inexorably resulted in widespread and systematic war crimes against both prisoners of war and civilians in the NEI.

A second factor, however, combined with the "Asian for the Asians" ideology to make Japanese war crimes unusually vicious, cruel, and sadistic in nature: The "Code of *Bushido.*" Inculcated in Japanese military personnel from the most senior to the most junior ranking individual, this "way of the samurai" or "way of the warrior" was a martial ideology that was "the imperial military's most important morale building tool."[2] Central to *Bushido* was the concept of "surrender as a mortal shame."[3] Since Dutch, American, British, and Australian soldiers had all surrendered to the Japanese, when the only honorable course of action was for them to choose death in battle, the Japanese considered them to be undeserving of respect. This attitude led not only to the mistreatment of POWs but, because military and naval personnel were also in charge of internment camps after April 1944, spilled over into the treatment given to European and Eurasian civilians interned

[2] Oleg Benesch, *Inventing the Way of the Samurai* (Oxford University Press 2014) 205.
[3] ibid 210.

during the occupation. This chapter discusses how the Asia for the Asians ideology and Code of *Bushido* are linked to the war crimes committed by the Japanese in the NEI.

"Japanization" and "Asia for the Asians"

Japan's goal in the NEI—and in other occupied areas—was to re-make Asia as a racially homogenous area, or at least an area free of white European imperialists. Just as the Germans ultimately sought to re-make Europe during World War II—as a greater Aryan *Lebensraum* emptied of gypsies, Jews, Slavs, and other undesirable *untermensch*[4]—so too did the Japanese seek to re-make Asia as a place devoid of all European influences. Nowhere was this intentional elimination of Europeans and their culture more pronounced than in the NEI, if for no other reason than that the Japanese sought to erase more than three centuries of Dutch civilization.

The origins of this goal—an Asia devoid of white Europeans—began some 2,500 years ago, when Jimmu, the first emperor of Japan, is said to have proclaimed that the Japanese were a "Chosen People" and that it was the "divine mission of Japan to conquer and rule other countries."[5] A popular Japanese song in the 1880s certainly encouraged the idea that it was Japan's destiny to rule the world: "There is a Law of Nations, it is true,/ but when the moment comes, remember,/ the Strong eat up the Weak." [6]

After the Japanese army and navy destroyed Chinese forces in the Sino-Japanese War of 1895, the island of Formosa became the first imperial colony. Ten years later, the crushing victory over the Russians gave the Japanese a foothold in Manchuria and paved the way for the acquisition of Korea as a colony. By the 1920s, Japanese schools (following government instructions) were teaching young students that "they belonged to a special race that was culturally and morally superior to the decadent and materialistic West."[7] By the 1930s, a very militaristic Japan expanded still more with the invasion of Manchuria and creation of Manchukuo as a puppet state.[8] Consequently, when the Japanese Foreign Minister announced in June 1940 "that the countries of East Asia and the regions of the South Seas are geographically, historically, racially, and economically very closely related" and that Japan would lead these countries in a "Greater East Asia Co-Prosperity Sphere," this proclamation was simply a continuation of long (and deeply) held convictions.[9]

[4] See Lucy Dawidowicz, *The War Against the Jews* (Holt, Rinehart & Winston 1975); Stephen G. Fritz, *Ostkrieg: Hitler's War of Extermination in the East* (University Press of Kentucky 2011).

[5] Muhammed Abdul Aziz, *Japan's Colonialism and Indonesia* (Martinus Nijhoff 1955) 3.

[6] John W. Dower, *Embracing Defeat: Japan in the Wake of World War II* (Norton Co. 1999) 21.

[7] Eric Bergerud, *Touched with Fire* (Viking Penguin 1996) 129.

[8] Harold H. Sunoo, *Japanese Militarism: Past and Present* (Nelson Hall 1975) 43–64.

[9] See Aziz (n. 5) 62–3.

For this new world order to be achieved, however, Asia must be reclaimed for the Asian people. Liberating the Asian races, however, required more than overthrowing the colonial powers. If Japan were to be the champion of a moral and cultural revival in Asia, then there must be an "elimination of all Western influence and penetration" in the Far East. According to Tokyo's Total War Research Unit, which operated under the auspices of Japanese Premier Hideki TOJO, Asia for the Asians could only be achieved with "the physical extermination of Western 'intruders,'" including thousands in Hong Kong, Indo-China, the Malay Peninsula (including Singapore), the Philippines, and hundreds of thousands in the NEI.[10]

Since the Japanese came to the islands "with the definite aim to eliminate all Dutch influence as quickly as possible from the life of Indonesia,"[11] it should come as no surprise that this ethnic cleansing began immediately after the Japanese conquest of the NEI. After more than 42,200 Allied military personnel were lawfully confined in POW camps,[12] the authorities focused their attention on Dutch citizens (including some Dutch Eurasians), and other European civilians.

In contrast to the legal basis for confining POWs, there was no legal authority for the raids that rounded up and interned thousands and thousands of civilian men, women, and children, simply on the basis of ethnicity or race. While the British use of concentration camps during the Boer War was certainly known to the Japanese authorities, their use during the armed conflict with the Afrikaaners did not make the camps legal under customary international law. On the contrary, Hague Convention IV of 1907, the international treaty containing provisions addressing the treatment of civilians during an enemy occupation, very much indicated otherwise. Article 43 of that convention, which the Japanese had ratified in 1911, stated clearly that an occupying authority was only permitted to take measures "to restore, and ensure ... public order and safety." This meant that the Japanese government in the Indies could seize and intern civilians who it believed posed a threat to good order and discipline. For example, civilians suspected of involvement in resistance activities certainly were subject to internment, if not arrest and prosecution.

In fact, during World War I, the belligerents did intern large numbers of male civilians, but only because they viewed them as potential spies. They did not, however, intern women and children and there was no legal basis for such an

[10] ibid 90. [11] ibid 166.

[12] ibid 285. Under both customary international law and the Geneva Convention of 1929, the Japanese were lawfully permitted to confine POWs for the duration of hostilities. Initially, the 42,200 European POWs (mostly Dutch but some Australian, British, and American) were held in various locations in the NEI. Within 12 months, however, most were shipped to camps in Burma, Japan, Formosa, Thailand, Manchuria, and other locations under Japanese control. They were forced to do "unbearable or dangerous work" building railroads (including the infamous Thai–Burma railroad) or working in coal mines in violation of the Geneva Convention of 1929. As far as the POWs were concerned, they were slaves. See John Franken, "Slave Labourer in Nagasaki," in Sheri G. Tromp (ed.), *Four Years Till Tomorrow: Despair and Hope in Wartime Dutch East Indies* (Vanderheide Publishing 1999) 22–6; Lodewijk Jan Weijgers, "A Dutch POW in Thailand," in Tromp (ibid) 89–101. Almost 20 percent of Allied POWs died in Japanese captivity.

internment. Rather, Hague Convention IV envisaged that life for civilians during an enemy occupation would be as normal as possible, which is why the treaty also required an occupier like Japan to respect, "unless absolutely prevented, the laws in force in the country."[13] Finally, as Hague IV stated that "family honor and rights, and the lives of persons ... be respected,"[14] it follows that the race-based internment of civilians in the Indies was simply illegal.

On Java, where the vast majority of Europeans resided, the internment of Dutch and Dutch Eurasian civilians began in May 1942. On the orders of General Imamura, the 16th Army commander, men and boys over the age of seventeen were rounded up and forcibly removed from their homes. Some prominent civilians, including high ranking civil servants, judges, and senior police officials, had already been picked up and interned in prisons. Presumably a few of those interned after May 1942 also went to prisons, but the vast majority of interned men went to "protected districts" or camps. Since male internees generally were not permitted to take anything with them from their homes, they had nothing with them except their underwear. From the beginning, conditions for them were harsh; in most men's camps there were no tables, chairs, beds, or cabinets.[15]

As for the internment of Dutch and Dutch Eurasian women and young children (both male and female), those residing in Batavia began to be interned in October 1942. The remainder of these women and children on Java were in camps by mid-1943. On the so-called Outer Islands (including Ambon, Celebes, (Dutch) Borneo, and Sumatra), the internment of civilians began at about the same time. But the process finished earlier than on Java, chiefly because there were smaller numbers of civilians to be interned. In contrast to the male internees, women were permitted to take some furniture and household possessions with them, which meant that their camp conditions were not as primitive as in the men's camps.

Two final points about the internment of civilians. First, although initially rounded up and removed to camps, many Dutch Eurasians later were released to return to their homes; on Java, for example, Eurasians earning less than 300 guilders a month were freed. Second, citizens of countries who were allied with Japan (like Germany), or were nationals of neutral states (like Switzerland), initially escaped internment.[16]

The internment was a huge undertaking for the Japanese, given that between 100,000 and 110,000 civilian men, women, and children were forcibly removed and placed in camps. On Java alone, more than 70,000 Europeans and Eurasians were interned by the end of 1943. Since the total number of civilians interned by

[13] 1907 Convention (IV) Respecting the Laws and Customs of War on Land (with annexed Regulations), signed at The Hague, (October 18, 1907) [hereinafter Hague Convention IV of 1907] art. 43; Japan ratified on December 13, 1911.

[14] ibid art. 46.

[15] See de Jong (n. 1) 433.

[16] By the end of the occupation, however, many of these Axis and neutral country citizens were billeted in camps for their own safety. See Andrew A. Van Dijk, "Overview of the Imprisonment Experience," in Jan A. Krancher (ed.), *The Defining Years of the Dutch East Indies, 1942–1949* (McFarland & Co., Inc. Publishing 1996) 15. In mid-1944, for example, the Japanese interned most Swiss businessmen and seized their assets. See also de Jong (n. 1) 496.

the Japanese in *all* Japanese controlled territory during World War II was about 125,000, the fact that four-fifths of these men, women, and children were interned in the NEI is significant, and reflects the clear intent of the Japanese to destroy forever the Dutch colony in the Indies.[17]

The map of Java shows the location of Batavia and other major cities and towns on the island; while most internees were housed near Batavia, there were also civilian internment camps in other locations, including Buitenzorg (south of Batavia), Tangerang (west of Batavia), and Pekalongan (central Java).

While there were some exceptions, Japanese camp personnel routinely mistreated internees under their control. As explained in Chapter 5, *Trials for the Mistreatment of Civilians and Prisoners of War and Civilian Internees*, beatings of both men and women were routine, for the slightest infraction (or perceived infraction) of camp rules and regulations, and delivered with exceptional brutality and cruelty. Medical treatment was frequently denied, even when the internee was likely to die (and in fact did die) without it. Civilians were also deprived of food, even when it was available and badly needed for nourishment. In June 1945, for example, then Lieutenant Kenichi SONE, the commandant of a camp for women and children, took bread intended for the internees and buried it in the ground. Sone then prohibited the distribution of any food for the next three days.[18] Chapter 7, *Trials for Forced Prostitution*, also shows that some civilian women in the internment camps also were forced to work in Japanese-licensed brothels. This forced prostitution was not only a war crime under the law, but was yet another illustration of the hostile conduct displayed by the Japanese occupation authorities toward internees.

The central mystery—unresolved to this day—is what Japan intended to do with the more than 100,000 civilian internees it held in the Indies at the end of World War II. Assuming that Japan was victorious in the Pacific, there is no doubt that any surviving POWs would have been repatriated to their home countries as required under Hague Convention IV of 1907 and the Geneva Conventions of 1929. As for the internees, there are no documents or other historic record in existence today that answer the question of what would have happened to these individuals had Japan been triumphant in her Pacific war. Perhaps the Dutch would have been sent to the Netherlands, and other European internees to their countries of origin, but this is speculation.[19]

What is known is that the health and welfare of European civilians in the camps was of little concern to the Japanese. From the beginning, the internees were informed that they should be "grateful for the special favor of being protected by the Japanese army" and "were not to do as they wished but were to accept their fate with cheerful diligence." While the Japanese did intend to supply those in the camps with sufficient food, there would be no clothing, shoes,

[17] See de Jong (n. 1) 429.

[18] Sone's war crimes—and his trial—are discussed in Chapter 5 in this volume.

[19] The Netherlands Institute of War Documentation believes that the Japanese "probably" intended "to send interned Westerners back to their own countries." See https://www.indischekamparchieven.nl/en (last accessed October 25, 2016).

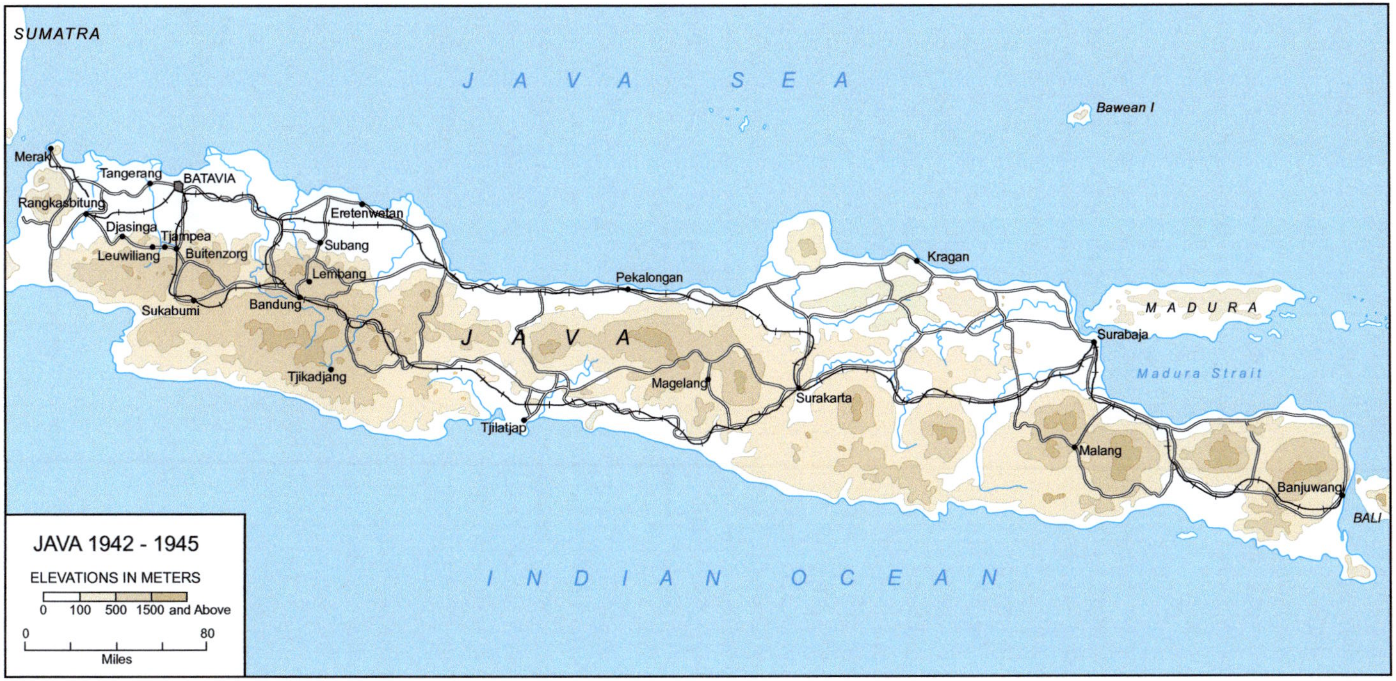

Map 3 Java.

Credit: U.S. Army Center of Military History, Washington, D.C.

or soap. The reason? According to the Japanese, "the internees had lived a life of luxury and had enough of everything to last for years."[20] Additionally, having lost their fatherland, they really had no right to anything. "You are like shreds of paper, blown away by the wind," the Japanese commandant of a men's camp once told the internees.[21]

With this attitude, it should come as no surprise that in 1944, the Central Military Administration (Japanese: *Gunseikanbu*) in the NEI reduced the quantity of food supplied to all internment camps. At least two historians have concluded that this decrease in rations reflected a Japanese plan intentionally to starve POWs and internees to death.[22] Certainly, there is evidence that the Japanese were totally indifferent to the fate of the internees. For example, Mr. D. M. G. Koch, who had been interned in a camp for elderly men at Ambarawa, Java, remembered that in early 1945,

> [t]he number of deaths [in the camp] was seven to eight a day, and it rose gradually to fourteen. At that point, I went to the Japanese commandant to ask him to improve the food supply. He replied that when we got up to fifteen deaths a day he would think about providing better food. If the liberation [August 1945] had come three months later, the whole camp would have been dead.[23]

More recent scholarship, however, concludes that shortages of rice, maize, sweet potatoes, and other foodstuffs resulted from Japanese mismanagement of the economy and that starvation was widespread in the islands; rations were reduced for Europeans in the camps simply because there was less food for everyone.[24] By early 1945, conditions *outside* the camps on Java and Sumatra were increasingly dire. De Jong estimated that, on Java alone, 2.5 million Indonesians died of starvation out of a population of 50 million men, women, and children. There were reports of bodies of Indonesians who had died of starvation lying in the city streets; "not a day passes that bodies are not found under viaducts, in air-raid shelters and in unfinished dwellings."[25]

Even if this is true, *i.e.* that people everywhere in the NEI were facing acute hunger, if not starvation, the situation for those in the camps was worse, because their captivity meant they had no opportunity to forage for food in the way that those living outside the camps did.[26] This author is convinced that, had World War II in the Pacific continued until 1946 or 1947, there would have been few whites still alive in the East Indies. The Japanese ethnic cleansing of the NEI would have been a success. As it was, the death rate among civilian internees was significant: One out of six internees died (13,120 or 13.6 percent).[27]

[20] Doetje van Velden, *De Japanse interneringskampen voor burgers gedurende de Tweede Wereld-oorlog* (Wolters 1963) 127, quoted in de Jong (n. 1) 435.

[21] ibid 223, quoted in de Jong (n. 1) 435.

[22] See Aziz (n. 5) 171; David Whel, *The Birth of Indonesia* (Allen & Unwin 1948) 4.

[23] See de Jong (n. 1) 438. [24] ibid 227–81.

[25] J. B. Bouwer, *Dagboek* (Diary), June 8, 1945 at 340, quoted in de Jong (n. 1) 279.

[26] See de Jong (n. 1) 280–1.

[27] Peter Post *et al.* (eds.), *Encyclopedia of Indonesia in the Pacific War* (Brill 2010) 167.

A final point about the ethnic cleansing of whites by the Japanese. While there is no doubt that the suffering of men, women, and children in the internment camps in the Indies played no role in President Harry S. Truman's decision to drop atomic bombs on Hiroshima and Nagasaki, there would have been no end to the war in the Indies—or the suffering of the internees—had this not occurred when it did. Truman's decision to use these new weapons, driven chiefly by his desire to save the lives of thousands and thousands of Americans who would have perished in an amphibious invasion of Japan, where "four to five million Japanese under arms awaited them,"[28] had the unintended consequence of saving thousands and thousands of Dutch lives in the archipelago.[29]

At the same time that the Japanese were separating the Dutch from Indonesian society, by concentrating them in camps, they also began a systematic elimination of Western influence in the archipelago. After all, as the "Dutch belonged to an inferior race," they must "understand that their civilizing role had come to an end forever."[30]

The Japanese, who saw themselves as liberators, now began implementing widespread changes in order to re-make NEI society and transform the islands forever. Within weeks of their victory over the Allies, the Japanese began trumpeting the *Tiga A* ("Three A") slogan, which was intended to convince both Europeans and non-Europeans that Asia now truly was for Asians, and that Japan would play a central role in the creation of the new Greater East Asia Co-Prosperity Sphere. While the "Three A" campaign—*Asia tjahaja, Asia pelindoeng*, and *Asia pemimpin* ("Japan the light of Asia, Japan the protector of Asia, and Japan the leader of Asia")—did not succeed in mobilizing the Indonesian masses, and was abandoned within months of its establishment, the fact that it had been created reflected Japan's commitment to revolutionary change in the NEI.

In the coming months, the Japanese implemented a variety of changes. On November 30, 1942, the occupation authorities announced that it was now illegal to speak Dutch on the telephone or send a telegram in the language. Using English on the telephone or when sending a telegram likewise was forbidden. German and French, however, were allowed.

The Japanese also closed primary and secondary schools at the beginning of the occupation. The following month, when the Japanese authorities on Java

[28] Richard B. Frank, "Why Japan Agreed to Unconditional Surrender," *Military History Quarterly* (Autumn 2015) 33.

[29] D. M. Giangreco, "Casualty Projections for the U.S. Invasions of Japan, 1945–1946: Planning and Policy Implications," 61 *Journal of Military History* (July 1997), 521–82. The atomic bombs also saved the lives of thousands and thousands of Japanese civilians who would have died in an Allied invasion of Japan. Historians who continue to criticize Truman's decision to use nuclear weapons fail to understand, much less accept, that it took the destruction of not one but two Japanese cities before Hirohito *forced* his military leaders to accept that the survival of Japan required surrender. John Toland, *The Rising Sun* (Random House 1970) 810–50. Certainly, the Imperial Army and Navy did not believe it had been defeated, as there were still 3.5 million soldiers and sailors in Asia, Siberia, and the Pacific Ocean area when Japan surrendered. In China alone, one million Japanese soldiers were ready for combat. See Dower (n. 6) 48–50.

[30] See Aziz (n. 5) 170.

permitted schools to reopen, all European schools were excluded. This meant that Dutch and Dutch Eurasian children resorted to home-schooling, but in any event this clandestine education stopped by mid-1943, when women and children were interned. Thereafter, the secret education of children continued to some extent in the camps.[31]

The possession of books and periodicals in all Western languages was also made a criminal offense. As the Japanese did not close libraries or archives in the NEI, this measure had little practical impact, except for those civilians interned in camps, who had no access to any library.

Ultimately, the authorities prohibited the use of the Dutch language in any correspondence. This meant that when postal service was restored in May 1942, only postcards written in Japanese or Indonesian were permitted to be mailed.

The use of foreign names was proscribed, so that all Dutch names of places, streets, and squares in all locations in the NEI were changed. The capital Batavia became Djakarta (today's Jakarta) and well-known streets like *Oranje* Boulevard became *Syoowa Doori*. Dutch language names of commercial enterprises, shops, and hotels were also changed into Japanese or Indonesian. Statues or monuments (including the famous "Lion of Waterloo" in Batavia) were removed.[32] The bank accounts of Dutch citizens were frozen and income and property tax were increased. Automobiles were confiscated.

Finally, the Western calendar was abolished and replaced by the Japanese *Kigenreki*; 1942 became 2602. On March 27, 1942, Japanese solar time also was introduced. This meant that those resident in the NEI were required to set their clocks ninety minutes ahead, starting the day one and a half hours earlier than had been the norm, simply because the day had already begun in Tokyo.[33] Dutch holidays also were abolished; the most important day of the year was now April 29, the birthday of Emperor Hirohito.

It is important to understand that the Japanese desire to turn the world upside down was not limited to the NEI. In December 1941, after quickly defeating U.S. forces on the island of Guam, the Japanese Navy adopted political, economic, and cultural policies in order to achieve "organic integration" (Japanese: *yūkiteki ketsugō*) of Guam into the Japanese empire. Japan, as the liberator of the Asian peoples, had an obligation to the indigenous people of Guam: To show them that they shared "a common destiny for Asia's coexistence and co-prosperity."[34] Just as Dutch influences were to be cleansed from the NEI, so too was the "disgusting Americanism" on Guam to be eradicated.

[31] See de Jong (n. 1) 72.

[32] The so-called *Oranje* Boulevard was named after the House of Orange-Nassau, the name of the Dutch royal family. As for the "Lion of Waterloo," it was a replica of the original lion erected at Waterloo by the Dutch after the Allied victory over Napoleon in 1815. Installed on top of a brick column in the main square of Batavia, near the Governor General's palace, this bronze lion was the major symbol of Batavia for more than 100 years. After its removal by the Japanese, the lion was destroyed.

[33] See de Jong (n. 1) 175.

[34] Wakako Higuchi, *The Japanese Administration of Guam, 1941–1944* (McFarland & Co., Inc. Publishers 2010) 11.

As *The Japanese Administration of Guam, 1941–1944* explains, the Navy took a three-pronged approach to rooting out American culture and thereby awakening the racial identity of the Chamorros as Asian constituents of Japan.[35] First, believing that discouraging the pro-American Catholicism of the islanders was the key to dismantling American influence, the Japanese replaced the American priests with Japanese priests. The latter subsequently worked "to dispel illusions of the old America [and] have the Chamorros grasp the lofty spirit of the imperial country."[36] The second prong of "Japanization" (Japanese: *Nihonka*) on Guam was the implementation of Japanese language training. This was important because Japan's language was its "spiritual blood," and Asian races could shake themselves "free of European and American colonial exploitation" if they learned Japanese.[37] The third and final prong was *kōminization*—transforming the Chamorros into "devoted subjects of the Emperor."[38] While *kōminization* was closely associated with the teaching of Japanese language (because it imparted culture), it was different in that its goal was to implant in the consciousness of the islanders that they were Emperor Hirohito's subjects and servants. The ultimate goal: The Chamorros would "be splendid Japanese nationals" and a part of Japan's vision to be a one hundred million people nation.[39]

While the Navy's program of organic integration on Guam failed with the U.S. reinvasion of Guam in July 1944, the parallels between what the Japanese implemented in Guam and the NEI are proof that Japan was willing to implement radical measures in order to eliminate any and all traces of Dutch rule in the NEI.

Code of *Bushido*

It follows that the widespread and systematic nature of war crimes committed by the Japanese was a manifestation of the "Asia for the Asians" policy and its implementation in the NEI from 1942 to 1945. But this only partly explains the type and magnitude of the war crimes committed by the Japanese during the occupation of the Indies. A second factor, the Code of *Bushido*, also had a profound impact on the Japanese in their day-to-day activities in the NEI. Consequently, while the racism inherent in the "Asia for the Asians" ideology resulted in Japanese mistreatment of the Dutch and their allies, *Bushido* exacerbated this mistreatment because it meant that the Japanese in the NEI also had utter contempt for the

[35] The island of Guam is the southernmost island in the Mariana Island archipelago. It was a Spanish possession until 1898 when, as a result of the U.S. victory in the Spanish-American War, sovereignty was transferred to the United States. The earliest inhabitants of Guam most likely arrived by sea from the Philippines. By the time of World War II, however, the people of the island, known as the Chamorros, were a mix of these original settlers and Spanish, Mexican, and Filipino soldiers, who were stationed on Guam and married local women in the 1700s and 1800s. When the Japanese took control of Guam in December 1941, there were 23,350 people on the island; most were Chamorros.

[36] See Higuchi (n. 34) 131. [37] ibid 133. [38] ibid 137. [39] ibid 144.

Dutch, especially those with a military or government connection. It was this contempt that inexorably led to the vicious, cruel, and sadistic acts inflicted on both the Dutch and other inhabitants of the islands.

Bushido has its origins among the Samurai of medieval Japan who, "no matter what rank, held their lives light as feathers when compared with the weight they attached the maintenance of a spotless name."[40] Family and personal honor meant everything and death was preferable to any dishonor.

As Japan continued its modernization in the early 20th century, her armed forces became convinced that success in battle would be assured if Japanese soldiers, sailors, and airmen had the "spirit" of *Bushido*. The belief was that if a human being had this spirit, he could overcome any obstacle. Japanese officers were convinced in their hearts, and taught their troops, that they could do things no other army could do simply because Japanese troops would not be denied.

The result was that the *Bushido* code of behavior "was inculcated into the Japanese soldier as part of his basic training."[41] Each soldier was indoctrinated to accept that it was the greatest honor to die for the Emperor and it was cowardly to surrender to the enemy. "Death was not only expected as a matter of duty, but was viewed as a rite of personal and national purification."[42] Those Japanese in uniform who did surrender (or were captured) consequently brought great dishonor upon themselves and their families. As a practical matter, this meant that Japanese soldiers and sailors were expected to fight to the death; most did, as reflected by the dearth of Japanese personnel taken prisoner by the Allies in the Pacific. Not only should Japanese military and naval personnel refuse to surrender, but they should keep their last bullet for themselves or, alternatively, assault the enemy in a final suicidal attack. Additionally, if a soldier or sailor were rendered unconscious and was taken captive, this made no difference under the *Bushido* code: He was disgraced forever, as was his family. This idea that a soldier or sailor must never surrender was so ingrained in the psychology of the Japanese armed forces that Japanese War Minister General Korechika ANAMI continued to insist in August 1945, after both Hiroshima and Nagasaki had been destroyed by atomic bombs, that there was "really no alternative but for us [Japan] to continue the war ... [because] our men will simply refuse to lay down their arms ... they know they are forbidden to surrender."[43]

Bushido also meant a willingness to accept orders that meant certain death, because death was the highest honor and the ultimate hallmark of courage. This explains why every Japanese soldier who participated in the attack on the NEI carried a copy of the Emperor Meiji's Imperial Rescript of 1882. The Rescript contains the image of a cherry blossom, which is beloved of the Japanese, falling to the earth in perfect form. The Rescript also said: "If someone should enquire

[40] Edward F. L. Russell, *The Knights of Bushido: A Short History of Japanese War Crimes* (Greenhill Books 2002) 55.
[41] ibid [42] See Bergerud (n. 7) 407. [43] See Toland (n. 29) 808.

of you concerning the spirit of the Japanese, point to the wild cherry blossom shining in the sun." So was the sanctity of death made clear to every soldier of every rank.

Bushido therefore explains why the Japanese in the NEI so mistreated POWs in their custody. Those who had surrendered to the Japanese—regardless of how courageously or honorably they had fought—merited nothing but contempt; they had forfeited all honor and literally deserved nothing. Consequently, when the Japanese murdered POWs by shooting, beheading, and drowning, these acts were excused since they involved the killing of men who had forfeited all rights to be treated with dignity or respect. While civilian internees were certainly in a different category from POWs, it is reasonable to think that there was a "spill-over" effect from the tenets of *Bushido*. Nothing else explains the vicious and cruel beatings of civilians for minor disciplinary infractions by Japanese military and civilian camp guards, and the repeated torture of civilians during interrogations at the hands of the Japanese civilian police, *Kempeitai* military police,[44] and *Tokketai* special naval police.[45]

One other point merits discussion, since more than a few war crimes were committed by Japanese military personnel on orders from their superiors. While not part of *Bushido*, orders from higher ranking individuals were considered to be sacrosanct, in that Japanese soldiers "should have the idea that the orders from their superiors are nothing but the orders personally from His Majesty the Emperor."[46] Consequently, when a superior officer or non-commissioned officer, acting in conformance with *Bushido* precepts, ordered a subordinate to commit murder, beat, torture, or otherwise mistreat a POW or civilian, this belief that an order was sacrosanct explains why so many Japanese participated in war crimes—and why there appears to have been little soul-searching, much less questioning, of the legality of the misconduct.

Kempeitai and *Tokkeitai*

Finally, as members of the *Kempeitai* and *Tokkeitai* were responsible for many of the worst war crimes committed during the occupation, some discussion of these organizations is required. Moreover, as the commission of war crimes came to be considered as such an inherent part of day-to-day operations of the *Kempeitai* and *Tokkeitai*, the Dutch decided when creating their temporary courts-martial system that both police organizations should be prosecuted as criminal groups. As shown in Chapter 8, *Criminal Group Responsibility*, such prosecutions at military tribunals are unique in the history of war crimes.

[44] *Kempeitai* is also spelled *Kenpeitai*; either spelling is correct.

[45] *Tokkeitai* is the shortened form of *Tokubetsu Keisatsu-tai*, and means "Corps of Special [Naval] Police." The unit was created in 1942, most likely because the Navy did not want the *Kempetai* in its areas of operations.

[46] Philip R. Piccigallo, *The Japanese on Trial* (University of Texas Press 1979) 77.

The *Kempeitai* was the Japanese Army's military police. The *Tokkeitai* was the navy equivalent and, as a practical matter, there was no difference between the two organizations in either mission or structure. While one might have thought that their chief roles would be to maintain order within the Army and the Navy, this was not the case during World War II. On the contrary, the primary responsibility of the *Kempeitai* and *Tokkeitai* in the NEI was to root out and destroy all individuals and groups who were resisting the occupation.

The senior *Kempeitai* officer on Java and Sumatra was a major general; on Borneo and other islands under the Navy's administration, the senior *Tokkeitai* officer was a colonel-equivalent. There were only a few *Kempeitai* or *Tokkeitai* officers; almost all personnel were noncommissioned officers and enlisted men.

On Java alone, there were more than 520 *Kempeitai* personnel by the end of 1942 and roughly 700 *Kempei* (a member of the *Kempeitai* was called a *Kempei*) on the island by 1945. While the *Kempeitai* headquarters in Batavia was in the School of Law building, most agents were assigned to small detachments in various geographic locations. These detachments, which consisted of one officer and a few dozen lower ranking personnel, enjoyed considerable freedom of action in their operations to stamp out clandestine resistance activities.

The *Kempeitai* and *Tokkeitai* were also in charge of the military court system that tried anyone—Dutch, Eurasian, Chinese, Malay, or Indonesians—suspected of refusing to "follow the imperial way," which meant that the police and courts were one and the same. Moreover, the senior *Kempeitai* and *Tokkeitai* officer also was the president of the military court, which suggests that there was little justice to be had at any trial. In any case, there were periods on both Java and Sumatra where no trials were held. From July 1943 to March 1944 on Java, and from August 1943 to March 1944 on Sumatra, the authorities decided that it was too much of a burden to send new criminal cases to the military courts for trial. Consequently, *Kempei* officers were given the authority to sentence men and women in their custody, including a sentence to death. On Java, for example, such a death sentence imposed by a *Kempei* officer had only to be approved by the head of the *Kempeitai* and by an officer at the 16th Army's General Headquarters. On Java, nearly 300 death sentences were carried out during these months—in secret. Just how many were carried out by the *Kempeitai* on Sumatra is unknown.[47]

The *Kempeitai* and *Tokkeitai* obtained some information about anti-Japanese activities from the *Beppan*, the armed forces intelligence service. Most of their information, however, came from a network of Indonesians who had previously been members of the Dutch-controlled Political Intelligence Service (Dutch: *Politieke Inlichtingen Dienst*) or "PID." No one knows exactly how many worked for the Japanese but there were hundreds, if not thousands. They assisted

[47] See de Jong (n. 1) 203. For a first-hand account of life in a *Kempeitai* prison see Robert Schultz, "Held by the Kempeitai," in Sheri G. Tromp (ed.), *Four Years Till Tomorrow: Despair and Hope in Wartime Dutch East Indies* (Vanderheide Publishing 1999) 117–27.

the authorities by listening to foreign radio broadcasts, searching for weapons, and finding spies and prohibited objects (such as radios, Dutch flags, and weapons). They also assisted in interrogation sessions and, according to historian Peter Post, "displayed a cruelty matching that of the *Kempeitai* and *Tokkeitai* under whom they worked."[48]

A final point. While one might think that the Japanese would cease committing war crimes after the surrender of imperial forces in August 1945, this was not the case. On the contrary, the collaboration of Japanese soldiers with Indonesian guerrillas gave rise to additional criminal offenses prosecuted at temporary courts-martial. These are examined in Chapter 9, *Trials for Violations of the Terms of the Armistice.*

[48] Peter Post, "Policing Society," in Peter Post *et al.* (eds.), *Encyclopedia of Indonesia in the Pacific War* (Brill 2010) 154.

3

Prosecuting the Japanese

Creating War Crimes Tribunals in the Netherlands East Indies

Before the end of World War II, teams of investigators working for the United Nations War Crimes Commission (UNWCC) began gathering evidence of war crimes committed by the Axis powers in Europe and the Pacific. While some of this evidence became the basis for prosecutions at the international military tribunals in Nuremberg and Tokyo, which tried high-level political and military leaders who had waged "crimes against peace" and "crimes against humanity" ("Class A" war criminals), the agreement among the Allies was that national military tribunals would prosecute those Germans, Austrians, Italians, Japanese, Koreans, and Formosans[1] who had committed "minor" war crimes and were labeled "Class B" or "Class C" war criminals.[2]

In the Far East, the Allies convened military tribunals for the trial of "minor" war criminals in a variety of locations. The United States convened military commissions in Yokohama, Manila, and Shanghai, and on the islands of Kwajalein and Guam. The British held trials in Singapore, Malaya, North Borneo, Burma, and Hong Kong. In Saigon, French authorities prosecuted 230 individuals for war crimes and the Australians held war crimes courts in eight locations, including Darwin, Morotai (Netherlands East Indies), and Singapore. After achieving independence on July 4, 1946, the Philippines utilized military commissions to prosecute Japanese war criminals in Manila. Communist and Nationalist Chinese officials also prosecuted both military personnel and civilians for war crimes.[3]

[1] During World War II, Koreans and Formosans were Japanese nationals, as Korea and Taiwan were Japanese colonies.

[2] For more on the Class A war criminals prosecuted at the International Military Tribunal (Nuremberg) and International Military Tribunal for the Far East (Tokyo) see Telford Taylor, *The Anatomy of the Nuremberg Trials* (Little, Brown & Co. 1992) and Yuma Totani, *The Tokyo War Crimes Trial* (Harvard University Press 2008).

[3] For an authoritative study of Class B and C war criminal prosecutions see U.N. War Crimes Commission, *Law Reports of Trial of War Criminals*, vols. 1–15 (London: His Majesty's Stationery Office, 1947–1949). For a unique study of Allied prosecutions in the Far East see Philip R. Piccigallo, *The Japanese on Trial: Allied War Crimes Operations in the East, 1945–1951* (University of Texas Press 1977). See also Yuma Totani, *Justice in Asia and the Pacific Region 1945–1952* (Cambridge University Press 2015). For a focused study on one jurisdiction see Suzannah Linton (ed.), *Hong Kong's War Crimes Trials* (Oxford University Press 2013).

Military Trials of War Criminals in the Netherlands East Indies 1946–1949, Fred L. Borch.

Map 4 Locations of War Crimes Trials in the Netherlands East Indies.
Credit: U.S. Army Center of Military History, Washington, D.C.

As for the Dutch, authorities in the newly liberated Netherlands East Indies (NEI) were adamant about prosecuting Japanese war criminals in their custody for war crimes committed against Allied prisoners of war (POWs) and inhabitants of the colony. From March 6, 1946, when a "provisional" or "temporary" court-martial (Dutch: *temporaire krijgsraad*) in Batavia began hearing evidence of war crimes until the last trial on NEI soil was completed in December 24, 1949, NEI authorities convened 448 courts in which a total of 1,038 Japanese, Koreans, and Formosans were tried.[4] Others who had collaborated with the Japanese, including Europeans, Eurasians, Chinese, and Indonesians, were also prosecuted at these temporary courts-martial.[5]

[4] Levinus F. de Groot, *Berechting Japanse Orloogsmisdadigers in Nederlands-Indie, 1946–1949* (Art & Research 1990 (privately published)) 21; Appendix B, 487–503.

[5] Note that these temporary courts-martial also had *in personam* and subject matter jurisdiction over Dutch soldiers who committed war crimes during the counter-insurgency campaign against Indonesian guerillas. While a few prosecutions of Dutch soldiers did occur, these war crimes trials are beyond the scope of this book. For more on crimes committed by Dutch soldiers against Indonesians see Rémy Limpach, "Business as Usual: Dutch Mass Violence in the Indonesian War of Independence, 1945–49," in Bart Luttikhuis and A. Dirk Moses (eds.), *Colonial Counterinsurgency and Mass Violence* (Routledge 2014) 64–90; Rémy Limpach, *De brandende kampongs van Generaal Spoor* (Boom, 2016). See also J. A. A. van Doorn and W. J. Hendrix, *Het Nederlands/Indonesisch Conflict: Ontsporing van Geweld* (De Bataafse Leeuw 1985).

The largest number of trials in the NEI were held in Batavia (today's Jakarta) which, as the seat of the colonial government and headquarters of the Government Office for Tracing War Crimes,[6] was the most logical site for judicial proceedings. But temporary courts-martial were also held in eleven other locations in the archipelago: Ambon (Ceram), Balikpapan (Borneo), Banjarmasin (Borneo), Hollandia (New Guinea), Kupang (Timor), Macassar (South Celebes), Manado (North Celebes), Medan (Sumatra), Morotai, Pontianak (Borneo), and Tanjung Pinang. The accompanying map of the NEI shows the archipelago and trial locations.

This chapter examines how, after a policy decision had been made to prosecute the Japanese for war crimes only, the Dutch authorities in the NEI established, organized, and operated temporary courts-martial for these prosecutions. It first looks at how the Dutch decided upon the war crimes that could be prosecuted, including six offenses that were unique to the NEI military courts. It also looks at an unusual prosecutorial charging method involving group criminal responsibility that likewise is unique. Next, this chapter discusses how NEI authorities structured these military tribunals. It finishes by looking at the rules of evidence and procedure, jurisdiction, and defenses used at temporary courts-martial, as well as explaining how these war crimes courts operated in practice.

Determining the Law

What was a war crime in 1945?[7] What war crimes and other war-related offenses could be (and should be) prosecuted at NEI military tribunals? These were important questions for colonial authorities in the East Indies, for they involved both customary international law and domestic law. Ultimately, the Lieutenant Governor-General chose to make thirty-nine offenses prosecutable as war crimes at temporary courts-martial. Thirty-three were already accepted "violations of the laws and customs of war," while six were war crimes made prosecutable by NEI domestic law.

[6] The Government Office for Tracing War Crimes (Dutch: *Regeringsbureau voor Opsporing van Oorlogsmisdrijven*) was responsible for gathering evidence of war crimes committed by the Japanese against NEI and other Allied nationals and, on the basis of that evidence, recommending individual soldiers, sailors, and civilians for trial.

[7] Since 1945, definition of a war crime under the law of armed conflict has evolved significantly. At the end of World War II, for example, the law was clear: an armed conflict between two or more nation states was required before there could be a war crime. Today, it is accepted that a war crime may occur in a noninternational armed conflict. See *Prosecutor v. Delalić (aka Čelebići)*, IT-96-21-T (November 16, 1998). Additionally, rape was not a war crime in 1945. The deliberate, massive, and egregious use of rape as a weapon during the conflicts in Bosnia-Hercegovina and Rwanda, however, changed international law. Today, rape and other acts of sexual violence are war crimes under the law of armed conflict. See *Prosecutor v. Akayesu*, ICTR-96-4-T (Sept. 2, 1998). See also Michael J. Matheson and David Scheffer, "The Creation of the Tribunals," 110-12 *American Journal of International Law* (April 2016) 173, 201; Gary D. Solis, *The Law of Armed Conflict* (2nd edn., Cambridge University Press 2016) 339–43.

The starting point for decision-makers in Batavia in 1945 was those war crimes falling into the category of "violations of the laws and customs of war." After World War I, a fifteen-member Commission on Responsibility,[8] which was part of the Paris Peace Conference of 1919, made a "formal list" of thirty-three war crimes that it determined were violations of the "laws and customs of war." Twenty-five years later, when the UNWCC developed its list of war crimes, it considered this 1919 list to be authoritative and adopted it in its entirety. The UNWCC recognized that there might be other violations of the laws and customs of war that had not been included in the 1919 list, but every UNWCC member agreed that those on the 1919 list were customary international law in 1944.[9]

The thirty-three war crimes on the UNWCC list were the basis of the war-related offenses prosecutable at temporary courts-martial in the East Indies. The crimes listed were:

- murder and massacres
- systematic terrorism
- putting hostages to death
- torture of civilians
- deliberate starvation of civilians
- rape
- abduction of girls and women for the purpose of enforced prostitution
- deportation on civilians
- internment of civilians under inhuman conditions
- forced labor of civilians in connection with the military operations of the enemy
- usurpation of sovereignty during military occupation

[8] The commission's formal title was "Commission on the Responsibility of the Authors of the War and on Enforcement of Penalties." Its members were the United States, the United Kingdom, France, Italy, and Japan (each with two members), and Belgium, Greece, Poland, Rumania, and Serbia (each with one delegate). The commission's task was to inquire into the crimes committed by the German Empire and its Central Powers allies during the 1914–1918 war, and to fix responsibility for those crimes. In its report of March 29, 1919, the Commission identified and listed thirty-three "breaches of the laws and customs of war." United Nations War Crimes Commission, *History of the United Nations War Crimes Commission and the Development of the Laws of War* (His Majesty's Stationery Office 1948) 32–35.

[9] Under the law of armed conflict, an act is a war crime only if it satisfies four requirements. First, there must be a "war" or armed conflict in existence at the time of act is committed. Second, there must be a nexus or connection between the act and that conflict. Third, if the act is to be successfully prosecuted, it must part of a criminal code. Fourth, if the prosecuting tribunal is a war crimes court, the charged offense must violate "the laws and customs of war." See Solis (n. 7) 328.

In 1944, the UNWCC agreed upon this definition of crimes that violated the "laws and customs of war": "any grave outrages violating the general principles of criminal law as recognized by civilized nations and committed in war time or connected with the preparation, the waging or the prosecution of war or perpetrated with a view to preventing the restoration of peace." See United Nations War Crimes Commission, *History of the United Nations War Crimes Commission* (n. 8) 444.

- compulsory enlistment of soldiers among the inhabitants of occupied territory
- attempts to denationalize the inhabitants of an occupied territory
- pillage
- confiscation of property
- exaction of illegitimate or of exorbitant contributions and requisitions
- debasement of the currency and issue of spurious currency
- imposition of collective penalties
- wanton devastation and destruction of property
- deliberate bombardment of undefended places
- wanton destruction of religious, charitable, educational and historic buildings or monuments
- destruction of merchant ships and passenger vessels without warning and without provision for the safety of the passengers and crew
- destruction of fishing boats and of relief ships
- deliberate bombardment of hospitals
- attack and destruction of hospital ships
- breach of other rules relating to the Red Cross
- use of deleterious and asphyxiating gases
- use of explosive or expanding bullets and other inhuman appliances
- directions to give no quarter
- ill-treatment of wounded and prisoners of war
- employment of prisoners of war on unauthorized works
- misuse of flags of truce
- poisoning of wells.

While almost all of these UNWCC war crimes are self-explanatory, two deserve additional comment, as they featured prominently in NEI war crimes prosecutions: "systematic terrorism" and "enforced prostitution."

After World War I, the Allies were convinced that the Central Powers had engaged in repeated and multiple violations of the rights of combatants and civilians. The Germans, in particular, had executed "a system of terrorism carefully planned and carried out to the end" of the war, and their intent had been to "strike terror into every heart for the purpose of repressing all resistance."[10] This explains why the Report of the 1919 Commission on Responsibility lists "murders and massacres; systematic terrorism" as war crimes. The Dutch believed that the Japanese likewise had committed multiple offenses against POWs and civilians

[10] United Nations War Crimes Commission, *History of the United Nations War Crimes Commission* (n. 8) 33–4.

with the intent to terrorize the local population, as part of their long-term goal to eradicate forever the Dutch presence in the islands. "Systematic terrorism" is therefore frequently encountered as a charge against the accused in NEI temporary courts-martial.

"Systematic terrorism" often took the form of unlawful or indiscriminate "mass arrests" by the *Kempeitai*, *Tokkeitai*, and Japanese civilian police. These mass arrests were war crimes because they were conducted for the purpose of terrorizing the population. As the court explained in *Prosecutor v. Shigeki MOTOMURA and 15 Tokkeitai Members*:

> Unlawful mass arrests are to be understood as arrests of groups of persons firstly on the ground of wild rumors and suppositions, and secondly without definite facts and indications being present with regard to each person which would justify his arrest.
>
> The aforesaid mass arrests [alleged in *Motomura*] already contained elements of systematic terrorism for nobody, even the most innocent, was any longer certain of his liberty, and a person once arrested, even if absolutely innocent, could no longer be sure of health and life.[11]

As for "abduction of girls and women for purposes of enforced prostitution," the commission included this war crime on its formal list, even though there does not appear to have been any substantiated allegation of such an offense occurring during World War I, even in Belgium, where the German occupation had been especially hard on civilians.[12] But as Article 46 of Hague Convention IV of 1907 had required belligerents to respect "family honor and rights," there was no member of the commission who opposed this offense being listed as a violation of the laws and customs of war. For the NEI authorities, "enforced prostitution" would be an important offense in the prosecution of war crimes, since both Japanese soldiers and civilians were eventually convicted of forcing European women to work as prostitutes in Japanese licensed brothels serving military clientele.[13]

In addition to these thirty-three generally accepted violations of the laws and customs of war, NEI authorities also decided that five more offenses should be prosecutable as war crimes. The five additional war crimes were:

- ill-treatment of interned civilians or prisoners
- carrying out of or causing execution to be carried out in an inhuman way
- refusal of aid or prevention of aid being given to shipwrecked persons
- intentional withholding of medical supplies from civilians

[11] *Prosecutor v. Shigeki Motomura and 15 Tokkeitai Members*, U.N. War Crimes Commission, *Law Reports of Trial of War Criminals*, Case No. 79, vol. 8, 143. See Chapter 8 for a discussion of this trial.

[12] The Allies concluded that German soldiers committed rapes and other sexual assaults while occupying Belgium, but there were no claims of forced prostitution. John Horne and Alan Kramer, *German Atrocities, 1914* (Yale University Press 2001).

[13] As explained in Chapter 7, the term "enforced prostitution" is a misnomer. The phrase "forced prostitution" more accurately describes the offense identified by the UNWCC as a war crime, in that women and girls were forced or coerced into working in brothels; they were not "enforced" into working as prostitutes.

- commission, contrary to the conditions of a truce, of hostile acts or the incitement thereto, and the furnishing of others with information, the opportunity, or the means for that purpose.[14]

It seems clear that some of these offenses (such as ill-treatment of internees or POWs) in fact did violate the "laws and customs of war." However, as a practical matter this seems not to have been the rationale for adoption, as the NEI authorities simply used the powers that they had to make any war-related offense prosecutable at a temporary court-martial simply by enacting colonial legislation through decree.[15]

While NEI authorities were expanding the list of offenses that would be prosecutable at temporary courts-martial, they also decided that they should remove any possible obstacle to a successful prosecution by suspending the prohibition on *ex post facto* laws contained in the existing NEI Penal Code. Article 1 of that code stated that:

> No act is punishable except by virtue of a legal penal provision which preceded such act. Should there be a change in the legislation after the date on which the crime was committed the provision most favorable to the accused shall then be applied.[16]

This language expressed the bedrock principle of Anglo-American and European law that no crime may be punished, or any punishment imposed, unless the crime violates a *previously* enacted penal law.[17]

The NEI authorities must have realized that, at least as in regard to war crimes that violated the laws and customs of war, Article 1 did not present any obstacle to a successful prosecution because, as these offenses had long been recognized as war crimes under customary international law, they were not *ex post facto* laws. Perhaps a stronger argument could be made that Article 1 applied to the five additional war crimes that were to be prosecutable offenses, but that is an open question. In any event, the NEI authorities avoided the issue by following the lead of the metropolitan authorities in the Netherlands, and preempted any *ex post facto* defense by suspending Article 1.

[14] United Nations War Crimes Commission, "Netherlands Law Concerning Trials of War Criminals," *Law Reports of Trials of War Criminals*, vol. 11 (His Majesty's Stationery Office 1949) Annex 94.

[15] War crimes violating "the laws and customs of war" are different from war crimes made punishable by domestic law, as were the war-related offenses that NEI authorities added to the UNWCC list of thirty-three crimes in 1946. By way of example, the U.S. Congress has declared that "material support for terrorism" is a war crime, but this does not make the offense a war crime under customary international law. Stated differently, while "material support for terrorism" is a war crime prosecutable at any military court or commission created by the U.S. Congress to try war crimes, it is not a war crime against the law of nations, and would not be an offense at any law-of-war tribunal convened by another nation. See Solis (n. 7) 801–805.

[16] ibid 86.

[17] The prohibition *on ex post facto* laws is found in a number of national constitutions, including the U.S. Constitution (Article I, section 9 "[n]o ex post facto Law shall be passed.") It also is found in the European Convention on Human Rights (art. 7(1)) and Treaty of Rome creating the International Criminal Court (arts. 22, 23).

The rationale offered by the colonial government for suspending Article 1 was "State Security." This was the same rationale advanced by the Dutch in the Netherlands when they took similar action in suspending Article 1 in the Netherlands Penal Code. As the metropolitan authorities put it, it was "urgently necessary to lay down extraordinary penal rules" so as to be able to prosecute "certain acts committed during the time of the present war, which acts were *gravely deserving of punishment*" (emphasis added).

Article 1 was suspended in the Netherlands so that alleged Nazi war criminals (and those *Quislings* and traitors who had collaborated with them) could be prosecuted for their offenses. In the NEI, Article 1 likewise was suspended because justice demanded extraordinary changes to criminal law if the five new categories of war crimes committed by the Japanese and those who aided them were to be punished. This decision to remove *ex post facto* obstacles was not an aberration at the time. Witness the prosecution of Nazi defendants in the International Military Tribunal (IMT) for "crimes against peace"—an offense that had not been recognized prior to 1945 and arguably was *ex post facto* in its application.[18]

On September 22, 1945, the colonial authorities announced in Statute Book (Dutch: *Staatsblad*) Decree No. 135 that the NEI Penal Code (Dutch: *strafrecht*) would be amended in the near future to add a number of war crimes as criminal offenses under NEI law. Decree No. 135 also stated that the first article of the NEI Penal Code was suspended, thus removing any *ex post facto* obstacle to prosecution.

With the suspension of Article 1 in effect, Lieutenant Governor-General Hubertus J. van Mook signed Statute Book Decree No. 44 on June 1, 1946. This "Definition of War Crimes Decree" defined war crimes as "*acts which constitute a violation of the laws and usages of war committed in time of war* by subjects of an enemy power or by foreigners in the service of the enemy" (emphasis added). This definition was followed by the thirty-eight offenses—thirty-three from the UNWCC list and the five additional offenses that NEI officials decided were required for war crimes prosecutions.

In addition to the thirty-eight offenses listed in Decree No. 44, NEI authorities announced in Decree No. 45, the "War Crimes Penal Law Decree," that the offense of "conspiracy" would also be prosecutable at temporary courts-martial. By including this offense in Decree No. 45, which Lieutenant Governor-General van Mook also signed on June 1, 1946, NEI authorities were making a radical departure from Dutch civil law. This was because "conspiracy" is an Anglo-American criminal concept that was not recognized in the civil code framework utilized by European and most other countries, at least in the 20th century.[19] "Conspiracy"

[18] See Taylor (n. 2) 37–9.

[19] Conspiracy is still not a crime in most countries with a civil law system of jurisprudence. Recently, however, in response to the post 9/11 (September 11, 2001) proliferation of nonstate armed opposition groups and the fear of domestic terrorism, some European civil law states have added conspiracy to their national penal codes, including Norway (2002), Sweden (2003), and the Netherlands (2004). See Erling Johannes Husabø and Ingvild Bruce, *Fighting Terrorism through Multilevel Criminal Legislation* (Martinus Nijhoff 2009) 79, 83, 89.

had not previously been prosecuted as a war-related crime by any Dutch military tribunal.[20] Yet Article 5 of Decree No. 45 states that "an attempt at or complicity and conspiracy in a war crime are equally punishable with the crime itself," with conspiracy defined as an offense in which two or more persons have agreed to commit a crime. This offense seems to have been added in order to give additional flexibility to the prosecutors and judges at temporary courts-martial. It does not, however, appear to have been utilized. This is probably because the offense was unfamiliar to Dutch prosecutors with a civil law background and, most importantly, because group prosecutions were permitted under Article 10 of Decree No. 45. This existence of this article, which is discussed next, was very much a satisfactory alternative to a conspiracy prosecution.[21]

Article 10 reads:

> If a war crime is committed within the framework of the activities of a group of persons in such a way that the crime can be ascribed to that group as a whole, the crime shall be considered to have been committed by that group, and criminal proceedings taken against and sentence passed on all members of the group.
>
> No penalty shall be imposed on the member for whom it is proved that he had taken no part in the commission of the crime.

Article 10 did not create a new offense. Rather, it created a method of charging war crimes at temporary courts-martial. It became critically important because it permitted NEI authorities to prosecute Japanese nationals (and their associates) for committing war crimes collectively as a group.

Why did NEI authorities create this collective responsibility (Dutch: *collectieve aansprakelijkheid*) provision in Decree No. 45? The answer is that the inhabitants of the Indies had been so brutally mistreated by the Japanese *Kempeitai* military police[22] and *Tokkeitai* special naval police[23] that NEI authorities regarded these as inherently criminal organizations. As they saw it, committing war crimes was an integral part of the day-to-day operation of the *Kempeitai* and *Tokkeitai* and this meant that virtually every man who served in either group had effectively

[20] The Dutch, however, had criminalized conspiracy in 1886, but only when the offense involved crimes against the state (such as conspiracy to overthrow the Kingdom of the Netherlands).

[21] Note that, as a matter of international law, the decision to make conspiracy a war crime prosecutable at a temporary court-martial did not transform conspiracy into a violation of the laws and customs of war. But that does not mean that it was any less legitimate as a prosecutable offense at NEI military tribunals.

[22] Created in 1881, the *Kempeitai* was the Japanese Army's military police but it had a Gestapo-like mission, too. A member of the *Kempeitai* was called a *Kempei*. *Kempeitai* is also spelled *Kenpeitai*; either spelling is correct.

[23] Created in 1942, the *Tokkeitai* (the shortened form of abbreviated name of *Tokubetsu-keisatsu-tai*) was the Japanese Imperial Navy's "Corps of Special Police." During World War II, the *Tokkeitai* were also responsible for recruiting "comfort women" for official brothels set up in areas under Navy jurisdiction. Many, perhaps most, of these women were recruited against their will. The *Tokkeitai* are also alleged to have massacred hundreds of persons suspected of involvement in Communist plots in Borneo, while the *Tokkeitai* at Kendari killed a number of prisoners of war, including all the surviving crew of the destroyer *USS Edsall*, sunk south of Java in March 1942. See Aiko Utsumi, "Local Military Trials," in Peter Post *et al.* (eds.), *Encyclopedia of Indonesia in the Pacific War* (Brill 2010) 410.

participated in a war crime by virtue of his membership. Consequently, it was both morally and legally appropriate to prosecute these organizations as criminal groups and, unless an individual defendant could prove that he had not been a full participant in the particular war crime(s) being prosecuted, he was guilty of a war crime by virtue of his membership in the *Kempeitai* or *Tokkeitai*.[24] Since one-third of the 1,038 Japanese convicted by temporary courts-martial between 1946 and 1949 were either *Kempeitai* or *Tokkeitai*, this indicates the dim view that the NEI authorities took of these two military organizations.[25] But despite Article 10's use as a charging vehicle in prosecutions involving the *Kempeita*i and *Tokkeitai*, the provision was not restricted to those two Japanese police organizations;[26] witness the prosecution of the 25th Army under Article 10, as discussed in Chapter 8, Group Responsibility.

There also were two important practical reasons for inserting a provision on collective responsibility under Article 10: Ensuring individual criminal liability and efficient use of legal resources. First, permitting prosecution of mere membership in a group ensured that no individual member of the *Kempeitai* or *Tokkeitai* would escape responsibility for participation in what was essentially an organizational war crime—but where actual evidence of acts by specific individuals belonging to that group might be limited.

Second, group prosecutions were a more effective and efficient use of judicial resources in the strained post-war situation. Rather than charging individuals with individual war-related offenses, a prosecutor charged a group that had committed a war crime collectively. The three-judge tribunal then decided three issues: Whether in fact there was a group within the meaning of Article 10 (this was completely up to the discretion of the court); whether the charged offense had been committed; and the collective nature of that crime.

It was a defense to this collective liability charge that the accused was not a part of the group or, even if a member of the organization, had not participated in the war crime. Once the prosecutor produced evidence of group membership, it was up to the accused to show he was not a member of the group or else had not been a part of the charged misconduct.

Assuming that the court determined that the war crime or crimes had been committed collectively, the tribunal found the members of the organization guilty as a group and sentenced them according to the extent of their participation in the war crimes charged. Those holding leadership positions in the group would naturally be considered to have a greater degree of guilt (and receive a more severe sentence), while lower-ranking persons would have lesser degrees of guilt (and

[24] L. F. de Groot, "De rechtspraak inzake oorlogsmisdrijven in Nederlands Indië (1947–1949)," in *Militair Rechtelijk Tijdschrift*, vol. LXXVIII (Ministerie van Defensie 1985) 85.

[25] Iris Heidebrink, "Military Tribunals in the Netherlands East Indies," in Post *et al.* (eds.), *Encyclopedia of Indonesia in the Pacific War* (n. 23) 415.

[26] See de Groot, *Berechting Japanse Orloogsmisdadigers in Nederlands-Indie, 1946–1949* (n. 4) 25–31; Lisette Schouten, 'Colonial Justice in the Netherlands Indies,' in Kirsten Sellars (ed.), *Trials for International Crimes in Asia* (Cambridge University Press 2016) 88.

receive lighter sentences). By way of example, in *Prosecutor v. Koonosuke CHOO and 33 Kempeitai Members*, the defendants were indicted as a group for systematic terror and mistreatment of prisoners. The trial, which began in Batavia in February and finished in May 1947, resulted in twenty-eight defendants being convicted, based on their membership in the group. Their sentences, however, ranged from five years to death, depending on their participation in group war crime activities between April 1942 and September 1945.[27]

Article 10's collective responsibility was unique in the history of war crimes, and was markedly different from the treatment given to criminal organizations at the International Military Tribunal (IMT) in Nuremberg. As Telford Taylor explains in his authoritative book *The Anatomy of the Nuremberg Trials*, there was considerable support at the IMT for declaring that certain groups, including the Gestapo and the SS, were criminal organizations, and then convicting individual members of those criminal organizations of war crimes *solely* on the basis of their voluntary membership in those groups.[28]

Ultimately, however, the IMT decided that even if its members supported the principle of organizational criminality, there would be no individual criminal liability based on mere membership. Rather, the IMT decided that "conviction of a defendant, prosecuted for membership in a criminal organization, required proof that the defendant had joined voluntarily *and* that the defendant knew that the organization engaged in crime" that violated international law.[29] Absent this proof, an individual could only be convicted at Nuremberg if the evidence showed that he had personally participated in war crimes. As a practical matter, however, no individual defendant was convicted by the IMT based solely on the voluntariness and knowledge test; in every case, there was proof that the individual defendant had personally participated in criminal behavior.

Note the difference between Article 10 and the IMT approach. At Nuremberg, the original concept was to find *individual* liability based on the official declaration, prior to the individual's trial, that he had been a member of a criminal group. Under Article 10 of Decree No. 45, however, there was no declaration of group criminality *prior* to the trial of the members of the group. In theory, the NEI provision permitted the prosecution of a group even if only a *single* war crime was committed *once* by the group, provided the war crime "can be ascribed to that group as a whole." This is quite different from the "organizational criminality" attached to the Gestapo, SS, and Nazi Party leadership by the IMT.

The thirty-eight war crimes listed in Decree No. 44, and the conspiracy and group responsibility provisions of Decree No. 45, were a radical step away from both tradition and existing jurisprudence in Dutch legal history. For the first time in Dutch history, the colonial authorities departed from the European civil law tradition (as reflected in the existing written NEI Penal Code) and used "the laws and customs of war" as a *direct* source for prosecutable offenses. This

[27] *Prosecutor v. Koonosuke Choo and thirty-two Kempeitai*, Vonnis No. 24/1947, Batavia.
[28] See Taylor (n. 2) 280–5; 555–9. [29] ibid 558.

is an important point because, while war crimes prosecutions being conducted by metropolitan officials in the Netherlands relied upon *existing* Dutch penal law provisions in prosecuting individuals for war crimes (so that war crimes were punishable by metropolitan courts if they fell within the scope of Dutch municipal law), the NEI made war crimes *independent* of existing written NEI criminal law. Given that Dutch lawyers—then and now—practice law in a civil law framework, one might have expected the NEI to follow the lead of Dutch authorities in Europe and look to the existing penal code for offenses. But they did not.[30] Consequently, while American, British, and Commonwealth prosecutors, schooled in the common law, were comfortable in looking to customary law in selecting offenses for prosecution as war crimes, this was something very new for NEI jurists.

Why did the colonial authorities in the Indies adopt this novel approach? There were at least two reasons. First, and most importantly, adopting offenses from the laws and customs of war provided extraordinary charging flexibility to prosecutors. There was, for example, no existing NEI civilian criminal statute that covered "ill-treatment of the wounded or POWs" or "systematic terrorism" or "employment of prisoners of war on unauthorized works." But these crimes could be charged as a violation of customary law, as occurred in *Prosecutor v. Kenitji SONE*,[31] *Prosecutor v. Shikegi MOTOMURA and 15 Tokkeitai Members*,[32] and *Prosecutor v. Koshiro TANABE, Nakao YAHAGI, Shozo YAMAMOTO, and Tetsuo FUHAJA*,[33] respectively.

Second, charging offenses as violations of the "laws and customs of war" better described the systematic and widespread nature of Japanese criminal conduct than could the existing domestic criminal code. Its penal provisions were designed to punish civilians committing criminal acts on a relatively infrequent basis in the East Indies; the legislation was not equipped to handle the repeated criminal acts of Japanese soldiers, sailors, and civilians (and those who aided them) during the occupation, especially the widespread *collective* misconduct of the *Kempeitai* and *Tokkeitai*. Even when the misconduct being prosecuted could be charged under the NEI Penal Code, this was simply not going to be satisfactory. For example, a Japanese soldier who killed an alleged spy could have been prosecuted for murder under existing NEI criminal legislation. But the war crimes prosecutor who charged him with "carrying out an [unlawful] execution in an inhuman manner" was able to charge an offense that better described the misconduct.[34]

[30] Later, Dutch authorities in Holland did incorporate some customary law into their war crimes prosecutions, but long after war crimes tribunals in the NEI were underway. See "Netherlands Law Concerning Trial of War Criminals," in U.N. War Crimes Commission, *Law Reports of Trials of War Criminals* (n. 14) Annex 88.

[31] *Prosecutor v. Kenitji Sone*, Vonnis 24/1946, Batavia (Aug. 14, 1946).

[32] *Prosecutor v. Shikegi Motomura and 15 Tokkeitai Members*, No. 17/1947, Macassar (July 18, 1947); U.N. War Crimes Commission, *Law Reports of Trials of War Criminals*, Case No. 79, vol 8, 138–45.

[33] *Prosecutor v. Moritake Tanabe, Nakao Yahagi, Shozo Yamamoto, and Tetsuo Fuhaja*, Vonnis No. 109/1948, Medan (December 29, 1948).

[34] *Prosecutor v. Jinshiro Ito*, Vonnis No. 51/1947, Balikpapan.

The NEI authorities most likely did not decide to adopt the "laws and customs of war" as a source for prosecutable offenses in order to synchronize their prosecutions with other major war crimes efforts in the Asia-Pacific area. But, in using customary law as the direct source for war crimes—the approach used by the United States, Australia, and the United Kingdom—synchronization was the practical outcome, and it offered at least two benefits. Australian, American, British, and Dutch investigators worked in concert in gathering evidence of Japanese war crimes. Having the same foundational thirty-three UNWCC offenses meant that investigators were familiar, regardless of nationality, with the crimes that would be charged and could more easily gather evidence necessary for a successful prosecution. An additional benefit was that, as other Allied military tribunals developed case law in the course of their respective war crimes prosecutions, NEI tribunals could look to decisions in these other courts as precedent, or at least consider them as guidance.

A final observation about the applicable law is the following. Having decided to break with tradition, in that Decree No. 44 defined war crimes as violations of the laws and customs of war, it might seem that a NEI military tribunal trying Japanese defendants would be prohibited from looking to statutory NEI law for any legal authority. This was not the case; in practice, there was some flexibility. An official "Explanation" (No. 15031) published by the NEI Department of Justice in 1946, provided that "the Netherlands East Indies existing criminal laws ... remain in principle applicable to war crimes."[35] What this "Explanation" meant was that general rules and principles in the existing NEI Penal Code—such as those governing modes of criminality—remained valid legal authority in any prosecution of acts categorized as war crimes. But the "Explanation" also stated that these rules and principles were not applicable "when a deviation from the general Netherlands East Indies Penal Code has been established by decree expressly for war crimes." As a practical matter, this meant that a temporary court-martial could use domestic legal principles and rules in its decision-making, but that there was *no requirement* for the court members to refer to existing NEI criminal law.

Legal Framework (Court Structure, Rules, and Procedure)

On June 1, 1946, NEI Governor-General van Mook signed four decrees. As already discussed, Decree No. 44 set out the substantive law for the trial of war criminals. Decrees No. 45 (except for Articles 5 and 10), 46, and 47 governed the configuration of the temporary court-martial, rules of evidence, the content of decisions, and review procedures.

[35] Explanation No. 15031/1946, Department of Justice, U.N. War Crimes Commission, *Law Reports of Trials of the War Criminals* (n. 14) 91.

Every accused was prosecuted by a temporary court-martial[36] consisting of one president and two members, all of whom were military officers of at least twenty-five years of age.[37] The Governor-General appointed the members of the court and, in accordance with Allied war crimes agreements reached in Singapore in December 1945, Allied officers were also eligible for appointment to the NEI military tribunals. In fact, British officers occasionally were appointed and served.[38] The accompanying photo shows a temporary court-martial sitting in Batavia in 1947.

There was no geographic restriction on the exercise of subject matter jurisdiction by the temporary court-martial. Under Article 3, Decree No. 45, the "Netherlands East Indies Statutory Penal Provisions with regard to war crimes are applicable irrespective of the place where the crime is committed."[39] Consequently, as a matter of law, a Japanese soldier in NEI custody could be prosecuted for war crimes committed against Dutch POWs in camps in Formosa. As a practical matter, however, the temporary courts-martial restricted themselves to hearing evidence of war crimes committed on NEI soil.

The proceedings commenced with a formal charging document drawn up by the prosecutor (Dutch: *Auditeur Militair*); this was akin to an indictment in Anglo-American common law. This document informed the defendant of the charge(s) against him, the punishment sought by the prosecutor if the accused were convicted by the court, and the date upon which war crimes proceedings against him would commence. Prior to this formal charging, the accused would have been interrogated by an investigator(s) gathering evidence of wrongdoing, and the accused's statements (if any) would have been reduced to writing. The prosecutor based his charges on any written statement from the accused, and written statements from witnesses having knowledge of the accused's criminal conduct. Whenever possible, these statements were taken under oath, and signed by the person making them.

A final point on charging war crimes. In drafting the charges, the prosecutor was permitted to charge in the alternative, which meant that the accused could be charged with a war crime using alternative theories of liability. In *Prosecutor*

[36] In addition to "temporary" courts-martial created for war crimes prosecutions, there were two other types of courts-martial under NEI law: ordinary and field general. Ordinary courts-martial were the regular military tribunals, and consisted of a civilian lawyer (as president) and four officers; they routinely heard cases involving NEI military personnel. Field general courts-martial were established only in wartime, and consisted of a president and two members, all of whom were officers. These field general tribunals usually were appointed only to hear a specific case. Although ordinary and field general courts-martial had jurisdiction to hear war crimes cases, in practice only temporary courts-martial tried these offenses. See U.N. War Crimes Commission, *Law Reports of Trials of War Criminals* (n. 14)Annex 106.

[37] One historian erroneously claimed that the senior member of the tribunal had to be a civilian lawyer. See Piccigallo, *The Japanese on Trial* (n. 3)) 175. In fact, all members of a temporary court-martial were *required* to be military officers. See de Groot, "De rechtspraak inzake oorlogsmisdrijven in Nederlands Indië (1947–1949)" (n. 24) 88.

[38] A British officer served on the temporary court-martial that tried Kenitji Sone in Batavia in August 1946 (see Chapter 5).

[39] Decree No. 45, War Crimes Penal Law 1946 art. 3,

Photo 1 Three military officers sat in judgment at every temporary court-martial convened in the Netherlands East Indies.

Credit: Netherlands Institute of Military History, Ministry of Defense

v. Tadashige DAIGO, for example, the accused was charged with either actually ordering a subordinate to conduct unlawful executions or, alternatively, with permitting or condoning the commission of these war crimes by his subordinate, with liability then based on a theory of command responsibility. Such alternative charging, however, was not required by the law. On the contrary, the prosecutor was entitled to amend any charge if the facts and evidence were at variance with the charge. More importantly, the prosecutor could add charge(s) if the evidence produced at an accused's trial revealed that he had committed other war crimes.[40]

Prior to his initial appearance before the temporary court-martial, the accused consulted with his defense counsel. A defendant had the right to be represented by counsel and most defense counsel were Japanese. Interestingly, the law required that the accused have counsel and, if he declined to choose someone to represent him, a defense counsel was assigned to him by the tribunal president. But there

[40] *Law Reports of Trials of War Criminals* (n. 14) Annex 107.

apparently was no right to *legally* qualified counsel since, in addition to lawyers practicing in the NEI, active and retired officers of the Army and the Navy were eligible to serve as defense counsel, as was "any other person who has been given permission to appear as counsel by the president of the court."[41]

At the first formal proceeding, the accused was given the right to challenge any one of the three-judge court-martial "on the ground of lack of impartiality." Article 38, Decree No. 74 (1946), states that:

> If a defendant has any reason to think that the president of one of the members of a court-martial might not be a suitable judge in his case on the grounds of hatred, enmity or for any other reason, he shall be allowed to place the reason for his objection with due respect before the court-martial and request a challenge.

Under NEI law governing temporary courts-martial, the challenge was "taken at the discretion of the court" and in the absence of the member being challenged. If granted, the member was replaced by another officer. This apparently was a unique provision; in American and British war crimes trials, for example, the accused was not entitled to object to the appointment of a court member.[42] Given that many of the officers who served on temporary courts-martial had been held as POWs from 1942 to 1945, and suffered at the hands of the Japanese, one might think that there would be a strong basis for granting challenges for cause. This does not, however, appeared to have often occurred, if at all.

When the temporary court-martial was formally opened, the court heard evidence presented by the prosecutor as part of the "Verbal Process" (Dutch: *Proces Verbaal*). Most evidence consisted of written statements, taken under oath, resulting from questioning by investigators. This was the only real practical course of action, as most witnesses had left NEI soil by the time the temporary courts-martial convened to hear evidence against the various defendants in custody. This was especially true where the witnesses were Dutch and Allied POWs, as most of these men were repatriated as soon as possible after their experiences in Japanese camps.

All documents, statements (written or oral, sworn or unsworn) and other evidentiary items obtained during the pre-trial phase were collected together as a dossier and presented by the prosecution to the three-member panel. This is the normal process in civil law proceedings, and was followed at temporary courts-martial. Article 22 of Decree No. 47 permitted the tribunal members to consider "all documents produced at the sitting [of the temporary court-martial] and all statements wherever made." Each judge was allowed to give such documents and statements

> such conclusive strength *as he thinks they may possess*, if, in his opinion, the particular circumstances under which the war crime was committed or in which piece of evidence would have to be furnished, would form an obstacle to the further production of evidence or

[41] ibid 108.

[42] Alexander Zahar, 'Trial Procedure at the British Military Courts, Hong Kong, 1946–1948,' in Suzannah Linton (ed.), *Hong Kong's War Crimes Trials*, (Oxford University Press 2013) 24.

would result in an inadmissible delay in the termination of the case, should further evidence have to be produced.[43]

In this regard, the NEI approach to evidence was no different from that taken by the United States in its war crimes tribunals, which were called "military commissions." Under the rules of evidence applicable to such commissions, the officers sitting in judgment could consider any relevant evidence that was "probative" to a "reasonable" person. Consequently, all hearsay was admissible, provided the tribunal considered it to be relevant to the proceedings.[44] This flexible approach was the same at all other Allied war crimes trials. British officers sitting in judgment, for example, could consider any relevant evidence, including hearsay, and an accused had no right to demand that any witness deposition be taken on oath, much less that such a deponent be subject to cross-examination.[45]

The defendant had an absolute right to present evidence on his own behalf, and to testify in open court. Some denied any wrongdoing. A few defendants insisted that the charges against them were a case of mistaken identity; some other Japanese national was the culprit. Self-defense and a lack of mental responsibility were valid defenses, depending on the charged offense. But many Japanese defendants also raised the defense of superior orders, insisting that any act(s) they had committed, even if a war crime(s), must be excused because they had acted pursuant to the order of a superior in committing that offense.

Prior to World War II, the general rule in most military legal codes—including that of the United States—was that a soldier could not be punished for acts done under the orders of a superior.[46] In the Dutch East Indies, this also was the rule. But the NEI authorities, recognizing that this defense would preclude the conviction of subordinates for war crimes committed during the occupation, announced in Decree No. 45 that the defense was "inoperative in the sphere of war crimes."[47] Additionally, to ensure that a superior officer or non-commissioned officer did not escape criminal liability when a subordinate committed a war crime, Article 9 in Decree No. 45 further provided that:

[43] Staatsblad van Nederlandsch-Indie 1946, No. 47 art. 22; *Law Reports of Trials of War Criminals* (n. 14) Annex 108, emphasis added.

[44] President Roosevelt established this evidentiary standard when he appointed the military commission that tried eight U-boat saboteurs in 1942. See *Ex parte Quirin*, 317 United States Reports 1 (1942).

[45] See Zahar, "Trial Procedure at the British Military Courts, Hong Kong, 1946–1948" (n. 42) 41–2.

[46] The October 1940 version of War Department Field Manual 27-10, *Rules of Land Warfare*, para. 347, provided that individuals "will not be punished for … offenses … committed under the orders or sanctions of their commanders or governments." As the Allies learned of the nature and extent of Nazi and Japanese war crimes, however, they recognized that permitting the defense of superior orders as an absolute bar to punishment was no longer appropriate. Consequently, the United States modified the language of Field Manual 27-10 in November 1944 by adding para. 345.1 to the *Rule of Land Warfare* manual. This provision announced that: "individuals and organizations who violate the accepted laws and customs of war may be punished therefor. However, the fact that the acts complained of were done pursuant to the order of a superior or government sanction may be taken into consideration in considering culpability, either by way of defense or in mitigation of punishment."

[47] See U.N. War Crimes Commission, *Law Reports of Trials of War Criminals* (n. 14) Annex 99.

He whose subordinate has committed a war crime shall be equally punishable for that war crime, if he has tolerated its commission by his subordinate whilst knowing, or at least must have reasonably supposed, that it was being or would be committed.[48]

Like the provision removing the defense of superior orders, this provision also became extremely important when more senior Japanese officers on trial at temporary courts-martial claimed ignorance of war crimes committed by their subordinates.[49]

Under Article 48, where a defendant could show that he had been "forced by necessity" to commit the offense, or had committed "a crime under duress," this might be a valid defense at trial. Although the U.N. War Crimes Commission Annex on Netherlands law states that these defenses "were relevant in cases of a crime being committed upon the orders of a superior or as a member of a criminal group," the defense was not allowed when the accused had murdered a POW or killed an innocent person. Duress or necessity could, however, affect the severity of a sentence, especially if the accused was a junior ranking soldier or sailor.

After completing its "Verbal Process," which might take a single day or might take a considerable period of time and require multiple court hearings, the panel delivered its findings and sentence in an opinion or "case" (Dutch: *Vonnis*). Unlike U.S. and British military commissions, which were not obliged to disclose the basis for their decisions, NEI tribunals were required to state the rationale for their decisions by Article 79 of Decree No. 74. That provision required "the reasons for the verdict and the description of the offense, together with a statement on the circumstances which … give rise to a severer or lighter punishment."[50] This intent of this requirement was to ensure that the judges on the tribunal not only identified the evidentiary basis for their decisions but articulated the rationale for both findings and sentencing. Presumably the idea was to prevent slipshod or sloppy work, and preclude a "rush to judgment," but requiring the reasons for a verdict and sentence also made it easier for the commanding general who had to issue a "fiat of execution" in the case (explained below) to make a decision.

The temporary court-martial could find an accused guilty only if it was "convinced by legal evidence that the act with which the accused was charged was committed by him." While this is not equivalent to the "reasonable doubt" standard for a finding of guilty in U.S. law, it was the functional equivalent.[51]

[48] ibid 100.

[49] This provision was in line with developments in other Allied war crimes trials after World War II. For example, the five American members of the military commission that found General Tomoyuki YAMASHITA guilty of war crimes in December 1945 concluded that he was liable because he knew or "must have" known (and permitted) individuals and units under his command to commit "widespread, repeated, constant atrocities of the most violent character." See U.N. War Crimes Commission, *Law Reports of Trials of War Criminals* (1948) Case No. 21, vol. 4, 1, 17.

[50] U.N. War Crimes Commission, *Law Reports of Trials of War Criminals* (n. 14) Annex 108–109.

[51] But note that there was no "reasonable doubt" standard required for a finding of guilty at U.S. war crimes tribunals during World War II. As a practical matter, however, most military commissions hearing evidence of war crimes used the reasonable doubt standard in the absence of a suitable prescribed standard. War Department, *Report of the Deputy Judge Advocate for War Crimes, European Command, June 1944 to July 1948* (1948) 67.

As Philip Piccigallo noted in *The Japanese on Trial*, a major criticism of Allied prosecutions was that there was wide disparity in sentencing of Japanese war criminals because "no set rules or pattern for sentencing" existed and that military tribunals "therefore wielded sole discretion over the handing out of punishments."[52] As Dr. Alexander Zahar puts it when discussing sentencing at British tribunals, "[b]ecause the judges recorded no reasons, we know little about how they went about sentencing the Japanese accused... verdicts were summarily pronounced without elaboration ... Sentences followed after submissions on mitigation. No attempt was made to justify them."[53] The Dutch, however, alone among all the Allies, muted this criticism by creating a unique provision governing permissible punishments. Article 4 of Decree No. 45 provided that anyone found guilty of a war crime "shall be punished with the death penalty, or imprisonment for life, or imprisonment for not less than one day, and more than 20 years." Consequently, while all other courts-martial and military commissions hearing war crimes in the Far East had complete discretion when it came to punishments, temporary courts-martial in the NEI were restricted when it came to sentencing (albeit having complete discretion in deciding which of these punishments to impose).

Why a restriction on imprisonment? The most likely explanation is that NEI authorities decided as a matter of policy that they did not desire to have jail sentences that constituted a life sentence without being labeled as such. For example, if a temporary court-martial sentenced a war criminal to forty-five years in prison, was there any meaningful difference between that sentence and life imprisonment? Restricting the maximum sentence of confinement to twenty years also arguably forced the three members of the tribunal to reserve life imprisonment for only the most serious offenders. After all, as with the death sentence, the court members certainly realized that too many life sentences would be criticized as unduly harsh.

While there was no appeal from the judgment of an NEI war crimes tribunal, the panel's judgment was required to be presented to the commanding general of the geographic area in which the tribunal was sitting for his confirmation of the sentence.[54] This "fiat of execution" (Dutch: *fiat van executie*) was the last step in the process, except that when the death penalty was imposed, the commanding general of the area was required to forward the case to the Governor-General in Batavia for his decision as to whether a pardon should be granted.

After the Governor-General made his decision not to pardon the convicted prisoner, the death sentence was carried out. According to Dutch historian Bart van Poelgeest, executions were by firing squad.[55]

[52] See Piccigallo, *The Japanese on Trial* (n. 3) 117.

[53] See Zahar, "Trial Procedure at the British Military Courts, Hong Kong, 1946–1948" (n. 42) 58–9.

[54] This senior officer, if he disagreed with the sentence, could decline the fiat of execution and return the case to the tribunal for further action. The tribunal could then alter the sentence or decline to take any action, in which case the matter was sent to the Governor-General for action.

[55] L. van Poelgeest, *Japanse Besognes: Nederland en Japan, 1945–1975* (SDU 1999) 44.

If the accused petitioned for mercy, then the Governor General was required to obtain an advisory opinion from the NEI Supreme Military Court (Dutch: *Hoog Militair Gerechtshof*). Ultimately, however, the Governor-General had the absolute authority to decide the case; the opinion of the Supreme Court was advisory only.

4

Preparing for Trial

Gathering Evidence and Selecting Cases for Prosecution

The decision to prosecute very much depended on whether the Netherlands East Indies (NEI) authorities had a Japanese defendant in custody when temporary court-martial operations finally commenced in 1946. What follows is a look at how war criminals were identified by the authorities, how evidence was gathered for prosecutions, and how cases were selected for trial at temporary courts-martial. The chapter closes with some thoughts on the challenges facing those who served as judges at these military tribunals.

Identifying War Criminals

Many of those Japanese soldiers and sailors who had committed war crimes during the conquest of the Indonesian archipelago in March 1942, or during the occupation that lasted until August 1945, were beyond the reach of NEI authorities. This was because they had left the islands for other duty assignments before the end of hostilities, and their whereabouts were unknown.

Many suspected war criminals also avoided military trials because they had been repatriated before Allied and Dutch authorities could complete their investigations. In 1946, the British repatriated almost 300,000 Japanese nationals from the NEI. Another 30,000 were repatriated from central Java a short time later. There was only "superficial screening" of these 330,000 individuals because a single Dutch officer, G. J. Jongejans, was responsible for identifying suspects. Jongejans had to match individual affidavits with individual suspects, which would have been a time-consuming task, even with a team of investigators.[1] Of the roughly 1,500 Japanese suspects remaining, 500 were transferred to the British for trial by military courts in Singapore.[2] All this meant that more a few guilty individuals were released.

[1] Robert Cribb, "Avoiding Clemency: The Trial and Transfer of Japanese War Criminals in Indonesia, 1946–1949," 31 *Japanese Studies* (September 2011) 155.

[2] Iris Heidebrink, "Military Tribunals in the Netherlands East Indies," in Peter Post *et al.* (eds.), *Encyclopedia of Indonesia in the Pacific War* (Brill 2010) 411.

Still other Japanese escaped justice because they had been killed in action, died of their wounds, or committed suicide. Rear Admiral Kōichirō HATAKEYAMA, for example, was in command of Japanese forces invading the island of Amboina in February 1942. Hatakeyama ordered a subordinate commander to kill all the POWs in his custody. His reasoning was that these men would likely become "a drag upon the movement of the Admiral's forces." But Hatakeyama was never prosecuted—and he likely would have been sentenced to death if convicted—because he was killed in an aircraft crash in China in 1945.[3] Similarly, Major General Sheiji NOZAKI and Colonel Tobo OKUBO, who would have been prosecuted for their involvement in the "Semarang forced prostitution affair," escaped lengthy prison sentences and perhaps even death when they took their own lives before they could be tried.[4]

That some war criminals were beyond the reach of the colonial authorities was not really the problem. Rather, the fundamental challenge was simply that it was extraordinarily difficult to identify *individuals*, especially ordinary soldiers or junior noncommissioned officers, who had actually killed or mistreated POWs and civilians. By way of example, the Dutch authorities certainly desired to identify, locate, and prosecute those soldiers in Colonel Toshinari SHOJI's brigade who had murdered British and Dutch POWs on March 1, 1942. But was there any Allied soldier still available in August 1945 who had witnessed the atrocity? Even if there was such a person, was he still able positively to identify the Japanese trigger-pullers some three and one-half years later? As shown in Chapter X, the Dutch did prosecute Shoji at a tribunal in Batavia in 1949, and that court did convict him for war crimes on the basis of command responsibility. The men who had actually done the killings, however, were never positively identified, much less prosecuted.

Even when the shooting ceased, and the chaos of the battlefield ended, identifying an individual who had committed war crimes was not necessarily any easier. Years after the event, a woman wrote that, in April 1942, she remembered seeing three dead Dutchmen tied to the barbed wire fence near the entrance of a Royal Netherlands Indies Army (Dutch: *Koninklijk Nederlandsch Indisch Leger* (KNIL)) prisoner of war (POW) camp on Java. She subsequently learned from her fiancé that all three men had escaped after hearing that American troops had landed nearby. This was not true, but rumors of Allied landings were widespread in the early months of the occupation. In any event, the POWs had been recaptured by the Japanese. To ensure that there were no more escape attempts, the Dutchmen were summarily executed by bayonet. "One of them spat blood at the Japanese officer—splattering it all over his uniform—and shouted "Lang leve Koningin

[3] Edward F. L. Russell, *The Knights of Bushido: A Short History of Japanese War Crimes* (Greenhill Books 2002) 100–2; War History Office of the National Defense College of Japan, *The Invasion of the Dutch East Indies* (University Press 2015) 371 http://pwencycl.kgbudge.com/H/a/Hatakeyama_Koichiro.htm (last accessed October 27, 2016).

[4] For more on Nozaki and Okubo see Chapter 8, Forced Prostitution nn. 36 and 37, and accompanying text.

Wilhelmina!" (Long live Queen Wilhelmina!)" These two acts so enraged the officer that he drew his revolver and killed the man.[5]

There is no evidence that this war crime was prosecuted. Assuming, however, that there were KNIL POWs who had witnessed the unlawful execution and that these POWs survived the war, would they have been able to identify with certainty the Japanese who bayoneted and shot their fellow POWs? And surviving the war was problematic, given that the vast majority of KNIL POWs were removed from the Indies and scattered to various locations, where they were forced to do dangerous work, including building railroads in Burma and Thailand or working underground in mines in Japan. Twenty percent of the KNIL POWs in Japanese captivity did not live to see the end of the war.

There were other identification challenges for the colonial authorities. Even when the NEI's Government Office for the Tracing of War Crimes (Dutch: *Regeringsbureau voor Opsporing van Oorlogsmisdrijven*) had a Japanese suspect in custody, victims and witnesses were not necessarily able to assist in the investigation. Europeans and Eurasians, as well Chinese, Arabs, Malaysians, British Indians, and Indonesians, simply did not understand or speak Japanese. Consequently, they did not know the names of those who had beaten, tortured, or mistreated them during the occupation. Only rarely did a Japanese person speak Dutch, and it was just as rare for a POW or internee to speak Japanese.

A related problem was that some Japanese surnames were so common that even when a suspected war criminal had been identified by name, the authorities were sometimes unsure about whether they had the right person on trial. By way of example, in the September 1946 trial of Saburo YAMURA at Balikpapan, the court-martial discussed the fact that Yamura's surname was common among the Japanese, and that it consequently was possible for there to have been a "mistake of persons." In this prosecution, however, the court was convinced that there was no mistaken identity since "it has been established at the trial that there was only one Yamura at Sanga-Sanga." Yamura, who had been charged with systematic terrorism, was found guilty and sentenced to death.[6]

Cross-racial identification was also a major issue. While familiar with Indonesian, Chinese, and Malay facial features, the white and Eurasian residents of the NEI had little experience with identifying Japanese faces. This factor, combined with the language barrier, complicated identification of perpetrators.[7] Additionally, the reliability of an eyewitness identification is very much dependent on the length of

[5] Sylvia Aart de Jong Klootwijk, "Life Outside the Camps and the *Bersiap* Time," in Sheri G. Tromp (ed.), *Four Years Till Tomorrow: Despair and Hope in Wartime Dutch East Indies* (Vanderheide Publishing 1999) 150–1. This may be the same war crime recorded in Louis de Jong (with an Introduction by Jeroen Kemperman), *The Collapse of a Colonial Society: The Dutch in Indonesia during the Second World War* (KILTV Press 2002) 332.

[6] *Prosecutor v. Saburo Yamura*, Vonnis, No. 1/1946 (September 13, 1946), Balikpapan. For more on Yamura's trial see Chapter 5 nn. 30 to 32, and accompanying text.

[7] Nothing has changed: today, cross-racial identification continues to be a problem in judicial proceedings, particularly in multi-racial societies. See Bell C. F. Chung, *Cross-Racial Eyewitness Identification* (Lambert Academic Publishing 2011).

time that the witness has contact with the suspect, and passage of time between that sighting and the actual identification. Consequently, unless a witness had frequent and repeated contact with a Japanese suspect, identification was often problematic.[8]

Remember also the legal procedure used at the temporary courts-martial did not give the accused any right to confront his accusers. There were many good reasons for this, starting with the fact that many witnesses who had been victims of war crimes wanted to go home after being released from a POW or internee camp. Some were in extraordinarily poor health. In any event, these persons simply could not be kept in the NEI waiting for an accused's court-martial to begin at some unknown future date. As a result, most of the evidence considered by the judges at temporary courts-martial consisted of affidavits rather than in-court testimony; often it was only the accused who gave evidence in person during the proceedings. But the Dutch were no different from the Americans or the British in permitting the use of sworn statements instead of requiring live testimony; other Allied war crimes tribunals also permitted such affidavits.[9]

These affidavits were generally reliable, and the result of good investigative work. But when the person giving the statement said it had been the accused who had tortured or otherwise mistreated him, this identification of the accused as the culprit did not necessarily mean that the witness had actually seen the accused during the course of the investigative interrogation. On the contrary, the witness might have simply identified the accused from a photograph. There was nothing improper about using a photograph, and perhaps that was the only feasible way for a witness to identify an accused, if that person was in one geographic location and the suspect in custody in another, or otherwise unavailable. Using a photograph did not, however, enhance the reliability of the identification process, and required the investigator to be more careful.

At least one judge recognized the problems with reliable identification of a Japanese accused. In 1985, Lieutenant Colonel Levinus F. de Groot, who is

[8] For more on the problems of eyewitness identification in general see Elizabeth F. Loftus, *Eyewitness Testimony* (Harvard University Press 1996).

[9] At British military tribunals convened in Hong Kong, for example, "the lifting of restrictions on hearsay was complete," which meant that "whole cases were sometimes proven through written testimonials alone." See Alexander Zahar, "Trial Procedure at the British Military Courts, Hong Kong, 1946–1948," in Suzannah Linton (ed.), *Hong Kong's War Crimes Trials* (Oxford University Press 2013). British war crimes courts sitting in other locations followed the same rule on the use of affidavits. At U.S. military commissions in Guam, Manila, Shanghai, and Yokohama, prosecutors likewise used affidavits and depositions instead of live testimony, as any evidence that "would have probative value in the mind of a reasonable man" was admissible. *In re Yamashita*, 327 U.S. 1, 9 (1946). Whether or not these written statements had "probative value" was determined by the commission members. Similarly, Australian military courts could consider any "document appearing on the face of it to be authentic," which meant that affidavits were admissible. See Philip R. Piccigallo, *The Japanese on Trial: Allied War Crimes Operations in the East, 1945–1951* (University of Texas Press 1977) 125, 203. French war crimes tribunals, operating in accordance with the Code de Justice Militaire, likewise had the discretion to consider any evidence "of value for finding the truth," and this meant out-of-court statements were admissible.

pictured in the accompanying photograph, and who had served as president of the temporary court-martial sitting in Batavia, wrote that:

> People were only too happy to testify against the Japanese, and they were not overly concerned about the truthfulness of the evidence they gave. Their testimonies were for various reasons often grossly exaggerated. *Their identifications of people from photos, or [from] face-to-face confrontations with those [who they believed] has mistreated them or with whom they had been in contact were performed with stunning ease and appalling indifference.* The people who were involved in the investigation (trained and untrained) often displayed a complete lack of objectivity and responsibility when interrogating witnesses [to obtain affidavits] or when collecting other data [for use in court].[10]

Despite Levinus de Groot's comments, and the general problems with identifying Japanese war criminals, there is no evidence that any of the 1,038 Japanese defendants tried at temporary courts-martial were victims of mistaken identity. Rarely did an accused claim that it was some other Japanese soldier, sailor, or civilian who had committed the war crime with which he was charged. After all, since a large number of those prosecuted at NEI tribunals had worked at POW or civilian internment camps, and consequently had frequent contact with the witnesses giving evidence against them, there was no reason to claim mistaken identity. It was no accident that the first Japanese soldier to be tried and executed for war crimes in the NEI was Captain Kenichi SONE, who had been the commandant of both a POW camp in Batavia and a civilian camp in Tjideng (Cideng). Hundreds of witnesses could positively identify Sone as the man who had mistreated them because they had seen him almost daily. Similarly, when a prosecutor brought charges against a Japanese soldier for the war crime of unlawful execution, the accused almost never denied having carried the killings. Rather, he admitted having shot or beheaded the victims, but insisted that he had been following the orders of his superior.

Where establishing individual identity was too difficult, however, the NEI authorities did have a unique work-around: Collective responsibility under Article 10 of Decree No. 45. As explained in Chapters 3 and 8, the theory was that if committing war crimes was an integral part of the day-to-day operations of an organization, then the persons assigned to that organization were collectively responsible as members of a criminal group. This meant that it was not necessary to identify and charge an individual member of the *Kempeitai* and *Tokkeitai* with a war crime if the group in which the individual had served was charged collectively with the offense. While membership alone did not guarantee a finding of guilty (there was no strict liability standard under Article 10), it was incumbent on the individual defendant to provide proof that he had not been a full participant in the particular war crime(s) being prosecuted. Absent such evidence, he could be found guilty of a war crime by virtue of his membership of the group.

[10] L. F. de Groot, "De rechtspraak inzake oorlogsmisdriven in Nederlands-Indië (1947–1949)," 78 *Militair Rechtelijk Tijdschrift* (1985) 86 (emphasis added), translation in Lisette Schouten, "Colonial Justice in the Netherlands Indies," in Kirsten Sellars (ed.), *Trials for International Crimes in Asia* (Cambridge University Press 2016) 86.

Photo 2 This poster of sixty *Kempeitai* members suspected of war crimes was published in a Batavia newspaper in 1946.

Credit: Netherlands Institute for War Documentation (NIOD), Amsterdam

Despite the existence of Article 10, the colonial authorities were sparing in using it. They almost certainly realized that it was better to find evidence of individual involvement in a war crime rather than convict on the basis of group responsibility and, in at least one case, the judges rejected the prosecutor's attempt to use it as a basis for criminal liability.[11] The importance of Article 10, however, was that it ensured that those whose day-to-day duties meant that they had almost certainly committed war crimes would not escape justice simply because evidence of their individual misconduct was lacking.

Gathering Evidence for Prosecution

Even when the authorities had identified a suspected war criminal, it was a challenge to gather evidence that would support a prosecution. Part of the problem was that the Dutch did not create their war crimes investigative machinery until September 1945, when they established the Government Office for the Tracing of War Crimes in Batavia. Only later was a satellite office set up in the Netherlands to obtain affidavits from Dutch citizens who had been victims of war crimes but had already left the Indies for the Netherlands after being liberated from POW or internment camps.

The Dutch colonial authorities, however, were not starting from scratch. During the war, the Netherlands Forces Intelligence Service had begun collecting evidence of Japanese war crimes, and teams of Australians and British investigators on the ground in the NEI (principally on the island of Java) in late 1945 and early 1946 also had collected information about Japanese war crimes.

Initially, the U.N. War Crimes Commission (UNWCC) was supposed to coordinate all Allied war crimes efforts in the Pacific, in order to ensure that there was a uniform approach to investigating and trying war criminals. At the end of hostilities against Japan, however, the UNWCC had still not decided upon any final arrangements. Unwilling to wait any longer, the British began arresting Japanese suspects and setting up war crimes tribunals in the South-East Asia Command (SEAC). The result was that, in October 1945, the UNWCC transferred responsibility over Class B and C Japanese war criminals to SEAC.[12]

That same month, the Allies agreed that they would work together and share information developed in their war crimes investigations. They also agreed that each Allied country would have the right to hold war crimes trials involving those persons (mostly Japanese) who had victimized its citizens. These trials could be held "in the most convenient place" and permissible punishments

[11] *Prosecutor v. Hitoshi Imamura and Seizaburō Okazaki*, Vonnis No. 1/1949, Batavia (March 16, 1949); see Chapter 10 nn. 28, and accompanying text.

[12] Nederlands Instituut voor Oorlogsdocumentatie (Netherlands Institute for War Documentation), "Voorlopige informative van het Departement van Justitie te Batavia over de berechting van orrlogsmisdadigers," collection 400, inventory no. 1926 (February 20, 1946).

were confiscation of property, death, fines, hard labor, and even flogging (although death and imprisonment were the only punishments ever used by war crimes tribunals).[13]

Meanwhile, investigators at the Government Office for the Tracing of War Crimes in Batavia did thousands of interviews of Japanese suspects and their victims. A starting point for many investigations was a simple questionnaire, which the colonial authorities distributed to all those who had been liberated from POW and internment camps. These questionnaires solicited reports of war crimes either inflicted on the person completing the questionnaire or about which he had knowledge. The information in these written documents were invaluable as a starting point for investigators because they provided names, dates, and descriptions of the offense(s). Moreover, since the Japanese had destroyed occupation records containing possible evidence of war crimes prior to their surrender, the questionnaires were critical in more than a few cases.

The Government Office for the Tracing of War Crimes also depended on members of the public to assist in investigations. Witness the photograph—depicting sixty *Kempeitai* members suspected of war crimes—published in Batavia's *Het Dagblad* newspaper in 1946. The intent of this "wanted poster" was not only to find and identify suspects but also to obtain witnesses who could testify against these Japanese suspects.[14]

While investigators labored in Batavia and elsewhere in the Indies, Dutch officers stationed at SEAC's headquarters in Singapore worked alongside their British, American, Australian, and French counterparts in investigating war crimes. These Dutchmen developed "the closest liaison ... with the result ... that everyone worked[ed] in complete harmony to achieve one aim."[15] The SEAC investigators compiled dossiers on war crimes committed in the NEI and against Dutch nationals elsewhere, including Burma, Formosa, and Manchuria. Eventually, the number of cases to be investigated increased to such a degree that the Netherlands established its own war crimes investigation team. Led by Captain J. G. BENDERS, this group initially focused on war crimes committed by Japanese, Koreans, and Formosans in the NEI. Later, the Benders team also investigated those who had collaborated with the Japanese during the occupation.[16]

In December 1945, SEAC and Dutch authorities agreed that the NEI would begin trying Japanese war criminals at temporary courts-martial. Some 200 Japanese suspects had already been identified, and forty-three had been taken into custody. Most were POW and civilian camp personnel, who had been the easiest to identify and build cases against.[17] Trials could not begin against the Japanese,

[13] See Cribb (n. 1) 156.

[14] Peter Post *et al.* (eds.), *Encyclopedia of Indonesia in the Pacific War* (Brill 2010) 158.

[15] See Piccigallo, *The Japanese on Trial* (n. 9) 179.

[16] See Schouten (n. 10) 79; Nederlands Instituut voor Oorlogsdocumentatie (Netherlands Institute for War Documentation), "Rapoort uitgebracht ingevolge mondelinge opdracht van den heer Procureur-Generaal," collection 400, inventory no. 442 (March 8, 1946).

[17] See Piccigallo, *The Japanese on Trial* (n. 9) 179.

Photo 3 Then Major Levinus F. de Groot served first as a member and later as the president of the temporary court-martial in Batavia; this photograph is circa 1990.
Credit: Moessen Maandblad, Amersfoort, Netherlands

however, until the NEI authorities promulgated laws and regulations that would define war crimes and create the process for conducting war crimes trials. When the "Definition of War Crimes Decree" and "War Crimes Penal Law Decree" were officially promulgated in June 1946, trials now commenced. The first Japanese war criminal was charged on July 30, 1946, when the prosecutor in Batavia alleged that Captain Kenitji SONE was guilty of systematic terrorism, mistreatment of POWs, and mistreatment of civilian internees.

Selecting Cases for Prosecution

The Government Office for Tracing War Crimes selected cases for prosecution based on the available evidence. Given the issues surrounding the identification of war criminals and gathering evidence, the cases selected by the Government Office fell into two major categories: POW and internee camp personnel and members of the *Kempeitai* and *Tokkeitai*. As previously explained, the former were readily identifiable because the Dutch POWs and internees had frequent contact with them and, as the camps were still operating in the NEI when the Japanese surrendered in August 1945, most of the men running those camps were still in the colony. Similarly, members of the *Kempeitai* military police and *Tokkeitai* naval police were readily identifiable, given their high profiles in the day-to-day Japanese occupation of the NEI. *Kempeitai* and *Tokkeitai* officials arrested and interrogated NEI citizens suspected of anti-Japanese activities, and the victims who had contact with these police officials usually had little problem identifying those Japanese who had beaten, tortured, or otherwise mistreated them while in *Kempeitai* or *Tokkeitai* custody. This explains why roughly one-third of the accused who appeared at temporary courts-martial belonged to the *Kempeitai* or *Tokkeitai*.

Challenges Facing Temporary Courts-Martial Judges

Those who served as judges between 1946 and 1949 faced a number of professional and personal challenges. There was a shortage of qualified legal staff, which made it difficult for the court machinery to operate smoothly. There also were too few judges, and most were overworked since they served in both the civilian (Dutch: *Landgerecht*) courts and the temporary courts-martial. The biggest challenge facing the judges, however, was that few were free of bias and prejudice. Having suffered personally at the hands of the Japanese or having family, friends, or colleagues who had been mistreated by the Japanese during the occupation, it was simply impossible for them now to sit in judgment of Japanese defendants without being affected by their own experiences.

Then Major Levinius F. de Groot, for example, had been mobilized as a Reserve Infantry captain in December 1941 and, while he apparently had not seen combat, de Groot had been held as a POW in various camps on Java from March 1942 until September 1945. This meant that when Major de Groot subsequently sat as a judge in Batavia, he was well aware that thousands and thousands of KNIL POWs had died because of mistreatment by the Japanese. Additionally, he knew that roughly 13 percent of civilians who had been interned by the Japanese also perished and that many of those who survived captivity suffered from starvation and disease. Given his personal experience, there is no way that de Groot could have been free of prejudice against a Japanese accused. In an ideal world, those sitting in judgment would have perhaps come from the Netherlands, and consequently be relatively free of anti-Japanese bias. But this was impossible, as there was a shortage of qualified men with a legal background and, in any event, metropolitan Holland was conducting its own war crimes prosecutions against the Germans and those who had collaborated with them, and so there were no judges available to send to the Indies.

Fortunately, the colonial authorities built in two safeguards that provided at least some protection for the accused against a judge's desire for revenge or retribution. As discussed in Chapter 3, a defendant at a temporary court-martial had the right to challenge the judge on the grounds that he was not impartial. While this rarely occurred, it meant that an accused did have the right to ask that a biased judge be excused from hearing his case. Additionally, the requirement that the judges give a "reasoned verdict" meant that, unlike other Allied war crimes tribunals which had no such requirement, the NEI judges had to explain how the evidence accepted by the court was legal and supported the verdict and punishment. As a result, even a biased judge would need to provide a rational basis for any decision.

Since all those who were judges at these temporary courts-martial, as well as any accuseds, have long since passed from the scene, there is no way to determine today the extent to which prejudice and bias affected the fairness of the proceedings. What can be said, however, is that at least some judges were aware of the issue, and tried to guard against allowing their personal feelings to color the decision-making process. De Groot, for example, later wrote that, while sitting as the president of the temporary court-martial in Batavia, he had tried "as far as possible—to keep up the standards of Dutch justice, while at the same time—as far as possible—keeping out the bad influence of ill-feelings toward the Japanese as a nation."[18]

Perhaps the best evidence that de Groot and his fellow judges succeeded in holding full and fair proceedings is that not every Japanese person who was tried was found guilty. Of the 1,038 convicted, fifty-five were acquitted (5.3 percent). While this is a smaller acquittal rate than at other Allied war crimes tribunals, it nonetheless reflects that the NEI judges were not in lock-step with the prosecutor or that a desire for retribution meant that no Japanese accused would ever walk away a free man.

The final challenge facing the judges was personal danger as a result of the ongoing revolution. As a former law clerk who had served in a civilian court in Batavia remembered:

> We held out first meeting in February 1946, in the former Supreme Court building at the Waterlooplein ... There we sat around a table with some chairs, all the carpets still dripping with blood of the murders that had happened just before. Indonesians had killed some Dutchmen. It was a real battle. Well, at that time there was no other building, we had just liberated that building and we did not have the opportunity to clean everything, so we just picked out the best room.[19]

Two months later, in April 1946, *pemudas* attacked and killed all members of an Australian team investigating war crimes working in Bogor, Java. Although one

[18] Letter from Major L. F. de Groot to General Imamura (September 8, 1950), quoted in Schouten (n. 10) 97. De Groot reprints and discusses other correspondence between Japanese defendants and himself in his two-volume monograph on war crimes. He insists that the warm feelings expressed by the Japanese authors of these letters indicates that he and his fellow judges were fair in judging Japanese war criminals. Since all the letter writers had either been acquitted or given relatively light punishment, their warm sentiments actually may only reflect gratitude at having escaped more severe punishment. See L. F. de Groot, *Berechting Japanse Orloogsmisdadigers in Nederlands-Indie, 1946–1949* (Art & Research 1990 (privately published)) 438–44.

[19] Statement by Van Rijckevorsel, "De Nederlandse Rechtspraak in Indonesië" (Dutch Law in Indonesia), VPRO radio broadcast, Pt VI, *Afscheid van Indië/Het Spoor Terug* (August 5, 1988) http://www.vpro.nl/buitenland/speel~POMS_VPRO_384592~afscheid-van-indi%C3%AB-6-de-nederlandse-rechtspraak-in-indonesi%C3%AB-het-spoor-terug~.html (last accessed May 4, 2017).

historian suggests that the Australians may have been murdered for reasons unrelated to their investigative work, the point is that the ongoing guerrilla insurgency meant that gathering evidence of war crimes was a risky business. There was every reason to believe that serving as a judge in a war crimes tribunal could be just as risky.[20] In any event, in the weeks, months, and years that followed, the security situation on Java and elsewhere only deteriorated even more.

[20] See Cribb (n. 1) 155. According to an NEI report, the murders included two former Japanese soldiers who deserted. See S. L. van der Wal, *Officiële Bescheiden Betreffende De Nederlands-Indonesische Betrekkingen, 1945–1950*, vols. I–XX (Martinus Nijhoff 1971) Pt 7, (January 6–March 20, 1947) 121.

5

Trials for the Mistreatment of Civilians and Prisoners of War and Civilian Internees

This chapter looks at representative cases involving the mistreatment of noninterned civilians by the Japanese occupation authorities and the mistreatment of prisoners of war (POWs) and civilian internees by Japanese camp personnel. It also examines two unusual war crimes prosecutions in which Japanese civilians working as supervisors in Japanese-owned companies were charged with mistreating their Netherlands East Indies (NEI) citizen employees. Finally, this chapter looks at an unprosecuted (and unpunished) war crime involving the death of 900 Indonesian civilian laborers.

It is appropriate to examine all these categories in the same chapter because the mistreatment meted out to them was similar, and included murder, beatings, starvation, torture, and other mental and physical cruelties. Additionally, since the Japanese Army was in charge of *both* POW and civilian internment camps on Java and Sumatra after April 1944, it is logical to discuss war crimes prosecutions involving both POWs and civilian internees at the same time, if for no other reason than more than a few Japanese defendants were tried at one criminal proceeding for mistreating both categories of people.[1] Army Captain Kenitji SONE, for example, whose case is discussed in this chapter, was prosecuted for mistreating both prisoners of war and civilian internees, as he had been in charge of both types of camps.

Mistreatment of Noninterned Civilians

Usually, the mistreatment of European and nonEuropean civilians occurred while these men and women were in the custody of civilian or military police officials, or were confined in Japanese-run jails. *Prosecutor v. Takeo SUGIBAYASHI*, and *Prosecutor v. Saikuro YAGUCHI, Yukiie FUKUI, and Nobuhiro TERUKI*, both

[1] On Java, all camps were under the Japanese 16th Army. On Sumatra, the 25th Army was in charge. On Celebes and Dutch Borneo, however, internment camps were under the Navy until early 1943, when they were transferred to the Navy Civil Administration or *Minseibu*. See Louis de Jong (with an Introduction by Jeroen Kemperman), *The Collapse of a Colonial Society: The Dutch in Indonesia during the Second World War* (KILTV Press 2002) 429.

Military Trials of War Criminals in the Netherlands East Indies 1946–1949, Fred L. Borch.

examined below, are a good examples of war crimes trials falling into this general category.

Prosecutor v. Takeo Sugibayashi

On September 5, 1947, the prosecutor in Medan charged police inspector Takeo Sugibayashi[2] with having "exercised a systematic reign of terror" by torturing civilian men and women in police custody. The defendant had either personally mistreated these civilians while interrogating them as a part of his work in the *Keimubu* (Japanese general police), or tortured them in concert with unknown Japanese nationals and with two Indonesian interpreters named BARKI and SJAFEI. These war crimes had been committed between March 1943 and August 1944 in the towns of Sawah-Loento, Padang, and Emmahaven, all of which are located on the west coast of Sumatra.

According to the charge sheet presented by the prosecutor to the temporary court-martial, the 27-year-old Sugibayashi had either performed the following war crimes or caused them to be committed against civilians during police interrogations:

- repeatedly struck civilians with his hand, fist, a stick, a leather strap, a hammer, a stick studded with nails, and an iron rod, until they bled and lost consciousness
- kicked civilians on all parts of their body with heavily-shod feet
- threatened to kill them
- flung civilians to the ground with jiu-jitsu holds
- hung them upside down by the feet and hung them up by their arms, which had previously been tied behind their backs
- stuck wood splinters under their finger and toe nails
- made civilians kneel with a stick or rod stuck through the hollow formed behind their knees and then exerted pressure on the projecting ends of the stick or rod
- pulled out their finger and toe nails with pincers
- poured large quantities of water into their bodies and then walked or "danced" on their abdomens, or otherwise exerted great pressure so that the water was expelled from their bodies
- burnt civilians with lighted cigarettes
- sent an electric current through them
- intentionally withheld food and water or otherwise starved them

[2] *Prosecutor v. Takeo Sugibayashi*, Vonnis No. 94/1947, Medan (October 16, 1947).

- intentionally withheld medicines from those needing medical treatment and
- shut civilians up for days on end in overcrowded rooms.[3]

In the prosecutor's view, these horrific acts of mistreatment had caused severe bodily harm to many civilians, as well as acute mental suffering. Consequently, he asked the tribunal to sentence the defendant to death.

When the defendant appeared before the tribunal on October 7, 1947, he was represented by counsel, Koichiro TADOKORO. In open court, the accused admitted that he was a Japanese national and had been a *Keimubu* official during the Japanese occupation of Sumatra. As for the charged misconduct, Sugibayashi admitted only to hitting a Chinese civilian in the face with his hand after the man had attempted to escape police custody; he denied that he had mistreated, much less tortured, any other civilians in police custody. He also denied that he had caused any other subordinates under his authority to mistreat civilians.

The defendant's problem was that the tribunal had more than a dozen sworn statements from civilians who had suffered at his hands during police questioning. The declaration of Mr. Hock Seng YO, who was questioned eight times by NEI war crimes investigators, was especially damaging. He stated under oath that he was present at an October 1943 interrogation of an Ambonesian named MATULESSY during which the accused kicked Matulessy and struck him on the head with his fist and then with a wooden ruler, before throwing him to the ground a number of times with jiu-jitsu holds.

Mr. Yo also told investigators that he was present at another interrogation in October 1943 in which the accused, assisted by the Indonesian Sjafei, tortured a Dutchman named COSIJN by putting the end of a bit of hose connected to a faucet into Cosijn's mouth and then turning on the water. After Cosijn's stomach filled with water, the accused and Sjefi put a board on his abdomen and sat on it until the water was forcibly expelled. The accused then took a lighted cigarette and burned Cosijn's head before beating him with a piece of wood and dragging him along the ground by means of a rope tied around his neck.

During this same period, Yo also saw the accused and his Indonesian colleague, Barki, beat a civilian engineer named LANZING on the head, body, arms, and legs with a stick. He also heard the accused threaten Lanzing with death after this beating. Sometime later, Yo witnessed the accused and the Indonesian Sjafei beat Lanzing on the head and all over the body with a whip composed of wires, bits of wood, and various other objects, until Lanzing was bleeding from multiple wounds. On another occasion, Yo witnessed the defendant repeatedly kick a civilian named VAN RAALTEN in the face and on the body during an interrogation. Van Raalten ultimately became so exhausted that he admitted all the misconduct with which he had been charged by the accused.

[3] For additional torture techniques used by the *Kempeitai* see de Jong, *The Collapse of a Colonial Society* (n. 1) 210–11.

Another witness, Herman Eugéne BROUWER VON GONZENBACH positively identified Sugibayashi as the police inspector who had interrogated him at Sawah Loentoh on June 26, 1943. According to Brouwer von Gonzenbach, the defendant charged him with being involved in an anti-Japanese conspiracy and, during questioning, beat him with a stick until he lost consciousness.

Mr. Henk de JONGH's affidavit, taken by Dr. W. BEUN, the prosecutor for Medan temporary court-martial, was also damning. De Jongh declared that, while confined in the Japanese police barracks in Emmahaven between December 1942 and July 1943, he had seen the defendant repeatedly strike a civilian named Wijckerheld BISDOM with an iron-tipped rattan cane. After this beating, according to de Jongh, Bisdom was carried back to his cell by other civilians who saw that he was bleeding from his mouth, nose, and eyes. At midday, de Jongh asked Bisdom if he would like something to eat, but the latter was no longer able to stand, much less speak. The next morning, Bisdom was gone; his cell was empty and de Jongh was told that Bisdom was dead.

Yet another witness, Mr. Johannes Marinus HANSEN declared under oath that during his confinement at Emmahaven, the defendant and his interpreter, Sjafei, came almost every day to the cells containing arrested persons in order to question them. According to Hansen, he often heard the shrieks and groans of these civilians who were mistreated during these interrogation sessions, including those of his brother, Leonard Hansen, who was repeatedly beaten by Sugibayashi with a stick. As for himself, he was tortured by the defendant when he was beaten and then forced to kneel with a stick placed behind his knees. Japanese soldiers then stood on the stick, which resulted in both intense pain and injury to legs.

Mr. Henri Theodor van HEERDT declared under oath that, in July 1943, the accused had thrown him to ground by means of jiu-jitsu holds, beaten him with a bamboo rod, and twice tied a rope around his feet and hung him upside down from a pulley attached to the ceiling. Van Heerdt was then beaten until he lost consciousness. According to van Heerdt, the defendant also tried to pull out his teeth with pincers, and as a result four of his teeth were broken off.

Despite the volume of evidence presented by the prosecutor to the military tribunal, the accused persisted in denying that he had committed any of the acts in question. Sugibayashi insisted that the declarations, all of which were read to him in open court, were lies and fabrications. The damaging testimony of Yo Hock Seng, for example, was nothing more than a "fanciful fairytale." Additionally, said the defendant, some of the false statements against him had been made by collaborators who wished to curry favor with the authorities at his expense or else had been made by men and women who simply hated the Japanese in general and were looking for revenge.

The judges heard testimony from the accused himself that he was knowledgeable about jiu-jitsu and other forms of Japanese wrestling because he had received training in them as a police officer. But Sugibayashi insisted that, as a result of an illness, he was incapable of having committed any crimes which demanded great physical effort, such as throwing individuals to the ground using jiu-jitsu holds. The tribunal rejected this defense, however, after hearing evidence that, while

Sugibayashi indeed had suffered from malaria while serving as a police official in Sumatra, this sickness had occurred early in his stay on Sumatra and consequently long before the alleged war crimes had occurred.

Probably the most viable defense offered by Sugibayashi, which the court-martial took seriously and addressed at some length in its decision, was his claim that he was a victim of mistaken identity. The accused believed that he was being mistaken for a Sergeant Major HOMMA, but judges rejected this claim because none of the witnesses had ever mentioned Homma by name, and the defendant looked nothing like a photograph of Homma that the tribunal had accepted in evidence. Additionally, the three military judges considered that several of the men and women who made declarations under oath had positively recognized the accused when able to confront him in person. The court did acknowledge that some witnesses had misspelled his surname in their statements, and that others had incorrectly identified him as a *Kempeitai* official or commandant of an internment camp. But, said the court, such misunderstandings were typical among interned Europeans who often did not know the names and official functions of Japanese officials.

Although the volume of testimony presented to the tribunal was both horrific and overwhelming, the judges were careful in writing their decision. For example, several witnesses provided statements in which they declared that "a great number of persons [who] were ill-treated [by the accused] later died." But the court reasoned that these declarations were not only hearsay but that it had not been shown that the defendant's actions (or that of his two Indonesian assistants) were the proximate cause of these deaths. Consequently, the judges expressly held that the accused was responsible only for the death of Wijckerheld Bisdom, for which there was more than sufficient evidence.

As for the prosecutor's charge that the accused also was responsible for the torture inflicted by his Indonesian interpreters Bakri and Sjafei on civilians in detention, because they were his subordinates, the Medan court-martial rejected this charge and acquitted Sugibayashi. The judges gave several reasons for this not guilty finding. First, the accused denied that the two Indonesians were officially subordinate to him. Second, the court concluded that from the depositions taken during the preliminary investigation into Sugibayashi's war crimes, it appeared that the two Indonesians took an active part in the torture of civilians in police custody, and that their actions were the product of free will rather than any duress applied by the accused. Since there was no evidence presented by the prosecutor that the accused had forced or otherwise ordered the Bakri and Sjafei to commit war crimes, their war crimes could not be attributed to him and he must be acquitted.

The tribunal judges, Major W. P. THOMAS, and Captains A. C. VAN HENGEL and H. J. C. VAN WIJK, concluded that the defendant was guilty of systematic terrorism, and torture and mistreatment of civilian prisoners. In their view, "the accused was guilty of the most repulsive ill-treatments and tortures" of a great number of defenseless civilians. Almost all of them were completely innocent of the accusations of sabotage and espionage with which they were charged, wrote the judges, but the accused's "inhuman" treatment of them resulted in forced confessions that were then used to inflict severe punishments upon them.

Having searched in vain for extenuating circumstances that could be taken into account in sentencing the accused, and concluding that the accused had tortured and mistreated civilians on his own initiative (and not because of any order from a superior authority), the temporary court-martial sentenced Sugibayashi to death on October 16, 1947. The fiat of execution was granted on October 27 by Dr. J. Gerritsen, the head of the Temporary Administration in Medan, and announced in open court by Major Thomas, in the presence of the accused and his counsel, that same day.

Prosecutor v. Saikuro Yaguchi, Yukiie Fukui, and Nobuhiro Teruki

On April 20, 1948, the temporary court-martial sitting in Batavia began hearing evidence against Yaguchi, Fukui, and Teruki.[4] During the occupation, all three men had worked as police officers in the Werfstraat prison complex in Surabaya (Dutch: *Soerabaja*), a town on the island of Java, located about 400 miles east of Batavia. The three defendants, all of whom had been born in Japan and were 56, 45, and 28 years old, respectively, were tried together for the war crimes of mistreatment of civilian prisoners, torture of civilians, and imposing collective punishments on civilians. Some of these prisoners were common criminals, but others had been tried, convicted, and incarcerated for more political offenses, such as possessing a radio. Since the majority of the offenses arose out of their work at the Werfstraat prison, the three defendants were prosecuted in a single proceeding. The prosecutor asked the court to sentence Fukui to death. As for Yaguchi and Teruki, he requested sentences of fifteen and twenty years, respectively.

The evidence presented by the prosecution consisted of both sworn and unsworn affidavits from twenty-one witnesses, all of which detailed the war crimes committed by the accuseds. These statements were read to the defendants in court, and each was permitted to respond to them, both individually and through their counsel.

The most damning evidence concerned Yukiie Fukui who, as the director or warden in charge of the entire Werfstraat facility, had overall responsibility for the prison's operations and set the day-to-day standards for the care and treatment of prisoners. Additionally, as the evidence also showed that Fukui personally inflicted beatings and torture on the prisoners, the court naturally concluded that he was a model for his subordinates in how they should treat the prisoners in their custody.

A statement from Mr. F. A. FRANZ, explained how, after being sentenced by a Japanese occupation court to life imprisonment in 1943, he had been confined

[4] *Prosecutor v. Saikuro Yaguchi, Yukiie Fukui, and Nobuhiro Teruki*, Vonnis No. 9/1948, Batavia (June 5, 1948).

in the Werfstraat prison where Fukui served as the director. Franz had been badly beaten when originally taken into custody, and as a result was unable to move his arms. When he asked for medical care, however, this was denied. The result was that he permanently lost the use of his left arm. As for the general conditions in the prison, not only were prisoners mistreated, but the food was so poor that men were dying from hunger, dysentery, and beri-beri.

An affidavit from Dr. In Tjhan GO, a physician who claimed to have examined some 500 prisoners in the facility between March 1943 and February 1945, insisted that mistreated prisoners received no medical care. He stressed that the prison doctors did their best under the circumstances, and even smuggled medicine and food into the prison in an attempt to alleviate the suffering of the inmates. As for Fukui, Dr. Go wrote that his sadism surpassed all the other guards in the Werfstraat complex, and that if a prisoner escaped and was recaptured, Fukui made certain that the man was tortured and starved until he died. This information was corroborated by other affidavits and the tribunal heard that the cruel treatment of prisoners under Fukui's regime eventually resulted in twenty deaths per month. Mr. Boen Ling OEI corroborated these facts in his affidavit. According to Oei, prisoners who committed the smallest of infractions routinely had food withheld for days, and the overall treatment of inmates in the Werfstraat prison was so bad that many men died from mistreatment and starvation.

While the affidavits of Franz, Go, Oei, and others spoke to Fukui's responsibility as the officer-in-charge, others addressed his personal involvement in war crimes. Mr. Tjwan Hian TIO stated under oath that he had been arrested on August 23, 1944. While being transported by truck from the court to the jail where Fukui was the warden, Tio witnessed his fellow prisoners being given food by their family members, who apparently had been able to intercept the truck as it was on its way to the prison. When Fukui discovered that these men had obtained food from outside the prison, he forced all the prisoners to undress and then repeatedly struck the men with a horsewhip on the back, buttocks, and genitals. After ordering the men to get dressed, Fukui then grabbed Tio by his shirt lapels and then twisted the cloth over Tio's throat so that he was unable to breathe and fell down unconscious; Fukui repeated this process with four or five other men, who of whom likewise fell unconscious to the ground.

Still unsatisfied with the punishment he had meted out, Fukui directed that Tio and the twenty-four other prisoners be tied together, with their hands behind their backs. They also were required to remain in their underwear and lie on the ground in a cell for the next week. Fukui also withheld food from the men for a week, except for a small amount of water and a teacup of rice. Tio's recitation of the events in the Werfstraat prison was corroborated by a sworn statement from Mr. E. C. H. ROBERT. Robert had been in the same cell with Tio in August 1944, and the two men had been tied together. According to Robert, when Fukui visited them in their cell, Fukui had smashed their heads against the prison wall, and also smashed their heads together. When shown a photograph of Fukui, Robert had positively identified him.

Perhaps the most damning affidavits came from Mr. J. W. J. ROMANS VAN SCHAIK. In his sworn statement, Romans van Schaik related that he arrived at the Werfstraat facility in the middle of 1943. From the beginning, there was little food available, and he was told that Fukui was responsible for deciding how much the prisoners received to eat. Breakfast, lunch, and dinner consisted of a small amount of rice (enough to fill a cigarette pack); the prisoners received a small amount of meat once a month. The end result was that between eighteen and twenty-two prisoners were dying from hunger every day.

Romans van Schaik also wrote in his statement that, while he was still confined in Werfstraat, he witnessed the recapture of an Indonesian prisoner who had escaped. Fukui repeatedly slammed the man into the ground and repeatedly kicked him. The man was so badly injured that he died a few days later. On another occasion, Fukui punished another recaptured escapee by beating him with a rattan stick and, when the man fell down, Fukui continued to strike and kick him while he lay on the ground. According to Romans van Schaik, Fukui also believed in collective punishment: When a prisoner lit a match at night in order to find his way to the latrine, Fukui handled the offense by turning off the water source to the latrine and refusing to give food or drink to the entire cellblock for a week.

Fukui was especially hard on anyone who escaped from Werfstraat, almost certainly because he believed it reflected badly on him. An affidavit from Mr. LA GATTA, for example, related that when an escapee named LAKATANI was recaptured after being absent for three months, the man was stripped of his clothing, and hanged by his wrists. Fukui and another Japanese prison warden then beat Lakatani with sticks until his skin was literally black and blue and blood flowed from his nose and mouth. Fukui and his colleague then took red-hot iron stakes and burned Lakatani on his stomach and genitals, which resulted in many large blisters. Lakatani was then returned to his cell where, deprived of any medical care, he died the following day.

As for Saikuro Yaguchi and Nobuhiro Teruki, the evidence against them was more than sufficient to find them guilty of the war crimes charged, albeit less damning than the evidence against Fukui. Yaguchi, who had been a district judge in Japan and was recruited by the Japanese Army to serve in a judicial capacity in the occupied NEI, instead had been employed as the chief inspector for prisons in Surabaya. The evidence presented to the tribunal was that Yaguchi had made daily inspections of all the prisons under his authority, including Werfstraat. Given these daily visits, the court wrote that Yaguchi "must have known about the deplorable conditions" in the prison and consequently was legally responsible. Additionally, since Yaguchi was Fukui's superior, and since the two men saw each other frequently, Yaguchi was guilty because he must have known that Fukui was mistreating prisoners and, as Yaguchi did nothing to prevent this mistreatment, shared Fukui's criminal intent and was an aider and abettor. The prosecutor did not specifically argue that Yaguchi was liable under any theory akin to command responsibility. This makes sense because all three defendants were civilians employed by the Japanese occupation forces on Java, and not commanders in any military organization.

As for Teruki, who had worked under Fukui as a prison warden in Werfstraat from February 1944 to August 1945, a number of affidavits addressed his participation in war crimes. Mr. E. PIMENTEL stated under oath that when he was caught smuggling letters into the prison, that Teruki tied his wrists and ankles together and then beat him. Pimentel also said that he was routinely mistreated by Teruki, who threw him on the ground using jiu-jitsu movements after which other Japanese guards "danced on his body." There were other affidavits confirming that Teruki participated in the beating of prisoners with his supervisor, Fukui.

The three-judge tribunal also considered an official statement (Dutch: *verklaring*) from Mr. Monod de FROIDEVILLE, who was serving as the chief of the Government Office for War Crimes Investigations. Mr. de Froideville provided information previously compiled by the Red Cross on conditions in Japanese-operated prisons in Surabaya. From December 1944 to August 1945, a total of eighty-one persons died, of whom fifty-seven were Indonesians, sixteen were Europeans, and eight were Chinese. About thirty of these deaths resulted from diseases that could have been prevented with proper nutrition or cured with medical care, such as malaria, beriberi, dysentery, and typhus. The military tribunal seems to have believed that the Red Cross report understated or underreported the numbers of prisoners dying in the Surabaya prisons but accepted the report into evidence because it buttressed the individual affidavits accepted by the temporary court-martial.

After considering all the facts and circumstances, the court found all three defendants guilty as charged, except that Teruki was acquitted of the war crime of torture. The prosecutor had asked the court to impose a jail term of twenty years for Teruki's war crimes but, given the finding of not guilty of torture, the tribunal imposed confinement for ten years. As for Yaguchi, the tribunal condemned his conduct and agreed with the prosecutor that fifteen years' imprisonment was an appropriate sentence; the tribunal might have imposed a more severe sentence had there been evidence showing that Yaguchi had personally mistreated any prisoner. As for Fukui, his punishment was death.

On June 5, 1948, the Resident of Batavia, Mr. M. A. F. Zwager, issued the fiat of execution in the case. Five days later, Major L. F. DE GROOT, Captain J. C. P. BAEL, and First Lieutenant W. GUERTS, the president and members of the court-martial, respectively, announced the sentence in open court in the presence of the Yaguchi, Fukui, and Teruki.

The two photographs of Yukiie Fukui were taken while he was in custody pending trial. He was shot by firing squad in Batavia on October 2, 1948.[5]

Two unusual prosecutions for mistreatment of civilians involved Japanese civilian defendants who, while working as supervisors in Japanese-owned companies, abused their Indonesian workers. Shozo WATANABE was a foreman in a Japanese shipbuilding firm in Balikpapan and Toshihide YAMAGISHI was a clerk in a Japanese owned mining company in Kidjang.

[5] Levinus F. de Groot, *Berechting Japanse Orloogsmisdadigers in Nederlands-Indie, 1946–1949* (Art & Research 1990 (privately published)) 514.

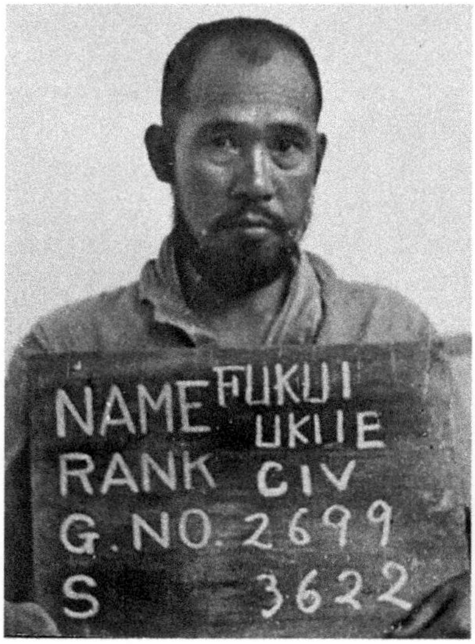

Photos 4 and 5 "Mug shots" of Yukiie Fukui. He was found guilty of torturing prisoners and other war crimes and was executed in October 1948.

Credit: Netherlands Institute of War Documentation (NIOD), Amsterdam

Prosecutor v. Shozo Watanabe

The accused was a 37-year-old Japanese civilian working as the foreman (Dutch: *hoofdmandoer*) in a Japanese shipbuilding firm located in the harbor at Balikpapan. He was charged with systematic terrorism because, between 15 January 1944 and August 15, 1945, Watanabe repeatedly beat Indonesian workers under his supervision with a wooden stick when they failed to meet his work standards. The evidence showed that these beatings resulted in broken arms for some of the victims and that three of the victims, deprived of medical care after being beaten, died of their injuries. Watanabe was found guilty as charged and sentenced to death.[6]

Prosecutor v. Toshihide Yamagishi

On May 31, 1948, the prosecutor charged Yamagishi with four war crimes, all of which involved the striking of local national employees under his supervision as a clerk with the Furukawa Company Ltd.[7]

[6] *Prosecutor v. Shozo Watanabe*, Vonnis No. 17501/R, Balikpapan (April 25, 1947).

[7] *Prosecutor v. Toshihide Yamagishi*, Vonnis No. 29/1948, Tandjong Pinang (June 11, 1948).

According to the record of trial, Yamagishi's job was to provide meals for those employed by the company. This meant that he supervised both the preparation of food, and how it was obtained. The most serious charge against Yamagishi was that he struck Mrs. PIAH on the right side of the head with such force that she died two days later. It seems the accused suspected that Mrs. Piah, whose job was making biscuits for consumption by the employees, also may have been making them to sell outside of the workplace. He confronted her and, after she denied any wrongdoing, struck her in the head with an iron-tipped stick; the blow was so severe that she lost consciousness and later died.

The three other charged offenses involved four other civilian employees, all of whom—like Mrs. Piah—had angered the accused because of a food-related issue. In this regard, Yamagishi repeatedly struck two Indonesian employees who were said "not to have been sufficiently energetic" in catching fish for the company's use in feeding its employees. According to the evidence, the men had failed to catch any fish for two weeks, and this failure so enraged the accused that he repeatedly struck the men in the head and legs. Since fish (along with rice) was a critical part of the local diet, a poor catch would explain the defendant's displeasure with his fisher employees.

The most interesting aspect of this trial was the jurisdictional defense raised by Yamagishi's defense lawyer. He argued that Yamagishi could not be prosecuted because he was a civilian working in a civilian company and, lacking any military status, could not be tried for a war crime. The court, however, took judicial notice of the fact that the Furukawa Company, at the direction of the Japanese Ministry of War, had taken over the Netherlands Indies Bauxite Development Company's operations in Kidjang, and was conducting business for the benefit of the Japanese government. In the words of the tribunal, "bauxite was of paramount importance for Japan" and the operations of the operations of the Furukawa Company were "under the supervision of the Japanese military authorities" in the NEI. Finally, the court also found that the defendant had been hired by the Japanese Ministry of War and sent first to Singapore and then to Kidjang to work in support of the war effort. While the tribunal agreed with the accused's counsel that Yamagishi played a relatively small role in the overall war effort, he nevertheless "played a part ... and in this part could violate the laws and customs of war."[8]

When the temporary court-martial sitting in Tandjong Pinang[9] began hearing the evidence against Yamagishi, it considered sworn affidavits from eleven witnesses. Without exception, the witnesses confirmed the prosecutor's allegations that the defendant repeatedly struck his employees with a stick when they did not meet his standards. Additionally, at the request of Yamigishi's lawyer, the tribunal heard live testimony from Taeeo TSUJI, who had been the commandant of the

[8] ibid 3. [9] Today the name is spelled Tanjung Pinang.

Kempeitai in Tandjong Pinang during the occupation. Tsuji told the judges that he had investigated the death of Mrs. Piah and interviewed five witnesses who confirmed that the accused had struck the deceased. As for the accused, he told Tsuji that he did not remember having hit Mrs. Piah, because he was drunk. Tsuji told the tribunal that, after completing his *Kempeitai* investigation, nothing was done by the military because of Yamagishi's civilian status. The case was referred to the civilian police, who did nothing.

Since Yamagishi continued to insist at his temporary court-martial that he could not remember striking Mrs. Piah because he was drunk, this may explain why his lawyer decided to present Tsuji's testimony. Perhaps he thought that the judges would be easier on the accused if they believed he had been intoxicated.

In its final decision, however, the court found Yamagishi guilty as charged. Moreover, it rejected the defendant's claim that he had been drunk, noting that none of the witnesses stated in any affidavit that he had been drinking that evening. But, while the court considered it "legally and convincingly proved that the accused struck Mrs. Piah in such a way that she died two days later from the injuries received," and also found him guilty of the other charged war crimes, it sentenced him to ten years' imprisonment. This seems relatively light, given that Mrs. Piah had died as a result of Yamagishi's assault. In its written decision, however, the court explained that there were two factors that supported this lighter punishment. First, the court found that the accused was someone who acted impulsively, and who "hit out immediately" when he believed that workplace rules and regulations had been violated. Second, the court took into the consideration that Yamagishi's role in providing food for employees was so difficult, and success so dependent on the timely arrival of sufficient fish, that his actions, while not excusable, were understandable.

An Unprosecuted War Crime

One final war crime involving Japanese mistreatment of NEI civilians deserves discussion: The use of 900 Indonesian conscripted laborers (Japanese: *rōmusha*) as test subjects in a massive vaccination experiment—all of whom died when the Japanese medical test went awry.

During the occupation of the NEI, the Japanese forcibly mobilized millions of poor and uneducated Indonesians to serve as laborers. These *rōmusha* (the Japanese word means 'laborer') were employed in a variety of tasks, including road building, construction projects, farming, and domestic work. On Java alone, there were several million *rōmusha*; about 10 percent were female. Some worked for a short period of time, while other *rōmusha* worked the entire occupation period. Most worked near their local villages but some were sent away from the NEI, some as far away as Japan. Generally, the Indonesian *rōmusha* were poorly treated by the

Japanese, and suffered from a lack of food and medical care. Millions died from malnourishment and disease.[10]

In July and August 1944, a group of 900 *rōmusha* were temporarily in Batavia, as they were waiting assignments to labor projects in other locations. While in this nonwork status, the workers were inoculated with an experimental serum that they were told would protect them from dysentery, typhus, and cholera—diseases that were a real danger to them as workers. Unfortunately, all 900 died within days of being vaccinated—but from tetanus.

Professor Dr. Achmand Mochtar, along with eight Indonesian doctors and five laboratory technicians from the famous Eijkman Institute,[11] were taken into custody and questioned by the *Kempeitai*. All denied any wrongdoing, and insisted that the Eijkman Institute had not participated in the preparation of the dysentery-typhus-cholera vaccine. In fact, Mochtar and his colleagues suggested to the *Kempeitai* that the experimental vaccine, which had been prepared by a Japanese drug manufacturer located in Batavia, might have been *accidentally* adulterated with tetanus during its production.

The Japanese refused to accept this explanation. They severely tortured Dr. Mochtar and his colleagues (two were so brutalized that they died in custody) and obtained statements from each person admitting that there had been a conspiracy to contaminate the vaccine deliberately with a tetanus toxin in order to embarrass the occupation authorities and undermine the Japanese war effort. At the time, the belief was that the Japanese were embarrassed by the accidental poisoning of the vaccine by a Japanese company and, to avoid the 'loss of face' that would have occurred if the families of the deceased *rōmusha* learned the truth, the Japanese were willing to blame Dr. Mochtar and his associates.

In the end, Achmand Mochtar was offered the opportunity to save his colleagues if he signed a confession admitting to the conspiracy; if he admitted guilt, and accepted full responsibility for the tetanus deaths of the 900 laborers, his fellow Indonesians would be released. Since Mochtar was a highly respected and internationally known bacteriologist, the Japanese must have concluded that his confession would be sufficient to cover up their own incompetence.

Late in the afternoon on July 3, 1945, Prof. Mochtar was blindfolded, made to kneel, and then beheaded. His execution was a war crime, since he was innocent.

[10] Shigeru Satu, "Rōmusha," in Peter Post *et al.* (eds.), *Encyclopedia of Indonesia in the Pacific War* (Brill 2010) 578–9.

[11] Originally called the Central Laboratory for Public Health (Dutch: Centraal Laboratorium van den Dienst der Volksgezondheid), the Eijkman Institute (it was renamed in honor of Nobel Prize winner Dr. Christiaan Eijkman in 1938), was world famous for its research into infectious tropical diseases. When the Japanese invaded the Indies in 1942, the institute was conducting scientific research into beri-beri, cholera, dysentery, leprosy, malaria, typhus, and other illnesses that afflicted the population of the archipelago. The work of Eijkman Institute continues today in Indonesia. See J. Kevin Baird and Sangkot Marzuki, *War Crimes in Japan-Occupied Indonesia: A Case of Murder by Medicine* (Potomac Books 2015) 57–60.

It now appears that the Japanese in fact were guilty of a much larger war crime in July and August 1944: Using 900 Indonesian civilians as human guinea pigs—without their knowledge or consent—in testing a newly developed tetanus vaccine intended for Japanese military and naval personnel. As *War Crimes in Japan-Occupied Indonesia: A Case of Murder by Medicine* explains, there was never any vaccine against dysentery-typhus-cholera. Rather, the truth was that Japanese Army had developed a new tetanus vaccine and, anticipating an Allied invasion of the East Indies and heavy combat with the enemy in the very near future, the Japanese concluded that they did not have time to test the new vaccine in a laboratory setting.

Unsure of the vaccine's efficacy, however, the Japanese did not want to take a chance with the health of their own troops. Consequently, they inoculated 900 Indonesians with the new serum and then, to see if it actually worked, exposed these *rōmusha* to the tetanus toxin. The Japanese must have been shocked when their human guinea pigs died, and they now had a serious political problem if the Indonesian public learned the truth. To cover up their botched vaccine trial, the Japanese transformed Mochtar into the lead actor of an imaginary conspiracy to sabotage the Japanese war effort, and then decapitated him to protect their web of lies.[12]

While the *Kempeitai* who tortured and murdered Dr. Mochtar were prosecuted for their mistreatment of him at a June 1947 temporary court-martial in Batavia, those Japanese responsible for the death of 900 *rōmusha* were never prosecuted for these homicides. Part of the reason for this lack of justice was that the Japanese destroyed any documents that might have proved that the deceased workers had been inoculated with a tetanus vaccine; it took more than sixty years for the evidence of Japanese malfeasance to be uncovered. Perhaps more importantly, the Indonesian nationalist leader Sukarno, who ruled Indonesia until 1965, insisted that Mochtar was guilty as charged. Apparently, it was politically expedient for Sukarno to blame Mochtar for the tetanus deaths, even long after the occupation had ended, given Sukarno's close cooperation with the Japanese in World War II.[13] This naturally meant that there was little incentive to search for the truth.[14]

Mistreatment of Prisoners of War and Civilian Internees

This section examines eight temporary courts-martial in which Japanese military or naval personnel were prosecuted for mistreating POWs or civilian internees,

[12] ibid 249–50.

[13] For more on Sukarno see Chapter 1 nn. 7 and 20, and accompanying text.

[14] Sukarno was so intent on blaming Mochtar that he liked to claim that thousands rather than hundreds had died as a result of Mochtar's vaccine. See Iris Heidebrink, "Military Tribunals in the

or both. It begins with a look at the trial of the infamous Kenitji Sone, who was shot by firing squad for his misconduct while the commandant of both POW and civilian internment camps on Java. The cases that follow *Sone* are presented in alphabetical order.

Prosecutor v. Kenitji Sone

Army Captain Kenitji Sone, the first Japanese national to be executed by the Dutch for war crimes committed in the Indies, was the commandant of both POW and internment camps. From September 1942 until March 1944, he was in charge of the 10th Battalion POW camp complex in Batavia, in which Dutch, Australian, English, and American military personnel were held captive, along with Royal Netherlands Indies Army (Dutch: *Koninklijk Nederlandsch Indisch Leger* (KNIL)) soldiers of Ambonesian background. In March 1944, Sone was transferred from Batavia to Tjideng where, until late June 1945, he was in command of a large internment camp containing Dutch women and children. When the war ended for the Japanese in August 1945, Sone headed the office in charge of all POW camps on Java.[15]

On July 30, 1946, Dr. R. J. Beer, the prosecutor for the temporary court-martial sitting in Batavia, charged the 36-year old Sone with three offenses: Systematic terrorism; mistreatment of POWs; and mistreatment of civilian internees. The language used in the indictment to explain how Sone had committed these war crimes is worth setting out in some detail because it illustrates how mistreatment of detained persons could rise to the level of "systematic terrorism:"

> [a]s Camp Commandant of the 10th Battalion POW camp ... and then the Tjideng internment camp, he ... committed and caused to be committed war crimes against Dutch, Ambonesian, Australian, English and American prisoners of war ... and civilians, women and children ... by treating them badly and exercising a systematic reign of terror ... repeatedly and in any case unnecessarily ill-treating them in a way that far exceeded the limits of a normal exercise of discipline, making them parade for roll-call for hours on end, including at night, denying them rest, food, medicines, care and attention, and further, causing the women and children especially to do excessively heavy work, which reign of terror and/or bad treatment exercised by him or by his orders caused the death of several prisoners and interned persons, or at any rate caused them bodily and mental suffering.

The proceedings opened on August 5, 1946, in the building of the former Supreme Court of Justice for the NEI. Colonel J. H. PETER, was the president. He was joined by Captain E. RIJKMANS. These two Dutch citizens were joined by British Army

Netherlands East Indies," in Peter Post *et al.* (eds.), *Encyclopedia of Indonesia in the Pacific War* (Brill 2010) 418.

[15] *Prosecutor v. Kenitji Sone*, Vonnis No. 24/1946; Batavia, Aug. 14, 1946. Captain Sone's surname is also sometimes spelled as Sonei.

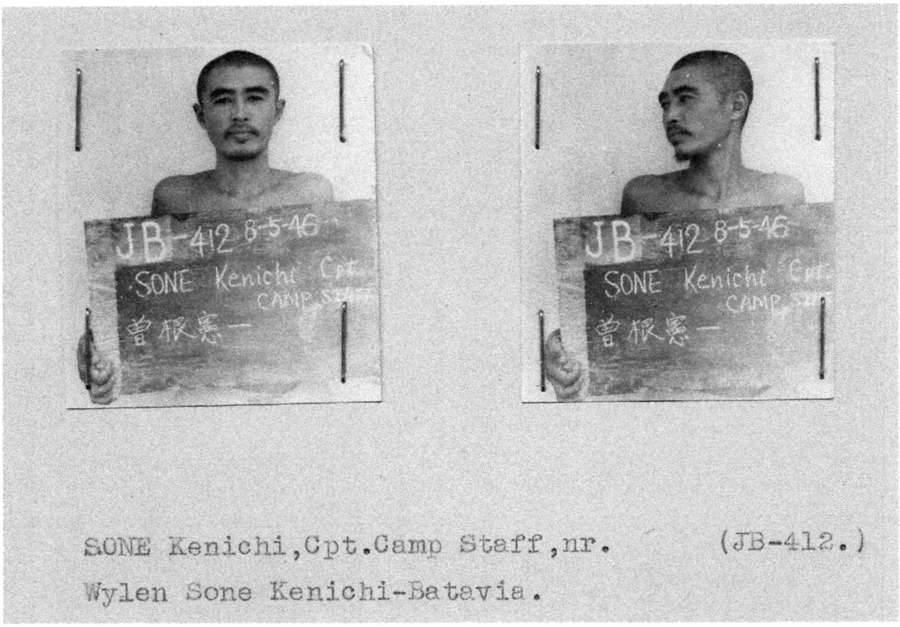

Photos 6 and 7 Captain Kenitji Sone's "mug shot" photographs, taken in May 1946 while he was in custody awaiting trial for war crimes committed against prisoners of war and civilian internees.

Credit: Netherlands Institute of War Documentation (NIOD), Amsterdam

Major J. F. HARTMAN and, while it was unusual for a nonDutch officer to sit on a temporary court-martial in Batavia, Hartman was participating because Australian and British prisoners of war had been victims of Sone's war crimes.

The tribunal first considered written statements from twenty-three men who had been prisoners of war in the Batavia camp under Sone's control. Almost all of these statements were signed and had been made under oath and they were the best evidence because, having been freed from captivity more than a year earlier, virtually all these ex-prisoners had left the East Indies. Certainly, those who were Australian, American, or English had been repatriated to their homes long ago. But the tribunal also accepted as evidence some statements lacking signatures and proof that the witness had been sworn, provided these statements were in "general agreement" with those signed statements made under oath. Finally, to ensure that Sone understood the evidence against him, every statement had been translated into Japanese and given to him.

Without exception the evidence showed that Sone was particularly brutal and cruel in his treatment of prisoners in Batavia. A witness with the surname FEYTES related that Sone routinely made the officers in the camp "stand at attention for hours on end" and, when an elderly lieutenant "fainted on that account and remained lying on the ground, bleeding from his mouth, no one [was] allowed to help him." Feytes also stated under oath that he witnessed the accused "smash Lieutenant VAN GOOR's wrist with a stick"—breaking it—because van Goor's "hair was not cut short enough."

An English-speaking prisoner with the surname HENRY wrote that, on one occasion in October 1943, the accused "hit 20 Dutch officers for about 1½ hours with his fist and then when his hand hurt struck them over the head with a stick." Another English-speaking prisoner with the family name of REILLY wrote that the "accused was a brute and a sadist who hit people for no reason at all" and he himself had been whipped by Sone "for 15 minutes and then imprisoned for 10 days" because he complained in a letter to Sone that it was wrong to make prisoners work who were suffering from dysentery.

Captain Sone reserved much of the worst treatment for those prisoners who were patients in the camp infirmary. He repeatedly reduced their food rations, even though nutrition was key to their recovery and he would sometimes "destroy medical equipment." On more than one occasion, Sone attacked doctors and patients. A statement from an ex-prisoner named PATTIE related how the accused "ill-treated Dr. GUNLACH" by "giving him 85 blows on the head and neck as a result of which his ear-drum burst;" Sone then put Gunlach "in a punishment cell" and denied him medical attention.

Captain Sone's brutality had grave consequences. The three judges heard from a Dutch ex-POW named LE CLERCQ that, on January 1, 1943, Sone had refused to permit medical care for two Dutchmen who had been seriously wounded by a Japanese sentry, with the result that the men died two days later. One Dutch soldier also testified that Sone's war crimes reflected his "intention to destroy the whites intellectually and physically, to which object he gave himself to wholeheartedly" and that Sone was responsible for "the worsening conditions in the camps" that caused "many cases of death."

While Sone's treatment of prisoners in the 10th Battalion camp was horrendous, civilians interned in the Tjideng camp fared no better. The "hygienic situation" for all the internees was "scandalously bad" but, despite pleas from the women and children in the camp, Sone did nothing to improve conditions. On the contrary, Captain Sone made the women and old people "parade for roll-call for hours on end, including at night" and denied them "rest, food, medicines and care and attention."

Dr. VAN WULFFTEN PALTHE, one of four medical doctors in the camp, testified that the accused "repeatedly, unnecessarily and cruelly ill-treated the civilian women and children" by withholding medical attention and requiring "women and young girls" to "do work which was much too heavy." Sone's "reign of terror" reached its zenith when, in June 1945, he punished the entire Tjideng internment camp of 10,700 women and children by withholding food for 48 hours. Shortly thereafter, Sone intentionally destroyed a large quantity of bread destined for these now starving civilians. In fact, Dr. van Wulfften Palthe testified that he believed that the lack of food seemed to him as if "a system of slow starvation was being applied and everything possible done to destroy the morale of the internees."

The court no doubt wanted to know why Sone had been so brutal in his treatment of both prisoners of war and civilians. There is some suggestion in the record of trial that the accused may have been mentally ill; Dr. Wulfften Palthe testified "that the accused was quite unaccountable in his behavior at full moon" and others who gave written statements confirmed that Captain Sone seemed often to be out of control. An Ambonesian prisoner named Halatoe described the accused as "a wild animal" during his tenure at the 10th Battalion camp and an English-speaking prisoner wrote that Sone "was a brute and sadist who hit people for no reason at all."

But the court also heard another rationale for Sone's misconduct. Dr. VEENBAAS testified that the "accused was the prototype of the Japanese European-hater and his criminal intention was to destroy the whites intellectually and physically, to which object he gave himself up wholeheartedly."

Captain Sone raised two defenses at this trial. First, his counsel pleaded *exceptio obscure libelli* or unclearness, a civil law plea that is akin to a bill of particulars in

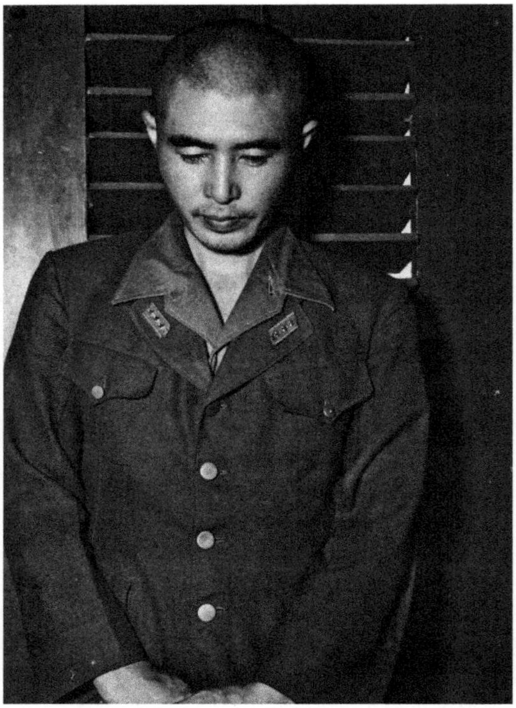

Photo 8 Captain Kenitji Sone at his trial in Batavia.
Credit: Netherlands Institute of Military History, Ministry of Defense

Photo 9 Captain Kenitji Sone is escorted from his trial. He was found guilty in September 1946 and executed in December 1946.

Credit: Netherlands Institute of Military History, Ministry of Defense

Anglo-American criminal law. The tribunal rejected this claim, as it found that the prosecutor's charging document did provide sufficient facts in support of the war crimes of systematic terrorism, mistreatment of prisoners of war, and mistreatment of civilians.

Sone's second argument was that he wanted only "to show himself as a first-class officer of the Imperial Japanese army and chiefly for that reason inflicted *disciplinary* punishments in order to maintain discipline" in both the POW and internment camp (emphasis added). The temporary court-martial, however, rejected this defense. On the contrary, the court concluded that: "[I]t has nowhere appeared that the prisoners of war or civilian internees … had any intention of seriously opposing camp regulations and orders issued by [Sone]. As the court put it, "the behavior of his victims … can never be a justification for the appalling cruelty and misbehavior by which he frequently made a whole camp of thousands of persons suffer for the misdemeanors committed by, or supposedly committed, by the few."

The tribunal did take into account that, in the Japanese Army, it was customary for physical force to be used; it was accepted for superiors to strike subordinates. But, while acknowledging this cultural difference, the court was quick to conclude that Sone's brutality went well beyond what would be acceptable even in the Imperial Army.

The court ultimately concluded that Sone was not legally responsible for the shortages of food and medicine in either camp, since his superiors determined the quantity of items delivered to both facilities. But, while the court did not hold Sone liable for the hardship resulting from these shortages, the remaining evidence against him was overwhelming.

Faced with evidence of this widespread mistreatment of both prisoners and civilian internees, the three-judge court consisting of Col. Dr. J. H. Peter, Capt. Dr. E. Rijckmans and British Army Major J. F. Hartman found Sone guilty as charged. He was sentenced to death and executed in Batavia on December 7, 1946.[16] As the first war criminal to be shot by firing squad, there was considerable media interest in his case.

Prosecutor v. Seitaro Fujiwara

On December 22, 1947, Navy Chief Petty Officer Seitaro Fujiwara was charged with having "committed a war crime by … treating the internees … badly" in the civilian internment camp at Bandjermasin, where he served as either the commandant or sub-commandant between May and October 1944. According to the indictment, this mistreatment included: Intentionally and repeatedly striking both men and women on the body with a stick; punching internees in the face with his fists; and beating and kicking civilians in the camp. The prosecutor asked the temporary court-martial sitting in Bandjermasin, where the trial was held, to sentence Fujiwara to fifteen years' imprisonment.

Nearly three weeks later, on Saturday January 10, 1948, 40-year-old Fujiwara appeared before the military tribunal for what was to be a one-day trial. He and his counsel were shown written sworn statements from twelve Europeans who had been interned in the camp and sworn statements from two Japanese nationals. All fourteen statements were read in open court and were considered by the three military judges, Major Dr. E. Rijckmans, and First Lieutenants H. F. WIEBOLS and P. BODEMAN.

[16] See de Groot (n. 5) 509.

Mr. VAN DER PLOEG wrote of his own mistreatment at the hands of the defendant. On June 30, 1944, he had gone to a guard with a razor case to ask permission to trade this case for cigarettes. The request was refused and van der Ploeg was accused of attempting to bribe the guard. He was disciplined. That same evening, the accused disciplined him a second time for the same event, by striking him on the back of his head, on his back, and on his legs. Although he had fallen down during the beating, the defendant continued to beat him until he was nearly unconscious.

Van der Ploeg's statement was corroborated by statements from Messrs. VAN OORT, ROMEYN, and SCHOOTS. The latter stated under oath that he saw the accused beating van der Ploeg but did not know the reason. Mr. Schoots also stated that van der Ploeg required medical treatment for some weeks after the ill-treatment. Finally, he added that "beatings took place for the slightest thing [and] it was the accused who did it."

As for civilian female internees mistreated by the defendant, Mrs. E. LANDMAN-DIEUDONNÉ gave a sworn statement in which she said that on July 9, 1944, in the camp at Bandjermasin, she had been struck in the hip and the back by the accused for some twenty minutes. This was because the accused said she had "given a rude answer" to a question put to her. "Her back showed great bruises and she had to remain in bed for three days;" the accused refused to permit her to be medically treated. Similarly, Mrs. Karstel VAN DER WOORD swore that the accused had beaten her when she was sick in her bed and could not attend roll-call. According to van der Woord, Fujiwara had struck her with a stick on her shoulder and leg because he thought she was faking her illness. Finally, a Mrs. ELBRACHT stated that Fujiwara was a "real brute who often used to hit people."

The defendant admitted only that he had struck Mrs. Landeman-Dieudonné with a bamboo stick. He otherwise denied that he had mistreated any civilian internees. In his defense, Fujiwara offered sworn statements from two Japanese nationals, HORII and TAKAHASHI. Mr. Horii stated that he had never heard or seen the accused beat internees and that he was a quiet, friendly man. Mr. Takahashi stated only that he knew from hearsay that the accused made every effort to do his work as well as possible and that he never heard that the accused had mistreated any internees.

Based on the twelve statements from the Dutch men and women who had been interned in the Bandjermasin camps, the tribunal concluded that the defendant's denial of wrongdoing was false. On the contrary, the three military judges wrote that the accused was both cruel and cowardly in his treatment of internees, especially "defenseless women." Consequently, the judges rejected the prosecutor's demand for seven years' confinement and imposed instead a more severe sentence of fifteen years.

The fiat of execution for the decision in *Prosecutor v. Fujiwara* was granted on February 10, 1948 by Mr. A.G. DEELMAN, the Resident of South Borneo. It was announced the following day at the public sitting of the temporary court-martial in Bandjermasin.

Prosecutor v. Hiroyuki Ishikawa

Sergeant Ishikawa[17] was the assistant commandant of Civilian Internment Camp No. 11, which housed women and girls, and was located at Banjoe Biroe on the island of Java.[18] The prosecutor charged that, in April 1945, Ishikawa "intentionally ill-treated" two girls, Joyce van der WOLK and Stans BRINK, by striking both girls a number of times in the face with a riding whip. After hitting the two females, he then made them kneel on the gravel and placed a piece of bamboo in the hollow behind their knees. According to the indictment, Ishikawa made van der Wolk and Brink remain in this position, exposed to the rain, wind, and cold, from about 8 p.m. until 9 a.m. the next morning, which resulted in both bodily injury and mental suffering. The prosecutor asked the temporary court-martial to find Ishikawa guilty of mistreatment of interned civilians and to impose a sentence of five years' imprisonment.

Colonel Dr. J. H. Peter, and First Lieutenants R. ROOSEGAARDE-BISSCHOP and J. A. SCHWANTJE, who were sitting as the president and members, respectively, considered written sworn statements from three women, one of whom was the victim, van der Wolk. In her affidavit, she wrote that:

> The Jap [Ishikawa] accompanied us with a dog-whip he had taken from the wall. He gave Stans and me in turns a few cuts on the face with it. Stans and I then had to kneel down on the gravel right in front of the guard and a *heiho* [local auxiliary soldier] who had beaten us in the morning put a long bamboo [pole] in the hollow behind our knees, and then tied our hands at the wrist with a cord behind our backs. All this was done at the Jap's [Ishikawa] instructions. He often used to hit people with his hand and was gruff and surly.

An affidavit from Mrs. J. W. RUYTER confirmed that "Ishikawa himself beat the girls" and that, after spending the night on their knees in the bad weather, "the girls were wet through, [and] their hands were swollen and blue." According to Ruyter, the girls could no longer feel their legs and had to be helped to walk back to their quarters. Similarly, Mrs. M. van ROSSUM DUCKKATTELL provided a sworn statement confirming the mistreatment of the two girls, including the placement of a bamboo pole behind their knees. But Mrs van Rossum Duckkattell also stated that Ishikawa "never hit people and treated us fairly reasonably." As she put it, "he never acted in a bullying and cruel way."

After having heard the evidence against him, Ishikawa and his counsel admitted that he "was guilty of ill-treatment of the interned girls ... but this was not as serious as specified in the charge." According to the defendant, the girls not only had failed to greet a sentry properly but had also "struck a sentry on duty" (although the record of trial does not explain why such an assault would have

[17] *Prosecutor v. Hiroyuki Ishikawa*, Vonnis No. 17/1948, Batavia (May 10, 1948).

[18] Today known as Banyubiru or Banyu-Biru.

occurred). He admitted to giving the girls two or three blows on the shoulder with a 50-centimeter long "dog whip," and ordering that they kneel in front of the guard room and have their hands tied behind their backs. Ishikawa further explained that, before going to sleep, he had asked a soldier to wake him at midnight because he intended to release the girls at that time. When the soldier violated his order to wake him, Ishikawa slept until the next morning and so van der Wolk and Brink were punished longer than he intended. Ishikawa denied having tortured the two internees with a bamboo pole. He also insisted that, had he not punished the two girls, their misconduct would have been brought to the attention of higher authorities, who would have punished them more severely.

The military tribunal accepted the defendant's testimony, but only insofar as it corroborated the statements of the victim and the two witnesses. But while it found Ishikawa guilty as charged, the judges declined to impose the five-year prison sentence demanded by the prosecutor. In its written opinion, the court emphasized that the war crime committed by the accused was serious in nature. But the prosecutor's recommended sentence was not "correctly proportioned to the gravity of the crime" and so the court instead imposed a sentence of three years in jail. The judges also noted that no evidence had been presented at the proceedings that Sergeant Ishikawa had mistreated any other civilian internees. Rather, given Mrs. van Rossum Duckkattell's statement that the accused had "treated the internees in a fairly humane way," the tribunal seems to have concluded that Ishikawa mistreatment of the two girls was an aberration that, while deserving of punishment, did not require the prosecutor's demand for a heavier sentence.

Prosecutor v. Seikon Kimura

On August 26, 1946, the prosecutor charged Seikon Kimura, who had been employed as a civilian guard at the civilian internee camps at Gedangan and Bangkong, with "carrying out a systematic reign of terror" against men, women, and children interned in these camps.[19] The hallmarks of the accused's "reign of terror," which had occurred between June 1, 1944 until the end of April 1945, were repeated and unnecessary "heavy blows" using his fist, leather straps, and clubs. Kimura also was alleged to have kicked internees and deprived them of all food for days at a time. As a result, many suffered serious bodily harm and "at any rate [his actions] hastened the death of many of them."

On September 9, 1946, the military tribunal sitting in Batavia began hearing evidence in the case. The prosecutor, who had demanded the death sentence for Kimura, presented sworn statements from twenty-two witnesses who had either been victims of the accused's beatings at the Gedangan camp, or else witnessed

[19] *Prosecutor v. Seikon Kimura*, Vonnis No. 28/1946, Batavia (September 11, 1946).

them. There were two affidavits from witnesses who had been personally mistreated by Kimura at the Bangkong camp; another six sworn statements reported witnessing beatings inflicted by the accused.

Mrs. SMITS stated in her affidavit that, while in the Gedangan camp, the accused struck her, her husband, and her daughter with his hand, a leather strap, or his rifle butt. He also told her that "I will kill you." She also reported that she had seen the accused beat Mrs. DE GROOT with a piece of wood because she was caught sitting while on fire-watch duty when she should have been standing. Kimura struck her with such force that her arm was broken in two places.

Mr. WENNEKES stated that he had seen the defendant "repeatedly hitting men, women and children" in both the Gedangan and Bangkong civilian camps. Another witness, Mrs. TAYLOR-KRAAY, wrote that she was caught smuggling cigarettes in the Gedangan camp in October 1944. As punishment, the accused ordered seven *heihos* to strike her in the face for thirty minutes. As a result of this beating, she fell unconscious and her head "swelled up to twice its normal size and she was [left permanently] deaf in one ear."

Mrs. PEETERS-LUYK stated in her affidavit "that the accused behaved like a beast and when once he started hitting he could not stop ... several women were so badly beaten by the accused that there flesh was in rags."

The Batavia tribunal also considered a series of witness statements about the accused's mistreatment of civilian internees in the Bangkong camp. These affidavits likewise reported that Kimura had repeatedly beaten men, women, and children, some of whom were as young as twelve years old. But the Bangkong camp witnesses also stated that the accused had withheld food and medical care as punishment. Mr. BRONKHORST stated that, after a "gang" of internees who were smuggling food and cigarettes into the camp were caught, Kimura "beat them with a thick club, straps and sticks." They were then "shut up in cells for a week and for the first three days were given nothing to eat." As a result, one of the internees, Mr. RENS, who had been so badly beaten that he had three broken ribs, later died.

When given an opportunity to defend himself, Kimura admitted that he had beaten internees "nine or ten times." But he denied having withheld food from the internees, or having ordered that it be withheld from them. Finally, Kimura denied that he had committed any type of "systematic terrorism," but instead insisted that he had only acted to maintain discipline in the two camps.

Colonel J. H. Peter, joined by Lieutenant Colonel M. L. Swaab and Captain E. Rijckmans, agreed with Kimura that there was not sufficient proof that he had withheld food as punishment, despite the witness statements to the contrary. But the judges rejected the defendant's claims that he otherwise was innocent of the war crimes with which he had been charged. The court wrote:

> [i]n the opinion of the Court, [the accuseds] acts were of the character of "systematic terrorism" as they were frequently applied over a lengthy period to a camp population which

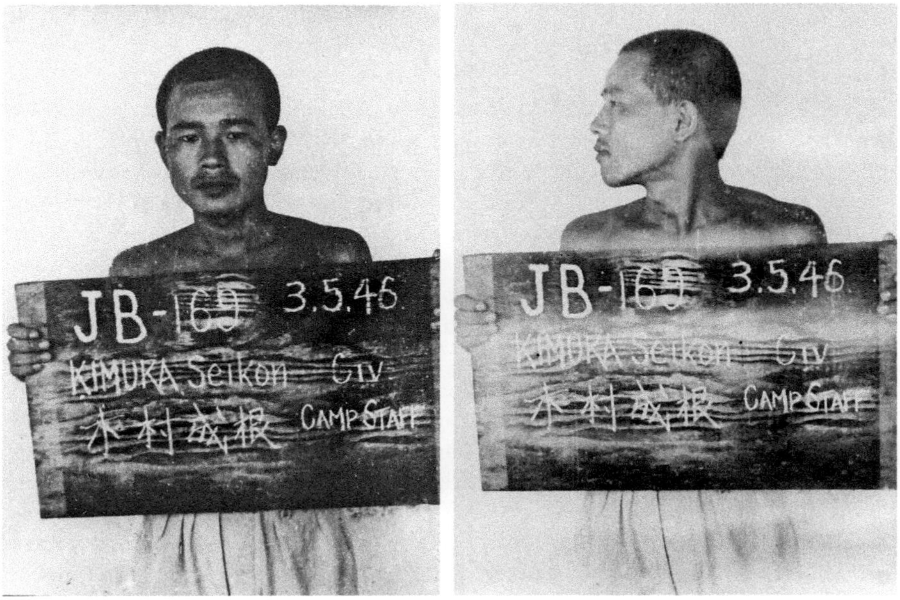

Photos 10 and 11 Seikon Kimura was convicted of mistreating prisoners of war. Sentenced to death, he was executed in January 1947.

Credit: Netherlands Institute of War Documentation (NIOD), Amsterdam

was a docile one, as the accused himself concedes, so that these grave ill-treatments entirely overstepped the bounds necessary for the maintenance of discipline.

Prosecutor v. Seikon Kimura closes by explaining the rationale for the tribunal's decision as to the accused's sentence:

> [t]hat the accused, who for about a year had given full reign to his sadistic tendencies, venting those on defenseless civilian internees, for the most part women, who through their long internment by the Japanese had been brought to the edge of starvation and despair, thereby committed a serious war crime and gave evidence of such a mentality that in connection with the severe standard accepted by the Allies for the trial and punishment of war criminals, the severest penalty must here be pronounced.[20]

Kimura was found guilty of systematic terrorism and sentenced to death on September 11, 1946. He was executed in Batavia on January 25, 1947.[21] The two 'mug shot' photographs of Kimura were taken by the NEI authorities while he was in custody awaiting trial.

[20] ibid 5.

[21] See de Groot (n. 5) 509.

Prosecutor v. Ryohei Miyazaki

At the end of the hostilities on Sumatra, about 4,500 Dutch and Dutch Eurasian and about 1,200 British and Australian soldiers were taken prisoner. In May 1942, some 2,000 were transferred to Burma; many would later meet their deaths working on the Burma Railway. The remaining POWs on Sumatra were put to work on the construction of a road in Aceh, and the building of the Trans-Sumatra Railway. Also known as the Pekanbaru Railway, it was to connect Pekanbaru on the River Siak, which was navigable for small vessels, with Maura, the starting point of the railway to Padang. The route to be built was about 120 miles long.

Captain Ryohei MIYAZAKI was the commander of a series of POW camps located along the route of the Pekanbaru Railway, and POWs from his camps provided the labor for the construction project.[22] The men were required to perform extremely heavy manual work yet, from the outset, had insufficient food and clothing. Almost all the POWs also suffered from malaria, at least one-third chronically. But they received no medical treatment for this debilitating disease, much less for dysentery (which was prevalent) or any other illness. Additionally, once a POW camp was infected it was almost impossible to get the disease under control. Since the Japanese believed that "the perfect remedy for illness was: Stop being lazy and work harder," any seriously ill POW was unlikely to recover.[23]

By July and August 1945, as the Japanese sought to finish the railway, POWs from Miyazaki's camps were working "at a feverish pitch, 36 hours at a stretch with only a two- to- three-hour break."[24] The men slept on boards in rat and lice infested barracks. Exhausted from the work, starving and sick, many died while working or while trying to 'recover' in a camp hospital. As a result, when the Pekanbaru Railway was finished on August 15, 1945, the day the Japanese surrender was announced, almost 700 POWs were dead.

The Medan prosecutor charged that Miyazaki had failed to uphold the 1929 Geneva Convention's requirement that all POWs be treated humanely and that they be protected from harm. Since he had not provided sufficient food, clothing, and medical supplies for the men working on the Pekanbaru Railway, they had died. Moreover, their deaths were foreseeable, given the heavy labor being required.

After an exhaustive look at the evidence, the military tribunal concluded—using the same rationale as the Batavia court in *Prosecutor v. Sone*—that there was insufficient evidence upon which to find Miyazaki criminally liable for the deaths. The court recognized not only that food, clothing, and medicine were in short supply, especially by early 1945, but that in any event it was

[22] *Prosecutor v. Ryohei Miyazaki*, Vonnis No. 16/1948, Medan (May 30, 1948).
[23] See de Jong, *The Collapse of a Colonial Society* (n. 1) 320. [24] ibid 386.

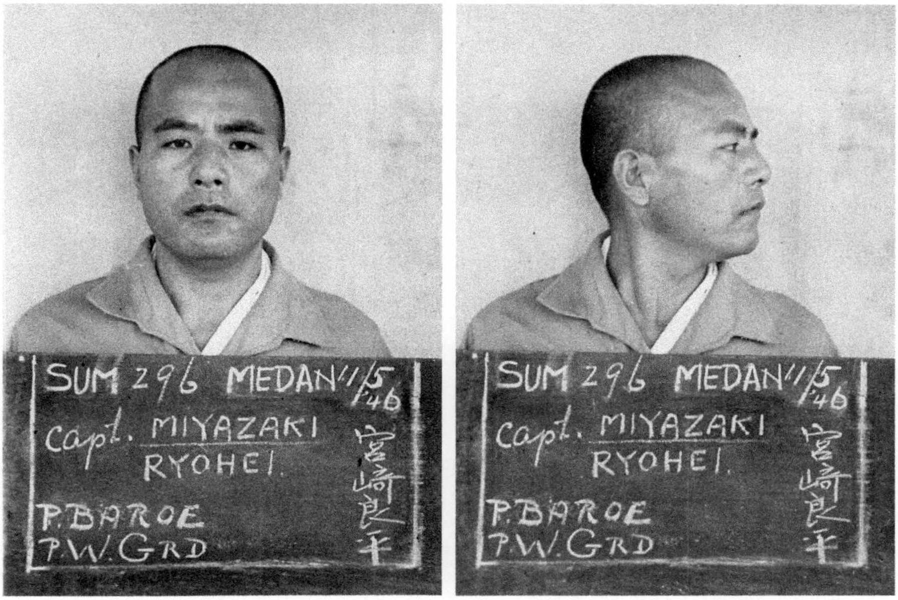

Photos 12 and 13 “Mug shots” of Captain Ryohei Miyzaki. He was found guilty of mistreating prisoners of war in Sumatra and executed.

Credit: Netherlands Institute of War Documentation (NIOD), Amsterdam

Miyazaki’s superiors who determined the quantity of supplies delivered to his POW camps.

But while the temporary court-martial determined there was not enough evidence to hold Miyazaki liable for the hundreds of POW deaths resulting from starvation and sickness, he did not escape responsibility for the brutal mistreatment of POWs in his camps by Korean guards. The court considered more than twenty affidavits from ex-POWs who reported beatings from these Koreans, including being struck in the face, head, torso, and legs with bamboo canes, iron bars, rifle butts, and whips. The injuries inflicted were severe; some POWs died as a result of the beatings. While the defendant denied knowing that his Korean guards were brutalizing POWs, the tribunal rejected this claim as unbelievable, given that the mistreatment was widespread and had resulted in the deaths of POWs. Additionally, as it was general knowledge that Korean guards were known for their harsh treatment of Allied POWs in the NEI, Miyazaki’s claims of ignorance must have rung very hollow.[25]

[25] POWs “as a rule” suffered “more at the hands of the Koreans than at hands of the Japanese.” This was because in their daily existence, the POWs had more contact with Koreans than with the Japanese, “who rarely appeared in the camps.” Additionally, “many Koreans tended to be more ‘Japanese’ in their behavior than the Japanese themselves.” See de Jong, *The Collapse of a Colonial Society* (n. 1) 311.

On May 30, 1948, Miyazaki was found guilty of mistreatment of POWs, and sentenced to death. The two photographs of him were taken while he was in police custody prior to trial.

As explained in Chapter 3, there was no formal appellate process after an accused was found guilty at a temporary court-martial. But a fiat of execution was required from the commanding general of the geographic area in which the tribunal was sitting, except that when the death penalty was imposed, the commanding general of the area was required to forward the case to the Governor-General in Batavia for his decision as to whether a pardon should be granted.

Because of this procedure, Miyazaki petitioned Lieutenant Governor General van Mook to spare his life. He also wrote this letter to KNIL Major J. J. VAN DE LANDE, whom he hoped would intervene with the NEI authorities on his behalf:

Dear Sir:

I would like to offer my hearty congratulation for you on your activity with best health in your new place and would like to express my cordial thanks for your kindness extended to me while you were in Medan.

I was sentenced to death by the Temporary Military Tribunal, Medan, on the 30th of 1948 and now spending lonesome days in a solitary cell waiting the last moment. I reproach myself, not others, I gave up myself as my destiny given by the God.

The verdict announced at the court, for me was quite reasonable which I understood very well with my appreciation. I was sentenced by the charge of high mortality in the camp and my insufficient supervision toward my Korean subordinates who ill-treated the POWs without my knowledge.

...

The charge about my responsibility of issuing foods, clothes and so on to the camp have been duty acquitted at the court by the President on the reason of insufficient evidence. It is really my great regret that I newly came to know the fact of the maltreatment inflicted by my Korean subordinates upon the POWs when I was examined at Medan in the time of the preliminary hearing after the surrender ... I would never tolerate any illicit conduct in the camp, if I were aware of it. I took all my possible steps within my competence to prevent them.

...

I frankly admit the high mortality in my camp. But as previously mentioned, the President has acquitted the supplying responsibility such as foots, clothes and so on to the camp and admitted other causes of the high mortality in favor of me. I am deeply convinced that it must have been difficult to get better results because of my poor position at the lower end of the line of command ... I dare say no POW died because of [my] personal conduct, whole through my tenure.

...

My last and best hope through the time was attend the funeral of my old mother in Japan, but all came to impossible at present. I would break my heart if I think over my old mother, wife and four children in Japan who are supposed to be in extreme poverty without any financial support.

Every minute and every second I am only waiting for the warm and merciful mitigation by His Excellence the Governor-General to whom I submitted by petition in due way.

I would be very much obliged if you will be so kind to bring forward the petition from you in favor of me to his Excellency, by taking my miserable situation into your consideration.

...

Your most grateful, I remain
Miyazaki Ryohei
c/o Medan Prison, Sumatra[26]

Miyazaki's petitions were unsuccessful; he was executed in June 1948.

Prosecutor v. Akio Takamura

On September 28, 1946, the prosecutor at the tribunal in Batavia charged Takamura with the war crime of mistreating civilian internees while serving as commandant of guards at an internment camp located at Semarang.[27] In particular, the accused was charged with "repeatedly" kicking men, women, and children, or else hitting them with an iron pipe while they worked in the camp's vegetable garden. Additionally, in July 1945, while working as a kitchen supervisor, the defendant "cruelly and repeatedly" struck Maria Elizabeth DIJKGRAAF. He hit her with his military belt and then with a thick tree branch until "blood flowed."

At this one-day trial, which began and finished on October 14, 1946, the prosecutor introduced five affidavits into evidence, all of which were read to the accused and his counsel in open court. Mr. George Johannes OEHLERS reported that he had witnessed the accused repeatedly striking women working in the vegetable garden, and that the reason for these beatings was that the accused objected to the women speaking to their children while they worked. Mrs. Anna H. A. M. COLLETTE wrote in her statement that, when she tried to speak with her small son, the accused "first pointed out to her that she was wrong," before striking her repeatedly with a leather strap. The result was that her back was "completely raw" and she had to be carried on a stretcher to the hospital for treatment.

As for the accused, he generally denied having committed any war crimes, much less mistreating internees in the Semarang camp. He also denied having mistreated Mrs. Collette. But Takamura did admit giving Maria Dijkgraaf "a number of slaps on the face, without causing her any harm other than a slight swelling." Takamura told the tribunal judges that he had struck Dijkgraaf because she "had accused him behind his back, of embezzlement or theft, at any rate she had spoken ill of him."

[26] Miyazaki's letter to Major van de Lande is reprinted in Peter Post *et al.* (eds.), *Encyclopedia of Indonesia in the Pacific War* (Brill 2010) 416–17.

[27] *Prosecutor v. Akio Takamura*, Vonnis No. 39/1946 (November 6, 1946).

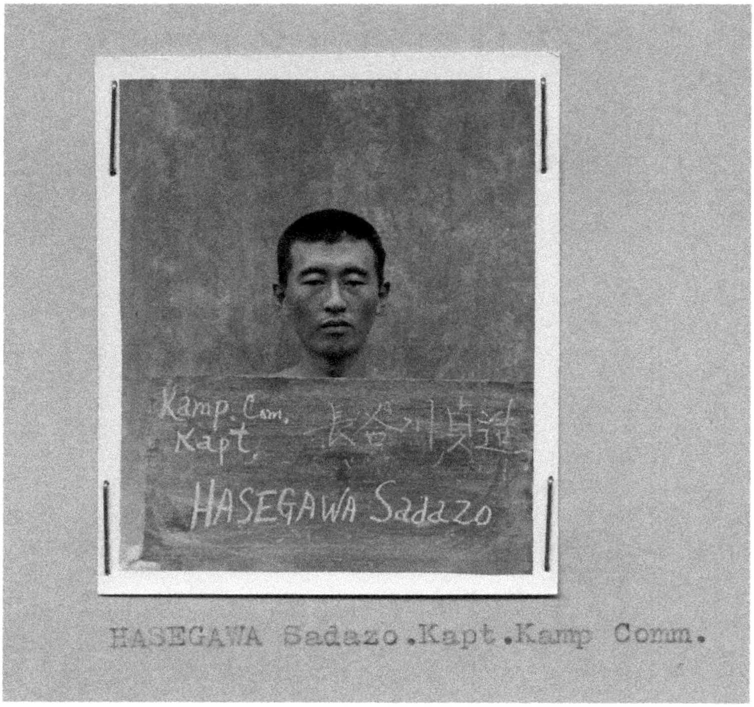

Photo 14 Captain Sadazo Hasegawa was convicted of mistreating civilian internees while serving as a camp commandant on Java. Found guilty of systematic terrorism, and mistreatment and torture of civilians, especially women and children, he was sentenced to death. Hasegawa was executed in August 1947.

Credit: Netherlands Institute of War Documentation (NIOD), Amsterdam

The tribunal determined that the evidence was sufficient to find the accused guilty of the war crime of mistreatment of civilian internees. But, while the prosecutor had requested a 10- year sentence of imprisonment, Colonel J. H. Peter, Lieutenant Colonel M. L Schwaab, and Captain L. G. Roetert STEENBRUGGEN instead imposed a five-year jail sentence. The written decision states that the judges decided upon this lesser punishment because, while Takamura "had a cruel and callous nature ... he certainly does not belong to the worst type of war criminal." But, continued the tribunal, "in connection with the mentality which forms the basis of these [war crimes], he must be severely punished by the United Nations in order to prevent a repetition."[28]

[28] ibid 4.

Photo 15 Captain Shigeyoshi Yamane was convicted of mistreating POWs and civilian internees while serving as a camp medical doctor. He was shot by firing squad on November 23, 1948.

Credit: Netherlands Institute of War Documentation (NIOD), Amsterdam

The fiat of execution was issued by J. E. YSEBAERT, the commanding officer of the Allied Military Administration Civil Affairs Branch, Batavia, on October 31, 1946.[29]

Prosecutor v. Koshiro Tanabe

On February 5, 1947, a tribunal sitting in Macassar found Navy First Lieutenant Koshiro TANABE guilty of using POW labor to build an ammunition depot.[30]

[29] The Allied Military Administration Civil Affairs Branch (A.M.A.C.A.B.), originally established in Australia in 1944 as the Netherlands Indies Civil Administration (Dutch: *Nederlandsch-Indische Civiele Administratie*), was responsible for the restoration of Dutch colonial rule after the end of the Japanese occupation of the NEI.

[30] U.N. War Crimes Commission, *Law Reports of the Trials of War Criminals*, vol. 11 (His Majesty's Stationery Office 1947–1949) Case No. 59, 13–16.

The legal basis for finding Tanabe guilty was clear-cut, as using prisoner labor in war work had been expressly prohibited by the Hague Convention of 1907 and the Geneva Convention of 1929, both of which had been signed by the Japanese. But Tanabe added insult to injury when he allowed the depot to be built only 50 meters away from the POW camp (containing Dutch, Australian, and British personnel), as this meant that he was "unnecessarily subjecting prisoners of war to danger."

The evidence presented at the trial—through the testimony of Dutch and Allied ex-POWs—was that the Allies had repeatedly targeted *both* the depot and the POW camp in their bombing operations. Why? Because the Japanese had placed anti-artillery guns in and around the POW camp, with the result that wounds to POWs caused by bomb splinters "were a regular thing." At least one prisoner died when his "head [was] smashed by bomb-splinters." On another occasion, a field where "hundreds of prisoners of war were daily employed was only missed [by Allied bombs] by some tens of yards."

The temporary court-martial sentenced Lieutenant Tanabe to seven years' imprisonment for this war crime.

Prosecutor v. Saburo Yamura

Finally, in *Prosecutor v. Saburo YAMURA*, a tribunal sitting in Balikpapan convicted a 32-year old Japanese interpreter of "systematically carrying out a reign of terror against civilians and prisoners of war ... by repeatedly and unnecessarily ... in a manner far exceeding the limits of the normal exercise of discipline ... giving them violent blows with his fist or with a thick piece of hard wood."[31] The evidence presented showed that Yamura

> [b]ehaved in a brutal fashion, that for no reason he beat people until they fell down unconscious, that he then threw water over them in order to bring them around and when they were again conscious beat them once more, that his mistreatment of two Indonesians, Oesman and Senen, was to such an extent that they died.[32]

The court concluded that, in addition to causing the deaths of OESMAN and SENEN, the accused also had "behaved in a very inhuman way, acted in an arbitrary and despotic fashion, [and] brutally beaten defenseless persons" on other occasions. On September 13, 1946, the three-judge panel, with Major J. L. PAARDEKOOPER presiding, found him guilty of systematic terrorism, and condemned him to death. Less than ten days later, the Commander of Dutch Forces in East Borneo confirmed the sentence.[33]

The mistreatment of POWs during the occupation was brutal and widespread. The beatings and other physical assaults may be explained, at least in part, by the

[31] *Prosecutor v. Saburo Yamura*, Vonnis No. 1/1946, Balikpapan (September 13, 1946). See also U.N. War Crimes Commission, *Law Reports of the Trials of War Criminals* (n. 30) 545.

[32] *Prosecutor v. Yamura* (n. 31) 2. [33] ibid 3.

Japanese military culture of the day, in that it was generally accepted for an officer or noncommissioned officer to strike or otherwise use corporal punishment on a recalcitrant subordinate. But the code of *Bushido*, and the disdain the Japanese felt for POWs who had chosen life instead of an honorable death are the key to understanding the harsh treatment meted out to many POWs. "Do not live to bear the shame of being taken prisoner" was the motto of the Japanese soldier. Those Allied soldiers, sailors, airmen, and marines who had not fought to the death deserved no better than to be treated like slaves. This inexorably led to the Japanese conclusion that the POWs were not worth feeding, much less protecting from harm, regardless of what the law of war required. Even those POWs who suffered debilitating illnesses received no sympathy: "Sick prisoners deserved to be punished for their arrogant rebellion against the Japanese Empire."[34]

As for the treatment of both noninterned and interned civilians, the contempt with which the Japanese held POWs inexorably spilled over to their treatment of civilians. Moreover, if Asia were to be cleansed of Europeans, and the Netherlands "eliminated" from the East Indies, then there was little reason to treat Dutch and Dutch Eurasian civilians with dignity or respect. As for those Indonesians, Chinese, and Malays who supported the colonial imperialists, they could expect no better treatment—and they received none.

The war crimes examined in this chapter show that there were many Japanese defendants who proved that, despite the passage of many years, Robert Burns was correct when he wrote in 1785 that "Man's inhumanity to man/Makes countless thousands mourn!" Captain Sadazo HASEGAWA, whose photograph is shown here, proves the truth of Burns's words. Convicted of mistreating and torturing civilian internees, especially women and children, while serving as a camp commandant on Java, Hasegawa was sentenced to death. He was executed in August 1947. Even medical personnel, who should have been caring for those in their custody, committed atrocities. Captain Shigeyoshi YAMANE, depicted here, was found guilty of mistreating POWs and civilian internees while serving as a camp doctor. He was shot by firing squad on November 23, 1948.

[34] See de Jong, *The Collapse of a Colonial Society* (n. 1) 320.

6

Trials for Mass Murder and Unlawful Executions

Temporary courts-martial heard evidence of "mass murder" and "unlawful executions" committed by the Japanese during the occupation. The former occurred when the Japanese carried out mass killings, chiefly of non-Europeans. These murders were either in retaliation for general resistance to their authority or because "military necessity" required it. An example of the latter was the March 1945 beheading of some thirty-five lepers (men, women, and children) by the *Kempeitai*, simply because the Japanese decided that the risk of infection was too great for the lepers to be evacuated.[1]

As for unlawful executions, the gist of this offense was that the accused had killed (or ordered his subordinates to kill) one or more Netherlands East Indies (NEI) citizens for some alleged crime or misconduct, but that the execution had occurred without any regularly constituted trial or hearing to determine guilt or innocence, much less pass sentence. These unlawful executions were very widespread, as reflected by the fact that, along with "systematic terrorism," this offense appears most often on the indictments at war crimes tribunals.

It might be argued that the distinction between mass murder and unlawful executions is simply semantic. After all, is not an individual killed in a mass murder incident also executed without a trial? An examination of the temporary courts-martial, however, indicates that large-scale killings done in retaliation reasons usually were charged as "mass murders," while the killing of individuals involved in (or suspected of being involved in) anti-Japanese activities (and therefore in violation of Japanese or international law, or both) was charged as unlawful executions. But the distinction between mass murder and unlawful executions can be blurry, as evidenced by the court-martial of Major General Toru TANAKA, which is examined in the first section of this chapter.

A final note on unlawful executions. In a number of prosecutions, including one examined in this section (*Prosecutor v. Gisaburo YOSHIDA*), the temporary court-martial found the defendant guilty, but imposed a relatively light sentence of imprisonment. This was because the victim of the unlawful execution

[1] *Prosecutor v. Goro Ogihara*, Vonnis No. 26/1947, Morotai (August 29, 1947) discussed below. See also Louis de Jong (with an Introduction by Jeroen Kemperman), *The Collapse of a Colonial Society: The Dutch in Indonesia during the Second World War* (KILTV Press 2002) 211.

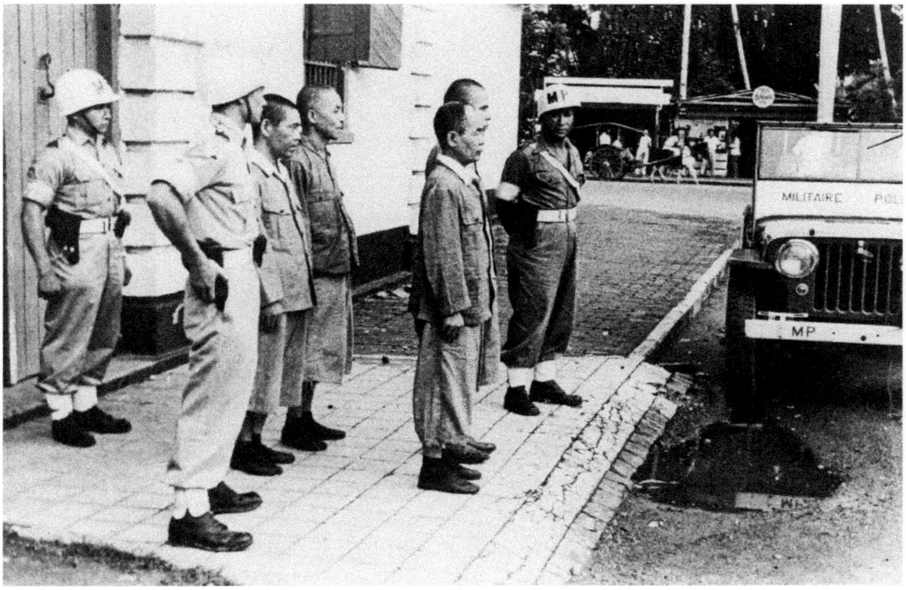

Photo 16 Japanese defendants under armed escort in Batavia, 1947.
Credit: Netherlands Institute of Military History, Ministry of Defense

in fact had committed a crime for which he could be lawfully tried and punished. Consequently, while the Japanese accused had committed a war crime because he had deprived the victim of a trial prior to his execution, the court considered the victim's criminal behavior as a matter in mitigation and extenuation when fashioning a sentence. The reasoning underlying this approach seems to have been that, as the Japanese could have put the victim to death if they had afforded him a trial, the accused should not be punished too severely. On the other hand, if the tribunal decided that the victim of the unlawful execution was innocent of any criminal wrongdoing, then the accused's sentence was not lenient.

Mass Murder

In addition to the *Tanaka* case, this chapter looks at the following four temporary courts-martial involving mass murder, in alphabetical order: *Prosecutor v. Gakuji IIMA, Yoshimitsu OCHI, Shinichi TAKEYAMA, and Yukio NARIKIYO*; and *Prosecutor v. Goro OGIHARA*, plus its companion cases, *Prosecutor v. Katzuaki SHIMIDZU, Toshiro ISHIGAKI, Sadao NAGASAKI, Kumedjiro FUKUCHI, and Nobuo SAKAMAKI.* Finally, this section examines the case of *Prosecutor v. Satsuki SANO.*

Prosecutor v. Gakuji Iima, Yoshimitsu Ochi, Shinichi Takeyama, and Yukio Narikiyo

All four defendants were civilians living in eastern part of Dutch Borneo. Iima functioned as a police inspector in the Borneo Civilian Administration; Ochi, Takeyama, and Narikyo were employed in a Japanese-owned transport company in Balikpapan.

The evidence presented at the tribunal sitting in Balikpapan was that all four men, at the instigation of the local Japanese military commander, participated in the mass murder of at least twenty-five Indonesian men and women early in July 1945. These killings had occurred because the Japanese believed that the Indonesians were organizing an anti-Japanese plot in anticipation of Allied landings in eastern Borneo. There was, in fact, no such conspiracy, but the Japanese believed otherwise.

In the Verbal Process conducted in December 1946, the four accuseds denied any knowledge of the killings. The three military judges, however, heard live testimony that all four Japanese defendants had participated in at least two separate killings of civilians. The first was a murder of "about 13" men, women, and children. The second mass murder occurred about seven days later, and involved "20 women and children between the ages of one and twenty." Additional corroboration was presented in the form of written statements from individuals having knowledge of the killings. There also were written statements from other witnesses, who affirmed that the four accuseds bound the victims and then shot them with pistols and rifles.

On December 3, 1946, Major J. L. PAARDEKOOPER, the president of the court-martial, joined by Captain B. van EYK and First Lieutenant O. van MEETEREN, found the four men guilty of "mass murder" and "murder" and sentenced them to death. The fiat of execution confirming the sentence was issued on January 1, 1947.

Prosecutor v. Goro Ogihara

On August 13, 1947, the prosecutor for the temporary court-martial sitting in Morotai charged *Kempeitai* First Lieutenant OGIHARA with nine different war crimes, all occurring between February and July 1945, and all involving murder or mass murder.[2] Two of the nine charges are examined in detail here, with the most important being the charge that, in February or March 1945, the defendant ordered his subordinates to kill about thirty-five lepers, all of whom were living near the village of Medi on the island of Halmaheira. The second charge involved the accused's July 1945 order to his men that they kill some twenty-five Indonesian

[2] *Prosecutor v. Goro Ogihara*, Vonnis No. 28/1947, Morotai (October 28, 1947).

men and women, all of whom were civilians. Ogihara ordered this mass murder because he believed that these Indonesians were going to escape from Japanese controlled territory to the Allied-held island of Morotai.

Trial proceedings began on August 24, 1947. When they were completed five days later, the tribunal had determined the following facts from affidavits and in-court statements from Ogihara.

In February 1945, anticipating Allied landings on the island of Halmaheira, Colonel MATSUNAGA ordered that all civilians be evacuated from a zone along the coast of the island. This meant that about thirty-five "completely innocent and defenseless" lepers resident in a village in the zone needed to be moved to another location. The defendant, however, did not want to evacuate the lepers. Consequently, he either proposed to his colleague, Captain Isao SUGAWARA, that the lepers be killed, and Sugawara agreed with the proposal, or else Sugawara ordered that the lepers be killed, and the accused carried out the order. In any event, at the beginning of March, the accused ordered his subordinate, Kempeitai Second Lieutenant Choguro KIMURA, to kill the lepers. On March 6, 1945, Kimura took a detachment of *Kempeitai* members and about twenty-five soldiers to the leper village, where they beheaded the lepers with their swords.

Ogihara did not deny that he had participated in the killing of the lepers, but he raised two defenses. First, he insisted that he should not be found guilty because he was only obeying the orders of his superior officer, Captain Sugawara, in carrying out the killings. As explained in Chapter 3, however, NEI Statute Book Decree No. 45 of 1946 had adopted the rule that a defense of superior orders did not relieve the accused from criminal liability. (This 1946 decree had also expressly suspended—and made inapplicable to temporary courts-martial proceedings—a provision of NEI *domestic* law, which provided that a subordinate could not be punished for a crime committed in the execution of an official order.) Consequently, it was up to the judges at the Morotai tribunal to decide the extent to which the defense of superior orders relieved Ogihara of culpability or, if found guilty, would permit a more lenient punishment.[3]

After analyzing the evidence, the judges decided that they need not address the accused's superior orders defense. The court acknowledged that Sugawara and the defendant were blaming each other, in that Sugawara claimed at his trial that it was the accused who proposed that the lepers be killed, while Ogihara insisted that he had simply carried out Sugawara's order because Sugawara was his superior officer. But the tribunal found it "fairly improbable" that Sugawara and Ogihara were in a superior–subordinate relationship, given the "special and independent position" that the *Kempeitai* occupied in the Japanese Army. At the same time, the judges were not persuaded that the evidence proved that Ogihara had proposed that the lepers be murdered and that Sugawara had consented to this proposal. Instead,

[3] There was nothing unusual about this approach to the superior orders defense. The U.S. Army's Field Manual 27-10, *Rules of Land Warfare*, provided that an unlawful act committed by a soldier pursuant to the order of a superior "may be taken account in determining culpability, either by way of defense or mitigation." See discussion in Chapter 3, n 52 and accompanying text.

the tribunal found that there was sufficient evidence that, regardless of who had the idea that the lepers should be murdered, the accused had agreed with the idea and, after consultation and coordination with Sugawara, planned and arranged for *Kempeitai* personnel and soldiers to carry it out.

In legal terms, Ogihara and Sugawara shared the same criminal intent and the tribunal noted that this explained why Ogihara had told the court that he believed the mass killing "to be a fully justified military measure in the circumstances." In fact, Ogihara did not believe that he had committed any crime, much less done anything wrong. Rather, the defendant told the judges that "he had only two objections to the execution." The first was that it might have "an unfavorable influence on the feelings of the population." The second was that "he found it *a very disgusting job to kill these lepers*" (emphasis added). The record does not expressly state why Ogihara was so disgusted with the lepers, but it seems that he (and Sugawara) thought leprosy was contagious. This is not true; there was no risk of infection. The tribunal also noted that "several entirely healthy and sound people" were living among the lepers, too. But this made no difference to the accused; he ordered them all to be killed.

As for the second charge discussed here, the court found that, as Japan's defeat became more and more certain, local men, women, and children fled from Halmaheira to the nearby island of Morotai, which had been occupied by the Allies. For the Japanese, this population movement had decidedly negative effects, because the Allies obtained intelligence from the locals about Japanese defenses on Halmaheira and this resulted in very effective Allied bombing of Japanese units.

To stop this flow of people and information, Colonel Matsunaga proclaimed that anybody who appeared to be attempting to leave Halemaheira for Morotai would be killed. The Japanese went to every village and announced this prohibition on travel, and the village headmen also passed the proclamation on to individuals over whom they had responsibility. On or about July 22, 1945, while the accused was on an inspection tour, he saw that despite Colonel Matsunaga's order, villagers were building rafts, which Ogihara believed was evidence that another "large-scale attempt to escape was planned." Believing that he had to take immediate action, the defendant ordered his *Kempeitai* personnel and soldiers under his authority to go down to the Koepa-Koepa river where he had seen the rafts. They were "to watch for possible fugitives and to kill them ... further, they were to kill all the natives they met" in that area near the river. The next morning, the accused's men reported to him "that a number of natives had dropped down the river on rafts" and that they consequently had captured, shot, and killed about twenty men and women who they believed were trying to escape to Morotai.

Once again, the accused admitted to the tribunal judges that he had ordered the killings of the local villagers, but he insisted that he was only acting pursuant to an order from Colonel Matsunaga. The court, however, determined that Matsunaga's order (even if it existed) was unlawful because it covered every attempt to escape to

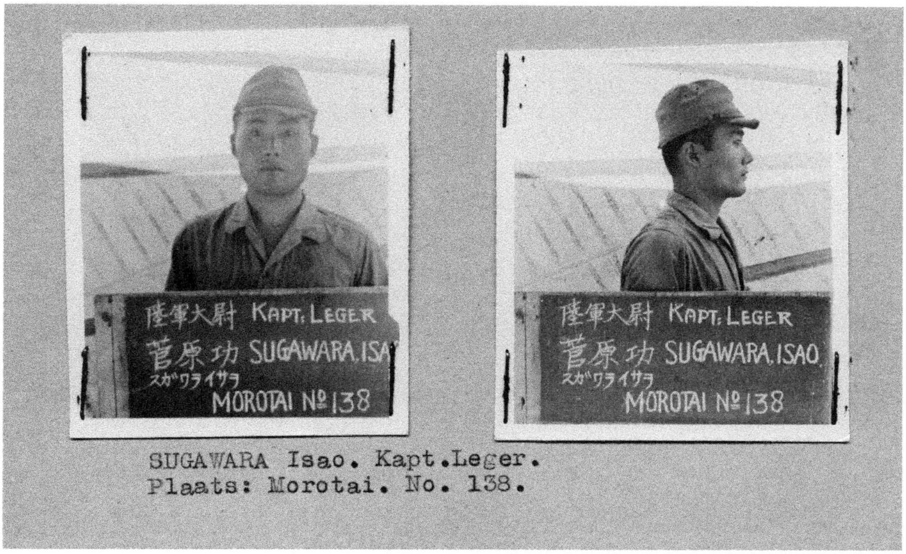

Photo 17 Infantry Captain Isao Sugawara was found guilty of participating in the mass murder of lepers near Medi in March 1945. He was sentenced to death and executed by firing squad.

Credit: Netherlands Institute of War Documentation (NIOD), Amsterdam

Morotai, even if such an attempt was or could be prevented. Finally, the tribunal heard considered affidavits from two witnesses, both of whom indicated that the twenty men and women were not attempting to escape but were simply moving to another village. Given these facts, the tribunal ruled that Ogihara bore "full responsibility for this second mass murder."

As a result of these two mass murders, and other war crimes, the military tribunal found him guilty. After expressly noting that the accused had served twenty years in the *Kempeitai* (including five years in China), the court raised an alternative basis for criminal liability: Article 10 of the War Crimes Penal Law Decree. That unique provision provided that an individual who was part of a group (like the *Kempeitai*) could be found guilty if the war crime at issue could be ascribed to the group as a whole because such crimes were part of the day-to-day conduct of the group. While the judges did not expressly state that the court was applying Article 10 to Ogihara's case, and the prosecutor did not charge the accused on the basis of Article 10, the tribunal's reasoning is persuasive, given the accused's lengthy association with the group.[4]

[4] For more on art. 10 and group criminal responsibility see Chapter 3, nn 21–28 and accompanying text and Chapter 10 'Collective Responsibility'.

"It is self-evident," wrote the judges, that "there can be no talk of exonerating circumstances" and that the accused, "entirely in the spirit of the *Kempeitai* system," carried out an "unscrupulous reign of terror ... upon the inhabitants of Halmaheira." Finding that "even the severest punishment seems too light a retribution for all the misery and suffering" inflicted by the accused, and "for the streams of blood with which he drenched the soil" of the island, the court sentenced the accused to death.

On October 28, 1947, Captain D. VERMEULEN, and First Lieutenants F. M. B. de BONT and F. J. REEMER, informed the accused that he was to be shot by firing squad.

A final note. Captain Sugawara, who helped plan the killing of the lepers, and Lieutenant Chimura, who had carried out the killings, were also both sentenced to death by temporary courts-martial sitting in Morotai.[5] The photograph of Sugawara was taken of him while he was awaiting trial for mass murder.

Prosecutor v. Katzuaki Shimidzu, Toshiro Ishigaki, Sadao Nagasaki, Kumedjiro Fukuchi, and Nobuo Sakamaki

In this companion case to *Prosecutor v. Ogihara*, all five defendants were members of the *Kempeitai*, and all had participated in the killing of lepers at Medi on March 6, 1945. Shimidzu and Sakamaki were lieutenants; Ishigaki, Nagasaki, and Fukuchi were sergeants.[6]

On September 3, 1947, the prosecutor charged them with the war crime of mass murder, and alleged that each defendant had used his sword to behead the victims, as follows:

Shimidzu	one woman and two children
Ishigaki	four women and one boy
Nagasaki	three men
Fukuchi	five women

As for Sakamaki, the prosecutor did not allege that he had personally killed any lepers. Rather, Sakamaki was charged as an accomplice, in that he had aided the four other accuseds in the commission of the mass murder. Sakamaki, who was the "commandant" with authority over the other four defendants, had helped locate and collect the lepers, stood guard over them, and then selected the spot where they were beheaded.

[5] Sugawara was sentenced to death on August 8, 1947; Kimura was sentenced to death on September 9, 1947.

[6] *Prosecutor v. Shimidzu, Ishigaki, Nagasaki, Fukuchi, and Sakamaki*, Vonnis No. 30/1947, Morotai (October 20, 1947).

In a trial that lasted but an afternoon on September 12, 1947, a tribunal consisting of Captain Vermeulen and Lieutenants W. RIDDER and C. SCHAGEN, considered written affidavits and oral testimony from each accused. All admitted that they had beheaded lepers, but explained that they had carried out these killings under orders from *Kempeitai* Lieutenant Kimura, who informed them that Lieutenant Ogihara had ordered the murders.

The testimony of Shimidzu is instructive, for it shows that the defendants were less than enthusiastic about carrying out the killings. At the same time, Shimidzu's testimony illustrates how a junior ranking soldier's desire to obey the orders of a superior trumped any sense that the killings might be unlawful. In fact, Shimidzu told the Dutch judges that he had questioned the order to kill the lepers, but not because he thought it was unlawful to kill them. On the contrary, he asked if the lepers could not be evacuated and, if this was not possible, if they instead could be poisoned. He also asked if other soldiers could carry out the killings. He suggested poison and that others do the killings because he was afraid of being infected by the lepers. The reply to Shimidzu's suggestion was "no," because military necessity required that the lepers be killed.

Shimidzu also provided a detailed description of the war crimes, which is worth setting out in full:

> At 8 AM, I went with Ishigaki and Fukuchi to Medi. At the village, we said that today the doctor was coming for a visit. All the lepers then came out. We collected all the men in one house, and the women and children in another house. Fukuchi, Ishigaki and I went to the house where the latter had been collected. There were about 40 lepers in total of whom 17 were women and three or four children. At that point, soldiers surrounded the houses so that no one could escape. Some soldiers were also sent out to guard the paths coming into the village.
>
> At this point the lepers were very afraid, so we bound their hands. Then the victims were taken one-by-one by one or two soldiers to the place of execution, which was about 50 meters from the houses. They were blindfolded while being taken there. The men and women were executed separately. After all the lepers had been beheaded, the soldiers dug one pit, and the bodies were deposited and covered with soil.

As for Nagasaki and Shimidzu, both made statements admitting to their participation in the mass murder. Nagasaki further said that, while it seemed possible that the lepers could have been evacuated, he believed that the order to kill them was lawful and that, in any case, an order must be obeyed. Interestingly, although the prosecutor had charged him with killing three men, Nagasaki told the court that he had beheaded five female lepers. Sakamaki similarly admitted to taking part in the mass murder, but as an organizer; he had ensured that the twenty soldiers who accompanied the *Kempeitai* to the leper village near Medi understood the mission.

The tribunal found Shimidzu, Ishigaki, Nagasaki, and Fukuchi guilty of mass murder. The fifth defendant, Sakamaki, was found guilty of the war crime of "complicity in mass murder" (Dutch: *medeplichtigheid aan massamoord*). Since Vermeulen had sat as the senior judge in *Ogihara*, he was already familiar with the facts surrounding the mass murder, and presumably Lieutenants Ridder and Schagen also were greatly disturbed by the massacre. The judges were especially unhappy with Lieutenant Sakamaki. According to the evidence, he had studied law in Tokyo at Waseda University, and the tribunal questioned how an educated man could not have realized that the order to kill lepers was unlawful and a war crime. Nonetheless, the court sentenced all five defendants to the same term of imprisonment: twelve years. The fiat of execution was given on October 19, 1947 and the defendants and their counsel were informed of the result on October 20.

While one might think that twelve years for the murder of innocent men, women, and children is too light, the tribunal undoubtedly considered that the five defendants believed that they had no choice but to obey the orders of a superior officer. Captain Sugawara and Lieutenant Ogihara, who had originated the plan for the mass murder, would pay for this decision with their lives. Those who had followed their orders, while guilty of war crimes, were deserving of at least some leniency.

Prosecutor v. Satsuki Sano

On October 24, 1946, Sergeant Major SANO was charged by the prosecutor in Pontianak with the war crimes of mass murder, torture of civilians, and mistreatment of civilian prisoners.[7] These offenses all occurred in the Sanggau district, located in the western part of Dutch Borneo, in late August and early September 1945. While this section examines all the charged crimes, it focuses on the mass murder.

The accused was the commandant of the Japanese garrison in Sanggau. On August 22, 1945, about 7 pm, he joined four other Japanese nationals in killing six Dayaks (the indigenous people of the island of Borneo) who were imprisoned in a jail under the accused's control. According to the prosecutor, Sano killed these men because he suspected them of involvement in a prior rebellion against Japanese authority; they were imprisoned while the Japanese authorities decided what to do with them. According to the prosecutor, after calmly planning this mass murder, and obtaining permission from the Japanese commander in Pontianak to implement it, Sano and his collaborators beheaded the Dayaks and then threw their heads and bodies in a nearby river.

The evidence for this war crime came from both witness affidavits and the accused himself. Hamid bin SOLEIMAN stated that one morning he saw that the door of the jail cell where the Dayaks had been confined was open, and that they were missing. When he asked a guard what had happened to the Dayaks, he was told that they had been beheaded by the Japanese the night before. Soleiman's statement was corroborated by Katje TUMBELAKA, who was the cook for the prisoners. One morning, she was told by her supervisor that she could now prepare meals for six fewer men and that she also should borrow a bucket to clean out the cell in which the Dayaks had been held.

[7] *Prosecutor v. Satsuki Sano*, Vonnis No. 14/1946, Pontianak (December 2, 1946).

As for the accused, he admitted that he had killed the Dayaks. He contended, however, that he had to put them to death because the "safety of the occupation was in danger" and moving the Dayaks to another location was impossible because of a lack of personnel to accompany the prisoners to another facility.

The tribunal rejected this defense. The judges wrote in the decision that it was impossible to believe that six unarmed Dayaks confined in a cell could be a danger to the well-armed Japanese occupation force. The court also noted that the accused had personally participated in the execution of the Dayaks. This meant he was guilty of both the war crime of murder and complicity in murder.

As for the other charged offenses, the court accepted an affidavit from Khim Min NG that, on or about September 8, 1945, Sano had either personally tortured or mistreated, or permitted his subordinates to torture or mistreat "many Chinese." One man, named TJONG, was so badly beaten that he later died in Ng's jail cell. The judges found Sano guilty of the war crime of torture and mistreatment of civilians.

When one remembers that the mass murder of the Dayaks occurred a week after Emperor Hirohito announced on the radio that Japan had surrendered to the Allies, and that the torture and mistreatment of civilians happened some three weeks after the Japanese capitulation, the Pontianak tribunal must have been outraged that Sano had committed these war crimes after hostilities had officially ended. Curiously, the decision does not mention that the Sano's crimes occurred after Japanese forces were supposed to have laid down their arms. Since the war was over, and Japan had lost, the judges must have been surprised when Sano had the audacity to claim that the safety of the occupation required murder of the Dayaks.

Sano was sentenced to be shot by firing squad. Captain C. VAN ESSEL, joined by Captain A.H. BOHM and Second Lieutenant F. M. SINNECKER, announced the decision in open court on December 2, 1946, after the fiat of execution was issued by J. VAN DER ZWALL.

Prosecutor v. Toru Tanaka

Major General Toru TANAKA was tried by the temporary court-martial sitting in Amboina for the mass murder of civilians and other war crimes. The prosecutor charged him on November 30, 1947, and Tanaka's trial began on December 20, 1947.[8]

Fifty-five year old Tanaka had a long record as a soldier, which included service in China and combat against American and Filipino troops in the Philippines in late 1941 and early 1942.[9] From September 1, 1944 to June 1, 1945, he was in

[8] *Prosecutor v. Toru Tanaka*, No. 27 J/1947 Amboina. Decided January 10, 1948; fiat of execution, January 22, 1948.

[9] Then Colonel Tanaka was the commander of the 2nd Formosa Regiment when it made an amphibious invasion of the island of Luzon on December 10, 1941. He subsequently saw hard fighting against U.S. and Philippine Army units as they withdrew into Bataan in January 1942. Lewis Morton, *The Fall of the Philippines* (Government Printing Office 1953, 1993) 103, 215–16.

the East Indies on the island of Timor, where he commanded the 2nd Formosan Infantry Regiment. Sometime after the Japanese surrender in August 1945, Tanaka was arrested in Timor by Australian troops, and taken to Darwin. He was taken into custody because his name appeared in the Australian Army "police gazette," which was a memorandum listing the names of Japanese nationals "wanted for war crimes" by the Allies. While Tanaka could have been prosecuted at an Australian military tribunal in Darwin (as soldiers of the 2nd Formosa Regiment were prosecuted in Darwin for war crimes committed against Australians), he was delivered to the Dutch authorities for trial in Amboina. This most likely occurred because the Dutch requested that Tanaka be handed over to them, and because his misconduct during the occupation of Timor was more egregious than any war crimes committed against Australian nationals.[10]

The facts developed at trial were that, in September 1944, some 1100 Indonesians living on Sermata, a small island located about 100 miles east of Timor, apparently believed that the Allies would soon be landing to liberate their island. Desiring to help the Allies, the Indonesians rose up against the Japanese stationed on Sermata. The rebels killed six enemy soldiers, and took their weapons. Most of the dead had been operating a radio station on the island, but a few were members of the *Kempeitai*.

To quell the rebellion, Major General Tanaka sent a punitive expedition (Dutch: *strafexpeditie*) to Sermata. After this expedition, under the command of Captain SHIMADA, investigated the circumstances of the uprising and reported back to Tanaka, he ordered Shimada "to kill a total of about 60 Indonesians" as a collective punishment. Shimada and his subordinates carried out these murders as instructed. Shimada later told Lieutenant Seidei OHARA, who was a member of the expedition, that he had ordered the execution of these sixty individuals.

During this same mission to Sermata, Lieutenant Ohara saw Captain Shimada order the execution of three men and two women. Three of these victims were the father, mother, and sister of a man named JOOST, whom the Japanese believed was the leader of the resistance group on Sermata. Captain Shimada had the parents and sister held as hostages and, when Joost refused to surrender to the Japanese after five days, Shimada had the three individuals executed. After the death of his parents and sister, however, Joost apparently did allow himself to be taken into custody. Tanaka subsequently ordered his execution in November 1944.

The evidence also showed that an additional thirty-four Indonesians were taken captive during the punitive expedition. All were transported from Sermata to the island of Moa. In November 1944, Major General Tanaka sent a telegraph to Lieutenant Ohara, who apparently was the senior Japanese officer on Moa, in which Tanaka ordered him to kill these thirty-four individuals. These killings likewise were carried out as instructed; all were executed by bayonet.

[10] "Wanted Jap Held in Darwin," *The Courier-Mail* (Brisbane, Australia) (March 15, 1946) 1.

Finally, in May 1945, Tanaka learned that a village official named Marthin NORIMARNA, his parents, and his brother, as well as two other individuals living on the island of Letti, were conspiring against the Japanese. These six men believed that a landing by Australian troops on Letti was imminent, and they were organizing an effort to aid the amphibious invasion. Tanaka had the six men taken into custody and subsequently ordered Lieutenant Ohara to bayonet them to death. Ohara carried out the killings as directed.

At the proceedings, Tanaka was defended by Yoshio IWASE and, because the accused did not speak Dutch or Indonesian (Malay), he had the full-time assistance of two translators, Wilhelm K. MALESSY and Kimizu TAKIMOTO.

Major General Tanaka denied that he was guilty of committing any war crimes. On the contrary, he argued that under Article 4 of the Japanese Penal Code, and the state of emergency that existed in the 2nd Formosa Regiment's area of operation, the execution of the Indonesians was lawful as required by "military necessity."

Major General Tanaka's chief problem was that his subordinate, Lieutenant Ohara, appeared as a witness at the temporary court-martial, and testified under oath. Ohara told the court that, acting under orders of Tanaka, he had participated in the punitive expedition led by Captain Shimada, and taken part in the murder of "about 100" Indonesians. Ohara also testified that, again on the orders of Tanaka, he had killed six Indonesians on the island of Letti, all of whom were conspiring to help the Allies if and when they landed on the island.

Captain C. M. SCHUDDEBEURS, the tribunal president, joined by Captain G. S. GASPERSZ and First Lieutenant H. P. J. M. van LOON, found the accused "guilty of causing the death of a great number of persons ... mostly done in a very cruel manner, namely by stabbing with a bayonet." Tanaka was found guilty of mass murder, murder (committed six times), murder (committed three times), and killing of hostages. Deciding "that only the severest penalty was adequate and just," the court sentenced Tanaka to death on January 10, 1948.

Unlawful Executions

Six cases are examined in this section in alphabetical order. They are: *Prosecutor v. Tadashige DAIGO; Prosecutor v. Michiaki KAMADA; Prosecutor v. Shigehiko KOKUBU; Prosecutor v. Shujiro MAKINO; Prosecutor v. Motosuke SUSUKI*; and *Prosecutor v. Gisaburo YOSHIDA*. This section concludes by looking at two events that were not unlawful executions, but might be thought to fall into that category: The executions of the "Haga Plot" and "Overakker Plot" participants.

While all the cases are instructive, three stand out: *Daigo, Makino*, and *Susuki*. The trial of Vice Admiral Daigo is important because he was a senior officer charged with ordering unlawful executions. The evidence presented at trial was that Daigo had ordered a subordinate "to execute in groups of 100, approximately 1054 persons." As for Makino, he ordered and participated in the unlawful execution of more than 400 men, women, and children, all of whom were killed as punishment for the deaths of a few Japanese nationals. Finally, the *Susuki* case is instructive because it shows that a seemingly straightforward case of an unlawful execution could have complex factual and legal issues. This is because the defendant was successful, at least in part, with arguing that he could not be prosecuted for a war crime where the Dutch victim had lost his nationality when he voluntarily joined the Japanese Army.

Prosecutor v. Tadashige Daigo

On September 22, 1947, Vice Admiral DAIGO was sentenced to death by the temporary court-martial sitting in Pontianak.[11] He had been found guilty of ordering the unlawful execution of 1,054 individuals between early February and the end of May 1944, although the evidence indicated there may have been as many as 1,200 victims.

The trial proceedings began on September 22, 1947, when the three-judge panel accepted witness affidavits as evidence and read them in open court to the accused and his defense counsel. The prosecutor had charged Daigo in the alternative, which gave the court additional flexibility in weighing the evidence against the defendant. In this regard, the charge was that Daigo, as the commander of the 22nd Naval Base at Balikpapan, had either ordered his subordinate, Keimei UESUGI to "summarily execute in groups of about 100, approximately 1054 persons" or, alternatively, that Daigo had permitted and condoned the commission of this war crime by Uesugi, while Daigo knew, or had good reason to believe, that the unlawful executions were committed or were going to be committed by Uesugi. In short, the prosecutor's theory was either that the accused had ordered the killings or had command responsibility for them.[12]

The tribunal eliminated the command responsibility theory fairly early in the proceedings. Sworn statements from Uesugi, who had been in charge of the *Tokkeitai* in Daigo's area of operations, and Soichi YAMAMOTO, the Deputy Commander of the Japanese garrison in West Borneo at the time of the executions, confirmed that Vice Admiral Daigo had ordered the executions.

Since Daigo also admitted that he ordered the deaths, the only issue before the tribunal was whether the killings were lawful. The accused insisted that he was not guilty of having committed any war crime because the 1,054 persons executed

[11] *Prosecutor v. Tadashige Daigo*, Vonnis No. 29/1947 (September 22, 1947). Born in 1891, Daigo graduated from the Imperial Japanese Naval Academy in 1912. He served on cruisers, battleships, and submarines in the 1920s and 1930s. Daigo was promoted to vice admiral on November 1943 and finished World War II as the Commander-in-Chief, 6th Fleet.

[12] As explained in Chapter 3 (see n 40 and accompanying text), the prosecutor at a temporary court-martial had the right to amend the charge(s) against the accused if, during the trial proceedings, evidence was at variance with the charge. He also could add a charge(s) if proof of additional war crimes were revealed at trial. Consequently, it was not necessary for the prosecutor initially to charge Daigo using an alternative theory of liability. He may have chosen this course of action, however, because the prosecutor was not entirely certain how the evidence would unfold. For cases on command responsibility see Chapter 10.

in Dutch Borneo had been part of a "conspiracy" to destroy Japanese authority. Drastic measures had been required to suppress this resistance, and Admiral Daigo told the judges in Pontianak that he had personally presided over an "Emergency Court-Martial" for each of the executed individuals to ensure that their executions were "entirely lawful." Apparently, Daigo had been the lone member of this emergency court.

The tribunal first decided that there was no evidence that such a widespread conspiracy had existed in West Borneo. The judges noted that, in early 1944, "Japan was at the height of her power," and this meant that any resistance to Japanese rule in Dutch Borneo had no reasonable chance of success, if for no other reason than those involved in any conspiracy did not possess the necessary arms.

Since Daigo and his counsel insisted that there had been a conspiracy, the court asked them to provide proof that a "great danger to the Japanese occupation" in Dutch Borneo had existed. When no such proof was forthcoming, the court rejected Daigo's claim that a conspiracy had existed. The view of the NEI judges was any so-called conspiracy had been manufactured by the Japanese in the course of their interrogation of suspected wrongdoers. The evidence presented showed that the Japanese had arrested "a few persons" thought to be unlawfully in possession of weapons. These persons, while being interrogated, were beaten. The "water cure" and the "electric cure" also were used during questioning. The result was that, while under such duress, "and under false promises of better treatment ... if they would state names of other persons" involved in the resistance, those being interrogated provided additional names. The Japanese then interrogated these newly identified persons and, using the same techniques, obtained yet more names. The "'conspiracy' thus gradually expanded to between 1300 and 1400 persons," although Admiral Daigo told the court that he believed that as many as 2,000 persons were involved.

Having concluded that a conspiracy had never existed, and that there was no basis to believe that the victims had committed any offenses in violation of Japanese law, the court proceeded to examine Daigo's claim that the executions were lawful because the death sentences had been imposed by an Emergency Court-Martial. The judges rejected the claim that there had been any formal judicial proceedings. Not only were there no documents or affidavits supporting the existence of such proceedings, but the court agreed with the prosecutor's argument that even if the Emergency Court-Martial had existed, the victims were denied the opportunity to present any defense. This meant that Daigo's emergency court was fundamentally deficient because all 1,054 suspects were denied a "true and fair" trial. The Pontianak court-martial concluded that the emergency tribunal, if it had ever existed, had been done only to "impart a lawful appearance to the executions."

Based on the evidence, the judges found that "a total of approximately 1,200 innocent persons" were executed. They found Daigo guilty of ordering the unlawful execution of 1,054. As the court members put it, they had "arrived at the opinion that the accused, who did not shrink from causing the deaths of hundreds of innocent civilians, can be meted out only one punishment." The court sentenced Daigo to death; he was shot by firing squad in Pontianak on December 6, 1947.

Prosecutor v. Michiaki Kamada

On July 29, 1947, the military tribunal in Pontianak began hearing evidence against Vice Admiral KAMADA.[13] He was charged with having ordered his subordinate, Captain Riki OKAJIMI, the commander of the local *Tokeitai*, to execute about 150 persons in December 1944. Alternatively, the prosecutor charged that Kamada was guilty as Okajimi's commander, because he had either permitted or condoned the executions, or had reason to believe they were occurring. The killings were unlawful because the victims had been arrested and then beheaded without trial.

Kamada had been the commander of the 22nd Naval Base in Balikpapan from August 1944; he had succeeded Admiral Daigo, whose court-martial is discussed above. Just as Daigo had suspected that the local people in his area were conspiring against the Japanese, so too was Kamada certain that there was an anti-resistance movement, albeit consisting mostly of individuals of Chinese ancestry.

During questioning by war crimes investigators, Okajimi explained that he and his deputy, Lieutenant Sōichi YAMAMOTO, had uncovered an anti-Japanese "Chinese conspiracy" among the Chinese inhabitants of the western part of Dutch Borneo. Okajimi and Yamamoto used waterboarding and electricity to inflict pain as part of the questioning of Chinese suspects and, after obtaining confessions, reported the existence of the plot to Admiral Kamada. According to Okajimi, the Chinese were attempting to create trouble between the native inhabitants and the Japanese, which the Chinese intended to accomplish by hoarding supplies and preventing raw materials from reaching local factories. Kamada's instructions to Okajimi were to act immediately to execute all persons who were a danger to the Japanese occupation.

Affidavits from other witnesses confirmed that Kamada had ordered the executions, and that Okajimi had asked for and received authorization in a telegraphic message to execute "dangerous persons." Okajimi carried out the killings between December 1944 and February 1945, with about twenty-five individuals executed at a time. They were beheaded with swords and buried in shallow graves.

Unlike Admiral Daigo, who admitted to executing 1,054 Indonesians, but claimed that his emergency court-martial made the killings lawful, Kamada denied

[13] *Prosecutor v. Michiaki Kamada*, Vonnis No. 34/1947, Pontianak (August 11, 1947). Born in Japan in 1890, Kamada graduated from the Imperial Japanese Naval Academy in 1911. He served on cruisers, battleships, and destroyers in the 1920s and 1930s. Promoted to rear admiral in October 1941, he subsequently saw action in New Guinea from 1942 to 1943. Kamada was a vice admiral when he surrendered to the Australians in September 1945. At the request of NEI authorities, the Australian government delivered Kamada to Dutch authorities in Pontianak.

that he knew anything about the unlawful executions. The judges, however, were convinced that he was not telling the truth. First, Kamada knew that his predecessor in command, Admiral Daigo, had ordered unlawful executions, and so he was on notice that such killings had been previously carried out by subordinates in his command. Second, the judges believed Okajimi's assertions that he would have never carried out such a serious order on his own initiative.

On July 29, 1947, Major C. van Essel, Captain C. A. MARTENS, and First Lieutenant H. O. LIM found Kamada guilty as charged and condemned him to death. The fiat of execution was issued by J. van der Zwaal on August 1, 1947. Kamada was executed by firing squad on October 18, 1947.

A final note. Post-war scholarship suggests that there was no Chinese conspiracy, and that any real resistance to the Japanese occupation was minimal in Dutch Borneo. But the members of the *Tokeitai*, who were from poor backgrounds and had little education, convinced themselves that trouble was brewing. As one historian puts it, they had created the Chinese conspiracy because, being "distrustful and fearful of the local population, they saw ghosts in the sunlight."[14]

Prosecutor v. Shigehiko Kokubu

In 1944 and 1945, Lieutenant Colonel KOKUBU was stationed near Sarmi, which was located on the northern coast of Netherlands New Guinea.[15] He was the Chief of Supply for the 36th Division, 2nd Army and, in this assignment, was in charge of three companies of *heihos*. These were local youths recruited by the Japanese in the NEI to serve as auxiliary soldiers.[16] While these Indonesian *heihos* were utilized in many ways by the Japanese, in Kokubu's division they were used to do heavy manual labor.

In April 1948, the prosecutor charged Kokubu with having mistreated the *heihos* under his command by forcing them to do heavy labor without sufficient food or medical care. He was also charged with "incitement to [commit] unlawful executions, committed several times" (Dutch: *uitlokking tot onwettige executies, meermalen gepleegd*).

Before discussing the unlawful executions with which Kokubu was charged, it is important to provide some context by looking at his mistreatment of the *heihos*.

[14] Ooi Keat Gin, "Calculated Strategy or Senseless Murder? Mass Killings in Japanese-Occupied South and West Kalimantan, 1943–1945," in Peter Post *et al.* (eds.), *Encyclopedia of Indonesia in the Pacific War* (Brill 2010) 219.

[15] *Prosecutor v. Shigehiko Kokubu*, Vonnis No. 54/1948, Hollandia (June 30, 1948).

[16] During the occupation of the NEI, the 16th Army, 26th Army, and the Navy, all recruited *heihos* to augment their forces. By 1945, most *heihos* were local Indonesian youths, although early in the occupation indigenous Royal Netherlands East Indies Army (Dutch: *Koninklijk Nederlands Indisch Leger* (KNIL)) soldiers who had surrendered were permitted to serve as *heihos*. At the end of the war, there were some 25,000 *heihos* on Java, 12,000 in Sumatra, and about 900 in New Guinea. They were used in a wide variety of assignments, including transport, anti-aircraft artillery, construction, mine sweeping, and as guards in prisons and camps. After the Japanese surrender, some former *heiho* joined the Indonesian guerrillas in their struggle against the re-establishment of Dutch colonial rule.

The tribunal considered affidavits from five witnesses; three were Japanese officers who had commanded the *heiho* companies under the defendant's supervision. Kansuke FURUTSUKA stated under oath that of the 461 *heihos* in his unit, only eighty survived the war, with 265 having died between February 1944 and August 1945. According to Furutsuka, he had told the accused as early as May 1944 that his men were so malnourished and unhealthy that they could not work. Colonel Kokubu's reply was that, "sick or not," the *heihos* must work. The result was that "many died."

Teiji YAYOSHI's affidavit was remarkably similar. He had started with 637 *heihos* in his company; 480 had died between February 1944 and the capitulation. While some had been killed by Allied bombs, the largest number had died from malnourishment and disease. Yayoshi reported that the accused told him that if a *heiho* could walk, he must work. Subsequently, the accused told him that every sick *heiho* who could walk, must work and that this meant that patients suffering from beri-beri, malaria, and dysentery were not excused from work. When Yayoshi protested that the work for his *heihos* was too heavy and their rations were inadequate, the accused ignored him.

Finally, Shigei WATANABE's sworn statement said that, of the 619 *heihos* in his company, only seventy-eight survived the war; 379 had died from malnourishment, malaria, and dysentery. While Watanabe—and Furutsuka and Yayoshi—acknowledged that the *heihos* were receiving the same food rations as junior Japanese soldiers, the difference was that the *heihos* were doing extraordinarily heavy manual labor and, when sick or malnourished, were not excused from work. As he too was concerned about the health of his men, Watanabe told the accused "at different times" that the labor being required of them was too heavy and that it would result in *heiho* deaths. Watanabe's concerns fell on deaf ears.

Colonel Kokubu was not helped when the judges informed him that they were considering an affidavit from Lieutenant General Hachiro TANOUE, who had commanded the 36th Division during this time. Tanoue stated under oath that the accused had never complained to him about the lack of rations for the *heihos*, or protested to him about the work assignments given to his *heiho* companies by the division. While this might have been a self-serving statement, the three judges concluded that it reflected that the accused did not care enough about the *heihos* to complain or protest.

As for the unlawful executions, the evidence presented was that the accused had personally ordered "many" *heihos* to be summarily executed, without trial or any judicial proceeding, when these *heihos* were caught stealing military supplies or leaving their places of duty without authority.

The defendant admitted that he had carried out these executions, but insisted that he was not guilty of a war crime because the killings were authorized by Article 22 of the Japanese Military Penal Code. The military tribunal, however, rejected this defense. Kokubu could not avail himself of Article 22 because it only allowed summary punishment (without any judicial process) when Japanese forces were "eye-to-eye with the enemy." The judges interpreted this to mean that if Japanese troops were in a combat environment requiring immediate discipline, then summary punishment was permitted. But since the evidence presented to the court showed that Kokubu and his *heihos* had not been engaged in hostilities with the Allies, he could not avail himself of this provision in Japanese military law.

The court found Kokubu guilty as charged. Out of three companies of 1,800 *heihos* under his supervision, only 180 were alive at the end of the occupation. The deaths of more than 1,600 men were the "direct result" of the accused's mistreatment of them as "work slaves" for the Japanese Army. As for his ordering that *heihos* be executed without trial for crimes they might have committed, this war crime simply demonstrated his complete lack of concern for them as human beings.

On June 30, 1948, Captain H. P. BLONK, joined by First Lieutenants A. Uyt DEN BOGAARD, and J. H. VAN WESTERNDORP, condemned Kokubu to death. His fiat of execution was issued by Mr. J. P. K. van EECHOUD, the Resident of New Guinea, on July 8, 1948.

Prosecutor v. Shujiro Makino

While one might consider the November 1944 massacre of more than 500 Indonesian villagers on Babar Island to fall into the "mass murder" category, the Dutch charged the war crime as an unlawful execution.[17] This was because the killings were punishment for the murder of several Japanese nationals.

On December 14, 1948, the temporary court-martial sitting in Amboina began hearing evidence against Shujiro MAKINO. During occupation, he had served both as a Navy adjutant and as head of the Japanese civilian administration in an area of the South Moluccas, which are located near New Guinea and Timor. The island of Babar[18] was under Makino's authority, and the prosecutor charged Makino with having "cruelly conducted unlawful executions" on the island. He also charged Makino with having committed "multiple rapes" of women who were from Babar, either personally or as an aider and abettor.

After considering sworn statements from eight Indonesians and hearing in-court testimony from the accused and his defense counsel, Yuichi YAMAGISHI, the military tribunal based its decision on the following facts. In mid-1944, a Japanese officer working at the navy supply unit on Babar agreed with a local man from the village of Emplawas to purchase 300 kilograms (660 lbs) of tobacco. At the time, Emplawas was renowned for the quality of its tobacco, and produced more than 6,000 kilograms (13,000 lbs) a year. The Japanese officer, whose name was SHINOHARA, had paid in advance and, when the tobacco was ready, sent an Indonesian named HETHARIA to pick it up.

17 *Prosecutor v. Shujiro Makino*, Vonnis No. 30/1948, Amboina (December 14, 1948).

18 Today, Babar Island is part of the Maluku Province of Indonesia. The island is located about 150 miles east of Timor.

When Hetharia arrived in Emplawas, he fell into an argument with the village headman, TIMERKAS, and insisted that he would now collect 400 kilograms of tobacco from the villagers. Timerkas was furious and demanded that Shinohara come to the village personally to resolve the dispute.

Five days later, on October 27, 1944, Sinohara arrived in Emplawas, accompanied by Hetharia and one other Indonesian employee from the naval supply unit. An argument ensued and Shinohara, known for his quick temper, struck Timerkas. Timerkas then stabbed Shinohara with a knife. The mutual assault now spiraled out of control as the villagers joined the fight, cut off Sinohara's fingers and toes, and then impaled him with a bamboo spear (through his anus). Then they hanged Sinohara upside down, and cut off his tongue (apparently a local practice to silence the dead). The two Indonesians who had come with Sinohara to Emplawas attempted to escape, but were caught and murdered by the villagers.

Knowing that the Japanese would retaliate, the Emplawas villagers decided to strike first. On October 29, the village men hid their women, children, and elderly in the forest. Then about sixty men, armed with machetes, spears, and bows and arrows, proceeded toward the naval base, which was located about three miles away. The Japanese had forty-six soldiers and about fifteen marines and sailors on Babar; there also were nine *Kempeitai* personnel. Perhaps the villagers intended to kill them all, but that did not happen. Rather, the locals managed to kill one Japanese guard and one *Kempei*, and wound one sailor. A large number of villagers then fled to the nearby mountains.

The Japanese now took a brutal and horrific revenge. Makino ordered two subordinates, Captain TASIRO and Lieutenant HIRONO, to conduct a punitive expedition against the Indonesians. As a result, starting on November 3, the Japanese soldiers and sailors captured, tortured, and killed about 100 villagers, who apparently had not gone into hiding. Then, on November 7, 1944, 100 more soldiers from Saumlaki arrived to carry out additional retribution. According to affidavits from Octavianus LEKAHENA and Thomas TANABORA, the Japanese sent a local villager into the mountains, who told the hiding villagers to return to Emplawas because all was forgiven and the Japanese now desired to make peace with them.

After 438 men, women, and children came out of hiding, the Japanese chose the twelve strongest from among them, including Timerkas. They tied these men and women to trees and then cut off their noses and ears. Then the Japanese killed them one by one, either with a sword or bayonet, as a warning to other villagers on Babar. On the orders of the accused, the Japanese also selected ten of the most attractive young women; the intent was to force them into prostitution at the local Army brothel.[19]

As for the rest of the men, women, and children? A sworn statement from Amaphilis IMEA explained that, under orders from Makino, the Japanese troops separated the men from the women and children, and then took all of them to a

[19] For more on the war crime of forced prostitution see Chapter 7.

nearby river. They tied them up and made them sit on the ground, all facing in the same direction. Makino watched while his subordinates set up two heavy machine guns behind the backs of the remaining 426 villagers and, when all was ready, the Japanese opened fire with these automatic weapons. An affidavit from Benjamin TARORE, who worked as a cook for the Japanese and witnessed the unlawful executions, stated that it took 30 minutes to kill all the villagers. Tarore also said that, when the machine gunning stopped, five Japanese inspected the bodies to be certain they were dead and those that still gave signs of life were finished off with a bayonet.

Since Makino was ordering his subordinates to execute the villagers, one might expect that he would not personally pull a trigger or wield a bayonet or sword. But one witness, Victor LIWIER, wrote in his affidavit that the defendant was "by far the cruelest" of those Japanese involved in the crime, having "taken great pleasure in personally striking individuals with a piece of wood, breaking their arms and giving them bloody wounds." Liwier also related that Makino had personally killed some of the villagers during the November 1944 punitive expeditions.

As for the rape charge, the affidavit from Lekahena stated that he had personally seen the accused take two of the ten young girls into his own home, for his own use. Lekahena also stated that the others were sent to the Army brothel as comfort women.

The final decision in *Prosecutor v. Shujiro Makino* does not record the accused's defense to the charges, or what evidence (if any) he offered in mitigation or extenuation. At least initially, however, the Japanese attempted to cover up this war crime by giving misleading information to the Allied investigators. When asked about the deaths of so many men, women, and children on Babar, the Japanese claimed that the villagers, believing that the Japanese defeat was imminent, had rebelled against the occupying authorities. The Japanese had been forced to counter-attack, and the deaths had resulted from necessary military operations.

On December 14, 1948, Lieutenant Colonel Dr. B. DAMEN, and First Lieutenants E. HAAK and W. Ridder found Makino guilty of unlawful executions and rape. The judges further agreed with the prosecutor that a death sentence was appropriate. Mr. Melkianus Augustinus PELLAUPESSY, the Resident, South Moluccas, issued the fiat of execution on December 17 and, three days later, the accused and his counsel were informed by the military tribunal that he would be shot by firing squad.

A postscript to this war crime. When Japan surrendered less than a year later, sixty to ninety villagers who had remained in hiding now emerged. They discovered that Emplawas had been burned to the ground, and that all their food and livestock had been confiscated. Moreover, the "stench from the rotting corpses still lingered, and people believed that whoever passed by the area could still hear the agonizing cries of the massacred." The surviving villagers subsequently built a new village about a mile away. In 1992, when a Japanese team of researchers visited the village, its population was still only slightly more than 300 persons.[20]

Prosecutor v. Motosuke Susuki

On Saturday, December 13, 1947, First Lieutenant Motosuke SUSUKI appeared before the military tribunal sitting in Amboina.[21] The charge was that, between August 1944 and December 1944, near the towns of Riring and Oewen Pantai in the South Moluccas district, the accused ordered his subordinates to execute four men by rifle fire, even though these individuals "had not been tried, at any rate in a legal manner." One of the men was a Dutchman named BARENDS, who had voluntarily joined the Japanese Army during the occupation of the NEI. The other three victims were Indonesians accused of anti-Japanese activities.

The prosecution charged Susuki with "the war crime of murder, committed four times" under Article 1, Decree No. 44, Statute Book 1946, in conjunction with Article 4, Decree No. 45, Statute Book 1946. The prosecutor demanded that the tribunal sentence the 27-year old Susuki to death.

When the proceedings commenced, the three military judges considered signed and sworn statements from both the defendant and Mr. Oei FERDINANDUS; these had been obtained during the preliminary investigation into the war crime. The judges also heard in-court testimony from Mr. Robert LATUMAHINA, Mr. Isamu NAKAMURA, and the defendant.

That evidence showed that Susuki, who was a member of the Army Engineer Corps, had been assigned to work in the *Hosikikan* (Japanese Intelligence Service) in the South Moluccas. According to Latumahina, an Indonesian who had volunteered to serve during the occupation with the Japanese army, he was one of four men who was ordered by the accused to form a firing squad. That squad then executed Barends by rifle fire. Barends had volunteered during the occupation to serve in the Japanese Army and was in the *Hosikikan* unit to which the accused belonged. At some point, Barends, who had been in charge of all non-Japanese volunteers in the *Hosikikan*, had fallen into a dispute with a Japanese soldier named

[20] Shigeru Sato, "Massacre on Babar Island," in Peter Post *et al.* (eds.), *Encyclopedia of Indonesia in the Pacific War* (Brill 2010) 419–21. Unfortunately, in writing about the unlawful executions on Babar Island, Sato erroneously claims that the war crime was never punished. He writes that: "the Dutch military tribunal, understaffed and overburdened, did not pay much attention to it [the massacre] or indict the Japanese involved." See Sato (ibid) 421. The existence of *Prosecutor v. Makino,* however, shows that Sato is simply wrong. The Dutch did investigate the war crime and the death sentence given to Makino demonstrates that the colonial authorities did care about the victims of this horrific event.

[21] *Prosecutor v. Motosuke Susuki*, Vonnis No. 25/1947, Amboina (January 28, 1948); U.N. War Crimes Commission, *Law Reports of Trials of War Criminals*, Trial of Susuki Motosuke, vol. 13, Case No. 77, 126–30. While the surname is spelled Susuki in both the Dutch court decision and in the U.N. Law Reports, it should be written as Suzuki in Romanized Japanese.

YAMAMOTO, and had shot at him. The result of this attack on Yamamoto was that Barends was shot by firing squad, and Latumahina testified under oath that Susuki himself gave the order to fire. Barends was hit by the rifle bullets and hung limply on the post to which he had previously been tied. While Barends was still bound to the post, the defendant approached him and shot him one more time to make certain he was dead. Barends was then put into a grave which was then filled with soil. All this occurred near Riring on the island of Ceram.

Latumahina also testified that in October 1944, three Indonesian nationals, MAILOA, SKALWIK and TARUMASELE, had been shot and killed by a firing squad on the orders of the accused. Although Latumahina had not participated in these executions, which had occurred near Oewen Pantai on Ceram island, he knew that Skalwik and Tarumasele were teachers who had been arrested in the middle of September 1944. The former had been accused of stealing a rifle from the Japanese and the latter was accused of setting ambushes in the path of the retreating Japanese. As for Mailoa, he also was a teacher and had been accused of shooting at the Japanese or robbing them, or both.

Latumahina's in-court testimony was corroborated by the written sworn statement of Oei Ferdinandus, which had been taken prior to Susuki's trial by the Deputy Chief Prosecutor, Dr. W. J. VAN DER VEEN. Ferdinandus told van der Veen that, in October 1944, he witnessed the defendant and other Japanese *Hosikikan* officers take Mailoa, Skalwik, and Tarumasele to a spot in the woods. When they did not return, Ferdinandus concluded that they had been murdered, since the defendant was the commandant of the *Hosikikan* execution squad.

At trial, the accused admitted that he had given his subordinates orders to shoot Barends, Mailoa, Skalwik, and Tarumasele. He denied, however, that he was guilty of any war crime, because these executions were legal under Japanese law. The temporary court-martial's discussion of the accused's defense is the most interesting aspect of *Prosecutor v. Susuki*, and makes it an important case in the history of war crimes prosecutions.

The judges, Major Dr. F. P. STÖCKER, and Captains C. M. SCHEDDEBEURS and Dr. H. P. J. M. VAN LOON, first examined Susuki's claim that he could not be prosecuted for the death of Barends because Barends had voluntarily relinquished his legal status as a subject of the Netherlands when he joined the Japanese Army. Since national tribunals conducted under the authority of the United Nations had *in personam* jurisdiction only where the victim was "a subject of the United Nations," the legal argument was that Barends was not a U.N. subject, given his voluntary decision to join the Japanese forces. As the accused and his counsel put it to the judges, even if the accused had failed to see that Barends received a fair trial and accordingly was responsible for his unlawful execution, the matter fell outside the tribunal's jurisdiction.

The three judges accepted the argument that the killing of Barends could not be prosecuted as a war crime because he was not a U.N. subject. But, wrote the judges in their decision, this legal conclusion did not end the inquiry. On the contrary, the issue was whether the Japanese had followed their own law in dealing with Barends because, if Barends had been executed by firing squad without due process under Japanese military law, then his death remained a crime over which the temporary court-martial would exercise jurisdiction *using NEI domestic law.*

The defendant and his counsel argued that it was lawful for Susuki to order the summary execution of Barends because the latter's act of shooting at Yamamoto was "actual insubordination, accompanied by the use of weapons" and a crime punishable by death under Article 22 of the Japanese Military Penal Code. The defendant and his counsel further argued that, while a Japanese court-martial ordinarily would have been required before Barends could be punished, summary justice was permitted when "face-to-face" contact with the enemy required immediate punishment (without trial) if summary punishment was necessary to maintain discipline in a Japanese Army unit. The NEI court rejected this argument, however, as it took notice of the fact that no Allied landings took place on the island of Ceram during the war, and that the *Hosikikan* unit to which the accused was assigned never saw any combat. Consequently, Susuki could not lawfully claim that military necessity permitted Barends to be killed without trial. Since the accused had failed to follow Japanese military law, he was guilty of the crime of "intentional incitement to murder by abuse of authority," which was a crime under the colony's domestic law. The judges concluded that, under the NEI Penal Code, the accused's misuse of his authority as a lieutenant over his subordinates in ordering them to shoot Barends constituted an "abuse of authority" under NEI domestic law.

As for the executions of Mailoa, Skalwik, and Tarumasele, the accused and his counsel claimed that he had acted lawfully in ordering the execution of these three Indonesians. Susuki insisted that he acted on the orders of his boss, Lieutenant Colonel HIRUNOGA, who he said informed him that a death sentence against each individual had been adjudged by a Japanese military court (Japanese: *Gunritsu Kaigi*). The problem for the accused was that the Dutch judges heard in-court testimony from Mr. NAKAMURA, who told the tribunal that, from October 1944 until the surrender of Japanese forces in the NEI, he was the prosecutor for all Japanese military courts in the area in which the defendant and his unit operated. Nakamura further informed the court any incident involving violence against the Japanese should have been brought to him, but that he had no knowledge of any Japanese courts-martial proceedings against Mailoa, Skalwik, and Tarumasele. Not surprisingly, the three judges concluded that no such trial had occurred. Consequently, when the accused ordered the *Hosikikan* firing squad to shoot the three Indonesians for their alleged misconduct, this violated the laws and customs of war because no citizen of an occupied nation may be punished by the occupier without due process of law.[22]

[22] Under art. 43 of the 1907 Hague Convention, the military occupier of a hostile state or territory was required to respect "the laws in force in a country;" under art. 47, that same occupier was

The court found Motosuke Susuki guilty of the crime of "intentional incitement to murder by abuse of authority" and "the war crime of murder." But while the prosecutor had asked for the death penalty, the three judges sentenced the accused to imprisonment for life. Why? The court acknowledged that Susuki's crimes were serious and had resulted in the deaths of four persons. But it also decided that it must take into account two extenuating circumstances. First, the tribunal conceded that all four victims "had committed punishable offenses" in violation of Japanese law, and that they presumably could have been harshly punished under Japanese law. Consequently, Susuki was guilty of unlawful executions only because the evidence at his trial showed that the victims had been punished without having received a fair trial. Second, the judges considered his relative youth (he was 27 years old) and the fact that Susuki was the commandant of a small isolated unit located in the middle of a hostile population.

One final point. While the decision does not discuss Barends' situation, the judges would have had little sympathy for him, given his voluntary collaboration with the Japanese enemy. Perhaps this also influenced the judges in their decision to give Susuki a more lenient punishment. As for the three Indonesians executed on Susuki's orders, it is also possible that the court members were not quite certain whether Susuki really understood that Lieutenant Colonel Hirunoga's order to shoot the three victims could not trump the requirement for a fair trial. After all, in all armed forces in the world, at all times and in all places, when a senior officer gives an order to a junior officer, the latter disobeys that order at his own peril. Did the three judges, all of whom were experienced officers, have some sympathy for the accused given his circumstances? Was it simply reasonable for a lieutenant to obey a lieutenant colonel under these circumstances? At this late date, no one can be certain, as all the participants in this trial are long gone.

The temporary court-martial in Amboina passed sentence on Susuki on January 28, 1948. The fiat of execution was granted by Mr. P.M. VISSERS, the Resident of Amboina, on February 13, 1948. The defendant began serving his life sentence a short time later although, as explained in Chapter 12, the life sentence intended by the tribunal was never completed.

Prosecutor v. Gisaburo Yoshida

On February 28, 1948, the prosecutor for the temporary court-martial sitting in Balikpapan charged Sergeant Major Gisaburo YOSHIDA with having unlawfully executed "six or at least some Indonesians" in Borneo July 1945.[23]

required to respect "the lives of persons." Since NEI law required a trial before an NEI citizen could be punished for a crime, the summary execution of the three Indonesians was also a violation of the Hague Convention.

[23] *Prosecutor v. Gisaburo Yoshida*, Vonnis No. 11/1948, Balikpapan (April 1, 1948).

Yoshida was alleged to have committed these war crimes both "intentionally and together" with other Japanese nationals because the Indonesians were involved in "anti-Japanese and pro-Allied" activities. According to the prosecutor, the victims had been executed without any trial. They had been beheaded or otherwise killed, and the defendant had personally beheaded one of the Indonesian victims.

In a one-day trial that began and finished on March 12, 1948, the three judges considered a number of affidavits from witnesses. They also considered a full confession from the defendant, who did not deny that he had participated in the executions but explained that he had been ordered to carry them out.

The three-page typewritten single space decision in *Yoshida* does not expressly acknowledge that the victims had committed any punishable offenses; it does not specify the type or scope of any anti-Japanese activities. But this is obvious given that the victims were killed in July 1945, when resistance activities were very much underway in the NEI. Anti-Japanese rebellions had broken out in Aceh in March 1945, and Allied troops had landed in Hollandia (Jayapura) and Biak in April. Allied bombings of Japanese units and defenses in the Indies were also increasing, and more frequent. Consequently, the temporary court-martial assumed that the victims had violated Japanese law and, having no protected status as combatants under the 1907 Hague Convention, could have been lawfully punished (including sentenced to death)—but only after a trial conducted in accordance with Japanese law.[24] The failure to conduct this trial, as required by the 1907 Hague Convention, was the war crime. But it is apparent from the decision that the three Dutch judges believed that had the Japanese conducted a trial proceeding, the six Indonesians could have been executed. These facts and circumstances explain why the prosecutor asked for five years' imprisonment for Yoshida.

It is also clear from the decision that the judges understood that Yoshida was guilty but, as a sergeant major, was simply carrying out orders that he probably did not know were unlawful. In the end, the court sentenced Yoshida to four years' imprisonment. The judges showed leniency chiefly because the defendant had given a complete confession that, after additional investigation, turned out to be completely accurate. The judges were also impressed by the fact that Yoshida expressed what the decision calls a "blind faith" in both his defense counsel and the fairness of the judicial process. This meant leniency was appropriate.

A final note about individuals prosecuted for unlawful executions. *Kempeitai* Major Yoshio KATSAMURA, depicted here, was convicted of systematic terrorism and unlawful executions. He was shot by firing squad in June 1948. Similarly,

[24] Under art 1 of the 1907 Hague Convention, lawful combatants (called "belligerents") must be (1) commanded by a person responsible for his subordinates; (2) have a fixed distinctive emblem recognizable at a distance; (3) carry arms openly; and (4) conduct their operations in accordance with the laws and customs of war. Failing to comply with (1)–(4) meant no protection for a combatant under the law of war.

Photo 18 *Kempeitai* Major Yoshio Katsamura was convicted of systematic terrorism and executed in June 1948.

Credit: Netherlands Institute of War Documentation (NIOD), Amsterdam

Captain Shoji ASHIDA, also shown here, was found guilty of having committed unlawful executions; he was executed in September 1947.

Execution of "Haga Plot" and "Overakker Plot" Participants

Two more episodes deserve mention, as they might be viewed as unlawful executions when they were not: The death by firing squad of some twenty-five individuals by the Japanese for their involvement in the "Haga Plot," and the executions of General OVERAKKER, Colonel GOSENSON, and other persons for their participation in the "Overakker Plot."

When the Japanese conquered the NEI in 1942, Bauke Jan HAGA was the Governor of Kalimantan. He had many years of experience as a colonial official and was a proponent of the "Ethical Policy" discussed in Chapter 1.

In mid-1943, while interned in Banjarmasin, Haga was accused by the Japanese of being the leader of a conspiracy to overthrow the Japanese administration in

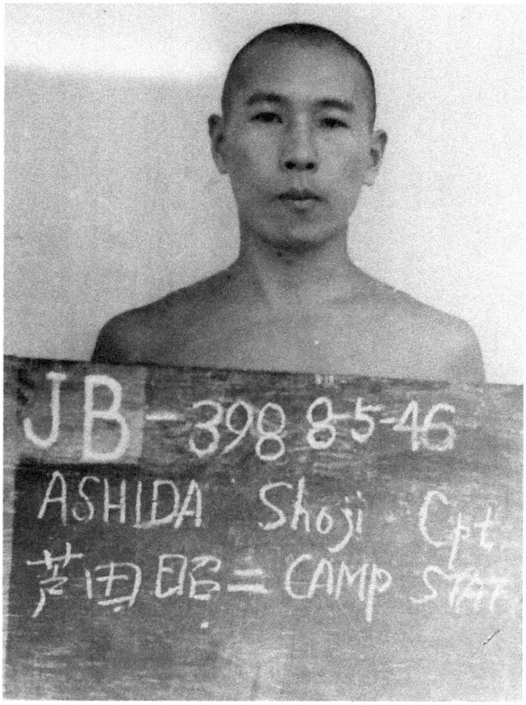

Photo 19 Captain Shoji Ashida was found guilty of having committed unlawful executions and shot by firing squad in September 1947.

Credit: Netherlands Institute of War Documentation (NIOD), Amsterdam

Kalimantan. Some 200 men and women, mostly indigenous people, were arrested and tortured by the Japanese, and they pointed to Haga and his wife, N. G. Haga-Witsenbrug, as the leaders of the "Haga Plot." The Japanese eventually were convinced that, when any Allied invasion of the NEI began, Haga and his wife would rise up and lead the male and female internees, respectively, in an attack on Japanese forces. Haga was tried and convicted by a Japanese military tribunal in December 1943. He was sentenced to be shot by firing squad but died as a result of torture before the execution could be carried out. His wife, however, was executed, along with some twenty-five other individuals on December 20, 1943. But this was not an unlawful execution, because it was not a violation of the law of war for the Japanese to prosecute Haga, his wife, and other individuals for their resistance activities. Under the 1907 Hague Convention, the Japanese were permitted to try those persons who violated Japanese laws, regulations, and orders, and even impose a severe punishment, provided that they conducted judicial proceedings in accordance with Japanese law. Consequently, because a formal trial was convened and completed, the execution of the Haga Plot participants was not unlawful.

While there is no real evidence that the "Haga Plot" existed, the same cannot be said for the resistance plan organized by General R. T. Overakker and Colonel G. F. V. Gosenson. In mid-1942, while both men were held as prisoners of war (POWs) in a camp on Sumatra, they established a secret organization that would prepare for the arrival of the Allied Forces—which they thought was imminent. As a result of their efforts, ex-KNIL soldiers (who were not interned or held as POWs) established so-called "V-groups" (V = Victory), which began gathering intelligence about the Japanese occupiers, as well as weapons and supplies, that would be used to help the Allies when they landed. Unfortunately for Overakker and Gosenson, the *Kempeitai* discovered the existence of the V-groups, which led back to the two Dutch officers. Both men—and many others involved in the "Overakker Plot"—were subsequently tried by a Japanese military court, convicted, and executed, although Overakker and Gosenson were not put to death until January 1945. Again, because their clandestine activities were illegal under Japanese law (and also not protected under the Hague Convention), [25] and because they were tried and convicted in accordance with Japanese military law, their executions were not unlawful.[26]

[25] Article 8 of the 1907 Hague Convention provides that: "Prisoners of war shall be subject to the laws, regulations and orders in force in the army of the State in whose power they are. Any act of insubordination justifies the adoption towards them of such measures of severity as may be considered necessary." This meant that POWs who had violated Japanese law imposed during the occupation must be tried by some form of regularly constituted court before they could be punished. It also meant that the death penalty was permissible if "considered necessary." The only exception to this rule was that POWs who escaped and were recaptured could not be punished severely. On the contrary, these POWs were subject only to "disciplinary punishment."

[26] See de Jong, *The Collapse of a Colonial Society* (n. 1) 190–2. For more on the Overakker Plot see Esther Zwinkels, *Het Overakker complot* (Spectrum, 2011). See also the discussion of *Prosecutor v. P. H. J. M. Maseland* in Chapter 11 nn 15–28, and accompanying text.

7

Trials for Forced Prostitution

While the Netherlands East Indies (NEI) authorities were bitter about the cruelty inflicted by the Japanese upon Royal Netherlands Indies Army (Dutch: *Koninklijk Nederlandsch Indisch Leger* (KNIL)) prisoners of war (POWs) and the suffering endured by Dutch civilians in internment camps, they were outraged by reports of the "forced prostitution"[1] of Dutch women and girls in brothels licensed by the Japanese military. As a result, for the first time in legal history, the offense of forced prostitution (which previously had been identified as a war crime by the United Nations War Crimes Commission) was prosecuted at a military tribunal. In fact, the Dutch were the only Allied nation to prosecute the Japanese for what one historian has called "a large-scale, officially-organised system of rape."[2]

The furor over "Japanese military sexual slavery"[3] continues to the present day, with news reports focusing on Korean women[4] forced by the Japanese to work as "comfort women"[5] during World War II. But Chinese, Filipina, and women of other ethnic and national backgrounds also had been forced to work as prostitutes in Japanese military brothels during the war and the Japanese who had established or operated these establishments could have been prosecuted by any one of the Allied tribunals having personal and subject matter jurisdiction. American

[1] The war crime of *gedwongen prostitutie* or *het dwingen tot prostitutie* translates as "forced prostitution." Dutch authorities providing English-language translations of NEI court-martial proceedings to the United Nations (U.N.) War Crimes Commission, however, translated it as "enforced prostitution" because the 1919 U.N. War Crimes list adopted by the NEI authorities calls the offense "enforced prosecution." See *e.g.* United Nations War Crimes Commission, *Law Reports of Trials of War Criminals* (His Majesty's Stationery Office 1949) *Trial of Washio Awochi*, Case No. 76, 122–5 (discussed below). Forced prostitution is a more accurate description and a more accurate translation, and this book uses "forced" rather than "enforced." There is no legal difference between "forced" and "enforced" prostitution.

[2] George Hicks, *The Comfort Women: Japan's Brutal Regime of Enforced Prostitution in the Second World War* (W.W. Norton & Co. 1995) 11.

[3] Christine M. Chinkin, "Comment: Women's International Tribunal on Japanese Military Sexual Slavery," 95 *American Journal of International Law* (2001) 335.

[4] "Saying sorry for sex slavery," *The Economist* (January 2, 2016) 27. During World War II, a number of young women living in the then-Japanese colony of Korea were forced to work as prostitutes in Japanese military brothels. These women began demanding compensation—and an official acknowledgment of wrongdoing by the Japanese government—in the early 1990s.

[5] "Comfort woman" (Dutch: *troostmeisje*) is a translation from the Japanese *ianfu*, a woman who worked at an *ianjo* or "comfort station;" this is a euphemism for military brothel. See William Bradley Horton, "Comfort Women," in Peter Post *et al.* (eds.), *Encyclopedia of Indonesia in the Pacific War* (Brill 2010) 196.

Military Trials of War Criminals in the Netherlands East Indies 1946–1949, Fred L. Borch.

authorities in the Philippines, for example, certainly knew that the Japanese had used coercion or trickery to "recruit" Filipinas to work as prostitutes in brothels in Manila and other locations in the islands.[6]

Just as he did with Japanese General Tomoyuki YAMASHITA, the "Tiger of Malaya," General of the Army Douglas MACARTHUR could have convened a military commission to prosecute those individuals who had forced Filipina women to work as "comfort women" for Japanese troops. The British government could have prosecuted similar offenders in Singapore and Hong Kong. The French government likewise could have pursued military brothel operators for war crimes committed in occupied Indo-China, assuming again that some of the women working in those brothels had been forced into prostitution.

Why did the Allies, other than the Dutch, not pursue such sex-related offenses at war crimes trials convened after World War II? There are at least four reasons. First, the Allies had limited resources and, because it was impossible to prosecute every Japanese offender, they focused on those miscreants who had committed the most heinous war crimes. For the Americans, British, and French officers in charge of war crimes prosecutions in the Asia Pacific area, this meant giving priority to trials of Japanese defendants who had murdered, beaten, and tortured POWs—and not those who had run houses of prostitution, even if some of the women in those brothels had been forced to work as prostitutes.

Second, while it is estimated that between 50,000 to 200,000 comfort women worked in Japanese controlled brothels during World War II, the vast majority of these women did not want to reveal how they had been victimized. In the conservative Asian culture of the 1940s, chastity was prized and a loss of virginity, even if by rape, meant a life of ostracism and misery. While some women certainly were willing to tell the Allies how the Japanese had sexually enslaved them, most were not. This reticence naturally affected Allied interest in pursuing forced prostitution as a war crime, if for no other reason than there was a dearth of victims who would be willing to testify in court proceedings.

Third, in the social and moral norms prevailing in America and Europe in the 1940s (long before the birth of feminism and a women's rights movement), it was generally accepted that men in uniform would seek out prostitutes, especially if they were far from home and engaged in military operations. Consequently, while the Allies did not establish brothels for their soldiers and sailors during World War II, and did not officially approve of their personnel visiting prostitutes, they were not surprised that the Japanese had "comfort women" for use by their troops. After all, military-sponsored prostitution did not originate with the Japanese. The Romans had a system of military brothels. In the sixteenth century, the Spanish Duke of Alva brought "400 mounted whores and 800 on foot" with his Army when

6 Ida Mae V. Fernandez (ed.), *International Symposium on Filipino Comfort Women: Papers and Proceedings* (Institute of International Legal Studies 1994) 5. In April 1993, forty-six Filipino comfort women filed a suit seeking compensation in the Tokyo District Court. Most were women who had been "young girls between 12 and 20 years old" when they were "forcibly detained and repeatedly raped" and then forced into prostitution in Japanese military brothels; ibid 46.

it invaded the Netherlands. The British Army in India maintained a "register" of prostitutes and insisted on compulsory medical examinations. The Germans established military brothels in occupied territories in World War II.[7] While this sort of sexist attitude is considered reprehensible today, at the time it would have been very easy for Allied authorities to see the Japanese military's use of comfort women as simply part of Japanese culture,[8] especially since U.S. troops occupying Japan in late 1945 and early 1946 also "were offered comfort women as an official policy."[9]

This is not to argue that having a system of military brothels is an excuse or justification for forced prostitution. It is not. Rather the point is that it was easy for the Allies to overlook the war crime of forced prostitution in Japanese licensed brothels given their acceptance of prostitution generally in military culture.

Racism was the fourth reason for the lack of forced prostitution trials by the Allies, because the vast majority of women forced to work as "comfort women" were Asian. There were no U.S. trials in the Philippines because no American women had been forced into providing sexual services to the Japanese. There were no British trials because no white females living in any Japanese occupied Crown colony had been sexually enslaved. The same was true in French Indo-China; no French women had been forced to work as comfort women. Given the lack of victims among their own nationals, the "pervasive racism of Western nations toward nonwhite people" (as one historian put it) made it easy to overlook the sex-related war crimes committed by the Japanese against other Asians.[10] However, had white women residing in Manila or Singapore or Saigon been repeatedly raped in brothels or otherwise been sexually enslaved by the Japanese, those running Allied war crimes programs would have taken a much different approach to forced prostitution.

There was one exception to this sexual enslavement of women by the Japanese during World War II: Caucasian Dutch women and girls had been forced into prostitution in military brothels in the East Indies.

Prostitution was illegal in the Indies, and the socially conservative Dutch living in the islands certainly did not approve of brothels. But they were sufficiently tolerant to accept military-related prostitution if that was required by the Japanese occupiers, and the Dutch knew that there were sufficient numbers of Chinese, Indian, and Malay women on Java, Sumatra, and the outer islands who could satisfy the sexual desires of Japanese troops.

What embittered the Dutch was their conviction that the sexual enslavement of Caucasian women was part of the overall Japanese effort to demonstrate the

[7] See Hicks, *The Comfort Women* (n. 2) 29–32.

[8] While Japanese military brothels existed chiefly to provide sexual satisfaction for Japanese troops, there was an additional rationale for having prostitutes available: At least some Japanese soldiers believed that having sexual relations "before going into battle worked as a charm against injury." Some also made amulets from the pubic hair of comfort women as a charm against injury. See Hicks, *The Comfort Women* (n. 2) 32–3.

[9] C. Sarah Soh, "Japan's Responsibility Toward Comfort Women Survivors," Japan Policy Research Institute Working Paper No. 77 (May 2001) 2.

[10] ibid.

racial superiority of Asians—to both the Dutch and to other ethnic groups living alongside them. The aggravating factor was that the Japanese had obtained Caucasian women by visiting civilian internment camps where they (or brothel operators collaborating with them) used heavy-handed techniques, if not actual force, to obtain "volunteers" to work as comfort women. Frightened, hungry, and separated from their husbands and male family members, many Dutch women found it impossible to resist these Japanese recruiting efforts. It was bad enough that one of every five Dutch civilian internees had perished in Japanese-run camps,[11] but to prey on vulnerable women and girls in those camps was both humiliating and outrageous.

This belief that they not only were the victims of Japanese racism but that the forced prostitution of Dutch women was a direct result of that racism certainly accounts for the language in *Prosecutor v. Awochi WASHIO* (examined below). In *Washio*, the three military judges wrote:

> CONSIDERING that, in view of where the power lay in this country during the Japanese domination and of the ideas held by the Japanese with regard to the relationship between them and their subordinates, especially if these latter belonged to another race, it may be taken on these grounds that the accused [a Japanese national] is directly responsible for the treatment to which the prostitutes were subjected …

While there is no doubt that the Dutch were victims of Japanese racism, the question remains whether the Dutch were also racist in selecting forced prostitution cases for trial, in that *only* women of European ancestry testified as victims at court proceedings. Historians Norma Fields and Yoshimi Yoshiaki argue that NEI authorities were uninterested in the fate of Asians in post-war trials because only European women provided sworn statements or live testimony at forced prostitution trials. There is undoubtedly some truth to this, if for no other reason than Western racism toward nonwhite people was widespread in the 1940s.[12] Assuming *arguendo* that this is true, however, this simply means that the Dutch were no different from the Americans, British, and other Allies when it came to prosecuting the Japanese for their victimization of nonwhite women.

As historian William Bradley Horton has pointed out, the claim that the Dutch were racist and consequently indifferent to the suffering of nonwhite females, even if valid, is only part of the story. While it is apparently true that *only* women of European ancestry testified at the forced prostitution trials, it is also true that initial investigations conducted by NEI war crimes investigators grew out of written questionnaires completed by Europeans interned in the camps. Having witnessed the Japanese recruiting of their fellow internees from the camps, and having been outraged when they learned these women had been sexually enslaved, these Dutch

[11] Louis de Jong (with an Introduction by Jeroen Kemperman), *The Collapse of a Colonial Society: The Dutch in Indonesia during the Second World War* (KILTV Press 2002) 420. In 1955, the Dutch government calculated "that there had been about 110,000 civilian internees, one in five of whom had died" in Japanese internment camps.

[12] See Horton, "Comfort Women," (n. 5) 195.

women naturally provided considerable details in the questionnaires—from which the investigators were able to make further inquiries.[13]

On the other hand, as most Eurasian and Asian women had not been interned by the Japanese, it was more difficult to obtain information from them about being forced into prostitution. As mentioned earlier, for cultural reasons, many Indonesians were unwilling to reveal that they had worked as prostitutes, even if they had been coerced by the Japanese.[14]

Finally, many nonEuropeans were uncooperative with the Dutch when it came to providing evidence of Japanese war crimes. Indonesia had declared its independence from the Netherlands in August 1945, and the ongoing insurgency between guerrillas fighting for freedom and the Dutch armed forces fighting to preserve colonial rule meant that many Indonesians now saw the Dutch as "foreign invaders" and had little desire to cooperate in any colonial war crimes investigations.[15] This was even more true when Indonesians themselves became the victims of war crimes committed against them by KNIL and Dutch Army troops.[16]

At least one historian suggests that the Dutch might have been unable to prosecute the Japanese for forced prostitution on legal grounds. The United Nations mandate governing war crimes trials provided that only offenses committed against a subject of a member country of the United Nations could be prosecuted as a war crime. The argument then is that no stateless person could be the victim of a war crime, and no individual who had "accepted" Japanese rule could be a victim either. The conclusion: That there was no jurisdiction over "cases in which Indonesians outside of Dutch government service were the primary victims."[17]

This is utter nonsense. The hundreds of Javanese, Balinese, and other Indonesian women forced into prostitution were all NEI citizens and, absent evidence to the contrary, they had not "accepted" Japanese rule in the archipelago. They most definitely did not accept Japanese authority when forced to work as prostitutes in brothels operated or licensed by the 16th Army in Java, the 25th Army in Sumatra, or those areas of eastern Indonesia under the administration of the Japanese Navy. Additionally, temporary courts-martial convicted hundreds of Japanese soldiers for murder and torture of Indonesian civilians with no official connection to the Dutch government—clear evidence that these civilians were subjects of the colony and consequently under the jurisdiction of NEI military tribunals.

[13] ibid.

[14] As a result, no accurate data exists on how many Indonesian women and girls were forced to work as prostitutes. Some historians believe it could be as high as 20,000, but this is speculation. See Y. Tanaka, *Japan's Comfort Women: Sexual Slavery and Prostitution during World War II* (Routledge 2002) 82.

[15] ibid.

[16] Rémy Limpach, "Business as Usual: Dutch Mass Violence in the Indonesian War of Independence, 1945–1949," in Bart Luttikhuis and A. Dirk Moses (eds.), *Colonial Counterinsurgency and Mass Violence* (Routledge 2014) 64–90. See Chapter 12, "Aftermath," for more on Dutch war crimes committed against Indonesians between 1946 and 1949.

[17] See Horton, "Comfort Women" (n. 5) 195.

Before examining the proceedings of four temporary courts-martial involving prostitution, some discussion of the Japanese "system of military-appointed brothels" is necessary. These had existed in the Japanese military since the late 1930s, when Japanese troops were deployed in large numbers outside of Japan. Originally, these brothels had been established in China but, as the conflict in Asia expanded, so did military-managed prostitution. By mid-1942, "there were reportedly 100 military brothels in Southeast Asia, and 400 in all of Asia."[18]

Official Japanese approval of "comfort women" and managed prostitution, however, did not make the practice legal in the occupied NEI. On the contrary, because prostitution—and the operation of brothels—were illegal under Dutch colonial law in March 1942, the Japanese decision to permit houses of prostitution that would provide sexual services and "relaxation" for Japanese military personnel residing on Java, Sumatra, Borneo, and other islands as part of the occupation was a violation of Dutch colonial law. It also was a violation of international law because the Hague Convention of 1907 required an occupier to respect "the laws in force in a country."[19] But it was a war crime because of the manner in which the Japanese operated these brothels, at least in those situations where they coerced women into prostitution or used force to prevent women working as prostitutes from ceasing to do such work.

Brothel managers were responsible for recruiting girls to work in their establishments, and it seems that women who were already working as prostitutes were recruited first. Soon, however, "local officials and other Indonesians were involved in persuading, tricking or forcing girls to sign up under a variety of pretexts, including study abroad or work as actresses or waitresses, both professions that were widely used as a cover for prostitution in Japan and Indonesia."[20]

While there is no doubt that coercion was used to obtain girls and women for prostitution, some females volunteered simply to survive the occupation. A Dutch Eurasian man who had escaped to Australia in September 1942 reported that, in Batavia, the " 'sole cause' " for " 'prostitution by European women was lack of money and hunger.' "[21] With their husbands and other male family members in either prisoner of war or internment camps, some women and their families were in desperate circumstances. "Brothels sprang up like mushrooms," and the "exploitation of women was completely open."[22]

This chapter examines three *forced* prostitution trials involving thirteen defendants: *Prosecutor v. Awochi Washio, Prosecutor v. Hiromu MITSUHASHI et al.*, and *Prosecutor v. Shoichi IKEDA*. Washio was a Japanese civilian and Ikeda was a Japanese Army colonel; Mitsuhashi and his ten codefendants were a mix of

[18] ibid 483.

[19] Hague Convention (IV), Respecting Law and Customs of War on Land, Annexed Regulations (1907) art. 43.

[20] See Horton, "Comfort Women" (n. 5) 191.

[21] See de Jong, *The Collapse of a Colonial* Society (n. 11) 76.

[22] ibid.

Japanese civilians and military personnel. All were tried for the war crime of coercing women into working in military brothels.

While the focus of this chapter is on forced prostitution, its discussion of a fourth court-martial involving a Dutch civilian, Franciska Hendrika ECKHART, is important because it provides a greater understanding of the sex trade during the Japanese occupation of the East Indies. The 35-year-old Eckhart was prosecuted for "trafficking in women" (Dutch: *vrouwenhandel*) and intentionally promoting "lechery" (Dutch: *ontucht*). The temporary court-martial exercised jurisdiction over her because her involvement in the sex trade supported the Japanese war effort.[23]

Prosecutor v. Awochi Washio

On October 25, 1946, a temporary court-martial sitting in Batavia delivered its decision in *Prosecutor v. Awochi Washio*.[24] The trial, involving a Japanese hotel keeper who operated a club and forced Dutch and Eurasian women into prostitution, is best known to scholars and the public today because it was the only forced prosecution case translated into English and published in the United Nations War Crimes Reports. The English language version, however, is incomplete; the original Dutch proceedings contain many more facts and a wealth of detail.[25]

The prosecutor charged that Washio had "in time of war and as a subject of a hostile power, namely Japan," committed "war crimes by, in violation of the laws and customs of war, recruiting women and girls to serve" the sexual needs of Japanese patrons. The indictment further alleged that the women and girls "were not able to leave freely" but rather were forced "to commit prostitution ... under the direct or indirect threat of the *Kempeitai*."

The three-member court, consisting of Colonel J. H. PETER, Lieutenant Colonel M. L. SWAAB and First Lieutenant J. G. H. van der STARP, began hearing evidence against the 60-year-old Washio on October 21, 1946.

Born in Nagasaki, Japan, in 1886, Awochi Washio had spent much of his adult life in Batavia, where he had worked from 1920 to November 30, 1941, when

[23] For more on the trials of Dutch and other nationals who collaborated with their Japanese occupiers see Chapter 11 of this book.

[24] The English language version of *Prosecutor v. Washio Awochi*, published by the U.N. War Crimes Commission in 1949, incorrectly identifies the decision by the accused's first name ("Awochi") rather than his surname ("Washio"), a mistake that has been repeated by numerous legal scholars over the years. In fact, Awochi is the first name for a boy; Washio is a family name. Additionally, based on the standard Romanization of Japanese, Awochi should be spelled Aochi.

[25] The English language version of *Washio* is only three pages; the Dutch "Vonnis" (Trial Court Decision) is sixteen pages, in addition to a ten page *Proces Verbaal* (written summary of the process). See *Prosecutor v. Awochi Washio*, Vonnis No. 40/1946, Batavia (October 25, 1946), translated into English at United Nations War Crimes Commission, *Law Reports of Trials of War Criminals*, vol. 13 (n. 1) 122–5.

he had returned to Japan. During his more than twenty years in the NEI capital, Washio had worked as a hotel keeper at least part of the time.

Despite having only recently come home to Japan, Washio told the court that he returned to Batavia "by order of his Government" in June 1942 and, at the direction of the Japanese mayor of the newly occupied city, opened up the *Akebono* restaurant.[26] Interestingly, despite his many years resident in the East Indies, Washio claimed that his understanding of Dutch was poor, so the tribunal provided him with a translator, 46-year-old Alexander Fedorischeff.

Under questioning by Colonel Peter, Washio explained that the all-female staff of his business served only food and drink. In June 1943, however, Washio was ordered by Japanese Colonel INAMI of the Central Military Administration to open a brothel that would be for the exclusive use of Japanese civilians.[27] Washio insisted at his trial that he had protested against this order, chiefly because he had no experience in running a brothel. Ultimately, however, he did rent a block of houses in Batavia and opened the *Sakura* Club, which included a brothel, in September 1943. According to Washio, he had seventeen or eighteen Dutch and Eurasian women working as prostitutes in his club. All were between the ages of 17 and 50.

The women had been recruited mostly by Mrs. Lies BEERHORST, a Dutch national who lived with Washio, although the latter did admit at trial that he had at various times between September 1943 and September 1945, when the brothel ceased its operations, gone "to places outside Batavia to recruit prostitutes for the *Sakura* Club." At least eleven of the women working as prostitutes had been Dutch civilians interned in the camp at Cideng.[28]

According to the evidence presented at trial, Beerhorst was responsible for the day-to-day operations of the house of prostitution, and Washio sought to minimize his involvement in the brothel by arguing that the business was really run by Beerhorst. But Washio did admit that no woman worked in the brothel without his approval and that he sent the names of all prostitutes in the brothel to the local *Kempeitai*, as these military police inspected the brothel "once every two or three months."[29]

When questioned at trial, Washio insisted that he had "never used any threat, force or trick to recruit women as prostitutes for the *Sakura* Club." He also denied that he had used forced to make them remain in the brothel when they wanted "to resign." Finally, Washio claimed that all the women working as prostitutes were at

[26] This is spelled *Akibono* in the trial transcript.

[27] The 16th Army's Central Military Administration (Japanese: *Gunseikanbu*) in Batavia was responsible for the day-to-day administration of the city. At first, it focused on law and order but, as the occupation continued, its administration focused more on providing services to those living in Batavia, including public utilities. The Central Military Administration was headed by a military administrator.

[28] For more on the camp at Cideng (spelled Tjideng in the court records) see de Jong, *The Collapse of a Colonial Society* (n. 11) 445–6. For war crimes prosecutions arising out of mistreatment of internees at Cideng, see Chapter 5.

[29] Washio explained that the *Kempeitai* inspected the brothel and determined who could visit it while the Central Military Administration inspected the brothel's financial accounts.

least seventeen years of age and "received a regular monthly salary plus a portion of the sum which the visitors who went to bed with them had to pay." Finally, Washio raised the defense of "superior orders" when he claimed that, in operating the brothel, he had done so under orders of the Japanese authorities.

The testimony of fourteen girls and women, however, directly contradicted Washio's claims. Mrs. Elisabeth V.,[30] who had "worked as a nurse for the prostitutes in the *Sakura* Club" told the three-judge tribunal that one of the prostitutes was only 12 years old and that a 14-year-old girl also worked in Washio's brothel.

Mrs. Elisabeth V.'s testimony was confirmed by Miss Mathilde H., who testified that she was only 14 or 15 (she had been born on June 13, 1929) and was living in Semarang with her mother when Lies Beerhorst "persuaded" her to go to Batavia to work as a waitress in the *Sakura* Club. "Within a very short time," however, Beerhorst threatened to turn the young girl over to the *Kempeitai* if she did not "receive at least two Japanese each evening." Under pressure, Miss Mathilde H. told the judges, she acquiesced and worked as a prostitute. She also told the tribunal that she fell ill in early 1945 and, after regaining her health in April 1945, was allowed to return home to Semarang. But "Mrs. Beerhorst had said to her she was to tell no one how old she really was and that she was to say she was seventeen."

Mathilde H.'s mother, Mrs. Henriette H., substantiated her daughter's testimony when she told the court that when Beerhorst first solicited her daughter to come to the *Sakura* Club, she was "not at all keen on the idea." But after Beerhorst "assured her that her daughter would only work in the restaurant and not be used for other purposes," and after Beerhorst also threatened to have the Political Intelligence Service[31] deport her daughter "to the outer districts" if she did not let her daughter go to Batavia, Mrs. Henriette H. reluctantly consented.[32] She later learned that her daughter had been forced into prostitution by Awochi and Beerhorst.

On the issue of voluntariness, all of the witnesses directly contradicted Washio's claims. Three of the women, Mrs. Maria K., Mrs. I. H., and Mrs. Wilhelmina P. told the temporary court-martial that Lies Beerhorst and a female associate had visited the Cideng internment camp in July 1943. Beerhorst had then addressed a group of women internees and "asked for ladies who would like to work in a Japanese club, the *Sakura* Club ... which consisted of a restaurant with a bar attached."

[30] The family names of the actual victims of forced prostitution (or those who testified on their behalf) have been replaced with initials to protect both their privacy and that of their surviving family members.

[31] The Political Intelligence Service (Dutch: *Politieke Inlichtingen Dienst* or *PID*) was a Dutch organization taken over by the *Kempeitai*. Many of its members were Indonesians, and they collaborated with the Japanese in performing a variety of police-related duties, including finding spies and prohibited objects (Dutch flags, radios, and weapons) and questioning prisoners. "In doing their interrogative work, the former PID officers displayed a cruelty matching that of the *Kempeitai* ... under whom they worked." See Peter Post, "Policing Society," in Peter Post *et al.* (eds.), *Encyclopedia of Indonesia in the Pacific War* (Brill 2010) 148.

[32] The outer districts were islands other than Java. Deportation to them would be a form of punishment given their remoteness from the more 'civilized' main island where the government was located and the majority of the European and Eurasian population resided.

Beerhorst informed the women with whom she spoke that there was a brothel attached to the club, but that there was no requirement to participate in any "intimate association with the Japanese." Relying on this representation, and believing that accepting Beerhorst's proposal to work in the restaurant or bar as a "service girl" or waitress would allow her to "get money for her children," Mrs. Maria K. agreed to the proposal. Similarly, Mrs. Wilhelmina P. agreed to go to the club because her three-year-old son was "very weak" and needed "strengthening food"—but only with the understanding that she would not be involved in prostitution. Mrs. I. H. likewise agreed to Beerhorst's proposal, but only to work as a service girl in Washio's restaurant.

Almost immediately, the Dutch women who had agreed to Beerhorst's proposal learned that they had been deceived. As Mrs. I. H. testified, during their first evening at the *Sakura* Club, "she and her companions" were told that they "had to give themselves to the Japanese ... that we must retire with at least two Japanese per evening." When Mrs. I. H. continued to refuse to work as a prostitute, Beerhorst threatened her with punishment from the *Kempeitai*. Believing that this meant a painful and severe beating, Mrs. I. H. gave in and worked as a prostitute in Washio's brothel.

Mrs. Wilhelmina P. wrote in a sworn statement admitted into evidence at Washio's trial that she had a similar experience: On her second evening in Batavia, "she and the other women recruited at the same time from the Tjideng [Cideng] camp" were placed in a house in the neighborhood of the *Sakura* Club and "forced to go to bed with visitors." When the women protested, Lies Beerhorst threatened to hand them over to the *Kempeitai*. Believing that they would be badly beaten by the military police, they agreed to work as prostitutes.

Mrs. Maria K. wrote in her sworn statement that she also acquiesced in the face of threats of physical harm after witnessing two other women being "severely beaten" when they refused to work as prostitutes. Maria K. also wrote that Beerhorst required each female internee forced into prostitution to "receive two people per evening," and that Beerhorst backed up this requirement "with threats of the *Kempeitai*." Mrs. Maria K. further stated that in January 1944, when she tried to stop working in the brothel, she was "fetched by the Political Intelligence Service" and accused of inciting other girls to leave the brothel. She was confined for nine days before being released.

Other women gave similar testimony. Mrs. Alexandrine G. told that court that she "came into contact" with Mrs. Beerhorst and her associate in April 1944. At the time, Mrs. G. was living in Semarang. Beerhorst asked Mrs. G. if she would like to work in a restaurant in Batavia; Beerhorst's associate "advised her to go with them [because] otherwise she would be fetched by the police and sent to the outer districts." Mrs. G. told the tribunal "that from fear of this threat she agreed to go and work in Batavia" and that on her first evening in the club she prostituted "herself out of fright." She also informed the judges that Lies Beerhorst told her and the other women in the brothel that if they attempted to leave the establishment "they would be fetched by the *Kempeitai*, thrashed, and sent to the outer districts." In fact, Mrs. G. was eventually taken into custody by the Japanese authorities and "whipped," with the result that her right leg was "now a few centimeters shorter" than her left leg.

The record of trial does not explain how this whipping resulted in a shortened leg; perhaps the leg was broken during the whipping and healed improperly.

In fairness to Washio, the three military judges did hear evidence from a few of the women that they had willingly worked as prostitutes at the *Sakura* Club, at least initially. But the evidence showed that Beerhorst, presumably with Washio's knowledge, used threats to induce the women to engage in prostitution or, if they wished to leave the brothel, used the threat of beatings, imprisonment, or deportation to force them to remain. The court also heard evidence that no woman could receive fewer than two visitors a night and that some were required to earn a minimum of 450 guilders per evening, which meant at least three customers.

Colonel Peter and the tribunal concluded that "contrary to the law and customs of war," Washio (and his female associate Lies Beerhorst) had forced Dutch and Eurasian women to work as prostitutes in the *Sakura* Club. The tribunal further determined that the brothel was "entirely under Japanese [military] control or direction," and for the exclusive use of Japanese nationals in Batavia. Finally, the court held that Washio or Beerhorst (or both) applied either direct or indirect force to compel these Dutch and Eurasian women to work as prostitutes, chiefly by threatening to turn over anyone who resisted to the Japanese military police.

After finding Washio guilty of the war crime of forced prosecution, the court sentenced him to ten years' imprisonment. In fashioning an appropriate punishment, the court stated in its decision that Washio's guilt "was greatly increased" for four reasons: He took advantage of women who were "mostly in very poverty stricken and difficult circumstances;" he employed very young girls in the brothel, some of whom were only 12 and 14 years old; he drew a very good income from the *Sakura* Club and ... had a very good time;" and the women "prostitutes were forced to work very hard in order to make the takings as high as possible."[33]

Sent to the Struiswijk prison in Batavia to serve his sentence, Washio died while incarcerated there in 1949.

Prosecutor v. Hiromu Mitsuhashi, Keiji Okada, Chiyomatsu Kawamura, Kuizo Murakami, Shiro Nakashima, Eiichi Ishida, Taranosuke Sai, Iwao Furuya, Shinji Shimoda, Yukio Morimoto, and Kenjiro Tsutaki

While *Prosecutor v. Washio* is arguably the best known forced prostitution war crimes trial, of equal importance are the proceedings against eleven Japanese accuseds[34] in what became known as the "Semarang forced prostitution affair" (Dutch: *Semarangse dwangprostitutie-affaire*).[35]

[33] See *Prosecutor v. Washio Awochi* (n. 25) 14; *Trial of Washio Awochi* (n. 1) 125.

[34] *Prosecutor v. Mitsuhashi, Okada, Kawamura, Murakami, Nakashima, Ishida, Sai, Furuya, Shimoda, Morimoto, and Tsutaki*, Vonnis No. 72/1947, Batavia (February 14, 1948).

[35] Levinus F. de Groot, *Berechting Japanse Orloogsmisdadigers in Nederlands-Indie, 1946–1949: Temporaire Krijgsraad Batavia* (Art & Research 1990 (privately published)) 32–3.

On January 26, 1948, the temporary court-martial sitting in Batavia began hearing evidence against Colonel Mitsuhashi, Majors OKADA, KAWAMURA, and Murakami, Captains Nakashima and Ishida, and Sergeant Major Sai. There were also four Japanese civilian defendants: Messrs. Furuya, Shimoda, Morimoto, and Tsutaki. Initially, the criminal proceedings also included a twelfth accused, Colonel Shoichi Ikeda, but the tribunal's concerns about Ikeda's mental health resulted in his case being severed from the trial proceedings against the other eleven codefendants. Ultimately, Ikeda was prosecuted separately and his trial is discussed below.

The gist of the indictment against Mitsuhashi and his codefendants was that, contrary to "the laws and customs of war," the men had forced a group of "some 35 women," who were interned in Japanese-run camps for civilians near Semarang on the island of Java, to work as prostitutes in Japanese brothels. The indictment alleged that some of the accuseds compelled the women "by threatening that they would be killed in the most horrible way and reprisals ... taken against their families if they ... refused to have sexual intercourse with each Japanese visitor." But other defendants forced the women to work as prostitutes by "repeatedly beating them" until they submitted. Additionally, the indictment charged that some of the defendants, including Major Ikeda, Captain Nakashima, Sergeant Major Sai, and Mr. Furuya, had raped one or more of the Dutch women who were being compelled to work as sex slaves in the brothels.

In deciding the guilt (or innocence) of the eleven defendants, Lieutenant Colonel J. la REVIERE, Major L. F. de GROOT, and Captain A. J. A. THEYS, considered written sworn statements from eleven victims. Each of these statements was read aloud in the judicial proceedings and each was shown to the accuseds. The Dutch Army officer judges also received in-court testimony from each of the defendants.

The evidence was that, in January 1944, Major General Sheiji NOZAKI was the commandant of Japanese occupation forces in Semarang, located about 250 miles east of Batavia. Nozaki was unhappy with the lack of control over local prostitutes, as the Japanese military personnel attending the Cadet Training Corps of the Southern Army in Semarang were visiting these women, and some were returning to duty with venereal disease.

According to a statement authored by Colonel Tomo OKUBO,[36] who was then serving as the school's commandant, Okubo proposed that a brothel be established for the exclusive use of the Japanese cadets, and that the women for the new brothel be "recruited" out of four European civilian internment camps located near Ambarawa and Semarang.

Major General Nozaki "felt good" about the proposal, although he questioned whether it was necessary to recruit women from the civilian internment camp.

[36] At the time of the trial, Colonel Tomo Okubo was dead. According to the trial record, he had "committed suicide in Japan in order to avoid being tried" for war crimes. He had, however, left behind a "declaration" explaining his involvement in the Semarang forced prostitution affair.

He agreed to Okubo's proposal, however, provided that Lieutenant General Shinshichiro KOKUBU, the chief of staff of the 16th Army, who was located in Batavia, gave permission for the plan. Okubo, in fact, did obtain authorization from 16th Army headquarters to establish four "comfort stations," and to solicit European women from the internment camps to work in them, but with the added provision that he must obtain a written "declaration" from each internee that she was volunteering to work as a prostitute.

In February 1944, Major Keiji Okada, who was the deputy logistics officer for the Semarang area, implemented the Nozaki–Okubo plan.[37] Teams of soldiers and civilians, acting under Okada's orders, began visiting five nearby internment camps. Ultimately, they "recruited" or otherwise obtained about thirty-five European women for the brothels. At one camp, some of the older women volunteered to work in the brothels, either to spare the younger women or else because they were suffering as internees and hoped for better conditions. But at the Ambarawa Six civilian internment camp, the Japanese forcibly took eight unmarried girls and two married women from this camp. When the Dutch female camp leader protested, she was informed that if the ten women resisted, the Japanese would shoot forty internees in retaliation.[38]

As for the young women taken from Ambarawa Six, they were told that they had two choices: Death or work as a prostitute in one of the four Japanese brothels in Semarang.[39] Five of the girls chose death, but were immediately informed that if they did not change their minds that their parents would pay for this resistance. In the end, the women who had chosen death were "driven into bedrooms and raped by Japanese officers … sometimes at gun or sabre point."[40] One of the young girls later reported that after arriving at the *Futabaso* brothel, she was taken to a room by a drunk Japanese officer who then raped her. He was followed by five other men, who also raped her. This pattern continued daily until the woman suffered a nervous breakdown and was admitted to a mental hospital. Another young woman, Paula van B., was so distraught "that she cut the artery in her wrist with a pen-knife and lost so much blood that she lay unconscious for 36 hours."[41]

The sworn testimony of the victims, recited at length in the court-martial decision, sets out in vivid detail the brutal treatment experienced by them. Miss L. F., who had been one of the young females taken from Ambarawa Six camp in February 1944, wrote that she had been taken by bus to a large building in Semarang. Upon arrival, she and the other women were sorted out by Major Okada. Miss L. F. "was ordered to go to the *Shoko* Club" and was made "to sign a printed declaration

[37] In the Imperial Army, the logistics (Japanese: *heitan*) officer was responsible for weapons, food, ammunition, and materiel necessary for success in military operations. He also was responsible for "everything connected with welfare and recreation of soldiers," including the running of brothels to service the sexual desires of military personnel.

[38] See de Jong, *The Collapse of a Colonial Society* (n. 11) 456.

[39] The "four premises" in Semarang were the *Shoko* Club (for officers and officer cadets only), the *Semarang* Club, the *Hinomaru*, and the *Futabaso*.

[40] See de Jong, *The Collapse of a Colonial Society* (n. 11) 457.

[41] See Hicks, *The Comfort Women* (n. 2) 59.

the contents of which she did not know nor were made known to her;" she later learned that the document purported to be her agreement to voluntarily work in a Japanese brothel. Miss L. F.'s statement continued:

> On 29th February 1944, Okada ... ordered her to go with him to her room; that he ordered her to lie on the bed which she refused whereupon he threw her onto her bed; that for fear of ill-treatment she did not then resist any further but that Okada during the sexual intercourse ... bit her on the face; that she had never had a man before and that she was raped by Okada; that after that she was compelled to go to bed every night with a Japanese; that Okada visited her once or twice a week [and raped her].

Similarly, Miss E. L., who was 21 years old at the time of the trial proceedings, had been taken from the Halmaheira Camp in February 1944. In her sworn statement, she reported that she had been made to work as a prostitute in a Semarang club where Iwao FURUYA, one of the eleven defendants, was the civilian "brothel keeper." As Miss E. L. explained, Furuya ordered her "to set to work [as a prostitute] which she refused." The following day, a Japanese sergeant appeared, seized her, and dragged her to her room. She was threatened and her clothing was torn off her body. The soldier then raped her. Miss E. L. "had never before had sexual intercourse with a man; after this she had to have sexual intercourse with [different] Japanese 7 or 8 times a day, sometimes with intervals of 5 minutes."

In the case of Mrs. D. A. J. van K., she was married and was interned in the Gedangan Camp with her two children, aged two and four. Although she protested against being removed, the Japanese nonetheless forcibly took her to a brothel, where the 24-year-old Mr. Yukio MORIMOTO, one of the defendants, was the manager. As Mrs. D. A. J. van K. put it, some days after her arrival at the house of prostitution, "3 Japanese came who said that we must receive men." The "reaction" of the women "was great [and] many of the women had thoughts of committing suicide but gave way for fear of being ill-treated" and, in fact, those who continued to resist working as prostitutes were hit in the face.

The temporary court-martial also considered statements from five Japanese officers. While these were unsworn, the contents of the statements were accepted by the tribunal because they underscored the gravity of the Semarang forced prostitution affair. Colonel Masayuki NAKATA, Captains Sadazo HASEGAWA, Iwao KOBAYASHI, and Hiroshi SUZUKI, and Dr. Shuichi KONDO, all testified that, in April 1944, 16th Army headquarters ordered the brothels to be closed. Why? Because an investigation conducted by Colonel ODAJIMA, who had come from Tokyo to inspect the civilian internee camps, revealed that women had been taken from the six camps and forced into prostitution. After the brothels were closed, about 100 women who had been working in these establishments were examined by medical personnel; "between 25 to 30 of the 100 were suffering from sexual diseases."

Lieutenant Colonel la Rivière, Major de Groot, and Captain Theys announced their initial decision in the Semarang forced prostitution affair on February 14, 1948. One accused was sentenced to death. Eight received terms of imprisonment. Two were acquitted of all charges and set free. This tribunal's decision was affirmed in a *fiat executie* signed by Dr. M. A. F. ZWAGER, the Head of the Temporary Administration in Batavia, on March 22. Two days later, the three-judge tribunal announced the verdicts and sentences in open court. All eleven accused and their assigned counsel were present.

Major Keiji Okada, then 38 years old, was identified as the most culpable of the eleven defendants. The judges recognized that, as Okada had "acted in accordance with Major General Nozaki's intentions" in compelling the Dutch women to work as prostitutes, that "it would not be right to make him alone responsible." But the judges also concluded that Okada knew that the 16th Army headquarters had agreed to the Nozaki–Okubo brothel plan only if the women recruited from the internee camps voluntarily agreed to work as prostitutes. The court concluded further that Okada knew or should have known or at least "reasonably suspected" that few of the women were volunteers, but rather that most were either tricked or compelled into leaving their camps and then forced into sexual slavery. To the court, what Okada had done was "a beastly and inhumane industry." He was found guilty of "abduction of women and girls for forced prostitution," "forcing prostitution," and "rape." As he had given "proof of a depraved mentality," Okada deserved the "extreme penalty" and was sentenced to death.

The tribunal concluded that Major Kawamura, who was Major General Nozaki's adjutant in March and April 1944, had actual knowledge or else "reasonably suspected" that "Netherlands women fetched out of the internment camps" were working involuntarily in brothels, and this forced prostitution was a war crime. The court held that, as a matter of law, Kawamura had a duty to prevent this war crime either by personally taking measures to close the brothels or convincing his superiors to close the establishments and stop the war crimes from occurring. But, as he had "associated himself with the [Nozaki–Okubo] plan which led to the peopling and maintaining of these brothels," the court found Kawamura guilty of "abduction of women and girls for forced prostitution" and "forcing prostitution." He received ten years' imprisonment.

As for Major Murakami and Captain Nakashima, aged 60 and 44, respectively, they both were found guilty of "mistreatment of prisoners;" Nakashima was also found guilty of rape. As a matter of law, it seems curious that they were found guilty of mistreating prisoners (rather than civilians) but the decision is clear on this point. Both officers, who were physicians and "inspecting medical officers," were responsible for providing medical care to the women and girls working as prostitutes in the *Semarang* Club and *Choko* Club. The tribunal concluded, however, that the females received "very superficial" examinations and that they were made to live (and work) "under bad hygienic conditions." Since a medical examination conducted after the Japanese-run brothels were closed disclosed that "25 to 30 out of the 100 women" working as prostitutes "were suffering from sexual diseases," the judges were convinced that Murakami and Nakashima had done little to alleviate the suffering of the women.

The court found as a matter of law that Murakami and Nakashima had a duty as medical professionals to alleviate and decrease the suffering of "fellow human beings," and in failing in that duty, the court found them guilty. Murakami received a sentence of seven years in jail; Nakashima was sentenced to a term of sixteen years, undoubtedly because he was also convicted of rape. Miss H. J. R stated that Nakashima "had ravished her by force after a struggle in which she had nearly fainted from exhaustion and misery." While the defendant Nakashima denied the rape allegation at trial (claiming consent), the judges rejected this defense. On the contrary, they believed the sworn statement of the victim's sister, Miss N. H. C. R., who had also been forced into prostitution and was working in the *Shoko* Club, and to whom Miss H. J. R. had reported the rape at the time it occurred. The judges also expressly took into account the fact that since the women, including Miss H. J. R., had been forced to work as prostitutes at the *Shoko* Club, it was not possible for Miss H. J. R. to consent to sexual intercourse with the accused.

Captain Ishida, who was 30 years old, was found guilty of aiding and abetting the "abduction of women and girls for forced prostitution." The court found that Ishida permitted his subordinates to "select ... women and girls from each of the camps near Semarang," when he either knew or should have "reasonably suspected" that these females "would not voluntarily go over to prostitution and that therefore compulsion would be used to make them do so." He was sentenced to a term of two years in jail.

Mr. Furuya, a 40-year-old civilian employee of the Japanese Army who had been born in Tokyo, was the manager of the *Semarang* Club. He was charged in the indictment with compelling seven women to engage in prostitution "by repeatedly beating them." Furuya also was charged with raping Mrs. Mies van H., who had been forced to work in the sex trade. The court found Furuya guilty of forced prostitution but not guilty of rape. This was because the only evidence of rape came from statements given by Miss E. N. and Miss E. L.; there was no statement in evidence from Mrs. Mies van H. The judges reasoned that since these two witnesses "only know the facts from hearsay, and have not stated their reasons for their knowledge ... no evidentiary value can be attached to their statements" in determining guilt or innocence. Furuya received 20 years' imprisonment.

Messrs. Shimoda, Morimoto, and Tsutaki, all civilians employed by the Army and all managers in those Semarang brothels in which the thirty-five women and girls had been forced to work in the sex trade, were found guilty of forced prostitution. The court concluded that each of the defendants knew that the "majority" of the women "allotted to them ... to work as prostitutes" in their respective brothels were not volunteers but rather had been deceived or tricked into leaving the internment camps. The court also held that each defendant had used force or threats of force to break down the resistance of the women who refused to work in the brothels. Shimoda was sentenced to ten years in jail and Tsutaki received a seven-year sentence of imprisonment. As for Morimoto, he was given fifteen years.

The temporary court-martial acquitted two of the accused. Colonel Mitsuhasi and Sergeant Major Tai were both found not guilty of rape. The prosecutor had charged the former with "compelling Jeanne A. O. through force to have sexual intercourse with him." The latter was alleged to have raped Mrs. Eugeni L. on ten occasions" in the *Semarang* Club.

Colonel Mitsuhashi admitted in court that he had visited the *Semarang* Club and engaged in sexual relations with the women working there. He denied, however, that he knew Jeanne A. O., much less that he had raped her. Additionally, Mitsuhashi denied that he had visited the brothel on the night it had first opened. The problem for the judges was that Jeanne A. O.'s out-of-court statement insisted that she had been raped on the evening the brothel opened, which was logical given that would have been the first occasion on which Jeanne A. O. would have been forced to have sexual relations with customers. As the court saw it, "this witness must have made a mistake about the person who raped her." Since her statement contained "no other confirmation on this point in any other evidence" before the court (for example, another victim's statement), the judges decided that the charge had "not been legally and convincingly proved."

Similarly, the court found the evidence insufficient to support the charge of rape against Sergeant Major Sai. The only evidence against Sai was the sworn statement of Miss E. L. and it is apparent that the three officer judges were uncertain about her reliability as a witness. Although the contents of 21-year-old E. L.'s statement were largely corroborated by the statement of the other victims, at one point she identified one of her rapists as Mario INOUE, a member of the *Kempeitai*. She wrote that he had visited her for two months in the brothel, where he "threw her on the bed, took off her clothes and in spite of her resistance and struggles compelled her to [have] sexual intercourse." But Miss E. L. continued that she had "to acknowledge that she was rather in love with this Japanese." In any event, the tribunal concluded that "the possibility of a mistake was too great to attach full credence to" E. L.'s identification of Sergeant Major Sai as the man who raped her, especially as there was no other evidence from any other victim statement of Sai's culpability.

A postscript—illustrating the lasting trauma caused by the Semarang forced prostitution affair. In 1992, almost fifty years later, a Dutch woman by the name of Jan RUFF, who had been one of the victims in the Semarang forced prostitution case, described her experience in excruciating detail. In February 1944, 20-year-old Ruff was in the Ambarawa Six Camp with her mother and two younger sisters when she was forcibly removed by a group of Japanese soldiers. After arriving at the *Shoko Club*, she was told what was required of her as a prostitute and was later dragged off to a room by a "large, fat and bald" officer she knew by the name of MIHASHI:

> I kick him in the shins. He stood there laughing. My fighting, kicking, crying and protesting made no difference. I screamed 'Don't, don't' and then in Indonesian, 'Djangan, djangan.' He pulled me up and dragged me into my bedroom, where I continued to fight him.
>
> Mihashi tore at my clothes and ripped them off. As I lay there naked on the bed, he slowly ran the [his Samurai] sword over my body, up and down, up and down. I could feel the cold steel touching my skin as he moved the sword over my throat and breasts, stomach and legs. He played with me like a cat plays with a helpless mouse. Then he started to undress. He threw himself on top of me, pinning me under his body. I tried to fight him off and kicked and scratched him, but he was too strong. The tears were streaming down my

face as he raped me. It seemed as if he would never stop. To me, this brutal and inhuman rape was worse than dying.[42]

Prosecutor v. Shoichi Ikeda

As for Colonel Ikeda, who was initially charged in the original indictment along with Mitsuhashi and the other ten defendants, concerns about his psychological health had caused the tribunal president, Lieutenant Colonel la Rivière, to "reserve" its decision while Ikeda was "put under observations in a mental institution." Six weeks after the decision in *Prosecutor v. Mitsuhashi et al.*, the same temporary court-martial announced its decision with regard to Shoichi Ikeda.[43]

In March 1944, Ikeda had been the senior logistics officer in the Semarang area. The evidence presented to the court (which it had already considered in the earlier Semarang forced prostitution trial) was that Ikeda was present at the conversation in which Major General Nozaki and Colonel Okubo decided to use European women to work as prostitutes in Japanese-run brothels.

Since Ikeda was aware of the Nozaki–Okubo plan from the outset, and knew that Major Okada and others had traveled to the nearby Semarang camps to recruit women internees to work as prostitutes, the indictment charged him with the war crimes of abducting women and girls for forced prostitution, forced prostitution, and rape. The prosecution's theory was that Ikeda had permitted civilians and soldiers "under his command to force a group of some 35 women" into prostitution because he knew or "must have reasonably suspected" that these women would not voluntarily engage in the sex trade. This meant he was charged in the alternative: Either Ikeda was guilty on the theory that he had aided and abetted the war crimes or he was guilty because he had a duty to prevent his subordinate logistics personnel from committing the war crimes, and failed in that duty.

When questioned prior to his trial, Colonel Ikeda claimed to have protested against the use of internees in the "brothel-plan." He insisted that, in a two-week period prior to his departure for a conference in Tokyo (where he was to learn about the newest Japanese fighting techniques), he had looked for women willing to serve as comfort women among the noninterned or "free people" in the area. But, wrote the court, Ikeda knew that Colonel Okubo was "enthusiastic about the plan." Consequently, it was no surprise to Ikeda when he returned to Semarang from Tokyo in March 1944 that the military brothels had been set up, and Dutch women taken from the camps to work in them.

While the tribunal apparently accepted Ikeda's testimony that he had never personally visited the brothels populated by Caucasian female internees, the judges were bothered by his lack of action as a senior officer in failing to speak more

[42] Jan Ruff testimony, Japan Lawyer's Association and Dutch Foundation for Honorary Debts, (December 9, 1992) Tokyo, Japan, cited in Hicks, *The Comfort Women* (n. 2) 62–3.

[43] *Prosecutor v. Shoichi Ikeda*, Vonnis No. 72 A/1947, Batavia (March 30, 1948).

forcefully against the initial plan to create them. The tribunal was convinced that Ikeda knew or should have known ("reasonably suspected" is the wording of the decision) that the girls and women would never volunteer to become prostitutes but instead would be raped and badly treated and that this "would weigh heavily on both their bodies and spirit."

The tribunal also faulted him for doing nothing further to investigate or otherwise examine brothel operations in Semarang. Ikeda could have followed up with Major General Nozaki, but he did not. He did nothing to investigate the use of Dutch women and girls in the brothels until after the 16th Army headquarters, learning that civilian internees had been coerced into prostitution, ordered that the brothels be closed in May 1944—just two weeks after Ikeda had returned from Tokyo.

Given the aggravating evidence surrounding the entire episode, especially the treatment of the young women taken from Ambarawa Six, the prosecutor asked for the death penalty. Lieutenant Colonel J. la Rivière, the tribunal president, joined by Major Levinus F. de Groot and Captain A. J. A. Theys, however, rejected this recommendation.

The record indicates that the judges showed leniency because Colonel Ikeda, while involved in the initial establishment of the brothels, was guilty more of nonfeasance rather than malfeasance; he had tolerated, but not encouraged, the brothel plan. The tribunal also accepted that his focus after returning from Tokyo was on teaching "modern fighting methods" to officer cadets at the military school in Semarang. Consequently, while it found Ikeda guilty, the court-martial took Ikeda's other duties into consideration and, instead of imposing the death as a punishment, was lenient in sentencing him to fifteen years' imprisonment.[44] The sentence was adjudged on March 30, 1948 and ordered carried out on September 8, 1948.

Two final notes. *Prosecutor v. Mitsuhashi et al.* explains that Colonel Okubo was not prosecuted for war crimes because he had committed suicide at his home in Japan in January 1947. As for Major General Nozaki? While pending trial, and held in jail in Batavia, he also committed suicide.[45]

As for Colonel Ikeda's mental health? The record reflects that Ikeda was suffering from some sort of psychosis, and had been examined by a physician to determine his mental fitness to stand trial. Dr. J. FERGUSON, a psychiatrist and neurologist, examined Ikeda at the Grogol hospital in Batavia, and cleared him for trial. But one has to ask why Colonel Ikeda was suffering from some sort of mental illness. Was he depressed because Japan had lost the war? Was the prosecutor's request that he be sentenced to death affecting his psychological health? Or could Ikeda, who was born in January 1902, and was 45 years old at the time of this trial, be mentally unhinged because he was a native of Hiroshima? Perhaps his home was

[44] See de Groot (n. 35) 66. This term of imprisonment was subsequently reduced to ten years.
[45] See Hicks, *The Comfort Women* (n. 2) 169.

destroyed and his family dead, injured, or missing in the aftermath of the August 1945 destruction of the city by an atomic bomb. But this is speculation and, whatever the reason, the record of trial does not give additional details about Ikeda's mental state—only that he had been declared mentally competent to stand trial for war crimes.

Prosecutor v. Franciska Hendrika Eckhart

On March 4, 1948, the Temporary Court-Martial of Batavia found 35-year-old Franciska Hendrika Eckhart guilty of two counts of "trafficking in women" (Dutch: *vrouwenhandel*) in "time of war during circumstances resulting from a hostile occupation" and "facilitating the commission of the crime." She was also convicted of intentionally promoting "lechery" (Dutch: *ontucht*) between an adult man and an underage girl and intentionally promoting "lechery" by others with third parties. The tribunal president was then Major Levinus F. de Groot; his fellow judges were Major J. P. TIDDENS and Captain C. CAMPEN. Note that Eckhart was not prosecuted for the war crime of forced prostitution, or any other war crime for that matter. Rather, the temporary court-martial exercised jurisdiction over her as a civilian because her prostitution-related offenses had occurred during the enemy occupation of the Indies and had occurred, at least in part, as the result of orders (Dutch: *opdracht*) made by Japanese authorities. The exercise of this jurisdiction was permitted under NEI Statute Book Decree No. 46 of 1946.

"Poppy" Eckhart's life is described in considerable detail in the thirteen-page single-spaced typewritten trial record, and this provides important context for understanding the military tribunal's decision in her case. Born in Batavia in August 1912, Eckhart had an unsuccessful first marriage, was divorced and then worked as a maid in three different hotels. In the last establishment, Eckhart claimed to have been offered the opportunity to be the hotel's manager, but she declined because she was "too young." De Groot and his fellow judges viewed this as evidence that Eckhart was a bright and capable person (although just how these two things are connected is not explained in the decision).

After working in the three hotels, Eckhart was given the chance to work as a bartender in the *Sante Clair* nightclub. She accepted the job because she would be paid a much higher salary and because she found the club's "happy nightlife" attractive. Her work tending bar also brought an unanticipated benefit, in that Poppy Eckhart met a musician who also was working in the nightclub, and married him.

After the Japanese invasion and the surrender of Dutch forces in March 1942, the *Sante Clair* closed its doors, and she was unemployed. After Eckhart's husband was interned in a Japanese camp, however, she needed money to support herself. The result was that Eckhart and the owner of the *Sante Clair* reopened the establishment.

Japanese officers frequenting the *Sante Clair* learned about Eckhart and her many connections in Batavia's nightlife. Consequently, they asked Eckhart to use her contacts to find women who would be willing to work in Japanese restaurants in Batavia. Eckhart agreed, but with the explicit understanding that she would not recruit women or otherwise participate in the sex trade.

In addition to her work with the *Sante Clair* nightclub, Eckhart took over the day-to-day management of the *Akebono* Club in Batavia (the same establishment that features prominently in the *Washio* trial previously examined in this chapter). While the women who worked in the *Akebono* were waitresses, some had an intimate relationship with a "settled friend" (Dutch: *vast vriend*) so they could pay their living expenses; what they earned as employees in the *Akebono* was not sufficient. Eckhart continued to resist prostitution in the restaurant, with the result that she was fired.[46]

Now without any means of financial support, and pregnant by a man named BARNAS with whom she was now living (she had a daughter in May 1944), Poppy Eckhart began helping other women who wanted to engage in prostitution. In December 1943, for example, she worked with another Dutch female to set up Mrs. C. F. as a prostitute in C. F.'s own home in Batavia. Mrs. C. F. was to be paid a monthly salary of 150 guilders and in exchange she would contract with the nearby *Telokbetong* Club to provide sexual services to Japanese officers frequenting that establishment.

The following month, in January 1944, working in concert with two other women, Shu Tok LIE (*alias* Shi Geru Hashiguchi), Wies RAP (described by the tribunal as an "international prostitute," albeit without further explanation), and Eckhart traveled to the Cihapit[47] female internment camp located in Bandung. Eckhart and her companions subsequently recruited fifteen Dutch women residing there to come to Batavia to work at a "specific salary" as prostitutes a Japanese licensed military brothel. The three military judges hearing the case did not hear evidence that this was forced prostitution, as had been the testimony in *Washio*, but they almost certainly thought that the willingness of these internees to accept Eckhart's offer to work as prostitutes may well have resulted simply from a desire to escape the dire conditions in the internment camp.

According to the record of trial, Eckhart remained unenthusiastic about her participation in organized prostitution. Significantly, she told police investigators that she did not believe she had any choice but to assist the Japanese since, in December 1943, an Army logistics captain with the surname JORA had "commanded" her to help him in finding Dutch women prostitutes for a Japanese licensed brothel named the *Theresian* Club. Jora told Eckhart that she "must" help him and that any "refusal" would bring "troubles" for her. In finding women to work in this and other brothels, the court noted that Eckhart showed little enthusiasm for the work

[46] The evidence presented in *Washio* was that Poppy Eckhart and her assistant manager, Lies Beerhorst, were "always quarreling," with the result that Washio "discharged" Eckhart and installed Beerhorst in her place. Given the testimony from Eckhart in her own case, it seems that these arguments were about prostitution in the *Akebono*, and were the basis for Eckhart being fired.

[47] In the court records, this is spelled "Tjihapit."

and de Groot and the judges recognized that any failure to obey Jora's order likely would have resulted in "terrible consequences."

Finally, the court-martial also heard evidence that Poppy Eckhart helped Mrs. W. J. C. A., a prostitute who was sick and no longer able to work in the sex trade, to prostitute her 12-year-old daughter, Miss W. A. The facts were that Mrs. W. J. C. A. was the sole provider for four children, the oldest of whom was a boy aged 16. Needing money to feed and otherwise care for her children, Mrs. W. J. C. A. first asked Eckhart if she could find a "settled friend" for her—someone who would help Mrs. W. J. C. A. financially in return for sex. When Eckhart told Mrs. W. J. C. A. that she was "too old" for such an arrangement, the latter proposed that her young daughter be prostituted. Eckhart tried to talk Mrs. W. J. C. A. out of this course of action, and in fact suggested that Miss W. A. work as a service girl or help in a bookshop. But Mrs. W. J. C. A. persisted and so Eckhart arranged for Miss W. A. to engage in "lechery" with a Japanese civilian named Asio YSO. This man, described in *Eckhart* as "an old and ugly Japanese," had sexual intercourse with Miss W. A. despite knowing that she "could not be older than twelve." Her involvement in this arrangement made Poppy Eckhart guilty of violating Article 295 of the NEI Penal Code.

Despite the lengthy recitation of organized prostitution activities, the tribunal viewed Eckhart with some sympathy, in that she admitted that some of the charges against her were true and she acknowledged that her actions were morally wrong. The court also recognized that she initially had resisted becoming a part of the sex trade, but that her dire financial situation had been the cause, at least in part, for her involvement in prostitution during the Japanese occupation. But this same tribunal rejected her claim at trial that she had not trafficked in women, but rather had only aided other females who desired to engage voluntarily in the sex trade. The issue of voluntariness, said the military court, was irrelevant to the charge. Rather, under Article 297 of the NEI Penal Code, the elements of the offense were satisfied if Poppy Eckhart had intentionally assisted those wanting to commit lechery with a third party.

As for Eckhart's claim that she had been an unwilling participant in *organized* prostitution, in that Captain Jora had commanded her to procure prostitutes for Japanese military brothels, the record of trial is silent. Under Article 48 of the NEI Penal Code, a defendant was "not punishable" if she "commit[ed] a crime under duress" but it seems that the tribunal was not persuaded that Jora's command constituted duress as a matter of NEI law.

In the final judgment rendered by Majors de Groot and Tiddens and Captain Campen, the court emphasized that Eckhart's actions had furthered the goals of the Japanese military in bringing Dutch women into their military brothels. She had engaged in "degenerate" behavior and had obtained a better life for herself at the expense of her fellow Dutch citizens. In passing sentence upon Poppy Eckhart, however, the court was lenient in sentencing her to be imprisoned for two years and six months, rather than the five years requested by the prosecutor. Eckhart had already spent two years in pre-trial confinement, and de Groot and his colleagues expressly stated that this time was to be credited against her sentence. As a practical matter, that meant that Eckhart had only six months remaining on her sentence after her conviction on March 4, 1948.[48]

Aftermath

The Dutch were the first to prosecute forced prostitution as a war crime, and this alone makes the *Washio, Mitsuhashi et al.*, and *Ikeda* trials important in the evolution of war crimes under the law of armed conflict, if for no other reason than the cases were precedent for future prosecutions of this offense. But it took another fifty years before a war crimes tribunal—the ICTY established by the United Nations in 1993—ruled that forcing women into prostitution was a war crime, as well as a crime against humanity under international law. In *Prosecutor v. Miroslav Kvočka*, the defendant and four coaccused were found guilty of various sex crimes arising out of their tenure at a notorious Bosnian Serb detention camp in the mining town of Omarska. The court found that the five defendants, all of whom were either police officers or camp guards, either raped or forced nonSerb female detainees to perform a variety of sexual acts.[49]

Kvočka and other decisions from the ICTY, the International Criminal Tribunal for Rwanda (ICTR), the Special Court for Sierra Leone, and the International Criminal Court (ICC), have ensured that the rape and other sexual violence experienced by Dutch women in World War II has not gone unpunished. In *Prosecutor v. Kunarac*, the ICTY convicted the defendant of rape and enslavement (as crimes against humanity) after finding that he took civilian women from a detention camp and then forced them to have sexual relations.[50] *Kunarac* also held that, because rape involves severe pain and suffering, it also constitutes the war crime of torture.[51] In *Prosecutor v. Issa Hassan Sesay, Morris Kallon, and Augustine Gbao*, the Special Court for Sierra Leone "imposed groundbreaking convictions for the crimes against humanity of sexual slavery and forced marriage."[52] Finally, in March 2016, the ICC broke new ground in *Prosecutor v. Jean-Pierre Bemba*, when it convicted the former government official and military commander in the Democratic Republic of the Congo of murder, rape, and pillage. The court found that Bemba knowingly permitted his troops to commit acts of sexual violence. This was the first

[48] *Prosecutor v. Franciska Hendrika Eckhart*, No. 76/1947, Batavia (March 4, 1948).

[49] *Prosecutor v. Miroslav Kvočka*, Case No. IT-98-30/1-T (November 2, 2001), http://www.icty.org/x/file/Legal%20Library/jud_supplement/supp29-e/kvocka.htm (last accessed November 30, 2016).

[50] *Prosecutor v. Kunarac et al.*, Case No. IT-96-23 & 23/1-A-T (February 22, 2001), http://www.icty.org/x/cases/kunarac/tjug/en/ (last accessed December 1, 2016). The leading decision holding that rape is a crime against humanity is *Prosecutor v. Akayesu*, ICTR-96-4-T (September 2, 1998), in which the mayor of a Rwandan town was found guilty of having encouraged rape and other forms of sexual violence by Hutus against Tutsis.

[51] For an excellent discussion of sexual violence as a war crime see Kelly D. Askin, "A Decade of the Development of Gender Crimes in International Courts and Tribunals 1993–2003," *Human Rights Brief* (American U. Washington College of Law, Spring 2004) 16.

[52] David J. Bederman (ed.), "International Decision," *American Journal of International Law* (Jan. 2010) 66, 74.

time that the Netherlands-based court, created by international treaty in 2002, has convicted anyone of a war crime involving sexual violence.[53]

Were the defendants in the Semarang forced prostitution affair being prosecuted for their misconduct today, they not only would be convicted of the war crime of forced prostitution, but would also be found guilty of torture and crimes against humanity. The defendant in *Prosecutor v. Washio* likewise would have been convicted of torture and crimes against humanity, either as a principal or as an aider and abettor. The bottom line is that the law has evolved markedly when it comes to sexual violence perpetrated during an armed conflict, and it was the Dutch who started the process.

As for the Dutch victims of Japanese sexual slavery? In 1990, the Foundation of Japanese Honorary Debts (Dutch: *Stichting Japanese Ereschulden*) was established in The Hague, Netherlands, to obtain financial compensation for Dutch "victims of Japanese military terror" in the East Indies, including those women who had been taken from the internment camps and then forced into prostitution.

The following year, the Netherlands government requested a group of international lawyers to explore whether it could submit a claim to the Japanese government for compensation payments to individual victims of the internment. After studying the relevant law, that commission concluded that a Dutch government claim for money was barred by the San Francisco Peace Treaty of 1951, since that treaty expressly resolved all outstanding claims between the Netherlands and Japan. The commission, however, also advised the Dutch government that the 1951 treaty did not prevent *individual* victims from making claims directly to the Japanese government.

While the Dutch government accepted that it was unable to pursue the issue of compensation country-to-country, the issue of Japanese mistreatment of Dutch civilians continued to be of considerable interest, especially the extent to which Dutch women and girls had been sexually enslaved during the occupation. As a result, in 1993, the Netherlands government commissioned a study into forced prostitution. That study, authored by the Dutch scholar Bart van Poelgeest, concluded that during the Japanese occupation of the NEI from 1942 to 1945, "military authorities were responsible for procuring the services of prostitutes for Japanese soldiers and civilians on the five large islands and a number of the smaller islands of the Dutch East Indies."[54]

Van Poelgeest's investigation confirmed what the temporary courts-martial sitting in Batavia likewise had concluded: That by late 1943, the Japanese military

[53] *Prosecutor v. Jean-Pierre Bemba*. Case No. ICC-01/05-1/08 (March 21, 2016); David P. Stewart (ed.), "International Decisions," *American Journal of International Law* (July 2016), 526–533. Bemba knowingly permitted his troops to commit acts of sexual violence, including rape. His conviction by the ICC signaled that the court recognizes that sexual violence plays a major role in many armed conflicts today. See also Kevin Sieff, "Ex-Congo Official Guilty in ICC War-rape Ruling," *Washington Post* (March 22, 2016) A8.

[54] Bart van Poelgeest, *Report of a Study of Dutch Government Documents on the Forced Prostitution of Dutch Women in the Dutch East Indies during the Japanese Occupation*, unofficial translation (January 24, 1994) 1.

authorities were making recruiting trips to civilian internment camps, where they sought volunteers who would provide sexual services in return for money, and who would do such work in a brothel approved by the military.

As illustrated in *Prosecutor v. Eckhart*, some women certainly did voluntarily agree with the Japanese authorities (and those collaborating with them) to work as prostitutes. Van Poolgeest wrote, however, that the "cruelty of the guards and extreme food shortages" in the internment camps, which resulted in "disablement, chronic illness and a very high death rate," meant that those interned women who accepted Japanese proposals to work as comfort women "could hardly be regarded as acting voluntarily." The Dutch government study also concluded that, at least in some cases of involving European women, the Japanese "applied physical force" to obtain females for their military brothels. Ultimately, van Poelgeest concluded that sixty-five of the 200 to 300 European women working in brothels in the NEI "were most certainly forced into prostitution."[55]

In 1994, shortly after van Poelgeest's study was published, some members of the Foundation of Japanese Honorary Debts filed claims against the Japanese government for compensation as individual victims. Their claims, which were brought in the Tokyo courts, were predicated on Hague Convention IV of 1907, which governed Japanese actions during World War II. Article 3 of the Convention requires that a "belligerent party" violating the convention "pay compensation" for all [illegal] acts committed by persons forming part of its armed forces." Since Article 46 of Hague IV expressly required that the Japanese respect "family honor and rights, the lives of persons, and private property" of all civilians residing in the NEI, and as Japanese troops had repeatedly violated this article as a "hostile army," the Dutch plaintiffs alleged that compensation should now be paid to them.

Testimony from a number of Dutch civilians who had suffered as internees left no doubt that the Japan had violated the Hague Convention and should pay compensation. But the Dutch plaintiffs ultimately failed to win a legal victory, since the Japanese courts concluded that Hague 1907 did not permit individual claims for compensation and, alternatively, that the issue of compensation for Japanese wrongdoing had already been settled by the San Francisco Peace Treaty.

While the Foundation of Japanese Honorary Debts was disappointed with the failure to obtain results in court for Dutch internees generally, those civilians forced into prostitution fared better after the July 1995 establishment of the Asian Women's Fund. Created "through the united efforts of the Government and people of Japan," the fund's goal is to express "the atonement of the Japanese people for the former comfort women."

On July 15, 1998, the Asian Women's Fund signed a Memorandum of Understanding with a "Project Implementation Committee" in the Netherlands. As a result of this memorandum, seventy-seven Dutch women who had worked as comfort women received medical and financial support totaling 255 million yen.[56]

[55] ibid 18–19.

[56] Women in the Philippines, the Republic of Korea, and Taiwan who had been forced into prostitution by the Japanese also received monetary support. Apparently, each woman received two million

Additionally, Ryutaro Hashimoto, the Prime Minister of Japan, delivered a letter to Willem Kok, the Prime Minister of the Netherlands, in which he expressed Japan's "deep feelings of apology and remorse ... for all the former comfort women who underwent numerous painful experiences and suffered incurable physical and psychological damage." A copy of the letter also went to each of the seventy-seven victims.

Some women who had been forced into sexual slavery wrote letters of gratitude to the Project Implementation Committee. One woman wrote the following:

> I thank you for all you have done and are committed to doing for me. I thank you not only for this monetary compensation, but also for having recognized the misery I experienced as a girl of 15. You have softened the pain of a wound that is still open, a wound I have endured through life.[57]

Today, the issue of forced prostitution and the agony of those who served as comfort women remains controversial and, as recently as late 2015 and early 2016, was front page news when the South Korean and Japanese governments inked "a landmark agreement" in an attempt to resolve the plight of Korean women who were forced to serve in wartime brothels.[58]

yen as "atonement money," with the funds being donated by Japanese people "who share feelings of apology and remorse." The Indonesian government declined to identify any former comfort women, but did agree to accept 380 million yen to provide social welfare services for elderly Indonesians. At 2016 currency exchange rates, 255 million yen is about US$2.4 million. See documents of the Japanese Government and the AWF, *Report on the Activities of the Asian Women's Fund* (September 1, 2000).

[57] ibid 4. [58] See also n. 4.

8

Criminal Group Responsibility

Prosecuting the *Tokkeitai, Kempeitai*, and 25th Army

During the Japanese occupation, the widespread and almost daily commission of war crimes by members of the *Tokkeitai* and the *Kempeitai* resulted in a unique post-World War II approach to the prosecution of war crimes. As explained in Chapter 3, Article 10 of Decree No. 45 created a special rule for individual liability based on membership in a criminal group (Dutch: *collectieve aansprakelijkheid*). The relevant language reads, in part:

> If a war crime is committed within the framework of the activities of a group of persons in such a way that the crime can be ascribed to that group as a whole, the crime shall be considered to have been committed by that group, and criminal proceedings taken against and sentences passed on all members of that group.
>
> ...
>
> No penalty shall be imposed on the member for whom it is proved that he had taken no part in the commission of the war crime.

Based on this provision, if a temporary court-martial determined that the commission of war crimes was an *integral* part of the day-to-day operations of a group or organization (and the tribunal itself decided what qualified as a "group" under the law), then the personnel assigned to that organization were collectively responsible for war crimes committed as part of a *criminal group*. This meant that every individual member of the group was guilty of the war crime(s) for which the group had been found collectively responsible, with punishment dependent upon the level of individual culpability. The only exception was that if the individual defendant could prove that he had not been a participant in the particular war crime(s) being prosecuted collectively, then he could escape liability. The burden of proof, however, was on the accused to show that he either was not a member of the group or, if a member that he had not participated in the war crimes being prosecuted.

No other war crimes tribunal operating in the Far East had such a provision, and no modern judicial system has ever accepted the idea of meting out individual punishments based solely on group or collective criminal liability. Even under Anglo-American conspiracy law, an accused must enter into an agreement to commit a criminal offense, or at least arrive at some common understanding

Military Trials of War Criminals in the Netherlands East Indies 1946–1949, Fred L. Borch.

about the criminal object of the conspiracy. American war crimes prosecutors at Dachau did use a "common plan or design" theory of criminal liability to avoid proving individual participation in a war crime, but that legal theory still required a shared criminal intent.[1] Article 10, however, was different in that it did not require the prosecutor to show, or the tribunal to find, that the individual members of the group *intended* to commit war crimes. Rather, the court need only determine if a war crime (or crimes) had been committed and if the group committed the war crime (or crimes) within the framework of its activities.

Note the difference between Article 10 of Decree No. 45 and Article 9 of the Nuremberg Charter. That article, which was applicable to the International Military Tribunal (IMT) in Nuremberg, addressed the trial of an *individual* member and provided that the IMT could declare, *prior* to that individual's trial, that the accused was a member of a criminal group. Under Article 10, however, there is no declaration of group criminality *prior* to the trial of the members of the group. More importantly, under the NEI provision, a group could be prosecuted even if only a *single* war crime was committed *once* by the group, provided the war crime "can be ascribed to that group as a whole." This is quite different from the "organizational criminality" attached to the Gestapo and the SS.[2]

A major reason for enacting Article 10 was that the inhabitants of the Indies had suffered so much from the actions of the Japanese *Tokkeitai* special naval police and *Kempeitai* military police that they regarded these as inherently criminal organizations akin to the Gestapo in Nazi Germany. By the end of the occupation, the Dutch were convinced from their own experiences that the commission of war crimes was an integral part of the day-to-day operation of the *Tokkeitai* and *Kempeitai*. Since this meant that virtually every man who served in either organization had participated in a war crime by virtue of his membership, the NEI authorities decided that it was both morally and legally appropriate to prosecute these organizations as criminal groups. Perhaps more importantly, finding a group collectively responsible for a war crime, and then punishing its individual members

[1] At the Dachau war crimes trials, held from November 1945 to August 1948, the prosecutor alleged that the defendants, all of whom had been employed in Nazi concentration camps, "acting in pursuance of a common design to commit the acts hereinafter alleged ... did ... willfully and deliberately, and wrongfully encourage, aid, abet and participate in ... cruelties and mistreatment, including killings, tortures, starvation, abuses and indignities, the exact names and numbers of such persons being unknown." See Joshua M. Greene, *Justice at Dachau: The Trials of an American Prosecutor* (American Bar Association/Ankerwycke 2017) 37.

[2] Telford Taylor, *Anatomy of the Nuremberg Trials* (Little, Brown & Co. 1992) 282. The German Secret State Police or Gestapo (German: *Geheime Staatspolizei*) was part of the *Schutzstaffeln* or SS during World War II. Both organizations were infamous for their brutal suppression of opposition to the National Socialist, or Nazi, Party (NSDAP). The Gestapo, working in concert with other organizations in the SS, ensured that there was no domestic opposition to the Nazi regime. The IMT declared both groups to possess "organizational criminality" because both organizations had "criminal aims" and their members committed criminal acts as a matter of routine.

Photo 20 Group trial of *Kempeitai*, Batavia, 1948.
Credit: Netherlands Institute of Military History, Ministry of Defense

based on that collective guilt, would ensure that no individual escaped responsibility for participation in what was essentially an organizational war crime—and where evidence of individual acts by individual members of that group might be limited, or even unavailable.

Since one-third of the 1,038 Japanese convicted by temporary courts-martial between 1946 and 1949 were either *Tokkeitai* or *Kempeitai*, this indicates the dim view that the NEI authorities took of these two military organizations.[3] But Article 10 was not only for the *Tokkeitai* and *Kempeitai*; it was intended for use against other groups that had committed war crimes as part of their normal operations.[4] Witness the Article 10 prosecution of the Japanese 25th Army discussed in this chapter.

[3] Iris Heidebrink, "Military Tribunals in the Netherlands East Indies," in Peter Post *et al.* (eds.), *Encyclopedia of Indonesia in the Pacific War* (Brill 2010) 415.

[4] L. F. de Groot, "De rechtspraak inzake oorlogsmisdrijven in Nederlands Indië (1947–1949)," 78 *Militair Rechtelijk Tijdschrift* (1985) 85.

Photo 21 *Kempeitai* officers on trial, Batavia, 1948.
Credit: Netherlands Institute of Military History, Ministry of Defense

Prosecutor v. Shigeki Motomura and 15 Tokkeitai Members

On May 5, 1947, the prosecutor for the temporary court-martial sitting in Macassar indicted the Macassar-based *Tokkeitai* under Article 10, alleging that this group "had committed war crimes within the framework of its activities" between March 1942 and August 1945.[5] These war crimes included unlawful mass arrests, systematic terrorism against criminal suspects, and "repeated, regular and lengthy torture." The charging document described the "systematic terrorism" committed by the *Tokkeitai* group as including:

[t]he seizing of men and women on the grounds of wild rumors, repeatedly striking them with the hand and with sticks during their interrogation, kicking them with the shod foot,

[5] *Prosecutor v. Shigeki Motomura, Chobei Sakai, Toshimitsu Tomita, Tooru Minami, Shigeo Manabe, Susumu Nakashima, Yoshio Ono, Yoshihiro Shiba, Tokyo Eguchi, Isamu Shimitzu, Tamotsu Masuda, Masashige Oku, Noboru Doi, Shoichi Terayama, Fusao Nakata, Shigeichi Senoo,* Vonnis No. 17/1947, Macassar (July 18, 1947); U.N. War Crimes Commission, *Law Reports of Trials of War Criminals*, Case No. 79, Vol. 8, 138–45.

hanging them up by the arm or leg, burning them with glowing cigarettes and bicycle bells, wrenching their knee-joints apart, stripping women and exposing them in this condition to the public view, withholding food from arrestees, compelling them to put their thumb print on blank sheets of paper ... these acts having led to or at least contributed to the death, severe physical and mental suffering of many and the condemning to death or imprisonment of several innocent persons.

The prosecutor identified four of the defendants as the most culpable in the group: Sub-Lieutenant Motomura, who was the highest ranking accused and second-in-command of the *Tokkeitai* in the South Celebes; Senior Petty Officer Sakai, who was Motomura's deputy; and Warrant Officers Minami and Ono (each in charge of a separate *Tokkeitai* detachment). They had "ordered, encouraged or allowed" personnel under their command or supervision to commit war crimes. The indictment alleged that the remaining twelve accused had committed unlawful mass arrests and engaged in systematic terrorism and torture. Two of the accused, Minami and Masuda, were also charged with rape.

The tribunal considered 114 statements, both sworn and unsworn, in determining whether the Macassar *Tokkeitai* had committed war crimes as part-and-parcel of its operations. While this meant that the sixteen defendants did not have the opportunity to confront, much less cross-examine, their accusers, this was not an unusual situation at a temporary court-martial. In any event, the prosecutor had brought the charges under Article 10, which did not require a showing of individual criminal liability. That said, it is apparent from an analysis of the nineteen-page, single-spaced typewritten decision that, while they were weighing evidence to determine collective guilt of the Macassar *Tokkeitai*, the judges also looked for evidence of individual guilt for all sixteen defendants. This almost certainly was because the judges wanted to find an alternative basis for criminal liability. Guilt under Article 10 may have been sufficient, but if the court-martial could also find evidence of individual wrongdoing in the 114 statements, then this would strengthen any group responsibility decision. Additionally, evidence that an individual had committed a war crime would give the judges more information when determining the degree of individual culpability and an appropriate sentence.

Some illustrations of individual misconduct follow. Mr. W. F. de QUILETTES stated that he had been "burned with a bicycle bell" by Doi and Shiba in July 1943. Mr. S. P. SOELEMANA wrote that Shimitzu had taken him out on a boat during questioning in November 1944, tied him to the boat's anchor, and thrown him (and the anchor) overboard three times. Mr. C. H. WENSVEEN stated that in between June and September 1943, Oku, Manabe, Doi, Nakashima, and Shimitzu hung him head down and forced him to put his thumb print (as a signature) to a blank piece of paper (the assumption being that a "confession" was added later). Mr. SAMAN gave a statement in which he alleged that, in July 1944, Shimitzu forced two persons to disrobe, one of whom "was in an advanced state of pregnancy;" Shimitzu then tortured them both. The tribunal considered a statement from Balie MASESE and Paul TANDI, who reported that during the months of December 1943 and January 1944, "people were brutally treated nearly every day by the *Tokkeitai* during interrogations" and that "an average of two people died per day in the *Tokkeitai* building in Macassar." There was also proof that at least two females in *Tokkeitai* detention were raped and that Motomura had "seriously ill-treated" three American airmen who had been captured and turned over to him in January 1945.

While all the defendants admitted being members of the *Tokkeitai* in Macassar, only a few were willing to admit some wrongdoing. Motomura acknowledged his responsibility—and his guilt—for the war crimes committed by his subordinates, but only when under his direct control; he was unwilling to accept any responsibility for their misdeeds when they were working at other *Tokkeitai* detachments. But Motomura also insisted that during his time in Macassar, there had never been any mistreatment of men or women during interrogations. On the contrary, "all confessed at once of their own accord." Motomura did acknowledge that, under Japanese law, there had to be a confession from a suspect before a case could be sent to a court-martial, but he categorically denied that he had personally mistreated any suspect.

Senior Petty Officer Sakai, who was Motomura's deputy, admitted that he had ordered mass arrests, but these were done under orders from superiors. As for personal misconduct, Sakai admitted only that he did "occasionally strike someone with the flat of my hand." While claiming that this occasional assault and battery was the extent of his misconduct, Sakai admitted that he

> did sometimes see and hear that the *Tokkeitai* beat people [but] I did not stop this because I did not have the power to do so. It was necessary ... that there should be beatings for *a confession had to be* forced; if beating had not taken place, there would practically never have been a confession, and without this a case might not be sent by the *Tokkeitai* to the court-martial. If they denied [their guilt] those being interrogated were struck with the hand or the stick. (emphasis in original)

As for the other defendants, they all denied having committed the acts with which they were charged, although most admitted having occasionally struck a suspect "with the flat of my hand."

At the conclusion of the proceedings on May 16, 1947, the tribunal determined that the 114 affidavits, combined with partial admissions from almost all of the accused, was more than sufficient evidence to find the *Tokkeitai* guilty as a "whole group ... seeing that these offenses were all committed within the framework of the *Tokketai* activities." In its written opinion, the judges emphasized the mission of the *Tokkeitai* in maintaining law and order in Macassar, and its clearly delineated powers under Japanese Navy regulations. In this regard, the court held that the group had used a "systematic" approach to obtain confessions from suspects, and adopted methods "in vogue with the *Kempeitai* ... German Gestapo and Russian G.P.U."[6] As a result, "legal and convincing evidence" permitted the court to find that the *Tokkeitai* "taken as a group ... was guilty of the aforesaid war crimes."

[6] The Soviet Union's Russian G.P.U. or "State Political Directorate" was a secret police organization; it was the forerunner of the K.G.B.

The court determined that there was sufficient evidence to find all of the sixteen individuals charged in the indictment guilty of war crimes, but with one exception: Chief Petty Officer Shoichi Terayama. There was "no legal and convincing proof" of his guilt and, consequently, the tribunal acquitted him and ordered his immediate release. (The court also did not enter a judgment against Yoshio Ono, as he had died during the trial proceedings.)

In passing sentence on the members of the remaining fourteen *Tokkeitai* members, the court noted that "the degree of responsibility must not be made the same for all the accused." The senior ranking defendant, Navy Sub-Lieutenant Motomura, was sentenced to death. Warrant Officer Chobei Sakai, the second named defendant, likewise was sentenced to death as he had been Motomura's deputy. Minami also was sentenced to be executed, along with six more defendants, based on their involvement in the group war crime as perpetrators or instigators; this meant that a total of nine defendants were destined to be shot by firing squad. Lieutenant Colonel N. M. VELLENGA, and Captains J. A. STRUYENKAMP and CLAPROTH, sentenced the remaining five accuseds to imprisonment ranging from one to twenty years.

Prosecutor v. Koonosuke Choo and 32 Kempeitai Members

On February 13, 1947, the prosecutor in Batavia charged thirty-three Japanese *Kempeitai* members as a criminal group under Article 10.[7] He alleged that, between April 1942 and September 1945, as part of the framework of its activities, the group had committed a variety of war crimes in Batavia, including: striking suspects on various parts of the body with their hands and fists; beating them with sticks; subjecting men and women in their custody to the "water cure;" applying electricity to various parts of the body; hanging suspects by their wrists and ankles; depriving them of food, water, and medical care; burning them with lighted cigarettes on various parts of the face and body; and throwing suspects to the ground using jiu-jitsu holds.

As many of those subjected to this mistreatment had died or been permanently crippled, the prosecutor asked the tribunal to find the *Kempeitai* group guilty of the war crimes of systematic terror and mistreatment and torture of civilians. He requested that nine of the defendants be put to death; almost all were officers or senior noncommissioned officers, including Majors Choo and Taniguchi, Captain

[7] *Prosecutor v. Choo Koonosuke, Kiyoshi Taniguchi, Kinjiro Iizuka, Michitaro Kato, Teruo Kobayashi, Yoshio Tomita, Keiji Shibao, Masayoshi Nakagomi, Nagamoto Sugiyama, Tsutomu Yamaguchi, Buichi Fukushima, Shigeo Goka, Shigeru Kobayashi, Hajime Komatsu (alias Sato), Kenji Matsunaga, Arata Moimoto, Yutaka Miki, Jitsuryo Nakahodo, Bunji Ogata, Chuji Ono, Tsumeno Takanami, Masayoshi Tsukamoto, Rijuji Aizawa, Yukio Chiba, Yoshio doi, Tatsuyi Maekawa, Yoshio Nara, Takuo Nishimura, Chiyoki Suzuki, Sumio Tanoue, Sohei Kobayashi, Liong Hone Tan (alias Nagita) and Nobuzo Adachi, all Kempeitai*, Vonnis No. 24/1947, Batavia, (September 15, 1947).

Kato, and Sergeant Majors Goka and Suzuki. As for the other accuseds, the prosecutor requested imprisonment between five and twenty years.

The trial, which began and finished in May 1947, resulted in a 100-page single-spaced typewritten decision. The judges concluded that there was sufficient evidence to find the *Kempeitei* group guilty under Article 10. The court, however, just as in *Prosecutor v. Motomura and 15 Tokkeitai Members*, also looked for individual criminal responsibility for each of the accuseds, and the 100-page decision carefully links each defendant to a war crime committed between April 1942 and September 1945. The judges wanted to find an alternative basis for criminal liability; guilt under Article 10 had been proven, but evidence of individual wrongdoing strengthened the group responsibility decision.

By way of example, in considering the evidence against the second named defendant, Major Taniguchi, the court noted that he had been the top *Kempeitai* officer in Struiswijk prison in Batavia between March 7, 1942 and February 24, 1943. While he was in charge, a large number of suspects had been arrested, interrogated, and tortured in the prison; the tribunal identified more than fifty by name. Similarly, in considering the culpability of Sergeant Major Ogata, the tribunal considered a sworn statement from Mrs. WEDDING, who testified that she was arrested because the *Kempeitai* suspected her of sabotage. During questioning, Ogata forced her to kneel in an open window, and then beat her with a stick until she was bloody. Later, she was burned on the palms of her hands with a lighted cigarette.

In all, the tribunal considered more than 200 affidavits. It also heard from each individual defendant and his counsel, with the exception of Ono, Maekawa, and Sugiyama. These three defendants had escaped prior to trial. While Maekawa and Sugiyama were still at large, Ono had been "shot down" and killed (Dutch: *neergeschoten*) during his escape attempt. Of the thirty remaining *Kempeitai* named in the indictment, 28 were found guilty. Two were set free on the grounds of insufficient evidence of their participation in the group war crimes. Six were sentenced to death, including Choo and Taniguchi. The remaining defendants were sentenced to between five and twenty years.

On September 15, 1947, Lieutenant Colonel J. la RivierE, Major L. F. de Groot, and Major J. G. H. van der Starp announced the verdict and sentences after the fiat of execution was issued by Mr. M. A. F. Zwager.

In addition to the *Motomura-Tokkeitai* and *Choo-Kempeitai* courts-martial examined here, there were other Article 10 collective responsibility proceedings in the NEI. Ten *Kempeitai* members were tried as a group in Medan in late 1948 for systematic terrorism, torture of citizens, and mistreatment of prisoners. All ten were convicted and received sentences ranging from eight years to death.[8] Similarly, some eighteen *Kempeitai* members were tried as a group in Batavia

[8] *Prosecutor v. Minoru Ichijo and 9 other Kempeitai*, Vonnis No. 119/1947, Medan, (October 18, 1948).

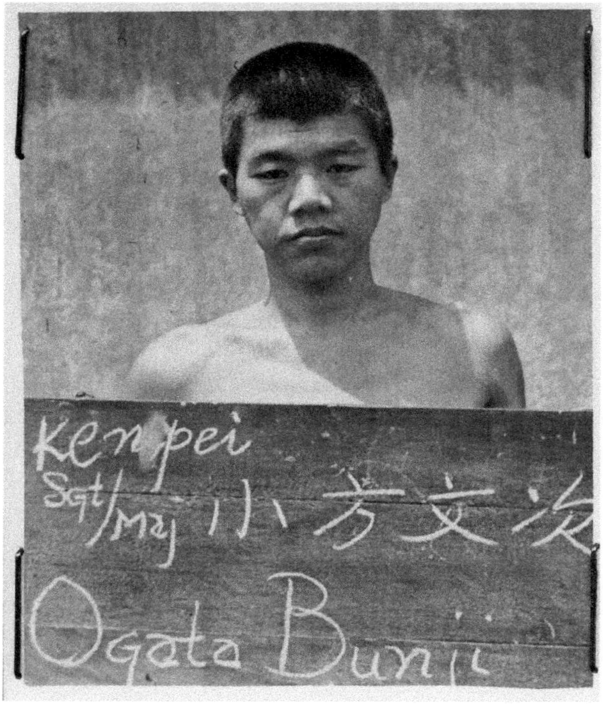

Photo 22 Sergeant Major Bunji Ogata was a defendant in *Prosecutor v. Koonosuke Choo and 32 Kempeitai Members*. Found guilty of systematic terrorism and mistreatment and torture of civilians, he was executed in Batavia in December 1947.

Credit: Netherlands Institute of War Documentation (NIOD), Amsterdam

in mid-1948 for systematic terrorism, torture of citizens, and murder. Almost all were found guilty; six were sentenced to death. The remainder were given between five and twenty years' imprisonment.[9] Some *Tokkeitai* in Banjarmasin also were apparently prosecuted as a group for the torture and execution of some 200 civilians, whom they believed were part of an anti-Japanese conspiracy. Thirty defendants in total were tried in ten different temporary courts-martial proceedings.[10]

Both Army Sergeant Major Isamu HANZAWA and *Kempeitai* Sergeant Major Yuko HAYASHI, whose photographs are shown here, were prosecuted and convicted in Article 10 group trials.

[9] *Prosecutor v. Kunishige Wada and 17 Kempeitai Members*, Vonnis No. 14/1948, Batavia, (September 11, 1948).

[10] Aiko Utsumi, "Local military trials," in Peter Post *et al.* (eds.), *Encyclopedia of Indonesia in the Pacific War* (Brill 2014) 410.

Photo 23 Army Sergeant Major Isamu Hanzawa was a defendant in a group trial of 18 *Kempeitai* in Batavia. He was found guilty of participating in murder, systematic terrorism, and torture of civilians and executed in September 1949.

Credit: Netherlands Institute of War Documentation (NIOD), Amsterdam

Prosecutor v. Moritake Tanabe, Nakao Yahagi, Shozo Yamamoto, and Tetsuo Fukaya

While the use of Article 10 against the *Kempeitai* and *Tokkeitai* was to be expected, the decision to prosecute the 25th Army as a criminal organization makes the proceedings against it—and Tanabe, Yahagi, Yamamoto, and Fukaya—much more interesting, especially because all four accuseds were senior officers.[11]

On November 19, 1948, the prosecutor for the tribunal in Medan charged that Lieutenant General Tanabe, Major Generals Yahagi and Yamamoto, and Colonel Fukaya were guilty of war crimes by virtue of their membership in a criminal group. His theory of liability was that the 25th Army, which had overall responsibility for

[11] *Prosecutor v. Moritake Tanabe, Nakao Yahagi, Shozo Yamamoto, and Tetsuo Fukaya*, Vonnis No. 109/1948, Medan, (December 29, 1948).

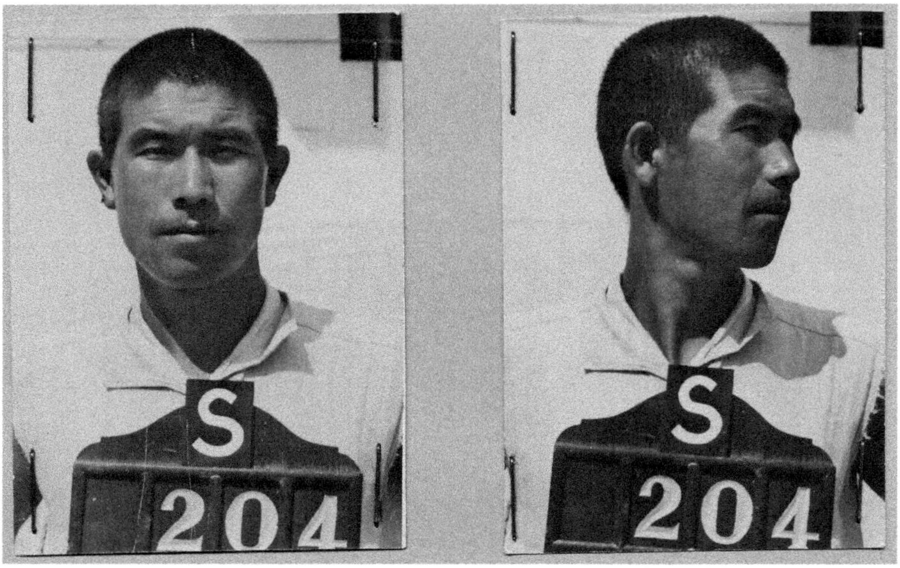

Photo 24 *Kempeitai* Sergeant Major Yukio Hayashi was a defendant in a group prosecution. Found guilty of systematic terrorism and torture, he was sentenced to death and executed in September 1948.

Credit: Netherlands Institute of War Documentation (NIOD), Amsterdam

the Japanese occupation on Sumatra, had systematically mistreated prisoners of war (POWs) and civilians on the island between mid-1944 and the end of hostilities in 1945.

This systematic mistreatment arose out of the Japanese Army's decision to build a railroad that could transport coal and move troops across Sumatra. When construction of the trans-Sumatra railway began in Paken Baroe in May 1944, however, the project was of little or no military value; Sumatra was remote, and already on the periphery of the war in the Pacific. Yet the 25th Army, which had been tasked with building the railroad, persisted with the project. Japanese engineers and Korean guards, acting at the direction of the 25th Army, forced some 5,000 POWs (mostly Dutch but some British, Australian, and American), at least 10,000 *rōmusha*, and a number of civilian internees, to build this militarily irrelevant project. When the Japanese surrendered in August 1945, the trans-Sumatra railway was complete. Not a single Japanese soldier was ever moved on its tracks. But the 25th Army's persistence in constructing the railroad had come at a great cost: about 7,000 POWs were dead, along with some 5,000 *rōmusha*, and 983 interned civilians.

The gist of the prosecutor's charge that these deaths were the direct result of the collective mistreatment of POWs and civilians by the 25th Army. Lieutenant General Tanabe and Major General Yahagi, the unit's commander and chief of staff, respectively, had taken no interest in the health and welfare of these laborers. Major

General Yamamoto, the head of the Army's Commissariat[12] (Dutch: *Intendance*), had failed to give sufficient food and clothing to the men. Compounding this lack food and sustenance was a failure of Colonel Fukaya, the 25th's senior medical officer, to provide adequate care to POWs and civilians suffering from beri-beri, dysentery, malaria, ulcers, and other illnesses. Just as guilty were those Japanese officers and noncommissioned officers in the 25th Army who participated in the railway construction efforts, since they did nothing to alleviate the suffering of the men, much less prevent the foreseeable and unnecessary deaths that followed from systematic mistreatment. These subordinate officers and noncommissioned officers knew, or had reason to know, that the 25th Army was committing a grave war crime against POWs and civilians, because "there were more than 100 deaths per kilometer" for a 200 kilometer railroad.[13]

Under Article 10, if the Medan tribunal ruled that the 25th Army was collectively guilty, then the prosecutor—in theory at least—could bring criminal proceedings against *all* members of the 25th Army. Sentences would be passed on all members of the group, with their level of culpability in the collective war crime determining their individual punishments. The Medan prosecutor, however, did not choose to pursue all members of the 25th Army. This almost certainly was because there were thousands and thousands of soldiers who belonged to the unit, and it was not an efficient use of judicial resources to pursue every individual who had served in the 25th Army from mid-1944 to the end of hostilities. Instead, the prosecutor indicted the four senior leaders in the organization who were most culpable in the systematic mistreatment of POWs and civilians.

The trial proceedings began on November 24, 1948. The Medan tribunal developed evidence of collective guilt by considering sworn written statements from more than thirty individuals who had worked on the railway project. It also accepted into evidence a September 1945 Red Cross report which addressed the ill-health of civilian internees in camps in north and central Sumatra. The judges also expressly relied upon evidence developed in at least fifteen earlier temporary courts-martial proceedings. By way of example, more than twenty affidavits that had been used by the Medan court to find Captain Ryōhei MIYAZAKI guilty in May 1948, were accepted into evidence. Miyazaki had been the commander of POW camps along the trans-Sumatra railway line, and consequently was in the 25th Army's area of operations; he was convicted in May 1948 and shot by firing squad the following month.[14]

The four defendants were defended by two Japanese lawyers, Mitsuji IWASAKI and Seisuko MIYAUCHI.[15] They presented a number of defenses to the court.

[12] In the 25th Army, the commissariat was responsible for providing food rations and other subsistence for soldiers in the organization, and POWs and civilian internees since these personnel were under its occupation authority.

[13] Gavan Davis, *Prisoners of the Japanese* (William Morrow 1994) 326.

[14] For more on Miyazaki, see Chapter V nn. 22–6, and accompanying text.

[15] Memorandum from Mitsuiji Iwasaki and Seizuko Miyauchi, to President, Temporary Military Tribunal [sic], Medan, Defence of the accused Tanabe Moritake, Ex-C in C 25th Army, and three fellow accuseds (December 17, 1948); see Allied Papers, *Prosecutor v. Tanabe et al.*

First, the two counsel argued that the 25th Army was only responsible for feeding and providing medical care for POWs on Sumatra. The public works contractors who employed the *rōmusha* were responsible for their rations. As for the civilian internees, the 25th's higher headquarters, the Japanese Southern Expeditionary Army, was responsible for their well-being. Consequently, it was unfair to blame the 25th Army for anything other than the suffering of the POWs. Second, Iwasaki and Miyauchi insisted that Lieutenant General Tanabe and his coaccuseds had done their best under the circumstances. In the spring of 1944, the 25th Army was ordered to prepare for "the final battle with the allied forces and [so] all affairs in Sumatra were prepared from the standpoint of [future] military operations." With their energies now focused on war, the senior leaders of the 25th inexorably had less time to ensure that those men working on the railroad were adequately fed and given good medical care. Additionally, as Japanese supply lines to Sumatra were increasingly disrupted in late 1944 and early 1945, rations had been reduced for the POWs and civilians. But this was only because food was scarce; rations had been reduced for Japanese soldiers, too. Similarly, medical supplies were reduced, but this was not done intentionally to harm POWs. Rather, medical support was reduced for all Japanese personnel as well.

A third argument from the two defense lawyers concerned only the three more junior defendants. It was unfair, they claimed, to hold Yahagi, Yamamoto, and Fukaya responsible for the deaths of POWs and civilians because they were merely staff officers and not commanders. Only the latter, men like Tanabe, had the authority to give orders to subordinates. The claim was that Yahagi, Yamamoto, and Fukaya, lacking command authority, could not have improved conditions for the POWs and civilians even if they had so desired. Fourth and finally, the two counsel asked the court to consider that, after the Japanese surrender, the 25th Army had helped transport Allied POWs and civilian internees from Sumatra to Java and had prevented Indonesian revolutionaries from harming them. The Japanese in fact had paid a price for protecting these POWs and internees, as the guerrillas belonging to the "radical Indonesian independence movement" had killed "several hundred" Japanese soldiers. The defense counsel insisted that this sacrifice by the 25th Army should be a matter in mitigation in deciding the fate of the four accuseds.

On December 17, 1948, Major H. C. A. VERMELEN, joined by Captain W. P. SCHRIJVER and First Lieutenant J. T. MEINESZ, found all four defendants guilty by virtue of their membership in the 25th Army. All four were sentenced to death. As the commander of the 25th Army, Tanabe was the most culpable. The judges wrote that, since taking command in April 1943, Tanabe had the most authority of any Japanese officer on Sumatra. Nothing occurred on the island without his approval or acquiescence. Yahagi was only slightly less guilty. As the Army's chief of staff, he was responsible for the work of the entire General Staff. The court concluded that he must have known about the ill-health and deaths of POWs and civilians working on the railway, if for no other reason than regular reports on the progress of the trans-Sumatra railroad would have come to him as the most senior staff officer in the 25th Army. Yamamoto and Fukaya likewise were

Photo 25 Major General Nakao Yahagi was convicted along with three other senior Japanese officers for his criminal membership in the 25th Army. Yahagi was the unit's chief of staff. Tried by a tribunal sitting in Medan, he was found guilty and executed in July 1949.
Credit: Netherlands Institute of War Documentation (NIOD), Amsterdam

highly culpable in that they failed to ensure that food and medicines, respectively, were available in sufficient quantities to ensure the health of the POWs and civilian workers. When food and supplies were running short, it was their responsibility to raise the issue with Generals Tanabe and Yahagi. Yamamoto and Fukaya both knew that the extraordinarily heavy work being done on the railway required sufficient food and adequate medical care, yet they failed to provide these items to the workers, as it was their duty and responsibility to do.

E. LUURING, the commanding officer of Medan, issued the fiat of execution approving the trial results and death sentences on December 29, 1948. All four accused were informed of the trial results on the following day.

Yahagi was shot on July 8, 1949; Tanabe was executed three days later.[16] An official photograph of Yahagi, taken while he was pending trial, accompanies this chapter.

[16] Born in 1889, Tanabe graduated from the Imperial Japanese Army Academy in 1910. He served in China in the 1930s and was Vice Chief of Staff of the Japanese Army's General Staff from 1941

A final note about the trial of the 25th Army for its treatment of POWs and civilians on Sumatra. As previously explained, the Japanese persisted in building the trans-Sumatra railroad despite its irrelevance to the war effort. The deaths of thousands and thousands of civilians was bad enough, but what made the Dutch authorities so bitter was that so many POWs had died for nothing. The colonial authorities were also very much aware of the experience of the Dutch held in POW camps in Europe when compared to the experience of those men held as POWs in the Pacific. About 13,000 Dutch soldiers were held in Germany as POWs. Between 300 and 400 perished, or about 3 percent. In the Pacific, 19.4 percent of Royal Netherlands Indies Army (Dutch: *Koninklijk Nederlandsch Indisch Leger* (KNIL)) POWs died in Japanese captivity. These numbers, however, really do not tell the whole story because the POWs held by the Japanese "were subjected to traumatic experiences" that virtually all the POWs in Germany were spared.[17] Today, we would say that almost all who survived Japanese captivity suffered from post-traumatic stress disorder or "PTSD"—which went untreated because it was not yet recognized as a serious mental disorder.[18]

to 1943. He then was sent to Sumatra, where he took command of the 25th Army; when the war ended, he was still in command. Since Tanabe was the brother-in-law of General Hitoshi IMAMURA, who had been found not guilty of war crimes at the temporary court-martial in Batavia, it must have seemed ironic to many observers that Tanabe was shot by firing squad while Imamura, who arguably was just as guilty, and likewise was facing capital punishment, was spared. See Chapter 10 nn. 26–41, and accompanying text for more on Imamura.

[17] Louis de Jong (with an Introduction by Jeroen Kemperman), *The Collapse of a Colonial Society: The Dutch in Indonesia during the Second World War* (KILTV Press 2002) 419.

[18] PTSD is a secondary effect caused by witnessing or experiencing a traumatic event. It is widespread among soldiers who participate in military operations; up to 20 percent of Americans who served as soldiers or marines in Iraq or Afghanistan suffer from PTSD.

9

Trials for Violations of the Terms of the Armistice

An armistice, also known as a truce or cease-fire, is the first step taken by parties engaged in armed conflict when they decide that fighting between their armed forces should stop—and peace be restored. It does not end a war; it merely suspends hostilities.

In modern history, the importance of an armistice cannot be overstated. Witness the end of fighting in World War I, when the Allied and Central Powers decided upon the eleventh hour of the eleventh day of the eleventh month in 1918 as the date of the armistice. Thirty-five years later, the armistice agreed upon by the U.S. and North Korean delegations at Panmunjom was no less important. This cease-fire ending the fighting on the Korean peninsula is still the only basis for peace; no treaty formally ending the Korean War has ever been negotiated, much less signed.[1]

In the Netherlands East Indies (NEI), the end of hostilities with Japan—and the armistice that followed—was much more complicated than what had occurred in 1918 and 1953. There were at least two reasons for this complexity. First, when those living in the NEI heard on August 19, 1945 that Japan had capitulated and the war was over, there were no Dutch troops in the archipelago. In fact, it would be six weeks before the first Allied units arrived in the NEI, when British paratroopers landed near Batavia on September 8. As a result, the more than 300,000 uniformed Japanese present in the NEI after the surrender found themselves in the unusual position of having to disarm themselves and start "self-internment." Then, when a new and bloody conflict broke out between the Dutch and Indonesian nationalists (the so-called *Bersiap* period), the Japanese were now in the unusual, if not unenviable, situation of being asked to protect Dutch ex-prisoners of war (POWs) and civilian ex-internees from the revolutionaries. For the most part, Japanese troops did well in maintaining law and order in the NEI until late September 1945, when sufficient numbers of Allied troops began arriving in the islands.[2]

Not all Japanese nationals in the NEI, however, observed the armistice or assisted the Allies in maintaining law and order. On the contrary, the second

[1] For more on the armistice on the Korean peninsula, see Howard S. Levie, "How It All Started—And How It Ended: A Legal Study of the Korean War," 35 *Akron Law Review* (2002) 205–25.

[2] For more on the *Bersiap* period see Chapter 1, "Setting the Stage," nn 21–23, and accompanying text.

Military Trials of War Criminals in the Netherlands East Indies 1946–1949, Fred L. Borch.

reason that the armistice in the NEI was so complicated was that more than a few Japanese soldiers resident in the archipelago were in sympathy with Indonesian nationalists, if for no other reason than the "Asia for the Asians" philosophy that dominated Japanese thinking about race and culture meant they could not support the reestablishment of white Dutch colonial rule. Historian William H. Frederick estimates that 800 of these men took up arms against the Dutch during the Indonesian revolution. About 250 of these "Japanese freedom fighters" were killed; roughly the same number disappeared. Whether or not these Japanese nationals were important to the success of the Republican guerilla military effort is not at all clear, but the Dutch military "implicitly considered them to be superior to any Indonesian military or militia forces."[3] This makes sense in that even the ordinary Japanese soldier had military training and probably combat expertise that would have been lacking among many insurgents.

With this as background, it should come as no surprise that the NEI authorities took a hard view toward any Japanese soldier who took up arms on behalf of Indonesian nationalists. The Dutch certainly believed that, having been a part of the Allied victory over the Japanese, it added insult to injury now to face soldiers of their defeated enemy on the side of Indonesian insurgents trying to prevent the reestablishment of Dutch authority in their colony. But there was a more practical reason as well, since if Japanese military personnel joined the anti-colonial guerrilla conflict, their knowledge and experience would be passed on to the insurgents, and make it more difficult for the Dutch colonial government to defeat them in battle.

The law certainly was clear on the matter, and had been set out in the 1907 Hague Convention IV Respecting the Laws and Customs of War on Land. Article 35 required that "capitulations agreed upon ... must be scrupulously observed," while Article 36 stated that an "armistice suspends all military operations ... between the belligerent parties." Consequently, NEI Decree No. 44, Definition of War Crimes was breaking no new legal ground in making it a war crime to commit any "hostile acts" (including furnishing information resulting in hostile acts, providing the means or opportunity to commit hostile acts, or inciting others to commit them) "contrary to the conditions of an armistice."

This chapter looks at three temporary courts-martial involving war crimes committed during the armistice in effect in the NEI from late August 1945 to early September 1951. In *Prosecutor v. Iwanaga*, tried in Timor in 1948, a Japanese infantry lieutenant was accused of unlawfully killing an ex-POW in October 1945. In *Prosecutor v. Hatada, Kanai and Ikeda*, tried in Macassar in 1947, three Japanese soldiers who had deserted from the Imperial Army and joined the insurgents were tried for committing hostile acts during the armistice. Finally, in *Prosecutor v. Katsuno*, which was heard by a temporary court-martial sitting in Medan, a deserter from the Japanese Army who had joined the Indonesian guerrillas was tried for the same war crime.

[3] William H. Frederick, "The Aftermath," in Peter Post *et al.* (eds.), *Encyclopedia of Indonesia in the Pacific War* (Brill 2010) 55–56.

While there is nothing unusual about the legal issues in *Iwanaga*, the two military trials involving Japanese nationals who had joined the Indonesian guerrillas are unique in legal history. There does not appear to be another situation in which an international or national court has tried, much less convicted, any individual for the war crime of violating the terms of a cease-fire, truce, or armistice.

A final point: it was not until September 8, 1951 that the Allies signed a formal peace treaty ending World War II with Japan; the armistice maintaining the peace in the NEI was in force until that day.

Prosecutor v. Satoro Iwanaga

On March 24, 1948, a temporary court-martial sitting in Kupang, West Timor, began hearing evidence against Infantry Second Lieutenant Satoro Iwanaga.[4] The defendant was alleged to have violated the terms of the armistice by committing manslaughter (Dutch: *doodslag*), in that he had unlawfully killed an ex-POW named TOASOEN, who had previously been confined in a Japanese camp on Timor.

In October 1945—some two months after the armistice was in place—Iwanaga was the commander of a group of Japanese soldiers who were rounding up ex-POWs (almost all of whom were former Royal Netherlands Indies Army (Dutch: *Koninklijk Nederlandsch Indisch Leger* (KNIL)) personnel) who had escaped from nearby Japanese POW camps. Instead of remaining in these camps after the surrender of Japanese forces in the NEI, which these men were supposed to do until they could be officially processed and released, these ex-POWs had fled into the surrounding countryside and were hiding among the local population. Since the Japanese were responsible for these POWs until such time as they were officially released, they went looking for those who had left their camps without authority.

While searching for these escaped POWs, Iwanaga and his men found an Ambonese soldier named Toasoen. According to the prosecutor, when Toasoen resisted being taken into custody, and then began running away, Iwanaga fired his pistol at him. Toasoen was struck by a bullet and later died of this wound. The prosecutor asked the military tribunal to convict the defendant of manslaughter, and sentence him to twelve years imprisonment.

The three judges heard from the accused, and from his counsel, Kenzo KANEDA. They also considered written sworn statements from four witnesses, and in-court testimony from a fifth individual.

According to the written statement from Mr. Petrus Poring TOENGGARA, Toasoen came to his house in the village (*kampong*) of Kabor about 4 o'clock in

[4] *Prosecutor v. Satoro Iwanaga*, No. 14/1948, Temporary Court-Martial, Timor Kupang (March 25, 1948).

the afternoon one day in October 1945. Toasoen asked for some water, which Toenggara gave him. While Toasoen was still with him, two Japanese soldiers, accompanied by a tall Japanese officer, came looking for ex-POWs who might be present in the village.

The Japanese, suspicious of Toasoen, began to question him. One of the soldiers then hit Toasoen in the cheek with the butt of his rifle. Toasoen did not fall down after receiving this blow. Rather, he raised both his hands above his head and then, with a jump, fled towards the river. When Toasoen was about 25 meters away, the tall Japanese officer—who was the defendant—fired his pistol at him, and the bullet struck Toasoen in the lower back. Toenggara told his interrogator that he had heard that Toasoen later died of this bullet wound.

Mr. Andrias Dewa MINGGOE confirmed Toenggara's recollection of the event. In his sworn statement, Minggoe wrote that he had witnessed Toasoen come to Toeggara for a drink of water. Shortly thereafter, three Japanese soldiers arrived and Minggoe saw a Japanese soldier strike Toasoen in his cheek with the butt of a rifle. He then watched Toasoen flee, and saw a tall Japanese officer fire a shot in Toasoen's direction. He later heard that the man was hit and had later died from the gunshot.

In a third sworn written statement, Mr. Andrias Lair LODANG told his interrogator that he had seen a dead Ambonese (Toasoen) who had a bullet wound in his lower back, and that he had seen a tall Japanese soldier (Iwanaga) standing guard over him.

The fourth written sworn statement, from Mr. Johan TALLANE, was markedly different from the other three descriptions of the killing. Tallane claimed to have been with Toasoen when he was shot and killed. According to Tallane, this all happened on October 13, 1945, when he, Toasoen, and another ex-POW were eating rice in a *kampong*. When a local man warned them that six Japanese soldiers were coming, the men fled in three different directions. Tallane claimed that he then heard two shots, and that he later heard from a villager that the defendant had shot and killed Toasoen, while he was on his knees praying. Tallane also stated that he had seen Toasoen's wound, which appeared to him to have resulted from a bayonet, as there was lots of blood on the ground. Finally, Tallane insisted that the Japanese had dragged Toasoen's corpse away as if he had been a pig.

One witness, Mr. Elisa PATTISINA, testified under oath in court. He told the three judges that he and his fellow Ambonese and Menadonese had been tricked into working for the Japanese Army as *heihos* (auxiliary soldiers) on the island of Timor. In February 1945, when Pattisina was working as a team leader, he first had contact with the accused. According to Pattisina, Iwanaga did not strike individuals under his authority, or otherwise mistreat them. Additionally, he took strong action against any subordinate Japanese who mistreated individuals. Interestingly, Pattisina also told the judges that he had heard the accused prohibit another Japanese soldier from firing on a man who was attempting to escape. Finally, it was Pattisina's opinion that Iwanaga was not capable of committing manslaughter.

In their decision, tribunal president Lieutenant Colonel Dr. B. DAMEN, and members Captain G. H. H. SCHRÖDER, and Navy Ensign F. H. BOS, held that it had not been "legally and convincingly established" that the defendant was guilty as charged. First, the court noted that the defendant denied that he was guilty of manslaughter. Second, the judges "were not in the least persuaded by the vague testimonies of Toenggara and Minggoe," although their statements certainly were more reliable than the sworn statement of Tallane, which the court rejected as "fantastic" and unreliable. Third and finally, the military judges were most persuaded by the in-court testimony of Pattisina, and his very favorable evidence about the accused's good character. The court in fact praised Pattisina's oral statements as "utterly reliable." In the end, the military tribunal based its decision based on a failure of proof. But the written opinion speculates that Toasoen's death perhaps had been an "accident" (Dutch: *ongeluk*).

The 28-year old Iwanaga, who had been in pre-trial detention since February 9, 1946, was ordered to be set free. After the Resident of Timor issued the fiat of execution confirming the acquittal, and the military tribunal announced this result on April 7, 1948, Iwanaga was released.

Prosecutor v. Iwanaga is an important case because it illustrates how a homicide committed during an armistice may be prosecuted as a war crime. Since all NEI temporary courts-martial also had subject matter jurisdiction over ordinary penal offenses (like manslaughter), there was no requirement for the prosecutor to charge the defendant with a war crime. He could have charged him with simple manslaughter under the NEI civilian penal code. That he did not most likely reflects a policy decision to prosecute any offense with a nexus to armed conflict as a war crime whenever possible. Since Iwanaga and his men were acting within the scope of their duties and responsibilities under the armistice when they sought to return Toasoen to a POW camp, Toasoen's allegedly unlawful death was a war crime.

Iwanaga also is an unusual case because of its unusual result. The tribunal concluded that the written sworn statements of Toenggara and Minggoe were "vague" but never explains what is actually vague about the statements of two eyewitnesses. (In fact, the statements do not appear to be at all vague.) Additionally, the military judges seem to have given great weight to the in-court good character testimony presented by Pattisina without explaining why it was reasonable to give it such weight, especially since Pattisina was not an eyewitness to Toasoen's death and some of his character evidence about Iwanaga was pure hearsay.

The decision also seems flawed in that, when the defendant fired his pistol at the fleeing Toasoen, it was foreseeable that Toasoen might be wounded or killed. Firing a pistol at Toasoen might not be grossly negligent, but the statements of Toenggara and Minggoe certainly were sufficient to support a finding of manslaughter resulting from simple negligence. It follows that even if the court determined that the death was an "accident," this finding does not preclude a manslaughter conviction if the accident resulted from Iwanaga's negligence. Finally, why did the tribunal need to discuss Toasoen's death as accidental? After all, if the accused was legally tasked with recovering escaped POWs, customary international law would permit the use of deadly force when an escaped POW flees rather than submit to being taken into custody.

Why did the court use good character evidence to acquit the accused? Were the judges sympathetic to Iwanaga because he was simply trying to do his duty in returning Toasoen to a POW camp? Did they think that the shot fired by Iwanaga was reasonable under the circumstances? There is not sufficient information in the tribunal decision to know with any certainty. The only clue to understanding the court's acquittal is the decision's holding that Pattisina was "utterly reliable" and was a "most favorably known witness" to the tribunal. This suggests that Pattisina had appeared as a witness in other temporary court-martial proceedings in West Timor, or otherwise was so known to the military judges that they trusted his good character evidence more than eyewitness reports of the killing.

Regardless of what the judges may have thought had happened on that day in October 1945, *Prosecutor v. Iwanaga* is an excellent example of how the officers sitting in judgment of the Japanese did not hesitate to reject the prosecutor's demand for a conviction where they believed justice demanded a contrary decision.

Prosecutor v. Minoru Hatada, Kioshi Kanai, and Suekichi Ikeda

On January 23, 1947, the prosecutor for the temporary court-martial sitting in Macassar charged Minoru Hatada, Kioshi Kanai, and Suekichi Ikeda[5] with having violated the terms of the armistice between the Netherlands and Japan by providing "information, opportunity or means" to the "extremist leader Andi Moesa and his *pemudas*."[6]

The three defendants, all Japanese civilians who were members of the *Tokkeitai*, a special branch of the Japanese naval police, had deserted after Japan's surrender and joined the Indonesian insurgents in their rebellion against the Dutch government. According to the prosecutor, the most serious misconduct committed by the three young Japanese men was that they had "placed a bomb against the back wall" of the home of a NEI government official, Assistant Resident BONE, on the night of February 17–18, 1946. While this bomb had exploded, no one had been killed; there was only structural damage to the building. But, said the prosecutor, the seriousness of the war crime required that the court-martial to sentence all three men to death.

The trial of the three defendants began and ended on February 7, 1947. The evidence against the three Japanese men consisted chiefly of admissions made by them during previous interrogations and testimony given in open court. These admissions were accepted as true by the military tribunal, at least insofar as they

[5] *Prosecutor v. Minoru HATADA, Kioshi KANAI, Suekichi IKEDA*, Vonnis No. 3/1947, Temporary Court-Martial, Macassar, March 28, 1947.

[6] See Chapter 1 n 20.

were consistent with each other or corroborated by statements from other witnesses, or both.

The evidence showed that on August 30, 1945, the three civilian defendants were residing in the town of Maros when they learned that Japan had lost the war. The men were told that they must remain in Maros and wait for future orders; they were not to desert or otherwise leave their place of duty. About September 13, however, they deserted along with a fourth man, Sergeant Major Rokura OTA, who was also a member of the *Tokkeitai*. Although all four men knew it was forbidden to take weapons, Sergeant Major Ota took two automatic pistols, six or seven revolvers, six hand grenades, one rifle, and twelve homemade bombs filled with explosives. The group also took a very large quantity of food with them.

According to Hatada, Kanai, and Ikeda, they deserted from Maros only to avoid being returned to Japan, where they believed that they would be living in poverty as a result of Japan's defeat. They claimed that it was only after deserting from the *Tokkeitai* that they learned about the independence movement in South Celebes, and that they then decided "to join it and fight on." Consequently, on October 23, 1945, the four Japanese joined the Indonesian guerilla leader Andi MOESA, who led *pemudas* in the town of Limpoe.

Moesa knew about the independence movement on Java, and had decided to organize a similar rebellion in the Celebes. He asked the four Japanese nationals "to help with it in every possible way." Moesa was particularly anxious to obtain more weapons but the Japanese told the Indonesian leader that this would be difficult and, in fact, the Japanese did not obtain additional rifles, pistols, or explosives for the insurgents. But they did take part in guerilla meetings on several occasions, including one attended by at least 300 *pemudas* in September 1945. Moreover, except for Sergeant Major Ota, who left the group at the end of November, the three defendants remained with Moesa and his rebels, and were still with them on February 16, 1946, when Dutch military forces attacked Limpoe.

Moesa and the three accuseds escaped. In revenge for the attack, however, the insurgents and their Japanese comrades traveled to the town of Watampone, where they placed a bomb against the back wall of the Assistant Resident's home. They intended for the bomb to blow up the house and kill high ranking Dutch and Australian officers who ordinarily resided in the home. Although the bomb did explode, it did only structural damage to the building; no one was injured, much less killed. It was this act of violence that the prosecutor considered the most grievous violation of the conditions of the armistice.

In their decision, Lieutenant Colonel N. M. Vellenga, Captain R. Claprogh, and Captain Abdullah DAENG MAPPOEDJI, all Reserve infantry officers sitting as judges, concluded that the three Japanese civilians had committed "hostilities contrary to the terms of an armistice." This war crime, which violated customary international law and was also prohibited by the 1907 Hague Convention, was especially egregious under the circumstances. It was bad enough that the actions of the defendants in joining the Indonesian insurgents directly contravened Tokyo's unconditional surrender to the Allied forces, and its pledge that all Japanese subjects would refrain from any military action. But what very much rankled the military judges was the evil intent of the Japanese defendants, which they considered in deciding the appropriate punishment. As the decision puts it:

> ... up to the present day [February 7, 1947] thousands have already fallen victim in the disorders in South Celebes since the Japanese capitulation, in which disorders the accused participated in the way explained above, and further that it was the intention of the accused to kill all those officers who as a rule were present in the house of the Assistant Resident, thus furnishing the proof that they did not shrink from employing any methods, so that the death penalty demanded by the Public Prosecutor is entirely in keeping with the gravity of the accuseds wrongdoing.

The military tribunal sentenced each defendant to death on February 7, 1947 and the findings and sentence were confirmed (fiat of execution) by Mr. Lion Cachet, the Resident of South Celebes, on March 7, 1947. The three defendants were informed of the decision in a public sitting of the court in Macassar on March 28, 1947. All three men were later executed.[7]

While *Prosecutor v. Hatada, Kanai and Ikeda* is an important decision in the history of NEI war crimes prosecutions, what is most interesting about the tribunal's written opinion is the lengthy discussion of what Lieutenant Colonel Vellenga and his two judge colleagues believed had motivated the defendants to desert the *Tokkeitai*, join the rebels in the South Celebes, and violate the terms of the truce. This provides not only insight into the thinking of the judges in this particular trial but also shows just why the Dutch were so alarmed by—and fearful of—Japanese involvement in the ongoing guerilla war against them.

All three accuseds admitted that they had been educated in Japan at a vocational school called the *Koa Sen Mon Gakko* or "vocational school for the uplift of Asia." Since the chief aim of this institution was to inculcate the Japanese ideology of *Hakko Ichiu* or "world family under Japanese leadership," Vellenga and his fellow judges were convinced that the three defendants had been sent to the NEI with the mission of furthering Japan's goal of "Asia for the Asians." The men first worked toward this goal in the *Hanakikan* (Intelligence Service) before being transferred to the *Tokkeitai* in 1944 and, when the three defendants deserted after the Japanese surrender and joined the insurgents, they were motivated by their original commitment to make Japan the dominant power in Asia. As the court put it:

> [i]n the opinion of the court-martial ... it was not their original intention *only* to escape in order not to be sent back to Japan where all was poverty ... when they learned of the independence movement in South Celebes, they decided to join in and in this way continue the fight for the sake of Japan; they have from the very beginning—*in*

[7] *Prosecutor v. Minoru Hatada and 2 others*, Vonnis No. 3/1947 (February 7, 1947) (Macassar); United Nations War Crimes Commission, *Law Reports of Trials of War Criminals*, Supplemental Cases vol. 15 (His Majesty's Stationery Office 1947–1949) 132.

complete accordance with the purpose for which they were sent—done everything possible to serve Japan's cause as far as they could, also and precisely since the defeat. (emphasis added)

As far as the three military judges were concerned, Japan's defeat and surrender in Tokyo on September 2, 1945 had not altered Japan's war aims. On the contrary, "the realisation of them has only been temporarily suspended and will be taken in hand again as soon as new possibilities for this present themselves." This meant that Hatada, Kanai, and Ikeda were part of a larger Japanese effort to accomplish its pre-surrender goals. "Japan," wrote the judges, "sees in an independent Indonesia a still easier prey for the future for the realisation of its world imperialism." The court concluded by saying that the Japanese did not really seek to free the peoples of the Far East from the chains of white colonialism. On the contrary, the goal was "the whole world for the Japanese."

More than sixty-five years later, this judgment that the Japanese were violating the terms of the armistice and collaborating with the Indonesian independence movement to further Japan's wartime aims seems far-fetched. The success of the Japanese in overwhelming and destroying the KNIL in the East Indies simply accelerated a preexisting desire among many Indonesians for freedom—and they would have revolted against Dutch rule regardless of Japanese participation after Tokyo's surrender. At the time, however, Dutch authorities and the vast majority of Europeans residing in the Indies were convinced that the Japanese were still encouraging Indonesian nationalism and inflaming resistance to any restoration of Dutch colonial rule.[8] The death penalty imposed on the young Japanese defendants—all of whom were in their twenties—reflected the belief that Japanese support for the rebellion was a very real danger.

Prosecutor v. Mizuo Katsuno

On May 7, 1947, 25-year-old Corporal Mizuo Katsuno appeared before the temporary court-martial in Medan.[9] The charge against him? That in August 1946, having deserted from the Japanese 25th Army, he had gone to the east cost of Sumatra, where he joined *Laskar Rakjat*, an Indonesian group "carrying on an armed opposition to the lawful Government of the Netherlands East Indies" and instructed members of that group "in the building of fortifications."

At his one-day trial, the accused admitted that he was a Japanese citizen but otherwise denied that he had violated the terms of the armistice or had otherwise aided the Indonesian rebels. On the contrary, he claimed that, after deserting, he

[8] See Chapter 2.

[9] *Prosecutor v. Mizuo Katsuno*, No. 18/1947, Temporary Court-Martial, Medan (May 7, 1947).

had gone to an estate near the city of Medan and devoted himself to agriculture. When Dutch troops conducted a military operation in the area, Katsuno had been arrested. While he admitted that he had a Japanese sword in his possession, he denied any wrongdoing.

The problem for Katsuno was that, in an earlier preliminary investigation conducted on January 23, 1947 by Dr. W. Beun, the deputy prosecutor in Medan, Katsuno had admitted having taught soldiers belonging to the *Laskar Rakjat* how to build fortifications. Presumably he had received training as a Japanese soldier on how best to construct defensive positions, bunkers, and the like, that he passed on to the insurgents. When this statement, which the accused had signed after it had been read to him in Japanese, was put into evidence by the prosecutor in open court, the defendant denied having made it. But the court accepted it over his protestations.

In addition to the defendant's statement, the military tribunal considered two other written statements, both of which had been obtained in January 1947. A Japanese soldier, Motoji IKEJIMA, confirmed under oath that the defendant had deserted from the Japanese Army. Mr. August Otto HERRNSDORF, also examined under oath, stated that when arrested, the accused declared that he had thrown his weapons into the river. Additionally, papers which were on Katsuno's person convinced the court that he belonged "to an armed native organization."

Convinced of the accused's guilt, the three-judge tribunal, consisting of Lieutenant Colonel J. M. F. Eskens, Captain R. E. Perdijk Rugebregt, and First Lieutenant E. Zondag, explained that a severe punishment was required:

> [t]he continuation of hostilities after an armistice has been concluded between the belligerents is so contrary to good faith and so hinders the restoration of normal conditions that a sharp punishment is rightly called for, but that the strengthening of the armed bands roaming the interior by adding to them a specially trained soldier has particularly serious consequences reigning at the present time so that a very heavy sentence ought to be imposed.

While the prosecutor had urged that the tribunal impose a sentence of fifteen years, the judges sentenced Katsuno to eighteen years' imprisonment. The findings of guilt and sentence were announced on the afternoon on May 7, 1947 and the head of the Temporary Administration in Medan confirmed it (fiat of execution) on May 28, 1947. That same day, the sentence was announced in open court by Lieutenant Colonel Eskens; the defendant and his counsel were present.

The judgment in *Prosecutor v. Katsuno* does not contain a lengthy discussion of the defendant's motivation to join the insurgents. It is likely, however, that the three judges in Medan would have agreed with their three colleague judges in the case of *Prosecutor v. Hatada, Kanai, and Ikeda*. The sentence in *Katsuno* certainly reflects a deep concern about the role of Japanese soldiers in the Indonesian struggle for independence.

10

Command Responsibility

Prosecutor v. Shoji, Prosecutor v. Maruyama, and Prosecutor v. Imamura and Okazaki

The horrific nature of the war crimes committed by the Japanese and German armed forces in World War II—ranging from the "Rape of Nanking" in China to the killing of millions of Jews in Germany, Poland, and the Soviet Union—reinforced the Allied decision to prosecute commanders for the war crimes committed by their subordinates, even though these commanders had not personally participated in the criminal acts and perhaps did not even know that a particular individual under his command had violated the law of war.

The legal theory upon which these trials was predicated is "command responsibility," also called "superior responsibility."[1] The concept is straightforward when a commander gives a manifestly unlawful order (*e.g.* "kill all prisoners captured in this military operation") to a subordinate, and that subordinate carries it out. Both are equally guilty of a war crime. Prior to World War II, the commander's culpability in this situation was viewed as a form of aiding or abetting.[2] In the war crimes trials conducted by the Allies after 1945, however, this aiding or abetting theory was replaced by new concept: a commander is guilty of a war crime when, having either actual or constructive knowledge that his subordinates are committing war crimes, he fails either to prevent or halt these violations of the law of war or fails to punish the responsible subordinates when the commander learns of their war crimes after they have been committed. This means that command responsibility is not predicated on the theory that the commander aided or abetted any war crimes committed by those individuals under his command. Rather, the superior's criminal responsibility is based on his own omission in failing to act. This criminal liability "flows from the neglect of a specific duty to take measures that are

[1] Some international law scholars also refer to command responsibility as *Respondeat superior* ("let the master answer"). While the term is a broader legal concept than command responsibility, and is based on accomplice theory, there is no practical legal difference between command responsibility, superior responsibility and *Respondeat superior* under the law of armed conflict today. See Gary D. Solis, *The Law of Armed Conflict* (2nd edn., Cambridge University Press 2016) 417.

[2] Aiding means giving help to someone, "while abetting involves facilitating the commission of an act by being sympathetic thereto, including providing mere exhortation or encouragement." Kriangsak Kittichaisaree, *International Criminal Law* (Oxford: Oxford University Press, 2001) 241.

necessary and reasonable in the given circumstances" to prevent the commission of war crimes by subordinates.[3]

The concept of command responsibility is relatively old. In 1439, Charles VII of France "promulgated an Ordinance providing ... the King orders that each captain or lieutenant be held responsible for the abuses, ills and offenses committed by members of his company ... If, because of his negligence or otherwise, the offender escapes and thus evades punishment, the captain shall be deemed responsible for the offense as if he had committed it himself."[4] In the 1600s, the Dutch legal scholar Hugo Grotius wrote that: "a community or its rulers may be held responsible for the crime of a subject if they knew of it and did not prevent it when they could or should prevent it."[5]

After World War I, the Allies intended to prosecute the most senior German military officer, Kaiser Wilhelm II, "for a supreme offense against international morality and the sanctity of treaties."[6] While "international morality" and the "sanctity of treaties" are not war crimes, and while the Kaiser escaped trial by fleeing to the Netherlands, his case illustrates an early effort by the international community to hold the superior commander responsible for what is arguably the greatest offense against humanity, *i.e.* starting a war.

While Dutch colonial authorities prosecuting Japanese commanders for war crimes on a theory of command responsibility may or may not have known about these historical antecedents, they were very familiar with the U.S. military commission that convicted Japanese General Tomoyuki Yamashita in December 1945. Since the *Yamashita* standard for command responsibility for war crimes committed by subordinates has become a foundational principle in the modern law of armed conflict, and the trial is frequently cited by legal scholars, the proceedings are worth examining in more detail—and provide a context for understanding the Netherlands East Indies (NEI) trials of a Japanese Army general, two lieutenant generals and a major general. As with *Yamashita*, the NEI temporary courts-martial addressed whether war crimes committed by lower ranking Japanese troops could be the basis for finding four general officer commanders guilty.

In October 1945, Yamashita was tried by a military commission in Manila, Philippines. The charge: that Yamashita "unlawfully disregarded and failed to discharge his duties as a commander to control the operations of ... his command, permitting them to commit brutal atrocities and other high crimes." The evidence presented by the prosecution was that, after the October 1944 American invasion of the Philippines, Japanese soldiers under Yamashita's command had raped, murdered, mutilated, tortured, and beheaded thousands and thousands of civilians;

[3] Chantal Meloni, "Command Responsibility," 5-3 *Journal of International Criminal Justice* (July 2007) 619, 628.

[4] Leslie C. Green, *Essays on the Modern Law of War* (2nd edn., Transnational 1999) 283.

[5] Hugo Grotius, 'De Jure Belli ac Pacis Libri Tres' ['The Law of War and Peace'] Bk. II, Ch. XXI, Sec. ii in Francis W. Kelsey (trans.) *Classics of International Law* (Clarendon Press 1925).

[6] Treaty of Versailles art 227, 14 *American Journal of International Law* (1920) (Supp) 95.

at least 8,000 men, women, and children were killed and nearly 500 women and girls were raped. Additional proof of Yamashita's guilt included that he had failed to inspect prisoner of war (POW) camps, where hundreds of men were tortured, starved, and killed, despite having the duty to make such inspections to ensure proper treatment, and that he had allowed the widespread and "unparalleled burning and destruction of entire villages, homes, churches, hospitals and schools, all without military justification."[7]

At trial, Yamashita denied knowledge of any unlawful killings or other war crimes committed by his troops. Additionally, he and his defense counsel argued that because the invasion meant that he "was constantly under attack by American forces [and] under pressure day and night," he was "completely out of touch with the situation [in the area around him]."[8] The gist of Yamashita's argument was that the massive ground and air attack on his forces had resulted in such chaos that it was impossible for him to exercise command and control over his subordinates, even if he had so desired. Consequently, insisted Yamashita, even if he had known about the widespread war crimes (which he claimed he did not), he could not have prevented them, much less punished those committing them.

Unfortunately for Yamashita, the military commission rejected this defense, finding instead that there was proof beyond a reasonable doubt that he was guilty as charged.

The importance of the Yamashita trial was that the defendant was not accused of having *personally* committed any war crimes; the prosecution did not claim that he ordered, or even knew about, the murders and rapes committed by his subordinates in late 1944. Rather, when Yamashita was convicted on December 7, 1945, and sentenced to be hanged, the basis for his guilt was command responsibility. As the commission wrote in its opinion:

> The prosecution presented evidence to show that the crimes were so extensive and widespread, both as to time and area, that they must either have been willfully permitted by the accused, or secretly ordered by the accused ... Where murder and rape and vicious, revengeful actions are widespread offenses, there is no effective attempt by the commander to discover and control the criminal acts, such a commander may be held ... criminally liable, for the lawless acts of his troops ... The Commission concludes: ... that during the period in question you [Yamashita] failed to provide effective control of your troops as was required by the circumstances.[9]

Yamashita was not convicted of committing war crimes himself; he did not pull a trigger or wield a sword in an unlawful manner. But he nonetheless was convicted of a war crime because he was responsible for the criminal actions of the soldiers under his command. While Yamashita had not ordered his subordinates

[7] Courtney Whitney, *The Case of General Yamashita: A Memorandum* (War Department 1946) 81.

[8] ibid 73.

[9] Howard S. Levie, *Terrorism in War: The Law of War Crimes* (Oceana Publications 1993) 157; William H. Parks, "Command Responsibility for War Crimes," 62 *Military Law Review* (1973) 1, 30 (quoting military commission's written opinion).

to violate the law of armed conflict, he had failed to stop their crimes and, because the war crimes committed by Yamashita's men were so widespread *and* had occurred over a long period of time, he *must* have known that they were being committed.

This "knew or must have known" standard is an important point because it means that Tomoyuki Yamashita was not convicted on the basis of strict liability; he was not found guilty merely because of his status as the commander, without a showing of fault on his own part. Rather, he was convicted because the military commission hearing his case was convinced that Yamashita knew or must have known about the war crimes committed by his men, and had failed to prevent these atrocities, much less punish them.[10] His guilt was based on his responsibility as a commander.[11]

In addition to the legal reasoning of *Yamashita*, the NEI judges about to hear evidence against senior Japanese officers in Batavia knew that Yamashita had been executed in February 1946. They also knew that another senior Japanese officer, General Masaharu HOMMA, had been tried by an American military commission sitting in Manila for the same offense. Homma had been convicted of permitting members of his command to commit "brutal atrocities and other high crimes" against Americans and Filipinos during the Bataan death march in 1942. Homma had been executed by firing squad in April 1946.

Finally, the Dutch military judges knew that the Americans were not alone in prosecuting senior Japanese officers for failing to control their subordinates. The Australians too had tried and convicted Japanese generals for their command failures: a military court sitting in Rabaul, New Guinea, adopting the same legal language used by the Americans in prosecuting Yamashita, had convicted Japanese Lieutenant General Masao BABA of "unlawfully" failing to "discharge his duty as

[10] See Solis (n. 1) 420. Critics of the *Yamashita* tribunal's command responsibility rule have been vociferous in claiming that General Yamashita was either innocent of the charges against him or else that the "command accountability" rule announced in *Yamashita* should be abandoned because countries like the United States have failed to apply the rule to their own senior commanders. See *e.g.* Allan A. Ryan, *Yamashita's Ghost* (University Press of Kansas 2012). Both arguments are nonsense. Yamashita's trial may have been flawed when measured by contemporary legal standards of due process, but he was guilty as charged. More importantly, the commission's "must have known" rule is the formulation used today by virtually all Western nations in regard to command responsibility, although the rule is now phrased as "knew or *should* have known." See U.K. Ministry of Defence, *The Manual of the Law of Armed Conflict* (Oxford University Press 2004) para. 16.36: "A commander will be criminally responsible if he participates in the commission of a war crime ... he also becomes criminally responsible if he knew or, owing to the circumstances at the time, should have known that war crimes were being or were about to be committed." See also *e.g.* Department of the Army, U.S. Army Field Manual, *The Law of Land Warfare* (Government Printing Office 1956) para. 501: "The commander is ... responsible if he has actual knowledge, or should have knowledge, through reports received by him or through other means, that troops or other persons subject to his control are about to commit or have committed a war crime and he fails to take the necessary and reasonable steps to insure compliance with the law of war or to punish violators thereof."

[11] Note that the U.S. Supreme Court never addressed Yamashita's guilt or the appropriateness of his death sentence; *In re Yamashita*, 327 United States 1 (1946) dealt only with an application for *habeas corpus* and prohibition writs.

commander to control the conduct of the members of his command" who were committing "brutal atrocities and other high crimes."[12]

Baba had been the commander of the 37th Army in Borneo. The evidence presented at his trial was that he had ordered about 1,000 British and American POWs to be moved from one location in Borneo to another location, a distance of 165 miles. The men were moved in two groups. The first group, which left in December 1944, was made to walk through very difficult terrain. Unfortunately for the men in this group, they were in such poor health that "a great number of prisoners died as a result ... many were severely ill-treated and some who could not keep up with the marching column were shot by guards on orders from the officer in charge of the party."[13]

Although the accused knew what had happened to the first group of POWs, he ordered the second group, numbering 540 POWs, to make the same march in May 1945. This long journey was even more disastrous. Only 183 POWs survived the march and, of these, 150 died shortly after their arrival. By the end of July 1945, only thirty-three of the whole party were alive. They were killed on August 1, 1945, on the orders of an officer who was under the command of Baba.

Lieutenant General Baba argued that the POWs had to be moved because Allied landings near the POW camp were imminent, and consequently "operational necessity" required the men to be evacuated. The accused also insisted that he had done his best to provide food and medical supplies for the POWs on the march. As for the killing of the thirty-three survivors, Lieutenant General Baba argued that he had been cut off from his subordinates during this period by Allied amphibious landings in the area, and "therefore could no longer exercise any effective control over officers ... under his command."

The Australian court rejected these defenses. It concluded that the POW deaths on the forced marches were the "natural consequences" of Baba's orders, and that he was responsible for them. As for the murder of the thirty-three surviving POWs, the Australians concluded that their deaths "were due to the failure of the accused in his duties as a commander." In addition to arguing that command responsibility was a "well-settled rule" of international law, the prosecutor in *Baba* proceedings cited the *Yamashita* decision as his authority for Baba's guilt.[14] Lieutenant General Baba was convicted on June 2, 1947 and hanged on August 7, 1947.

[12] See Whitney (n. 7) 60; *Trial of Baba Masao*, Case No. 60, vol. 11 U.N. War Crimes Commission *Law Reports of Trials of War Criminals* (Hi Majesty's Stationery Office 1949) 56–60; Philip R. Piccigallo, *The Japanese on Trial* (University of Texas Press 1979) 133–4.

[13] See *Trial of Baba Masao* (n. 12) 56.

[14] ibid 59. *Baba* was not the only command responsibility decision handed down by an Australian military court, nor was it the first. A tribunal sitting at Morotai, NEI in January 1946 had convicted Japanese Major General Shimichi ENDO of "neglecting to issue or enforce ... proper orders ... to provide for the treatment of prisoners of war ... by reason of which neglect the prisoners of war were unlawfully killed." Endo was found guilty and sentenced to five years' imprisonment. In April 1947, Lieutenant General Hatazou ADACHI (this is misspelled as Hatazo Artachi in the *Law Reports of Trials of War Criminals*) was convicted by an Australian military court as the responsible commander. Troops under Adachi's command murdered Australian and Chinese POWs and killed and mistreated civilians in territory occupied by the Japanese 18th Army. He was given a life sentence.

While *Yamashita, Homma*, and *Baba* are not mentioned in any decision from a NEI temporary court-martial (and there was no reason for these decisions to be cited, given the existence of Article 9 of Decree No. 45 as the basis of command responsibility), the point is that the Dutch judges knew that, given these American and Australian decisions, they were on firm legal ground in pursuing senior Japanese commanders for war crimes committed by their subordinates. They also knew that a decision to impose the severest punishment on a commander for the crimes committed by his subordinates would not be viewed as excessive by the Allies.

In 1948 and 1949, the temporary court-martial in Batavia heard evidence against four Japanese general officers. They were charged with having either allowed or having failed to prevent soldiers in the 16th Army, in which all four individuals were serving as commanders, from committing various war crimes during the Japanese invasion of the Indies from January to March 1942, and during the early years of the occupation of Java. The four defendants were Major General Toshishige SHOJI, Lieutenant General Masao MARUYAMA, Lieutenant General Seisaburo OKAZAKI, and General Hitoshi IMAMURA. The war crimes committed by the soldiers in the 16th Army included murder, rape, torture of civilians, and mistreatment of prisoners.

Prosecutor v. Toshishige Shoji

During the February 28–March 1, 1942 Japanese landings on West Java, Major General Shoji was a colonel commanding a separate 5,000-man brigade.[15] His mission was to capture a strategically important airfield at Kalijati, about forty-five miles from the landing site. After wading ashore, Shoji's troops moved quickly. Within a short time, they arrived at their objective and then "simply drove onto the airfield and in less than an hour the British and Dutch defenders were overpowered."[16] The Japanese soldiers then immediately killed about sixty British soldiers whom they had taken prisoner.

Six days later, on March 6, Shoji's men defeated a company of Royal Netherlands Indies Army (Dutch: *Koninklijk Nederlandsch Indisch Leger* (KNIL)) infantry who had been blocking their advance toward Bandung, where the KNIL General Headquarters was located. They took seventy-two men prisoner and, a few hours after capturing them, took them to a clearing in a wood and killed them. About March 10, Shoji's troops entered a hospital near the village of Soebang and

Adachi committed suicide in Papua New Guinea on September 10, 1947. See Sachi Sri Kantha, "Suicides of 84 Newsworthy Japanese between 1912 and 2015," 22 *International Medical Journal* (October 2015) 353.

[15] *Prosecutor v. Toshishige Shoji*, Vonnis No. 28/1948, Batavia (July 18, 1949). In some sources, Shoji's first name is spelled Toshinari. See Louis de Jong (with an Introduction by Jeroen Kemperman), *The Collapse of a Colonial Society: The Dutch in Indonesia during the Second World War* (KILTV Press 2002) 37.

[16] See de Jong, *The Collapse of a Colonial Society* (n. 15) 37–8.

murdered another twenty wounded POWs who were patients there. The Japanese also killed the European medical staff, including the nurses. At Shoji's trial, the prosecution also charged that soldiers under his command had taken prisoner three KNIL chaplains, identified as MOSTERD, Van HOEK and La HAYE. The Japanese then tied the three pastors to an armored vehicle, and then drove the vehicle in such a manner as to kill the chaplains. A report authored by the Central Bureau of Graves Registration (Dutch: *Centraal Bureau van de Gravendienst*) stated that the remains of the three victims were found in a mass grave near Soebang in 1945.

The prosecutor asked the court to impose the death penalty on Shoji for the murders and mass murders committed by the soldiers in his brigade. But the basis for Shoji's criminal liability was not that he had committed these war-related killings. Rather, it was that Shoji either "knew, or at least had reasonable suspicion" that these war crimes were being committed by his men.[17] In arguing command responsibility, the prosecutor relied on Article 9 of Staatsblad 1946 No. 45, which stated that "he whose subordinate has committed a war crime shall be equally punishable for that crime, if he has tolerated its commission by his subordinate, while knowing, or at least have reasonable suspicion, that it was being or would be committed." The prosecutor's reasoning was that the war crimes committed during the early days of March 1942 were so widespread that Major General Shoji not only must have been aware of the crimes, or suspected that they were occurring, but that he tolerated their commission.

The evidence was overwhelming that the Japanese in Shoji's unit had committed the war crimes identified by the prosecutor. The tribunal considered more than twenty-five statements from various witnesses. For example, KNIL First Lieutenant Henri Gerard CHRISTAN, who had been taken prisoner on March 2, stated in a sworn affidavit that he saw the bodies of KNIL soldiers a few days after being captured; it was clear to Christan that the men had been tied together and then shot. J. G. HOOGSTRATEN stated that he had been taken prisoner by the Japanese on March 6, 1942, and witnessed a Japanese soldier kill another POW by stabbing him with a bayonet. A sworn statement from an Indonesian named TIRTA, who resided in the village of Soklat, explained that the Japanese had taken him from his home to a trench near his village, where he saw at least twenty dead bodies. The Japanese ordered Tirta to cover the bodies with soil; he recognized some of the dead as nurses who worked in the hospital near Soebang.[18] Another Indonesian named SOEDARMI, who also had been directed by the Japanese to cover the dead in the trench with soil, confirmed Tirta's statement.

The accused also testified before the tribunal. While he did not contest that his troops had committed war crimes, he denied any knowledge of the misconduct. As Major de Groot put it, Shoji's claims of ignorance about the murder of KNIL and British POWs were "lies," if for no other reason than Shoji must have realized

[17] Levinus F. de Groot, *Berechting Japanse Orloogsmisdadigers in Nederlands-Indie, 1946–1949: Temporaire Krijgsraad Batavia* (Art & Research 1990 (privately published)) 330–1.
[18] ibid 337.

that it was virtually impossible for his soldiers to have advanced so quickly and had such battlefield success without having taken a single POW. De Groot and his fellow judges also concluded that when Shoji was present in the village of Soebang, he must have seen dying or dead POWs along the side of the road and in other places. In any event, the court concluded that even if Shoji had given instructions to his men on the proper treatment of POWs, it was clear that such instructions were not followed.[19] Just as in *Yamashita* and *Baba*, where the American and Australian military tribunals rejected the claims of ignorance and instead concluded that both defendants were guilty of having "unlawfully disregarded and failed to discharge" their duties as commanders "to control the operations of members of [their] commands, permitting them to commit brutal atrocities and other high crimes," so too the Dutch judges refused to accept Shoji's claims that he did not know his troops were committing war crimes. Consistent with the Allied decisions in *Yamashita* and *Baba*, the Dutch judges applied the law and found Shoji accountable as a commander.

Concluding that Major General Shoji deserved the "heaviest punishment" for failing to prevent the murder and mass murder of POWs and civilians, much less punish those responsible for the war crimes, Major de Groot, Captain J. G. M. van der STARP and Captain Th. L. DOORNWEERD, the tribunal judges, sentenced him to death on January 21, 1949. The fiat of execution was confirmed on July 8, 1949. In the end, however, Major General Shoji was lucky. On December 19, 1949, the High Representative of the Crown reduced his sentence to ten years as an "act of grace" (Dutch: *bij wege van gratie*).[20]

Prosecutor v. Masao Maruyama

Born in 1889, 59-year-old Lieutenant General Maruyama was a 1911 graduate of the Imperial Japanese Army Academy.[21] Having served as a military attaché in London in the 1920s and 1930s, Murayama spoke English and was more familiar with European culture than were most of his fellow officers. But he also had seen combat as a regimental colonel in China from 1937 to 1938 and consequently was well aware that some Japanese troops had committed war crimes in China.

During the invasion of Java, Lieutenant General Maruyama had been in command of the 2nd Division, 16th Army and, like Colonel Shoji, had come ashore with his men in the initial assault. But while soldiers in Maruyama's division may have committed war crimes during the initial assault on Java, Maruyama was not charged with any invasion-related misconduct. On the contrary, the prosecutor charged him with command responsibility for war crimes committed by his men between March 10 and September 10, 1942—a six-month period that began ten days *after* the initial Japanese attack on Java. During this time frame, Maruyama

[19] ibid 340. [20] ibid.

[21] *Prosecutor v. Masao Maruyama*, Vonnis No. 33/1948, Batavia (December 24, 1949).

had been the "commandant of the territory of West Java" and had control over all Japanese military personnel in this geographic area; this command duty position was the basis for the prosecution's command responsibility theory of criminal liability.

The indictment identified four specific events in which Maruyama's soldiers had committed the war crimes or murder and mass murder, and further charged that these offenses occurred because Maruyama had "failed to exercise sufficient control" over the actions of his men or had failed to give "directives and orders" on the care and treatment to be given KNIL and Allied POWs, or both. First, on or about April 22, 1942, three KNIL POWs escaped from the POW camp at Djatinanggor. After being recaptured, all three were summarily executed. Second, about the same time, three other POWs escaped from the POW camp located at Bandoeng. After being caught, all three men also were killed by their captors. Third, about May 5, 1942, between seven to nine POWs held at the camp near Tjimahi escaped. They also were soon recaptured, and murdered. Fourth, on or about May 10, 1942, two Allied POWs escaped from the POW camp at Soekaboemi. When they were recaptured, they too were immediately killed.

The prosecutor charged that these killings of fifteen to seventeen POW escapees were a violation of Article 50 of the Geneva Convention of 1929. Since it was the duty of captured combatants in 1942 to escape if reasonably possible, Article 50 permitted only "disciplinary punishment"[22] for POW escapes. This provision was nothing new; Article 8 of Hague Convention IV of 1907 similarly permitted only disciplinary punishment for recaptured POW escapees. The prosecutor argued that the killing of recaptured POWs by the Japanese was an obvious war crime and that Maruyama was guilty of murder and mass murder because he "knew or at least had reasonable suspicion that these unlawful executions were or would be committed" by soldiers under his command.[23] The prosecutor requested that the tribunal convict Maruyama as charged and sentence him to death.

As the tribunal began hearing evidence against Maruyama, however, it soon was apparent that there was no proof that Maruyama had ordered the executions of POWs in West Java. On the contrary, it was clear that Maruyama had instructed his subordinates that they were to adhere to the "international rules" for the treatment of POWs during and after the invasion, and that Maruyama had every reason to believe these instructions would be followed.

But if this was true, why were the POWs killed after attempting to escape? Statements from Colonel ISHIZAKI and Lieutenant Colonel KIMURA, both of whom had served under Maruyama in West Java, revealed that his chief of staff, Colonel OKI, had ordered the summary executions. Ishizaki, who had commanded

[22] "Disciplinary punishment" includes fines, discontinuation of privileges, extra labor, and imprisonment. Disciplinary punishment is distinct from punishments that a court-martial or other judicial proceeding might lawfully impose; brutal and inhumane punishments are expressly prohibited. See Jean S. Pictet (ed.), *Commentary on the Geneva Convention relative to the Treatment of Prisoners of War* (International Committee of the Red Cross 1960) art 93, 436.

[23] See de Groot (n. 17) 342, 350.

an artillery regiment in the 2nd Division, further stated that he believed that Colonel Oki had given this order on his own initiative, and that Maruyama knew nothing about it. As Oki had been killed in combat on Guadalcanal, he could not be questioned about this order to kill POWs who escaped and were recaptured. No doubt the tribunal would have preferred to hear from Oki, but it is clear from the record of trial that the judges were satisfied with the statements given by Ishizaki and Kimura, and accepted them as credible evidence.[24]

The only remaining issue was whether Murayama should have had reasonable suspicion that these killings of POWs were occurring. Major de Groot, Captain Doornweerd and First Lieutenant J. te HAVE concluded that Murayama was so focused on operational issues during the period that these war crimes occurred that it was not reasonable for him to have suspected any wrongdoing. His superior officer, General Imamura, had ordered him not only to maintain law and order on West Java, but also to be ready to repel and defeat any Allied counter-attack that might be coming. Finally, the court recognized that Murayama had also been tasked by the 16th Army commander with preparing his division for combat outside the Indies, which in fact occurred when the 2nd Division left for Guadalcanal in late September/early October 1942.

The tribunal concluded that Maruyama's guilt had not been proven, and ordered his release on February 25, 1949. As the prosecution resisted this decision to acquit Maruyama, however, the fiat of execution confirming the acquittal was not issued until December 24, 1949. Now a free man, Masao Maruyama returned to Japan the following day on the passenger ship *Tjisdane*.[25] He died there in November 1957. He was 68 years old.

Prosecutor v. Hitoshi Imamura and Seizaburō Okazaki

While the acquittal in *Maruyama* may have been disconcerting to some observers, the results in the temporary court-martial proceedings against General Imamura and Lieutenant General Okazaki caused a firestorm of protest in both the Indies and the Netherlands.[26] Both men were charged with the war crimes of murder, mass murder, torture of civilians, rape, and mistreatment of POWs, in that they had failed as commanders to prevent their soldiers from committing these crimes on the islands of Java and Borneo. The public uproar resulted because the military tribunal acquitted them of the charges.

Imamura had been the senior commander in the Japanese 16th Army; Okazaki was his chief of staff. Prior to the start of the criminal proceedings in Batavia in

[24] ibid 349. At the time Colonel Oki was killed on Guadalcanal, Maruyama was leading the 2nd Division on the island. The Japanese were subsequently defeated and evacuated Guadalcanal in February 1943.

[25] For more on the repatriation of Japanese war criminals to Japan on the *Tjisdane*, see Chapter 12, "Aftermath".

[26] *Prosecutor v. Imamura and Okazaki*, Vonnis No. 1/1949, Batavia (March 16, 1949).

early 1949, Imamura had already experienced a war crimes trial: in May 1947, an Australian military court sitting in Rabaul, New Guinea, had found him guilty of failing "to discharge his duty to control the members of his command, whereby they committed brutal atrocities." That court had sentenced Imamura to ten years' imprisonment. Imamura was now in Batavia to face the death sentence for war crimes committed by his soldiers on Java. Okazaki had not previously been tried for any war-related offenses, but was now in a joint trial with Imamura. While technically not in a command position as the 16th Army's chief of staff, Okazaki had been a key player in the day-to-day operations of the military government on Java and had decision-making powers akin to a senior commander.[27] Consequently, the prosecution theory was that Okazaki, like Imamura, could be found liable on the basis of command responsibility.

As in the *Shoji* and *Maruyama* cases, the Dutch Indies prosecutor charged Imamura and Okazaki under Article 9, alleging that both men either knew or had a reasonable suspicion that their subordinates were committing war crimes, and then failed to prevent them or take action to punish them.[28] Imamura's command responsibility was for war crimes committed between early March until November 11, 1942, when Imamura relinquished command of the 16th Army and transferred to the Eighth Area Army.[29] Okazaki's command responsibility was for offenses committed on Java and Borneo between early March 1942 and May 1943; Okazaki left the Indies in June 1943.

Both general officers pleaded not guilty, and insisted that they knew nothing about any war crimes committed by Japanese soldiers in the 16th Army.

The court conducted an exhaustive examination of command and control in the 16th Army during the period in which the war crimes occurred. De Groot and his fellow judges concluded that a large number of atrocities had been committed by soldiers under the command of the two accuseds. The murders of POWs and civilians on West Java by Colonel Toshishige Shoji's brigade certainly fell into this category. Another particularly gruesome war crime alleged to have been committed by the Japanese during Imamura's period of command involved 16th Army soldiers

[27] In all Imperial Japanese Army units commanded by a general officer, the chief of staff was the key staff officer responsible for translating the ideas and guidance of that commander into practical plans for soldiers to execute on the battlefield. While it depended on the personal relationship between the commander and the chief of staff, the latter usually emerged as the commander's alter ego and wielded considerable authority. The Dutch authorities believed that Okazaki had this type of relationship with Imamura. For a general study of the role of the chief of staff see David T. Zabecki (ed.), *Chiefs of Staff* (2 vols.) (Naval Institute Press 2008).

[28] See de Groot (n. 17) 57. The prosecutor also charged the two senior officers under Article 10, alleging that the 16th Army General Headquarters was a criminal group and that this criminality could be imputed to Imamura and Okazaki. The tribunal rejected this theory of liability. It reasoned that because Imamura and Okazaki were the only two men from the headquarters element to be prosecuted, and because no evidence of war crimes committed by the headquarters had been discovered, there was insufficient evidence of group criminal liability. For more on this subject See Chapter 8, "Group Responsibility."

[29] This newly organized Eighth Army had command authority over the Japanese 17th Army in the Solomon Islands and the Japanese 18th Army in New Guinea.

putting hundreds of Australian POWs into bamboo cages and then throwing the cages into the sea.[30]

The judges also found that the two Japanese general officers might have had a reasonable suspicion that these crimes were being committed. But the judges were also persuaded that the defendants had tried to prevent the commission of war crimes and had otherwise made sincere efforts to control their subordinates. Consequently, the tribunal concluded that it lacked sufficient evidence to support a finding of guilty, and that Imamura and Okazaki could not be held accountable as commanders. On March 16, 1949, after a six-day trial, both defendants were acquitted.

The tribunal's judgment identified a number of factors in support of the not guilty verdict. The chief reason was that the judges were convinced that Imamura and Okazaki had made good faith efforts to prevent the commission of war crimes. Imamura insisted in a written statement that he had issued directives to his men that the rules of warfare enunciated in the Hague and Geneva Conventions were to be followed. As Imamura explained, he had been so alarmed by the misbehavior of Japanese troops in China in the 1930s that, while serving as Inspector General of Military Education at the Ministry of Defense in Tokyo in 1940, he had prepared a booklet called "Moral Instructions on the Battlefield." This was later approved by War Minister Hideki TOJO and distributed to every Japanese soldier.[31] Imamura argued that this was evidence that he took seriously his duties and obligations as a commander under the law of armed conflict.

The Dutch judges also were very much impressed with the behavior of the two accuseds during the court-martial proceedings; de Groot later told Imamura that he "personally, during the investigation of your case[,] appreciated your attitude as well as the attitude of your Chief of Staff."[32]

This "attitude" was one manifestation of a generally favorable opinion that the three Dutch judges had of Imamura and Okazaki. In part, this was because it was widely known to the inhabitants of the NEI that Imamura, in implementing the military occupation of Java in March 1942, had adopted a relatively lenient policy toward civilians. The Dutch judges also knew that Imamura had been criticized by other Japanese Army officers for his permissiveness toward these civilians. But the judges also knew that Imamura had refused to change his views on the treatment

[30] Postwar research indicates that perhaps no living POWs were put in bamboo cages. Rather, dead Australian soldiers may have been transported in bamboo crates, which were then thrown into the ocean. At the time of the war crimes trials in Batavia, however, it was generally believed that the Australians were murdered in this manner. See de Jong, *The Collapse of a Colonial Society* (n. 15) 39 n. 16.

[31] See de Groot (n. 17) 57. General Hideki Tojo (1884–1948) was a key Japanese leader during World War II. He served as Prime Minister from 1941 to 1944, and as War Minister from 1940 to 1944. Tried as a Class A war criminal after the Japanese surrender, he was found guilty and hanged in December 1948. For more on Tojo see Robert J. C. Butow, *Tojo and the Coming of the War* (Stanford University Press 1961).

[32] Levinus F. de Groot, letter to Imamura, (September 8, 1950), quoted in Lisette Schouten, "Colonial Justice in the Netherlands Indies," in Kristen Sellers (ed.), *Trials for International Crimes in Asia* ((Cambridge University Press 2016) 75, n. 103.

of the local civilian population (because he had learned in China that harsh and brutal treatment provoked resistance to Japanese rule). They also believed that Imamura's policy had moderated "Tokyo's ruthless war spirit,"[33] and thus reduced the suffering of those living under Japanese occupation.

Another reason for the favorable attitude of the judges toward the defendants was simply racist. The tribunal judges—all of whom were white Europeans—believed that Imamura and Okazaki were more "civilized" than the typical Japanese Army officer because they had lived and worked in Europe, and been exposed to Western culture and ideas. Imamura had served as a military attaché in London during World War I and in British India in the late 1920s. Okazaki also had served as an attaché in London and Geneva prior to World War II. Both men spoke some English. For de Groot and his colleagues, this exposure to Western civilization meant that the two general officers not only were more "enlightened," but apparently also more credible and trustworthy. In the words of the tribunal's decision:

> The court martial during this trial is firmly convinced that both the first and second defendant by their extended and repeated stays abroad ... have acquired *international views and insights*. (emphasis added) These go far beyond the level of development and civilization of the average Japanese warlord of the genre of Harada[34] and Kokubu[35] and many others who, as notorious representatives of the unscrupulous Japanese war spirit, have been tried as war criminals.
>
> For this reason, and because the defendants did not shun the responsibilities associated with their high positions, more value may be attached to their statements than to those of other Japanese defendants, *even though they are not entirely confirmed by legal evidence.*[36]

Prosecutor v. Imamura and Okazaki is an important trial for several reasons. First, it was the last war crimes tribunal to be held in Batavia, and so was heard as the 300-year Dutch rule in the Indies was crumbling. Second, the court's acquittal of the accuseds was severely criticized in the Netherlands and in the NEI; Imamura in fact was dubbed by newspapers as the "Seyss-Inquart of Java," after the brutal Nazi Reich Commissioner of German-occupied Netherlands.[37]

Raden A. Hilman DJAJADININGRAT, the Governor of Batavia, who was required to confirm the court's decision, tried to overturn the acquittal and instead obtain a death sentence.[38] He was unsuccessful. After nine months, the High

[33] See *Prosecutor v. Imamura and Okazaki* (n. 26) 30.

[34] Lieutenant General Kumakichi HARADA succeeded Imamura as the commander of the 16th Army, and served as its senior leader until April 1945. After the war, he was prosecuted in Singapore by an Australian military court. Found guilty for the mistreatment and murder of POWs by soldiers under his command, Harada was hanged in Singapore in May 1947.

[35] Lieutenant General Shinshichiro KOKUBU was the 16th Army Chief of Staff and Chief of the Military Administration on in the Army's area of operation from June 1943 to November 1944. He escaped liability for any wrongdoing in the NEI and died in Japan in 1984.

[36] See *Prosecutor v. Imamura and Okazaki* (n. 26) 23 (emphasis added).

[37] After World War II, Artur Seyss-Inquart (1892–1946) was tried and found guilty of summary executions, mass deportations, and the shooting of hostages. He was executed in 1946. See "Boek van Haarlemmer over Japanse oorlogsmisdadigers," *Haarlems (Netherlands) Dagblad* (November 30, 1990) 18.

[38] De Groot later wrote that Djajadiningrat's reluctance to approve the acquittal may have resulted from Djajadiningrat's fear that his close wartime relationship with Okazaki might be revealed to the

Representative of the Crown, Mr. A. H. J. LOVNINK, ordered Djajadingrat to give a fiat of execution to the military tribunal's decision. But although the decision to acquit Imamura and Okazaki was ultimately upheld, de Groot was very much stung by the criticism that followed the decision. He spent years defending the result in letters and various articles, insisting that he had always wanted "to keep up the standards of Dutch justice, while at the same time, as far as possible, keeping out the bad influence of ill-feelings toward the Japanese as a nation."[39]

Several general conclusions may be drawn from an analysis of the *Shoji, Maruyama, Imamura*, and *Okazaki* decisions. As to the applicable law, the "knew or at least had reasonable suspicion" standard for command accountability used by the Dutch in the NEI, while different from the "knew or must have known" standard announced in *Yamashita*, were equivalent in one key respect: there was no requirement that the prosecution prove (or the judges conclude) that the defendant had actual knowledge that his soldiers were committing war crimes. For the Dutch, it was sufficient that a commander, under the circumstances, would have reason to suspect that his subordinates were violating the law of armed conflict,

As to the process for determining guilt used by the judges in the three courts-martial, it is reasonable to conclude that, as Major de Groot was the senior judge in all three trials, he not only led the decision-making process, but applied it uniformly in each proceeding. This means that the judges, with de Groot as the senior member, likely adopted the same approach when weighing evidence and applying the command responsibility standard enunciated in Article 9.

Finally, since three of the four defendants were found not guilty, it is obvious that de Groot and his fellow judges were not predisposed toward a finding of guilty and, at least as regards senior Japanese officers, did not let any racial prejudice or bias affect their evaluation of the evidence—at least adversely to the accuseds. The Dutchmen certainly were not going to apply a "strict liability" standard when deciding command responsibility of senior Japanese leaders. The Batavia court-martial arguably could have decided—as did the military commission that tried Yamashita in Manila—that Imamura and Okazaki were responsible as senior leaders for the many horrific war crimes committed by Colonel Shoji's brigade and Lieutenant General Murayama's division during and after the invasion of Java and Borneo, since the brigade and division were part of the 16th Army. It seems that a different panel of judges, looking at the same evidence, might well have concluded that Imamura and Okazaki should have been found guilty.

In this regard, consider that a key component of Yamashita's defense against the charge that he was liable as a commander was that the American attack on his forces so disrupted his command and control that he could not have prevented war crimes committed by his men on Luzon, much less punished them. When

Dutch authorities if he was too quick to approve the tribunal decision. But it is also possible that Djajadiningrat believed that Imamura and Okazaki were guilty as charged and should not escape their justice. See Schouten (n. 32) 96 n. 106.

[39] Letter from de Groot to Imamura (n. 32).

one remembers that Imamura and Okazaki had no such chaos in the 16th Army on Java, but in fact crushed KNIL and Allied forces in a very well-planned, organized, and controlled advance, this is another reason to think that different military tribunal examining the same evidence could have concluded that the defendants were guilty as charged. In this regard, different judges might have believed that once the fighting on Java was at an end, Imamura and Okazaki would have had actual knowledge that Japanese soldiers continued to murder POWs and unarmed civilians. The two defendants certainly did not have Yamashita's excuse for failing to know about war crimes, much less act to prevent them. It follows that Imamura and Okazaki's claim that they made genuine efforts to prevent war crimes rings hollow given the cessation of hostilities on Java after mid-March 1942.

As for specific conclusions, it is clear that the difference between the conviction in *Shoji* and the acquittals in *Maruyama, Imamura*, and *Okazaki* was the location of the defendants in the chain of command, and a firm belief by the judges in both trials that very senior level commanders were less likely to know about, or suspect, that war crimes were being committed by their subordinates. The court seems to have reasoned that Shoji, as the commander of a 5,000 soldier unit, was physically close enough to combat operations that he would have had frequent contact with his front-line troops. This physical proximity, combined with Shoji's relatively low place in the chain-of-command (at least when compared to a division or army-level commander) meant that he knew about or at least had reason to suspect that war crimes were being committed by his men in West Java.

As for Maruyama, Imamura, and Okazaki, their commands during the invasion and early days of the occupation of the NEI were relatively large in terms of personnel. Maruyama's 2nd Division had an operational strength of about 14,000 men. Imamura's 16th Army consisted of three divisions (the 2nd, 38th, and 48th) and other smaller detachments, totaling some 97,800 soldiers.[40] This meant that Imamura and Okazaki, located as they were at 16th Army General Headquarters, were physically distant from the front lines during combat operations and, even when the fighting had stopped, were out of contact with day-to-day military operations in smaller subordinate units. Major de Groot and his fellow judges seem to have believed that this physical distance meant all three accuseds were less likely to have knowledge of misconduct, as opposed to the commander of a 5,000 man unit.[41]

Additionally, in terms of the chain-of-command, Imamura and Okazaki, and even Maruyama, were at the top of hierarchical pyramids that had numerous platoon, company, battalion, and regimental commanders between them and the

[40] For more on the personnel, equipment, and organization of the 16th Army and its subordinate units, see Willem Remmelink (ed. and trans.), *The Invasion of the Dutch East Indies* (Leiden University Press 2015) 69–102.

[41] In *United States v. von Leeb et al.* ("the *High Command* case"), the court adopted similar reasoning when it acknowledged that because modern warfare is "highly decentralized ... a commander cannot know everything that happens within the command, so the prosecution must prove knowledge." See Solis (n. 1) 423, quoting *United States v. von Leeb*, XI T.W.C. Before the Nuremberg Military Tribunals under Control Council Law No. 10 (Government Printing Office 1950) 509.

Japanese troops who were pulling rifle triggers and firing artillery rounds at KNIL and other Allied personnel—and committing war crimes.

A final note: At least one of the stated reasons for finding Imamura and Okazaki not guilty does stand up to scrutiny. The idea that "international views" and exposure to Western civilization made the two accuseds more credible is nonsense, and that the NEI judges would allow this opinion to influence their decision is disappointing. Long before World War II, men of culture and sophistication committed or allowed the commission of unspeakable crimes against humanity. De Groot and his fellow judges knew that intellectuals and sophisticates in national socialist Germany had only recently implemented a "Final Solution" that murdered millions and millions of Jews, gypsies and Slavs. In fact, given the prevalence of *Bushido* and the "Asia for the Asians" ideology in the Imperial Army, and the behavior of Japanese troops in China in the 1930s, it would have been reasonable for de Groot and his fellow judges to conclude that Imamura and Okazaki should have suspected that the commission of war crimes would be an integral part of Japanese combat operations on Java and elsewhere. Certainly, the conduct of Shoji's brigade in the early days of the invasion should have put the two most senior defendants on notice.

Finally, the fact that Imamura had already been convicted by an Australian military court on the basis of command responsibility should have caused the Dutch judges to think twice about their decisions to acquit the two defendants. All of this means that perhaps the greatest significance of the *Prosecutor v. Imamura and Okazaki* is that it stands as an example of a trial in which the facts were arguably similar to those in *Yamashita*, and yet the military tribunal reached a very different result when applying the command responsibility standard.

A postscript on Imamura. He served the ten-year sentence imposed on him by the Australian court at Sugamo Prison, in Japan. Released in 1954, he died in 1968.

Command responsibility continues to be part of the modern law of armed conflict, with the "knew or should have known" standard for liability being the rule today.[42] The legislation creating both the International Criminal Tribunal for the Former Yugoslavia (ICTY) and International Criminal Tribunal for Rwanda (ICTR) provided the following guidance on command responsibility:

> The fact that ... [crimes were] committed by a subordinate does not relieve his superior of criminal responsibility if he knew or had reason to know that the subordinate was about to commit such acts or had done so and the superior failed to take the necessary and reasonable measures to prevent such acts or punish the perpetrators thereof.[43]

More recently, the ICTY has addressed command responsibility in a number of cases, with *Prosecutor v. Halilović*, decided in 2005, being one of the most

[42] Robert Cryer, "Then and Now: Command Responsibility, the Tokyo Tribunal and Modern International Criminal Law," in Kristen Sellers (ed.), *Trials for International Crimes in Asia* (Cambridge University Press 2016) 55. See also n. 10 above.

[43] ICTY art. 7(3),; ICTR art. 6(3).

important. In this decision, which tacitly affirms the judgments of World War II tribunals described here, the ICTY ruled that command responsibility "is responsibility for an omission" because a commander is responsible "for the *failure* to perform an act required by international law" (emphasis added). In the view of the ICTY, a commander is guilty for the acts of his subordinates not as an aider or abettor. Rather, he is guilty where he either knows about the acts, or had reason to know about them, and failed to act to either prevent the acts or punish them.[44]

The International Criminal Court (ICC) decision in *Prosecutor v. Bemba* illustrates how firmly rooted is the concept that commanders must be accountable for the misconduct of their troops. Jean-Pierre Bemba Gombo was the commander-in-chief of the Armée de Libération du Congo. Soldiers under his command committed numerous acts of pillage, rape, and murder against civilians. The court unanimously decided, beyond a reasonable doubt, that Bemba knew that forces under his effective authority and control were committing or about to commit these crimes. Consequently, they found him guilty of the war crimes because he had failed to exercise control over his troops properly. In June 2016, Bemba was sentenced to eighteen years' imprisonment.[45]

The temporary courts-martial decisions in *Shoji, Maruyama, Imamura*, and *Okazaki* demonstrate that the Dutch not only appreciated that command responsibility was a respected battlefield concept, but one that required prosecution when a commander's failure to control his subordinates resulting in those subordinates violating the law of war. This was because the Dutch—like the other Allies—understood that unless a senior military leader is held criminally liable for failing to control the members of his command, there is a greatly reduced incentive for that commander to emphasize obedience to the law of war. Prosecuting these four Japanese general officers, however, signaled that a commander who neglected to give orders requiring that POWs and civilians be treated humanely, or who failed to take disciplinary action against his subordinates who committed war crimes, did so at great peril.

Regardless of whether they found the defendants guilty or not, the NEI military judges were making legal decisions that were not only in accordance with the law of armed conflict, but were consistent with the legal decisions in other Allied war crimes tribunals. This is an important point. While it is true that the *Yamashita* "knew or must have known" standard is different from the "knew or at least had reasonable suspicion" standard utilized by the Dutch in the Indies, the important takeaway is that the Dutch had a rational legal test for holding senior officers accountable for their failures as commanders.

Finally, it is clear that, in applying the command responsibility standard, the NEI judges were meticulous when considering evidence of wrongdoing and genuinely tried to give each Japanese defendant a full and fair trial.

[44] *Prosecutor v. Halilović*, IT-01-48-T (November 16, 2005).

[45] *Prosecutor v. Jean-Pierre Bemba*, Case No. ICC-01/05—1/08 (March 21, 2016); David P. Stewart (ed.), "International Decisions," *American Journal of International Law* (July 2016) 526–33.

11

An Unfortunate Sideshow

The Trials of Collaborators

There have always been men and women who collaborate—provide aid, comfort, and support—to the enemy in time of war. History shows that these collaborators have a variety of reasons for their actions. They may support the enemy because they accept his ideology, or because, believing that the enemy ultimately will be victorious, they desire to be on the "winning side." Some collaborate to obtain better living conditions or privileges for themselves or their families. Finally, some collaborate simply to obtain remuneration.[1]

During World War II, there was collaboration between the Germans and the Dutch in the occupied Netherlands. Initially, more than a few Dutch citizens were persuaded that the overwhelming victory of the Wehrmacht in the early summer of 1940 meant that Hitler's Third Reich would dominate Europe for years to come, and that they must learn to live—and cooperate—with it. Additionally, some found fascism attractive as an ideology and believed that as the Dutch were a "Germanic" people, the Netherlands would have a place in Hitler's "Greater Germanic State." This certainly accounts for the increased strength of the Dutch fascist party, the National Socialist Movement (Dutch: *Nationaal-Socialistsiche Beweging* (N.S.B.)) during the war, although N.S.B. membership never exceeded 103,000, about 1.25 percent of the population of the Netherlands.[2] Inspired by German propaganda to join with them in the fight against Bolshevism, between 22,000 and 25,000 Dutchmen (most of whom were not N.S.B. members) also

[1] Collaboration with the enemy was a problem for all the Allies in World War II. After the end of the fighting in Europe, the French arrested more than 350,000 men and women for collaboration, tried 125,000, and convicted 100,000; 26,000 served prison sentences. See Richard Vinen, *The Unfree French* (Allen Lane 2006) 342–3. The Belgians deprived some 43,000 collaborators of their civil and political rights (including the right to vote). They also sentenced about 3,000 Belgians to death and executed 242 for aiding the Germans in World War II. See Rolf Michaelis, *Belgians in the Waffen-SS* (Schiffer Publishing 2012) 15. Even Americans willingly joined with the enemy to fight against the United States, with the most infamous being U.S. Army Air Force fighter pilot Martin James MONTI. In October 1944, First Lieutenant Monti stole a Lockheed F-5E Lightning, flew it to Axis-occupied Milan, Italy, and then delivered both the aircraft and himself to the Germans. Monti then joined the Waffen-SS and served as an SS-Untersturmfuhrer (second lieutenant) until the end of the war. See Ron Soodalter, "A Yank in the SS," *Military History* (January 2017) 40–7.

[2] Gerhard Hirschfeld, *Nazi Rule and Dutch Collaboration* (Berg Publishers 1988) 285. During World War II, the population of the Netherlands was 8.2 million.

Military Trials of War Criminals in the Netherlands East Indies 1946–1949, Fred L. Borch.

collaborated by joining the Waffen-SS and fighting alongside the Germans during the war, mostly on the Eastern Front.

While the overwhelming majority of Dutch men and women were opposed to German rule during the war, Dutch authorities nevertheless conducted "mass arrests" of "between 120,000 and 150,000" collaborators after the restoration of Dutch authority in May 1945.[3] Thousands were interned for as long as two years.[4] Dutch authorities also prosecuted some of these collaborators for treason and related offenses, with the trial (and execution) of Dutch N.S.B. leader Anton MUSSERT by a Special Court (Dutch: *Bijzonder Gerechtshof*) being the most high-profile prosecution.[5]

When Dutch authorities returned to power in the Netherlands East Indies (NEI) in 1945, they too faced the reality that thousands of Indonesians had collaborated with the Japanese. Although disappointing, this collaboration was foreseeable in light of the "Asia for the Asians" ideology trumpeted by the Japanese and the resulting belief among many Indonesians that the Japanese would help them in their struggle for independence from the Dutch. Men like Sukarno certainly fell into this category.[6] Additionally, like the Dutch in the occupied Netherlands, there were more than a few Indonesians who believed that the crushing defeat of the Royal Netherlands Indies Army (Dutch: *Koninklijk Nederlandsch Indisch Leger* (KNIL)) in 1942 meant that the Japanese were in the NEI for the foreseeable future and that Indonesians must cooperate with them if they were to survive.[7]

This chapter, however, does not focus on Indonesian collaborators. Rather, it focuses on five war crimes trials of Europeans charged with aiding the Japanese during the occupation of the NEI. These military prosecutions were permitted because, as explained in Chapter 3, temporary courts-martial had *in personam* jurisdiction not only over Japanese war criminals but also over Europeans, Eurasians, Chinese, Arabs, and Indonesians who had committed war-related offenses, including providing comfort, help, or support to the Japanese enemy. Of the five proceedings examined here, three (*Prosecutor v. Van Dienst*, *Prosecutor v. Duursma*,

[3] ibid 321.

[4] Hendrick C. Verton, *In the Fire of the Eastern Front* (Helion Publishing 2005) 244–5.

[5] Born in 1894 in Werkendam in the Netherlands, Anton Adiraan Mussert was the son of an elementary school teacher. He completed his examinations at the Delft Institute of Science and Technology in 1918 and became an engineer with the Utrecht provincial Department of Public Works. In 1931, Mussert founded the N.S.B. and the party gained considerable public support in a short period of time. Dutch middle-class voters were deeply disappointed with the existing government's failures to deal with the mass unemployment and social distress of the 1930s and consequently were attracted by the N.S.B.'s promise of an authoritarian and corporate state. After the German occupation of the Netherlands, Mussert collaborated extensively with the Germans, and styled himself as the "Führer of the Dutch People." On May 7, 1945, Mussert was arrested in the N.S.B.'s headquarters in The Hague. He was condemned to death in December 1945 and executed on the first anniversary of his arrest. See Hirschfeld, *Nazi Rule and Dutch Collaboration* (n.2) 310.

[6] For more on Sukarno's collaboration with the Japanese see the discussion of his involvement with the *rōmusha* (forced laborers) in Chapter 5.

[7] For more on Indonesian collaboration with the Japanese see Taufik Abdullah, "Nationalist Activities during the Japanese Period," in Peter Post *et al.* (eds.), *Encyclopedia of Indonesia in the Pacific War* (Brill 2010) 113–32.

and *Prosecutor v. Maseland*) resulted in convictions, while two (*Prosecutor v. De Haan-De Vries* and *Prosecutor v. Banning*) were acquittals. While all five prosecutions began as temporary courts-martial, only three were completed at that level; judgment in the other two cases came from the Military High Court in Batavia.

Prosecutor v. William Josias van Dienst

On April 22, 1948, the temporary court-martial sitting in Batavia began hearing evidence against 50-year-old William Josias van Dienst.[8] Described in the record of trial as a Buddhist priest and author, he was charged with the war crime of aiding the enemy. The gist of van Dienst's crime was that, although he was a Dutch citizen, born in The Hague in June 1897, he had supported enemy propaganda efforts by working in Tokyo as a radio announcer for the Japanese Broadcasting Corporation between December 8, 1941 and November 1944. These actions were "in time of war" and "aided the Japanese enemy" by "promoting" and "spreading" Japanese propaganda. The prosecutor asked the court to find van Dienst guilty as charged and sentence him to six years' imprisonment.

The facts developed by the military tribunal showed that van Dienst had traveled from the NEI to Japan as early as 1936 and had started working in 1938 as a news announcer in Dutch-language radio programs conducted by the Broadcasting Corporation of Japan. After the outbreak of hostilities between Japan and the Allies (the Netherlands declared war on Japan on December 8, 1941), van Dienst's Japanese boss had offered him the opportunity to remain in this radio job. While he apparently could have left Japan and returned to the NEI, van Dienst instead elected to stay in Tokyo and was employed as a news announcer until November 1944, when the Japanese disbanded the Dutch-language section of their radio operations and his job was terminated. Although the record of trial does not reveal how van Dienst came to be present on Java in 1948, he must have been repatriated from U.S.-occupied Japan to the NEI at the request of Dutch authorities, as the record states that van Dienst had been in pre-trial detention since September 14, 1945, and in Batavia's Struiswijk prison since June 9, 1946.

The prosecutor in *van Dienst* had transcripts of radio broadcasts made by the accused on behalf of the Japanese and the trial record identifies with great specificity the words and phrases that supported the charge against him. In early December 1941, van Dienst had broadcast the following words: "Why did little Holland declare war on Japan? We have not taken this war declaration seriously and threw it in the trash [can] since the Netherlands Indies with its puny Army of 100,000 men can do nothing against the powerful Imperial Army." During this same time period, the defendant also said: "Japan is conducting war not to expand

[8] *Prosecutor v. William Josias van Dienst*, Temporary Court-Martial, Batavia, No. 16/1948, decided April 24, 1948; fiat of execution, May 12, 1948.

area but to bring prosperity to Greater Asia and raise consciousness in areas where the Japanese come."

From the end of December 1941 or in the month of January 1942, or both, van Dienst also encouraged Indonesians to ignore the Netherlands declaration of war against Japan and instead provide aid to the Japanese because Japan was conquering the NEI to establish a "new Asia."

In early March, as fighting between NEI forces and the Japanese invader continued, van Dienst aided the enemy by broadcasting the following: "Soldiers of the KNIL, you cannot hold out against all-powerful Imperial Army. Give up and count on the mercy of the Japanese Army" and "Give up. You cannot win against us. So think hard about what you are doing. It will be good for the Netherlands East Indies [if you give up]. Otherwise, it will be a disaster for the Netherlands Indies."

Prior to the surrender of the colonial authorities in March 1942, van Dienst also broadcast the following, which the prosecutor alleged had undermined the morale of both the military and civilians inhabitants: "You have heard what I have said to the Governor General [Van Starkenborgh]. If he will not willingly give up, then it is up to you to force the government to surrender."

Finally, after the collapse of Dutch resistance, and the capitulation to the Japanese, the prosecution alleged that the accused did everything he could to convince his listeners that the Japanese Army had conquered the Netherlands Indies in a "few days" because it was "invincible" and "irresistible." He continued this collaboration by telling his Dutch-language listeners that now was the time to support the Japanese because they had come to the Indies "without any bad intent" and because working with the Japanese was in the best interests of all NEI citizens.

Van Dienst and his defense counsel did not deny that he had worked as a radio broadcaster for the Japanese. But they raised a number of defenses to the charge. First, van Dienst argued that he qualified for the general amnesty proclaimed by Lieutenant Governor-General Hubertus J. van Mook in May 1947. The military judges quickly rejected this defense on two grounds. First, the court decided that van Dienst's crimes were not covered by the amnesty provisions and that, second, van Mook's amnesty was limited to offenses committed in the NEI. Since van Dienst had committed his crimes in Japan, the amnesty proclamation did not apply to his case.

Van Dienst's second defense was that he had remained in Tokyo chiefly because he was afraid that if he declined to work as a radio announcer, he would be subject to arrest and mistreatment by the Japanese police or *Kempeitai*. Van Dienst told the military judges that he had a wife and four young children and that while he knew he would have to answer for his actions after the war was over, he felt he had no choice but to protect his wife and children.

The accused's third defense was that he had been but a reader of Japanese news and commentary, and had taken no part in authoring propaganda. He acknowledged that he had used his knowledge of Japanese and Dutch to improve the grammatical quality of the Dutch language used in the broadcasts, but denied having written or otherwise composing any radio news or commentary.

Lieutenant Colonels J. la Rivière and K. L. H. M. van der Vijver and Major L. F. de Groot, the three judges considering the evidence against van Dienst, found him guilty as charged. But instead of imposing the six years requested by the prosecutor, the judges sentenced the defendant to three years in jail. The tribunal justified the lesser sentence on several grounds. First, van Dienst had not created the Dutch language broadcasts; the court accepted his claim that, as a radio announcer, he was simply an "instrument" of the Japanese propaganda machine, and consequently was less culpable. Second, the judges acknowledged that van Dienst's concerns for his family's safety were reasonable; had he refused to work for the Broadcasting Corporation of Japan, his wife and his children might have been tortured or otherwise mistreated. The judges also noted that van Dienst had been "honest" in his dealings with the court and that he had already spent nearly three years in pre-trial confinement. Consequently, the three-year sentence imposed by the military tribunal meant that van Dienst was freed shortly after being convicted on April 24, 1948. The fiat of execution was issued on May 12, 1948.

The *van Dienst* court-martial illustrates that the Dutch authorities were convinced that propaganda played a key role in undermining the war effort, especially in the early days of the Japanese invasion. In this belief, they were not alone. Witness the high-profile prosecutions of Captain Norman BAILLIE-STEWART and William JOYCE (colloquially known as "Lord Haw-Haw"), who were prosecuted for high treason by the British for their roles in broadcasting German propaganda during World War II.[9] Similarly, the United States prosecuted second-generation Japanese-American Ivo Ikuko TOGURI ("Tokyo Rose") for treason for her radio broadcasts of Japanese propaganda during the war in the Asiatic-Pacific Theater.[10]

Prosecutor v. Douwe Duursma

On June 18, 1948, the High Military Court in Batavia found Mr. Douwe Duursma[11] guilty of "giving aid to the enemy in time of war." This was a high-profile trial by court-martial because, prior to the Japanese occupation, Duursma had been a prominent member of the Padang community as the chairman (Dutch: *voorzitter*) of the local district council (Dutch: *Landraad*). Additionally,

[9] Captain Baillie-Stewart was the original Lord Haw-Haw. Imprisoned in the Tower of London, he was released from jail in 1949 and died of a heart attack in 1966, at the age of 57. William Joyce, also known as Lord Haw-Haw (his broadcasts always began with the words, "Germany calling, Germany calling") was found guilty of high treason for his role in broadcasting German propaganda. Sentenced to death, he was hanged in London's Wandsworth prison in January 1946. See Rebecca West, *The New Meaning of Treason* (Viking Press, 1964) 1–133.

[10] Found guilty of treason in U.S. District Court in 1949, Ivo Toguri was sentenced to ten years' imprisonment. President Gerald Ford pardoned her in 1977. See Yasuhide Kawashima, *The Tokyo Rose Case: Treason on Trial* (University Press of Kansas 2013).

[11] *Prosecutor v. Douwe Duursma*, Military High Court of the Netherlands East Indies, Batavia (June 11, 1948).

Duursma had been set free after earlier proceedings at the temporary court-martial in Batavia had adjourned after finding insufficient evidence to support the charge against him, and so his subsequent trial and conviction at the Military High Court increased public interest in his case.

Born in Rijperkerk, the Netherlands, in April 1897, Duursma was living on Sumatra in the town of Padang when war broke out in the Pacific in December 1941. According to the record of trial in his court-martial, he remained free after the surrender of the NEI government, but was interned in April 1942 in a Japanese camp near Padang. With him in this camp was a fellow European named Willem VAN DIJK, who formerly had been a police chief on Sumatra's west coast.

The facts developed at Duursma's trial were that van Dijk had set up a secret organization shortly after the KNIL's surrender in March 1942. Van Dijk's goal was to have this organization assist the Allied landings that he and others believed would soon occur—and would defeat the Japanese invaders. Van Dijk was helped in these organization efforts by several Eurasian, Ambonese and Manadonese men, all of whom had been former KNIL soldiers.

In June 1942, van Dijk and Duursma were taken from the internment camp to the Japanese officers' club in Padang, where they were put to work as laborers maintaining the grounds. It was here that van Dijk made contact with an ex-KNIL sergeant named Jacob "Pat" PATTINAMA, who apparently had been ordered by a KNIL officer in Medan to set up a clandestine resistance organization in Padang; this officer probably was acting under orders from Major General R. F. Overakker, whose efforts to create "V-groups" are explained in detail in *Prosecutor v. Maseland*, below.

In any event, now that van Dijk was outside the internment camp, Pattinama visited him regularly and updated van Dijk on the clandestine work that had been accomplished since March. Pattinama also acted as a go-between and smuggled letters to and from van Dijk. Finally, at some point Pattinama delivered a revolver to van Dijk, although just what the latter was supposed to do with this weapon is unclear.

Although they were both Dutchmen—and were fellow internees—van Dijk initially did not trust Duursma. The latter had made statements that led van Dijk to view him as pro-Japanese in his leanings and consequently van Dijk did not share with Duursma the details of his early meetings with Pattinama. But Duursma had witnessed these meetings, since he was standing less than four meters away when van Dijk and Pattinama held their whispered conversations.

Despite his misgivings, van Dijk ultimately confided in Duursma to some extent and, either because of what van Dijk revealed to him or because of what he had managed to learn by overhearing subsequent conversations between van Dijk and Pattinama, Duursma knew that Pattinama and his comrades were operating a clandestine organization involving as many of 150 Ambonese.

According to the Military High Court prosecutor, Duursma had reported to the *Kempeitai* in November 1942 that van Dijk was conducting secret meetings with Pattinama, and involved in letter smuggling. This denunciation led to the arrest of van Dijk, Pattinama, and another ex-KNIL sergeant by the name of VAN DER

TORREN, and all the members of the organization. Van Dijk, van der Torren, and Pattinama were taken to Singapore, where they were tried by a Japanese military court. All three were sentenced to death on April 22, 1943.[12] They were executed the following year.

At his trial, Duursma denied that he was guilty of any war crime, and insisted that he had betrayed no one, much less aided the enemy. Unfortunately for him, there was sufficient evidence that proved otherwise. The most damning proof came from the Japanese. First, there was a written statement from HASHIMOTO, who had been the head of the Japanese *Kempeitai* in Padang in late 1942. During questioning by an investigator gathering evidence for the war crimes trials, Hashimoto had revealed that a Lieutenant UTSUMI, the head of Army intelligence in the area, had told him that a Dutch informant had revealed to him the existence of Pattinama's anti-Japanese organization. While Utsumi had not given Hashimoto the name of the informant, he had described the Dutchman as the former head of a local court. The tribunal concluded that, based on all the evidence in the proceedings, this must be Duursma since he had, in fact, been the chairman of the local district council and in that position, had also acted as a quasi-judicial official.

The second piece of Japanese proof was the written decision from the Japanese military court that had condemned van Dijk, van der Torren, Pattinama, and others to death on April 22, 1943. That decision identified Duursma as having been a witness in the proceedings. Presumably this was a written, signed declaration, since the case was heard in Singapore.

The tribunal also accepted as trustworthy the sworn written statements of Messrs. MONTI, TOFOHR, Gin Toen TJOU, SALAMONY, and LASAMAHU, all of whom stated that van Dijk had told them, prior to his death, that Duursma had betrayed the existence of the secret resistance organization to the Japanese.

The Military High Court found Duursma guilty of aiding the enemy by betraying van Dijk, Pattinama, and others to the *Kempeitai*. Mr. J. C. BERENSCHOT, Major General M. E. A. VAN GOOR, and Head Administrative Officer H. J. G. VAN GIESSEN, the president and members of the court, respectively, sentenced Duursma to eighteen-year imprisonment, with credit for the time spent in pre-trial confinement between December 24, 1945 and December 1, 1947. The court also ordered that Duursma be taken immediately into custody to begin serving his prison sentence. Like many defendants serving prison sentences in the Indies, Duursma's fortunes changed with Indonesian independence; Sukarno ordered his release in 1950.[13]

Duursma's involvement in the "Padang Betrayal Case" (Dutch: *Padang verraad zaak*) is not entirely clear, and this is reflected in his sentence. The three Military High Court judges found sufficient evidence to support a finding that he was guilty of the war crime of aiding the enemy, but the court seems to have accepted

[12] Louis de Jong (with an Introduction by Jeroen Kemperman), *The Collapse of a Colonial Society: The Dutch in Indonesia during the Second World War* (KILTV Press 2002) 194; see also Esther Zwinkels, *Het Overakker-complot* (Spectrum, 2011) 183.

[13] See Zwinkels, *Het Overakker-complot* (n. 12) 254. See also Chapter 12, Aftermath, infra.

that there were others who had betrayed the resistance plotters to the Japanese. Had there not been this shared culpability, the High Military Court likely would have imposed a much heavier sentence.[14]

Prosecutor v. P. H. J. M. Maseland

On October 29, 1946, Head Police Commissioner Petrus "Piet" Hardewijnus Johannes Marie Maseland was arrested and placed in pre-trial confinement in Medan.[15] Initially, he was housed in a cell measuring just one by two meters, and a sign with the words WAR CRIMINAL was placed above his cell door. His subsequent trial by court-martial is far and away the most significant—and most controversial—of the collaboration prosecutions conducted in the NEI.

Mr. P.R. VETTER, the prosecutor assigned to the temporary court-martial in Medan, began interviewing witnesses and gathering evidence almost immediately. But the criminal investigation moved at a glacial pace and, although Maseland wrote three times to the Prosecutor General in Batavia requesting that the judicial proceedings against him be accelerated, it was not until September 1947 that Maseland himself was formally questioned by Vetter—eleven months after he had been jailed.

On April 27, 1948, Major General Pieter SCHOLTON, the senior commanding officer in Medan, referred Maseland's case to the temporary court-martial in Medan and on June 21, 1948, the tribunal formally began proceedings against him. A new prosecutor, Mr. J.B. de BEAUFORT, charged Maseland with one count of voluntary service with the enemy (by working for the *Kempeitai* during the occupation) and three counts giving aid to the enemy through the betrayal of persons (by identifying twenty-two NEI citizens as involved in anti-Japanese activities during the occupation).

Prosecutor v. Maseland was the most high-profile case involving a collaborator, and there was intense public interest in the proceedings, if for no other reason than Maseland was a high ranking NEI police official with more than twenty-five years of government service. Additionally, while KNIL prisoners of war and Dutch civilians suffered horribly during the Japanese occupation, Piet Maseland not only had worked for *Kempeitai* but, as a result of this service, he and his family had avoided internment and instead had enjoyed a comfortable lifestyle that stood in sharp contrast to the poor living conditions of their fellow Europeans. Perhaps most importantly, while working with the *Kempeitai*, Maseland provided some information about soldiers and civilians involved in the so-called "Overakker Conspiracy" (Dutch: *Overakker Complot*). His statements were later used by the

[14] A Moluccan named NOERSALE was identified by the tribunal as another person who betrayed van Dijk and his fellow conspirators. See Zwinkels, *Het Overakker-complot* (n. 12) 134.

[15] *Prosecutor v. P. H. J. M. Maseland*, Temporary Court-Martial, Medan (June 1948); *Prosecutor v. P. H. J. M. Maseland*, High Military Court, Batavia, March 1949; A. G. Vrouwmans, *De Zaak 'Maseland'* (unpublished 1962); see Zwinkels, *Het Overakker-Complot* (n. 12) 254–61.

Japanese in their prosecution of two high-ranking Dutch officers, Major General Roelof T. Overakker and Colonel George F. V. Gosenson. Since both officers were sentenced to death, and later executed by the Japanese, more than a few in the East Indies blamed Maseland, at least in part, for their deaths—yet another reason that his trial for treason-related war crimes was of great interest. Finally, Head Police Commissioner Maseland was the only European to be sentenced to death by a NEI war crimes tribunal. While he ultimately escaped this death sentence, the strong feelings aroused by Maseland's cooperation with the enemy changed his life forever.

Born in Enschede, the Netherlands, on October 13, 1895, Piet Maseland graduated from high school (Gymnasium), completed mandatory military service, and then completed the police school in Amersfort. In 1918, he sailed from Holland to the NEI, where he entered government service as a police commissioner.

According to the facts developed at Maseland's trial, he did excellent work as a young policeman. In 1929, after a decade working as a detective in Semarang, Medan, and Batavia, and investigating cases in which Japanese criminals were involved, Maseland began learning Japanese. Presumably Maseland believed that a knowledge of the language would aid him in future police work.

After the capitulation of Dutch forces in the Netherlands in May 1940, now Head Police Commissioner Maseland (he had been promoted to this high rank in 1937) was stationed in Medan. In December 1941, after the Japanese attack on the Philippines and Hawaii, and in anticipation of a possible attack on Sumatra, Maseland was appointed the leader of a 1200-man military "field police" unit located in Medan.

On March 8, 1942, the main island of Java fell to the Japanese. Major General Overakker became the senior commander on Sumatra. According Maseland, Overakker contacted him by telephone on March 11 and appointed him as a lieutenant colonel, although no written orders or other proof confirming this appointment have ever been located.[16] General Overakker also told Maseland that he, Overakker, was withdrawing his KNIL forces in the face of an expected Japanese attack on north Sumatra, but that Maseland was to remain on duty in Medan and gather information of value to the Army.

On March 13, 1942, Japanese forces reached Medan. On his own initiative, Maseland went by automobile to meet the advancing enemy troops. He addressed the Japanese soldiers in Japanese and told them that Medan was an "open city." Shortly thereafter, although Maseland was under house arrest (on the first day of the occupation, the Japanese ordered all Europeans to be interned in their homes), *Kempeitai* Lieutenant Colonel YOKOTA began releasing Maseland for various tasks, chiefly involving the translation of Japanese documents into Dutch and vice versa.

By the middle of 1942, Kempeitai officials had sufficient trust in both Maseland and his abilities that they tasked him with investigating a black-marketing case

[16] See Zwinkels, *Het Overakker-complot* (n. 12) 106.

involving rice and reports of suspicious nighttime lights that might indicate signaling of some sort. He solved both cases, and earned enough respect from the Japanese that, by August 1942, Maseland was working in the office of the "Gunseibu" (military government) in Medan. In that office, he continued to translate documents and also compiled a Japanese-Dutch dictionary.

Maseland was friendly with his Japanese co-workers and one soldier, Sergeant Major Kiyoshi SATO, visited Maseland on a regular basis in the latter's home. In return for his service to the Japanese, Maseland was permitted to remain in this home, with his wife and children. He also had an automobile at his disposal, which gave him considerable freedom of movement. By the end of 1942, Maseland was increasingly viewed by the Japanese in Medan as a valuable asset—and by his fellow Dutch citizens as a collaborator.

During the months that Head Police Commissioner Maseland was working with the Gunseibu in Medan, Major General Overakker, Colonel Gosenson (who had been the territorial commander in Aceh prior to the surrender), and all KNIL soldiers who had been captured on north and east Sumatra in March 1942, were imprisoned in a camp at Belawan, located about fifteen miles north of Medan. In mid-May, believing that landings by Allied forces on Sumatra were imminent—landings that would liberate the Indies from the Japanese—Overakker and Gosenson formed secret resistance organizations. These organizations, called "V-groups" (V for Victory), would aid the expected invasion by collecting military intelligence, manufacturing weapons, and undermine the Japanese "in any way possible."[17] In retrospect, the belief in imminent landings seems farfetched but at the time, broadcasts from Radio Melbourne and Radio San Francisco convinced Overakker and Gosenson that the Allies would be arriving "on Java and elsewhere in the archipelago, not in a few years but in a few months, and perhaps in just a few weeks."[18]

Since Overakker believed that he was unlikely to remain on Sumatra (he suspected that the Japanese would transfer him to another location, perhaps to Burma), he signed an order on May 18, 1942, in which he selected KNIL Reserve Captains Klaas TEN VELDE and Cornelis WOUDENBERG as the leaders of this resistance. By July 1942, when the Japanese had, in fact, removed Overakker and Gosenson from the Belawan camp and transported them first to Singapore and then to Formosa, the V-groups were making bladed weapons, and gathering revolvers and machine guns. They also were collecting Dutch East Indies money and amassing intelligence about Japanese troop numbers and movements. The V-groups were aided in their resistance efforts by Ambonese, Manadonese, and Timorese ex-soldiers who, having served in the KNIL, remained loyal to the Dutch crown. To identify themselves to each other, the members of these secret organizations used a red handkerchief or a white feather as a sign that they were members.[19]

[17] See de Jong, *The Collapse of a Colonial Society* (n. 12) 190.

[18] ibid 89. See Chapter 2 n. 1.

[19] ibid 192.

In March 1943, some eight months after Overakker and Gosenson had left Sumatra, the *Kempeitei* arrested a former KNIL sergeant major and learned from their interrogation of him about the V-groups. As a result, the Japanese arrested every Indonesian ex-KNIL soldier in possession of a red handkerchief or a white feather. During this manhunt, a second ex-KNIL sergeant major fell into the hands of the *Kempeitai*, and he soon revealed that Major General Overakker and Colonel Gosenson were the organizers of this anti-Japanese conspiracy, and that they had organized it while POWs in Belawan.

In August 1943, Overakker and Gosenson were returned to Sumatra for questioning. Overakker was interrogated from August 18-20; Gosenson on August 24. As Dutch historian Dr. Esther Zwinkels explains in *Het Overakker-complot*, the only comprehensive history of the conspiracy, the Japanese were convinced that they had uncovered a wide-ranging, extensive, and organized conspiracy against them. Overakker, however, insisted during interrogations that what he had ordered on May 18, 1942 amounted to much less. As he put it:

> What I have planned was not as basically systematic as you state. To Capt. Ten Velde, Woudenberg, and others, I only ordered that they keep an eye on the situation, collect information and submit [it] at the same time of allied counterattack, and to cooperate therewith through all ways and means, and did not have any concrete plans.[20]

The legal problem for Overakker was that, having surrendered and accepted prisoner of war status, he had violated the Geneva Conventions of 1929. As far as the *Kempeitai* were concerned, creating V-groups violated Article 45, which required a prisoner to "obey current laws, regulations and orders of the Forces of the country by which he is held as a POW." As the Japanese saw it, Overakker, Gosenson, ten Velde, Woudenberg and others in these V-groups had violated the law, and deserved severe punishment.

Interestingly, Japan had signed the 1929 Geneva Conventions, but not ratified them, so it might be argued that it was wrong for the *Kempeitai* to insist that Japan had been wronged by the "Overakker Conspiracy." Since the Netherlands had both signed and ratified the conventions, and the Japanese government had announced in 1942 that it would follow the conventions, this argument is not persuasive. Not surprisingly, an Allied War Crimes Investigation Team later concluded that Overakker had violated international law in organizing clandestine resistance groups.[21]

As the *Kempeitai* investigated the "Overakker Conspiracy," they interviewed those accused of being part of the criminal plan, and others who might have information about it. On September 12, 1943, *Kempeitai* Lieutenant Haruji HISAMATSU questioned Piet Maseland about his knowledge of anti-Japanese activities. Maseland told Hisamatsu that he had "heard something" about the "Overakker Conspiracy" but knew no details. But Maseland did identify twenty

[20] See Zwinkels, *Het Overakker-complot* (n. 12) 159.

[21] "From our initial investigations, it was clear that the execution of General Overakker by the Japanese was probably justified." See Zwinkels, *Het Overakker-complot* (n. 12) 233.

individuals involved in "anti-Japanese activities," including Overakker, Gosenson, ten Velde and Woudenberg. Maseland also told his Japanese interrogator that Police Commissioner P. A. J. de BRUIJN, whom Maseland had known since the 1920s, but with whom he had a poor relationship, was involved in the anti-Japanese resistance.[22]

On October 6, 1943, General Toyoji HIRANO, who had been the head of the 25th Army *Kempetai* on Sumatra since November 1942, informed his superiors that the "Overakker Conspiracy" had been "rolled up" and that Maseland's collaboration, at least in part, made this possible. Maseland's testimony was subsequently used in the trials of Overakker, Gosenson, and others. Eighteen months later, on January 9, 1945, Overakker and Gosenson were executed by the Japanese at Fort de Kock. Woutenberg was executed in Singapore on January 31, 1945.[23] De Bruijn was put to death near Medan in November 1944.[24] As for ten Vrede, he died in June 1944 when the *Harikiku Maru*, a Japanese transport ship in which he was travelling as a prisoner of war, was torpedoed and sunk by a British submarine in the Malacca Straits.[25]

In June 1948, when tribunal president Van MEERWIJK and his two military colleagues began hearing evidence in *Prosecutor v. Maseland*, the issue before them was not whether Overakker and his colleagues had violated international law, or whether the Japanese had acted legally in executing these Dutch soldiers. Rather, the question was the extent to which the information Maseland had given the *Kempeitei* was linked to their deaths and how this collaboration should be punished.

With this as background, it was no surprise that Maseland was placed into pretrial confinement in Medan in October 1946. Eleven months later, on September 8, 1947, criminal proceedings began against him in Medan. He was charged with voluntary service to the enemy (*i.e.* the *Kempeitai*) and giving aid to the enemy by betraying persons.

On May 15, 1948, Mr. J. C. H. M. van Meerwijk, the president of the temporary court-martial, opened the proceedings against Maseland; there were two military officers who joined him as part of the three-judge tribunal. On August 23, 1948, the court accepted as evidence the statement of Lieutenant Hisamatsu, who had questioned Maseland about the Overakker plot and anti-Japanese activities on both September 12, and November 13, 1943. While a variety of statements from other witnesses also were introduced into evidence, the statement of Hisamatsu was the key piece of evidence against Piet Maseland. This was true not only because Hisamatsu insisted that Maseland had provided him with information about those involved in General Overakker's conspiracy but also because it was Hisamatsu who told his interrogators that General Hirano had praised Maseland in a written report to his superiors. Since Hirano had committed suicide in August 1945,

[22] See Vrouwmans, *De Zaak Maseland* (n. 15) 8, 33, 67.
[23] See Zwinkels, *Het Overakker-complot* (n. 12) 209. [24] ibid 187–8.
[25] ibid 207–8.

there was no way to question him, much less know the exact wording of any laudatory missive about Maseland. As a result, the temporary court-martial relied on Hisamatsu for its information about the extent of Maseland's collaboration with Japanese authorities.[26]

In early October 1948, the Medan court-martial was prepared to issue its verdict and sentence: guilty and life imprisonment. Before this could occur, van Meerwijk, the tribunal president, was called to a meeting with Major General Scholton in Batavia. Scholton, who had been imprisoned with Overakker and Gosonsen in Formosa, and who believed that Maseland's collaboration was directly responsible for their deaths, wanted the ultimate punishment imposed on Maseland. Van Meerwijk, however, was opposed to this punishment, as he and his two colleagues desired instead to impose imprisonment for life.

On October 14, 1948, the proceedings of the Medan temporary court-martial were adjourned. Since there had never been any public pronouncement of a result in the Medan proceedings, it was a nullity as a matter of law. The following month, at the request of Dr. L. J. M. BEEL, the Crown's High Representative in Batavia, Maseland's case was transferred to the High Military Court.

In March 1949, Maseland was moved from Medan to Batavia. Five months later, in August, the proceedings against him formally began, when the high court began examining the same evidence presented at the temporary court-martial in Medan. The president was Mr. F. H. KEUZENKAMP, with Major General M. E. A. van GOOR and Navy Captain H. J. G. van GIESSEN as members. Because of the sensitivity of case, the court proceedings were held in secret; they were closed to the public.

Although the High Military Court did hear from Maseland himself, it apparently called only a single new witness: A. B. C. ALTING SIEBERG, who had been the jailer in the Soekamoelia prison in Medan. Alting Sieberg not only had been personally involved the anti-Japanese resistance but he told the high court that Maseland had given evidence at the Japanese prosecutions of those involved in the "Overakker Conspiracy."

On October 4, 1949, the court acquitted Maseland of voluntarily serving with the enemy. It found him guilty, however, of aiding the enemy, in violation of Article 124, of the NEI Statutes of September 22, 1945, and sentenced him to death.

But events in *Prosecutor v. Maseland* never went quite as expected. First, despite having convicted him and sentenced him to death, the president of the High Court asked for an official pardon for Maseland. This was denied. In the meantime, articles in Indonesian and Chinese newspapers also came out against the death penalty for Maseland.

On December 27, 1949, while Maseland was pending execution, the United States of Indonesia became a sovereign state. President Sukarno immediately suspended all pending death sentences, which meant that Maseland was spared—at least for the moment.

[26] See Peter Post *et al.* (eds.), *Encyclopedia of Indonesia in the Pacific War* (n. 7) 157.

In September 1950, Sukarno reduced Maseland's punishment to ten years' confinement. Then, on January 27, 1951, at his own request, Piet Maseland became an Indonesian citizen. As a matter of law, however, this resulted in the loss of his Dutch citizenship.

Slightly more than two weeks later, on February 15, 1951, Maseland got very lucky: three Indonesian judges tasked with re-examining his trial concluded that he qualified for the general amnesty previously proclaimed by Lieutenant Governor-General Hubertus J. van Mook in May 1947.[27] While provisions in van Mook's proclamation purported to give amnesty to those who had given aid and comfort to the Japanese during the occupation, NEI authorities insisted at the time that Maseland was ineligible for amnesty because van Mook's proclamation did not apply to existing criminal proceedings. Now, however, three Indonesian judges had interpreted the amnesty provisions otherwise and, as a result of their favorable decision, Piet Maseland was set free.

Maseland had hoped to remain in his new country of citizenship, and obtain employment with the Prosecutor General in Batavia. But there was such heavy opposition to him by Dutch nationals working in the office, that he was refused a job.

In May 1958, Piet Maseland, his wife, and his five children left Indonesia for Europe. His health had deteriorated (he had a mild stroke while imprisoned in Batavia in November 1949) and he wanted to return to the Netherlands. The Dutch government, however, denied him a visa and, given that he no longer held Dutch citizenship, he was denied entry into the land of his birth. Maseland consequently lived in Gronau, on the German side of the Dutch-German border. Piet Maseland never set foot on Dutch soil again; he died in Gronau on August 28, 1958. With Maseland's death, the Dutch government's hard views softened to the extent that Maseland's wife was able to bring his body into the Netherlands and have him buried in Eschede, his birthplace.

In the years since Maseland's trial, Dutch historians have debated the extent to which he collaborated with the Japanese, and whether any such collaboration was responsible for the execution of those involved in the "Overakker Conspiracy." In a lengthy unpublished monograph authored Captain A. G. VROMANS, who had served in the NEI and been a prisoner of war with Overakker and Gosonsen in Formosa, Vromans concluded that the evidence against Maseland was not at all clear. In Vromans' view, Maseland had a character flaw that led him to take the "wrong course" during the Japanese occupation of the Sumatra. Significantly, Vromans discounted both the import of Maseland's statements to the *Kempeitei* in September 1943 and General Hirano's October 1943 report in which Hirano credited Maseland for the successful "rolling up" of the "Overakker Conspiracy."

[27] When Lieutenant Governor-General Hubertus Johannes van Mook (1894–1965) returned to the NEI in October 1945, he realized that it would be impossible to reestablish Dutch colonial authority without negotiating with the leaders of the self-proclaimed Indonesian Republic. Van Mook's May 1947 amnesty was part of his efforts at reconciliation.

Vromans advanced a number of arguments in support of Maseland. First, he concluded that the Japanese were so convinced from evidence already in their possession that General Overakker had established a dangerous and widespread clandestine resistance organization on Sumatra that they likely would have executed him and his co-conspirators without any evidence from Piet Maseland. It follows that Maseland's statements to Hisamatsu were not the proximate cause, much less a necessary condition for the Japanese decision to ruthlessly stamp out the "Overakker Conspiracy."

Second, Vromans argued that Maseland should be given the "benefit of the doubt" because he believed that the key evidence against Maseland was unreliable. Maseland denied that he had been interrogated by Lieutenant Hisamatsu in September 1942 and, since only an English translation of this Japanese interrogation was introduced against Maseland at his trial, Vromans insisted that it impossible to know exactly what Maseland said when being questioned about the Overakker conspiracy. Additionally, as General Hirano's written report lauding Maseland was not introduced in evidence (presumably because it had been sent to Hirano's superiors), and since Hirano was dead, it likewise was not possible to know exactly what Hirano wrote. From an Anglo-American legal perspective, this was a classic case of hearsay, in that Hisamatsu's statement that Hirano credited Maseland with "rolling-up" the Overakker plot was being used to prove the truth of the matter asserted.

Vromans' first argument is sound. Had Maseland provided no information to the *Kempeitai*, the Japanese still most likely would have dealt ruthlessly with Overakker and those whom they believed were members of the conspiracy.

Vromans' views about the evidence against Maseland, however, are problematic. While Vromans had only the English language translation in his possession when he was analyzing the *Maseland* case in 1962, the Medan and Batavia tribunals sitting between 1947 and 1949 had *both* the original Japanese language investigation and the English translation of the *Kempeitai* investigations of the Overakker conspiracy—some 400 pages translated by British War Crimes Investigations Teams.

In the ordinary course of questioning a witness, the Japanese would write down the substance of any statement in block letters, and then have the witness affirm the accuracy of his statement with his thumbprint. Of course, unless the witness could read Japanese, he could not be certain that what had been written was accurate but the judges sitting in both Medan and Batavia were able to see at least one thumb print said to be that of Piet Maseland in the original Japanese documents. At the time, an expert witness confirmed that this was Maseland's left thumbprint. When the original Japanese documents in the Overakker-Gosenson investigation reappeared in March 1985, it was not only possible to see Maseland's left thumbprint, but also to confirm that the English translations were both complete and highly accurate.

With this as background, the following are reasonable conclusions about Maseland's involvement in the Overakker plot. First, since Maseland was working closely with the Japanese military government in Medan, it was logical for the *Kempeitai* investigating resistance activities to question him about General Overakker, Colonel Gosenson, and others whom they suspected of conspiring against them in Sumatra. In fact, it would have been illogical for the *Kempeitai* to fail to question Maseland.

Second, based on Lieutenant Hisamatsu's statements, it is clear that Maseland provided some information about Overakker and Gosenson, and that he likely did identify men whom he believed might be involved in resistance activities. Third, there would be no logical reason for General Hirano, the top *Kempetai* commander in Sumatra, to credit Maseland's collaboration as significant in "rolling up" the Overakker plot, or for Hisamatsu to relay this information, unless Maseland was a key player in the success of the Japanese investigation. Consequently, the real question is whether it was *reasonable* for both the temporary court-martial and High Military Court judges hearing the evidence against Maseland to find him guilty of betraying his fellow citizens. The answer is yes. After all, to paraphrase a well-known saying, "when you lie down with dogs, you should not be surprised to get fleas." Given that Maseland was working closely with the enemy, it was reasonable for the judges examining the evidence to conclude that he had aided the Japanese investigation and that this constituted treason.

Although it may have been reasonable for the tribunals to convict Maseland, the manner in which his case was handled was very much flawed. *Het Overakker-complot* shows that a desire for revenge played a role in Maseland's prosecution. He had avoided internment, and his family had enjoyed a relatively privileged life during the Japanese occupation. Not surprisingly, this meant that NEI authorities not only believed he had willingly collaborated but also that they were prepared to believe the worst about him when it came to his involvement in the deaths of General Overakker, Colonel Gosenson, and others. Certainly, there is no doubt that the decision to adjourn the Medan proceedings and move the prosecution to Batavia was motivated solely by a desire to obtain the death penalty—because General Scholton and his superiors were convinced that Maseland was to blame for the deaths of their fellow Dutchmen. This desire for revenge against Maseland does not cast the NEI authorities in a positive light. The most that can be said in their defense is that they had suffered horribly at the hands of the Japanese, and wounds that they believed had been inflicted by one of their own hurt more than those done by the enemy.

Unfortunately, the Dutch authorities were so predisposed to think badly of Maseland that they failed to understand—or care—that he probably did not have much choice when it came to answering questions about General Overakker and Colonel Gosenson. After all, he knew both officers from his many years as a police official in Sumatra, and the *Kempeitai* knew that Maseland knew them. Consequently, it was to be expected that the Japanese would question him about the "Overakker Conspiracy"—and that he would have to provide some information.

There are three other factors that favor Maseland. First, Maseland insisted at trial that his decision to cooperate with the Japanese invaders had not only spared Medan's destruction in March 1942, but that his actions had saved lives. This is probably true, and should have been considered in fashioning an appropriate sentence at his trial. Second, Maseland insisted that starting in June 1944, he had tried to negotiate with the Japanese for better conditions in the internment camps. This author might find this persuasive, however, if Maseland been agitating for better treatment in 1943, and not in June 1944, when it was clear that the Japanese were losing the war in the Pacific. Was Maseland perhaps thinking that he would soon be called to account for his collaboration, and that he would be wise to demonstrate concern for those who were suffering in Japanese camps? Finally, both Captain Vromans and Dr. Zwinkels believe that Maseland's twenty-five years of faithful service as a police officer, and his many accolades for his duty performance, are relevant in judging his guilt.[28] But this is misplaced. After all, history is replete with examples of men of good character who betrayed their governments and their fellow citizens, starting with General Benedict Arnold. A genuine hero of the American Revolution, who had proven time and again that he was brave and loyal to the colonial cause, and who held high military rank, Arnold nonetheless attempted to betray his nascent country to the British Crown.

To sum up: There was sufficient evidence for both the Medan and Batavia tribunals to find Piet Maseland guilty. But, as his collaboration was not the proximate cause of the executions of those involved in the "Overakker Conspiracy," the death sentence imposed upon him was excessive. Moreover, the prosecution—and the government—were infected by a desire for vengeance, and this tainted the fairness of the proceedings; Piet Maseland did not enjoy the due process enjoyed by others prosecuted for war crimes.

The extent of Piet Maseland's collaboration with the Japanese will never be known, but it seems fair to conclude that his story is very much one of "gray" rather than "black and white."

Prosecutor v. Gonda de Haan-de Vries

On January 12, 1948, 24-year-old Gonda de Haan (neeé Gonda de Vries) was summoned to appear before the temporary court-martial in Batavia and informed that she would be prosecuted for the war crime of "having intentionally aided the enemy in time of war."[29] The charge was very serious, as the prosecutor was asking the military tribunal to sentence Mrs. de Haan to death.

The gist of the offense was that, in August 1943, Gonda de Haan had informed Major Mitsuo MURASE, head of the *Kempeitai* headquarters on Java, that a European woman named Hannie HILGERS was either hiding three persons who were involved in planning anti-Japanese operations or else that Hilgers was in contact with these individuals, who were in hiding in Buitenzorg, a town located

[28] See Zwinkels, *Het Overakker-complot* (n. 12) 258.

[29] *Prosecutor v. Gonda de Haan-de Vries*, No. 80/1947, Temporary Court-Martial, Batavia (February 20, 1948).

about thirty-five miles south of Batavia.[30] As a result of this betrayal, Hannie Hilgers, and Tom POWELL, John APPLEBY, and a third man (whose name was either BERKHOLST or BETTKLUFT), were arrested by the *Kempeitai* and then killed by beheading.

On Monday, February 9, 1948, at 8:30 a.m., Gonda de Haan appeared before the military tribunal to answer the charge against her. The three-judge tribunal, consisting of Lieutenant Colonel J. la Rivière, Major de Groot, and Captain Theys, considered written statements of witnesses who had been interrogated by police officials investigating the charge against de Haan. In accordance with normal procedure, each written statement, ordinarily signed by the individual making the statement, was shown to the defendant and was read aloud in the courtroom.

The military judges also heard live testimony from the accused, de Haan, and five other witnesses, all of whom had previously made at least one written statement as part of the investigative process. These were: de Haan's mother, Mrs. IPSEN; Major Murase; and Milly Langlois VAN DEN BERG, who was Murase's mistress. The other two witnesses who appeared personally to testify before the tribunal were Mrs. M. GÖTTGENS and Miss J. M. VAN DER MEER; both women had come to know Hannie Hilgers (and had spoken with her) while all three were in Kempeitai custody prior to Hilgers' execution.

The defendant, her mother, and Milly van den Berg all knew each other because, in 1943, Milly was living in the dwelling being rented by Gonda de Haan and her mother. The three women knew Major Mitsuo Murase because he was regularly visiting Milly at the home. The Japanese *Kempeitai* officer and Milly van den Berg had formed a romantic relationship and their nightly meetings in her room, which often lasted until morning, had to be conducted in secret because the Japanese were officially forbidden to have relationships with European women.

The original basis for the charge against Gonda de Haan were several out-of-court statements made to investigators by Milly and her one-time lover, Major Murase. On August 8, 1947, when Milly was herself suspected of having betrayed Hannie Hilgers to the *Kempeitai*, Milly was asked if she knew who might have told the Japanese about Hilgers. She denied knowing who might have betrayed Hilgers or anyone else. A month later, however, on September 8, 1947, when Milly van den Berg was no longer a suspect in the Hannie Hilgers case, she accused Gonda de Haan and de Haan's mother of having told Major Murase about Hilgers and the latter's involvement in anti-Japanese activities.

This conversation between Gonda, her mother, and Murase had supposedly occurred in August 1943, when Milly van den Berg was living in the home being rented by the defendant and the defendant's mother. According to Milly, Gonda's mother had recently had a bitter argument with an acquaintance named Mrs. BÜTNER, and she was now afraid that Mrs. Bütner would falsely report to the

[30] *Buitenzorg* (Dutch for "without a care") was the summer residence of the Governor General of the Netherlands East Indies. Known today as Bogor, it is part of metropolitan Jakarta, and an important cultural and tourist center, as well as a mountain resort.

Kempeitai that she was involved with Hilgers. Milly told the police investigator questioning her that, to preempt this false report, both Gonda and her mother told Major Murase about the argument with Mrs. Bütner. During the course of this conversation with Murase, Gonda and her mother necessarily revealed to him the allegation that Hannie Hilgers might be hiding two or three persons involved in anti-Japanese activities.

As for Major Murase, his statements to police investigators and his testimony before the tribunal likewise were inconsistent. When Murase was first interrogated on July 8, 1947, he stated that he could not remember who betrayed Hannie Hilgers. "Perhaps Milly had given him a report," said Murase, which "he handed over to the Batavia or Buitenzorg *Kempeitai*."[31]

Then, on July 30, 1947, Murase remembered—after much thinking—that it could have been either Milly or Gonda. But on September 3, 1947, perhaps now fearful that he had somehow incriminated his former lover, Murase "remembered" that Gonda told him about Hannie Hilgers—in the presence of both Gonda's mother and Milly.

Finally, on September 10, 1947, Murase provided more details about the betrayal: he was now certain that Gonda had told him that Hannie Hilgers was hiding persons who were involved in anti-Japanese activities. For the first time, Murase also stated that he remembered asking Gonda for Hannie's name and address, which Gonda she gave him. Murase further claimed to have written this information down in his black pocket notebook. At another interrogation on September 17, 1947, Murase affirmed his statement of September 10th, except that he now remembered having recorded Gonda's statement to him in his official *Kempeitai* notebook.

At trial, Major Murase testified in accordance with this last statement. He confirmed that it was Gonda who betrayed Hannie Hilgers to him.

The facts developed further by the court-martial tribunal very much called into question the truthfulness of both Milly van den Berg and Mitsuo Murase's statements. First of all, Murase spoke only French—and only Milly was fluent in that language. On the other hand, Gonda spoke very limited French and her mother, Mrs. Ipsen, was even less familiar with the language. Consequently, the tribunal found it unbelievable when Milly van der Berg and Major Murase stated that Gonda and her mother did most of the talking about Hannie Hilgers, when it was unlikely that their French was good enough to set out the facts in such a complex dispute in that language. Additionally, the military judges noted on the record that Milly was not a truthful or honorable person. Initially, for example, she

[31] See *Prosecutor v. Gonda de Haan-de Vries* (n. 29) 13. Interestingly, the military court deduced from Murase's July 8, 1947 incrimination of Milly van den Berg that Murase probably did not know that the police investigators had found insufficient evidence of her involvement in the betrayal of Hannie Hilgers. The court's reasoning was that Murase mentioned her as "perhaps having given him a report" because Murase thought that the NEI authorities in fact had other evidence that his ex-lover had committed a war crime. When Murase subsequently discovered that Milly was no longer a suspect in Hannie's betrayal, he changed his story and identified Gonda de Haan and her mother as the guilty parties.

had denied having a romantic relationship with Murase; only later did she admit that she had been his mistress. Additionally, she informed the investigators that although Murase had forbidden her from dating another Japanese man, she had done so anyway—and the court inferred that she had then lied to Murase about this involvement with another man.

The three judges also learned from both the witness statements and in court testimony that Milly van den Berg and Gonda de Haan knew each other from before the Japanese invasion, as they had gone to school together. But it also was clear that they disliked each other. In fact, when Gonda made it known to Milly that she did not approve of Milly's relationship with Major Murase, at least in part because the relationship was forbidden by the Japanese authorities, Murase called the defendant to Milly's room and informed her that if she were not nicer to Milly, then her whole family would be arrested.

Besides her poor relationship with the defendant, Milly van den Berg also disliked the now deceased Hannie Hilgers. Hannie had been engaged to marry Tom Powell, the Englishman or Australian who was arrested along with Hannie and later executed by the *Kempeitai*. The record of trial infers that Milly was jealous of Hannie's relationship with Powell, and that Hannie's engagement to him did not sit well with Milly.

The facts developed at trial also revealed that Milly was jealous of Hannie's intimate relationship with a Japanese man by the name of KAWANA. According to the record of trial, Milly was jealous because Kawana previously had painted Milly in the nude, and apparently had an intimate relationship with Milly. But, when Kawana began showering Hannie with beautiful gifts, including a necklace about which Hannie bragged, this only increased Milly's jealousy and had led to some fights between them. While the temporary court-martial was careful to refrain from stating on the record that Milly's dislike of Hannie might be evidence that it was Milly who betrayed Hannie Hilgers to Murase, the inference is certainly in there.

In contrast to the statements and testimony of Milly van den Berg and Mitsuo Murase, Gonda de Haan consistently gave the same version of events. She insisted she would never had betrayed Hannie Hilgers because they were best friends. After Milly van den Berg introduced the defendant to Hannie in the middle of 1942 (and so after the invasion), it was Hannie who had found the defendant a job in a Japanese-run oil company. The defendant worked in that job from January 1943 to August 1944, and she and Hannie and their respective Japanese bosses became such good friends that the four individuals would periodically join each other for an evening of playing the game of Monopoly at the defendant's home.

An additional factor in Gonda de Haan's favor was that, while she knew that Hannie Hilgers had been arrested by the *Kempeitai* and executed, she insisted that she had not learned until after the war that Hannie had been accused of hiding individuals involved in Resistance activities. The defendant had assumed that Hannie had gotten in trouble for having had a radio (which was forbidden by the Japanese) and so she was amazed to hear after the war that Hannie had been accused of being involved in anti-Japanese activities.

A final piece of evidence considered by the tribunal was the testimony of Mrs. M. Göttgens and Miss J. M. van der Meer. Both had been imprisoned with Hannie Hilgers and spoken with her after the latter had been arrested and interrogated by the *Kempeitai.*

Mrs. Göttgens told the tribunal that Hannie had reported to her the circumstances of her interrogation by the *Kempeitai* in Batavia. Hannie Hilgers had asked her Japanese interrogator who had betrayed her. At first, the Japanese would not tell her. After she asked a third time, however, the Japanese showed Hannie a handwritten postcard—which contained an anonymous allegation that Hannie was hiding three anti-Japanese operatives. According to Göttgens, Hannie recognized the handwriting as belonging to a girlfriend whom she had known before the war. Since the tribunal knew that the defendant had only become acquainted with Hannie Hilgers after the Japanese invasion, this was additional proof that someone other than the accused was responsible for the fate of Hannie Hilgers.

As for Miss van der Meer, who had been locked up with Hannie Hilgers in Buitenzorg, she told the tribunal that Hannie told her that she had been betrayed by a girlfriend who worked at the same office with her. The court, however, did not accept van der Meer's statement as evidence of Gonda de Haan's culpability, as Hannie did not reveal the identity of this girlfriend to van der Meer and so there was no way to know if Hannie was referring to Gonda or one of the other young women working in the office at the time Gonda and Hannie were there.

On February 20, 1948, the temporary court-martial announced that the guilt of Gonda de Haan had not been proven. Consequently, she was to be set free and the charge against her dismissed. This decision was confirmed on March 30, 1948.

Prosecutor v. Gonda de Haan is a particularly interesting case for at least three reasons. First of all, the twenty-three page decision—single-spaced typewritten—is totally fact-based; there is no discussion whatsoever of the law, much less the application of the law to the facts. But the facts, as carefully developed by the court, were very much in conflict. The statements and testimony of Major Murase and his mistress, Milly van den Berg, were both individually inconsistent and at odds when considered together. On the other hand, the statements and in court testimony of Gonda de Haan and her mother, Mrs. Ipsen, were entirely consistent, and had been delivered in a very calm manner. The court placed great emphasis on the fact that Mrs. Ipsen had testified under oath on her daughter's behalf even after being advised that she was not required to offer any evidence before the tribunal. While one might find it curious that the tribunal would attach much credibility to the testimony of a parent for her child—who was facing the death penalty if convicted—Mrs. Ipsen's in-court demeanor clearly impressed the court and made her highly believable.

Second, while the facts developed in *Prosecutor v. Gonda de Haan* would seem to point toward her innocence, the court was not willing to state on the record that de Haan was not guilty of the charge of *intentionally* aiding the enemy in time of war. Did the court believe that there might have been an accidental betrayal of Hannie Hilgers in the course of some conversation that Gonda or her mother had with Major Murase? We will never know. But perhaps this uncertainty about what really happened explains that the tribunal decided only that the charge against Gonda de Haan was not proven; that there was insufficient evidence of guilt.

Third and finally, *de Haan* reflects that there was no "rush to judgment" in the trial of collaborator. On the contrary, a defendant could be set free despite being accused of a war crime that had resulted in four killings, and a prosecutor's request for the death penalty.

Prosecutor v. Ferdinand Christiaan Marie Banning

On Friday May 9, 1947, at 8:30 a.m., Ferdinand C.M. Banning appeared before the temporary court-martial in Batavia, which was holding its proceedings in the NEI Supreme Court building.[32] Banning was charged with having aided the enemy during August and September 1942 by informing the *Kempeitai* in Batavia that a Mr. G. M. BERENDS, who was working as a guard in the Struiswijk prison, was smuggling letters in and out of the prison. These letters were written by Europeans interned in the prison to their family members, and vice versa, and were the only source of contact between the two groups. As a result of Banning's betrayal of Berends, the latter was repeatedly beaten by a Japanese commander named YAMADA or another Japanese official, or both. Berends also was locked up in a cell for a month and then fired from his job as a prison guard.

The prosecutor charged that Banning's actions in betraying Berends to the Japanese enemy was in violation of article 124 of the NEI Criminal Code, as amended by Staatsblad 1945, No. 135. He asked the temporary court-martial to find Banning guilty as charged and punish him with one year in jail.

At trial, a tribunal consisting of Lieutenant Colonel J. la Rivière, Major de Groot, and First Lieutenant J. G. H. VAN DER STARP, considered written signed statements, all made under oath, from Messrs. A. VERSCHUUR, G. J. L. M. MEIJS, G. M. Berends, W. L. A. HESSEL, and M. VAN MINOS. These documents were read to the defendant and his counsel in open court prior to their consideration by the three judges. The judges also heard from D. J. GERRITSE, who testified in person and under oath. The accused, Banning, also testified in his own behalf.

From the tenor of the written decision in *Prosecutor v. Banning*, the court-martial found Banning to be both sympathetic and believable as a witness. According to Banning, he had been arrested in May 1942 and confined in the Struiswijk prison in Batavia. In July, the defendant had been moved from Struiswijk to the hospital in Tjipinang, where he obtained treatment for swollen knees. One evening in August, while still in the hospital, Banning had a conversation with his fellow patients, Messrs. Verschuur, Meijs, and OTTO, and learned more about the group of guards who were smuggling letters, notes, and packages in and out of Struiswijk.

[32] *Prosecutor v. Ferdinand Christiaan Marie Banning*, No. 21/1947, Temporary Court-Martial, Batavia (May 14, 1947).

It is worth noting that Banning already knew that these items were being smuggled in and out of the prison, since he had previously sent notes to his wife by this means. But he learned more details about this smuggling operation, including how it was organized, in this talk with his fellow patients.

That same night, Banning was suddenly pulled out of his bed by the *Kempeitai*, thrown into a cell in Struiswijk, and then interrogated by the Japanese about the conversation in the hospital about letter smuggling.

The Japanese told Banning that they already knew all about the conversation about smuggling and smugglers. But they still struck him in the head with a stick and struck him on the legs. They also told Banning that they were going to arrest and torture his wife. Faced with this threat, Banning revealed to the *Kempeitai* that he knew about the secret letter smuggling. He also told the Japanese that he knew that one of the Struiswijk prison guards was acting as a go-between in passing letters from inside to outside the prison, and vice versa, but Banning also told the court that he did not know the guard's name.

At the end of this interrogation, Banning testified, the Japanese put a document written in Japanese characters in front of him and gave him the order to "sign, sign"—which he did out of fear, although he did not know what was written. After Banning had put his signature to the paper, Mr. G. J. L. M. Meijs was brought by the Japanese guards into the interrogation room where Banning was present, and then repeatedly struck in the head with a baton. After witnessing this beating of Meijs, Banning said to Meijs that he had told the Japanese that he knew about the letter smuggling in Struiswijk, and advised Meijs to do the same.

After this interrogation by the *Kempeitai*, Banning was returned to Struiswijk and thrown into a cell, even though he was very sick with dysentery. A few days later, the same *Kempeitai* agents who had interrogated Banning came to his prison cell, accompanied by three prison guards, and confronted him. The men insisted that Banning reveal to them the identity of the guard smuggling the letters. Faced with this coercion, and perhaps more vulnerable because of the dysentery, Banning now identified Berends as the culprit. After he had revealed Berends as the smuggler, Banning insisted that he had no further contact with the *Kempeitai* and, after leaving Struiswijk, was interned in a camp until the end of hostilities in 1945.

As for G. M. Berends, he was arrested by the *Kempeitei* while on duty at Struiswijk, accused of being involved in the letter smuggling operation and beaten during a few days of questioning by a Japanese interrogator named YAMADA. Berends was subsequently imprisoned for a month and then fired from his job as a prison guard.

In addition to Banning's own statements, both before and during his trial, the court considered written statements from Berends and another witness, Mr. A. Verschuur. Both men stated under oath that they had "heard" that it had been Banning who had betrayed Berends and the letter smuggling operation to the Japanese, and that Banning had given a written statement to that effect.

Finally, the tribunal considered a sworn statement from Mr. W. L. A. HESSEL that the defendant had been a "fanatical" member of the N.S.B., which had been active in the NEI prior to the German attack on the Netherlands in May 1940.[33] Since Nazi Germany had been allied with Japan during World War II, Banning's Nazi affiliation might have made it more likely that he would collaborate with the Japanese. The military tribunal, however, learned that Hessel's statement probably referred to a Dutchman named "Bannink"—suggesting a case of mistaken identity because the Dutch pronunciation of "Banning" and "Bannink" is almost the same. In any event, Banning strenuously denied that he had been a member of the N.S.B., and the court accepted this denial. There was another major reason to doubt that Banning was a Nazi sympathizer: The defendant had been put in charge of running a German-owned hotel after that establishment had been confiscated by NEI authorities after Germany attacked the Netherlands on May 10, 1940. As the court saw it, it would have made no sense for a Nazi to have been asked to operate a German hotel.

After carefully considering all the statements offered into evidence, and the defendant's own testimony, the military tribunal concluded that the charge against him had not been proven. As the judges explained in their opinion, the war crime of *intentionally* aiding the enemy had *both* an objective and subjective element. The objective element was the actual betrayal in providing information. The subjective element was the intent to betray by providing information. In *Prosecutor v. Banning*, the court-martial considered it proven that the defendant had given the information about the smuggling to the Japanese and identified Berends as the smuggler. But the court determined that the second element of the war crime—the subjective intent—had not been proven.

The judges identified a number of factors that supported this conclusion as to the second element. First, Banning had never exercised any initiative in informing the Japanese about the letter smuggling operation. On the contrary, he had been repeatedly subjected to coercive interrogation techniques by the Japanese and this mistreatment, combined with the very real fear that his wife would be arrested and tortured, caused Banning to reveal details about the smuggling—details that the Japanese already knew. In the court's view, this mistreatment and fear vitiated any subjective intent on Banning's part to betray Berends. Second, the military tribunal considered the statements of Berends and Verschuur, both of which incriminated Banning, to be unreliable and consequently rejected them as evidence of Banning's guilt. This was chiefly because both Berends and Verschuur insisted in their sworn statements that Banning had betrayed Berends in a written statement to the Japanese. But as the court could find no evidence that Banning had made such any such written statement, this called into the question the accuracy of the

[33] Wealthy plantation owners and other Dutch nationals residing in the Indies were attracted to the N.S.B. because they feared the "loss of white predominance" in the colony, and the N.S.B.'s aggressive racism appealed to them. In 1935, there were more than 5,000 registered N.S.B. members in Batavia, although membership declined to about 1,800 in 1939. See Hirschfeld, *Nazi Rule and Dutch Collaboration* (n. 2) 252. After the German invasion of the Netherlands in May 1940, the NEI authorities arrested and interned about 500 N.S.B. members as a security measure. See de Jong, *The Collapse of a Colonial Society* (n. 12) 27.

Berends and Verschuur statements and caused the court to reject them as evidence that Banning had the requisite subjective *mens rea* to commit the war crime.

A final point. The tribunal also noted that Banning had been examined by Dr. R. J. PRINS on January 30, 1947, and that Prins had delivered a psychiatric report to the court. His conclusion: that in 1942, the defendant was "someone with diminished mental capacity of pathological origin" which was due to head trauma. The court considered this to be relevant because this head injury meant that Banning was unbalanced in his thinking at the time and consequently had "diminished psychological resistance" during his interrogation by the *Kempeitai*. This medical report was yet another reason for the tribunal to conclude that the second element of the offense—a subjective intent to aid the enemy—was lacking.[34]

The acquittal in *Prosecutor v. Banning* is interesting for three reasons. First, it shows that the NEI authorities were interesting in pursuing all those who aided the Japanese during the occupation, even those like Banning whose collaboration was relatively low-level in that the prosecution asked for merely a year imprisonment. Second, it shows that the three military judges were not rubber-stamps when it came to the prosecution evidence in collaboration cases. As *Prosecutor v. Banning* shows, a prosecutor's claim that a defendant had aided the enemy did not inexorably lead to a conviction; in *Banning*, the judges sided with the defendant in determining the facts. Finally, the court's consideration of psychiatric testimony—that Banning had a diminished mental capacity—shows that the judges not only obtained psychiatric testimony but were willing to consider it in their decision.

The temporary court-martial decision in *Prosecutor v. Ferdinand Christiaan Marie Banning* was announced on May 14, 1947. The *fiat executie* confirming the tribunal's decision was made by Mr. J. E. YSEBAERT, the Resident of Batavia, on June 4, 1947. The tribunal announced this final decision on June 9, 1947, and Banning was a free man.

The five collaboration cases examined in this chapter are interesting for at least three reasons. First, the military tribunals were inordinately detailed in explaining the factual basis for their decisions; while one might expect such detail in a conviction, the courts spent just as much time with the facts in deciding that a case was "not proven" and that the lack of sufficient evidence meant that the accused should be set free. Second, the acquittals of de Haan-de Vries and Banning reflect a careful and nuanced approach to deciding guilt or innocence, at least where a European defendant was charged; there was no rush to judgment based solely on the allegations set forth by the prosecutor. Third, and finally, all five cases show that Dutch authorities in the NEI took allegations of collaboration seriously, and were prepared to pursue criminal charges against those who were thought to have aided the Japanese during the occupation. In the end, however, the judges who determined the guilt or innocence of these alleged collaborators must have been disappointed, if not bitter, to see what their fellow citizens had done during the Japanese occupation.

[34] ibid 6.

12

Aftermath

War Criminals Return to Japan

End of Dutch Colonial Sovereignty in the NEI

War crimes prosecutions in the Netherlands East Indies (NEI) came to a halt on Christmas Eve 1949. This was not what the Dutch colonial authorities had contemplated when they began prosecuting Japanese war criminals in 1946. They almost certainly believed that temporary courts-martial would continue as long as there were war criminals to be prosecuted, if for no other reason than the NEI would continue to exist as a colony for an indefinite period of time, and because justice required trials for those who had committed brutal and cruel war crimes during the occupation. But this was no longer possible, as the end of Dutch sovereignty in the islands on December 27, 1949, and the birth of the Republic of Indonesia, meant that the war crimes structure created by colonial authorities in 1946 no longer existed as a matter of international law—since the NEI no longer existed as a sovereign state.

This termination of Dutch colonial sovereignty did not affect the legality of the proceedings that had been completed, and where firing squads had already carried out lawful death sentences, these too were finished business. But as for prison sentences imposed on Japanese war criminals as punishment, the end of the NEI meant that the new Republic of Indonesia was the new sovereign with jurisdiction over all Japanese nationals serving prison sentences in Tjipinang[1] prison in Batavia.

The Dutch knew that any new Indonesian regime was very unlikely to keep these Japanese war criminals imprisoned, even for a brief period. Sukarno, who had collaborated with the Japanese occupiers during World War II, was certainly sympathetic to the plight of those imprisoned. He almost certainly felt indebted to the Japanese for their support and encouragement of the Indonesian revolutionary struggle against the Dutch and, as shown in Chapter 9 ('Trials for Violations of the Terms of the Armistice'), some Japanese nationals had paid with their lives for their support of the Indonesian guerrillas. Sukarno also knew that freeing these Japanese prisoners, and permitting them to return home, would be welcomed in Tokyo, and

[1] Today spelled as Cipinang. Regardless of where they were tried in the NEI, all Japanese nationals sentenced to terms of imprisonment were transferred to Tjipinang.

he no doubt believed that this would enhance Indonesia's relations with Japan—which would be better for the infant Indonesian republic.

The Dutch, both in the Netherlands and the NEI, were completely opposed to the possibility that imprisoned Japanese war criminals might have their sentences cut short, or receive any form of clemency. There were two reasons for this uncompromising position. First, the Dutch firmly believed that any Japanese national prosecuted at a temporary court-martial had received a full and fair trial and, if sentenced to jail, should serve that sentence in its entirety. As Australian historian Robert Cripp explains: "To most Dutch observers, the Japanese invasion had been a predatory act marked by ... gratuitous violence. They saw Japanese war criminals as the worst kind of gangsters, whose punishment should continue as a deterrent."[2]

Second, while the Dutch were bitter about the Japanese occupation, many were just as angry about Japanese responsibility for the post-1945 revolution that had turned their colony upside down. The vast majority of the Dutch citizens, both in the Netherlands and in the NEI, believed that the guerrilla war being waged against them by Sukarno and his revolutionaries was the direct result of Japanese indoctrination and propaganda, which had turned the generally happy and content Indonesians against Dutch rule. This was not correct, as an Indonesian nationalist consciousness that had existed prior to World War II was the driving force behind the revolution. It was true that these nationalist aspirations had grown stronger during the occupation, but this was chiefly because Indonesians had awakened to the realization that the humiliating defeat inflicted by the Japanese on the Dutch signaled that they, too, could have a future free from white rule. The Dutch, however, believed that Japanese agitation was the root cause of the revolution. Consequently, the NEI authorities were adamant that there would be no clemency for Japanese war criminals.

In late 1948 and early 1949, after a second Dutch "police action" (Dutch: *Politionele Actie*) against the guerrillas failed to extinguish the revolution,[3] and it seemed increasingly possible that Dutch rule in the Indies might terminate in the not too distant future, the authorities began exploring a way out of this problem.[4]

[2] Robert Cripp, "Avoiding Clemency: The Trial and Transfer of Japanese War Criminals in Indonesia, 1946-1949," 31 *Japanese Studies* (September 2011) 165.

[3] While the words "police action" might appear to be a euphemism, the term accurately described the Dutch use of force against the Indonesian insurgents. The conflict that began in 1946 and ended in 1949 was a non-international armed conflict and, under the law of war as it existed prior to 1949, the guerrillas were not lawful combatants; they had no protected status under the law. On the contrary, the Dutch were entitled to treat the insurgents as criminals under the colony's domestic law. Consequently, although the Dutch ultimately deployed 100,000 soldiers to combat the revolutionaries, these soldiers were performing a police function as a matter of law. For a concise summary of the various police actions carried out against the insurgents see Rémy Limpach, *De brandende kampongs van Generaal Spoor* (Boom 2016) 52–9. See also Thijs Brocades-Zaalberg, "Civil Military Cooperation During the Faltering Pacification of Java, 1947–1948," 1–2 *British Journal for Military History* (2015) 67–83.

[4] See Cripp (n. 2) 167.

Transferring War Criminals

Since clemency was a no-go, and Sukarno could not be trusted to keep the Japanese imprisoned, transferring the prisoners to another geographic location was the only course of action. As a sovereign state, the NEI could transfer Japanese war criminals confined in Tjipinang to a prison outside its borders. As a matter of international law, however, because the temporary courts-martial had been created by the colonial government (and not the Netherlands), once the NEI ceased to exist, all legal authority over the prisoners would belong to the new Republic of Indonesia. This meant that, at least in theory, the new Indonesia could undo any transfer.

While NEI lawyers must have been aware of this legal issue, the colonial authorities nonetheless decided that a physical transfer of the Japanese to a location outside of the Indies was necessary. Presumably the incarcerated Japanese might have been sent to the Netherlands, but this made little sense given the geographic distance and, if the new Republic of Indonesia subsequently requested the return of the prisoners, there would be no legal basis to deny the request from the new sovereign state. A second possibility was to transfer the Japanese war criminals to West New Guinea, which would not become a part of any Republic of Indonesia but would instead remain a colony under Dutch sovereignty. Again, however, if Indonesia requested return of the prisoners, the Dutch would face the same legal issue. As a result, the NEI decided upon a third option: Transfer those confined in Tjipinang prison to the Sugamo prison in Tokyo.

This last option had at least five advantages. First, the large, secure prison was under U.S. control in American-occupied Japan and already housed Japanese war criminals convicted in Tokyo by the International Military Tribunal for the Far East and in Yokohama by American military commissions.[5] Second, as it seemed unlikely that this U.S. occupation would terminate soon, the Dutch could anticipate that the Japanese would serve out all the time on their sentences. Third, it seemed equally unlikely that the Republic of Indonesia would request the return of the prisoners from the Supreme Commander for the Allied Powers (S.C.A.P.)[6] in Tokyo, or attempt to exercise any other legal authority as a sovereign state over these Japanese war criminals if the men were physically present in Japan. Fourth, Sugamo was geographically close to the NEI, which reduced the practical difficulties in transporting prisoners. Fifth and finally, there was precedent as another

[5] Described as "sprawling," the four-acre Sugamo prison contained more than 700 jail cells and held more than 1,000 war criminals in 1949. Those Japanese who had been condemned to death were hanged at Sugamo; those with prison terms were guarded by more than 300 American military guards. See Arnold C. Brackman, *The Other Nuremburg* (William Morrow 1987) 227–9.

[6] After the surrender of Japan, General Douglas MacArthur was appointed as Supreme Commander for the Allied Powers, a position he held until his relief by President Harry S. Truman in 1951. While the post-1945 occupation of Japan was theoretically an Allied affair, jointly directed by an Allied Council in Tokyo, in reality MacArthur was in charge as S.C.A.P.

Allied nation—Nationalist China—had transferred 260 convicted war criminals to Sugamo in January 1949.[7]

On December 15, 1949, just days before the NEI would cease to exist as a state, the Dutch and S.C.A.P. agreed upon a framework for the transfer of Japanese war criminals from Batavia to Tokyo. The Dutch had insisted that the occupation authorities in Japan guarantee that they would uphold the sentences imposed by the NEI temporary courts-martial. When the Americans declined to give any such assurances to the Dutch, it was too late to do anything else other than accept S.C.A.P.'s terms for the transfer of prisoners—which were that the Japanese would be confined in Sugamo, and that S.C.A.P. would have jurisdiction over the prisoners. Left undecided was the extent to which the Americans would inform and consult with the Dutch before taking any action to grant clemency to any prisoner.

On December 26, 1949, 679 Japanese nationals who had either been convicted or acquitted of war crimes, plus a small number who had been charged with war crimes but whose trials had never been held, boarded the Dutch ship *MS Tjisedane*. The International Committee of the Red Cross was in charge of the prisoner transfer but, because the *Tjisedane* was a 9,000-ton merchant ship belonging to the Royal Interocean Lines, it had a cargo aboard that had to be delivered to a variety of locations, including Penang (Malaya), Singapore, Saigon, and Hong Kong. As a result, the ship with its prisoners did not arrive in Yokohama, Japan until January 23, 1950.[8]

War Criminals in Japan

The prisoners were met by Japanese Red Cross officials, as well as the Netherlands Military Mission (Tokyo) and U.S. military authorities. When the men walked down the *Tjisedane*'s gangplank and set foot on Japanese soil, fifty U.S. Army trucks that had been awaiting the ship's arrival took all the Japanese to Sugamo prison. But it was winter and it was cold, and so before the trucks departed from the dock, each prisoner was issued a military great coat.[9]

According to L. F. de Groot, those men who had been acquitted (and those who had never been tried because the Dutch authorities ran out of time) were not immediately released. Rather, they spent a month in Sugamo before being set free. Those who went home to their families included Generals Maruyama and Okazaki. Both officers had been charged with command responsibility for war crimes but acquitted by the Batavia temporary court-martial. As for General

[7] Barak Kushner, *Men to Devils, Devils to Men: Japanese War Crimes and Chinese Justice* (Harvard University Press 2015) 177–8.

[8] L. F. de Groot, *Berechting Japanse Oorlogsmisdadigers in Nederlands-Indie 1946–1949* (Art and Research 1990 (privately published)) 377–9.

[9] International Committee of the Red Cross, *Report: Japanese Prisoners and Repatriates on Board the "Tjisedane" from Djakarta to Yokohama* (March, 28, 1950), reprinted in de Groot, Appendix F, 573–80.

Imamura, who also was aboard the *MS Tjisedane* and, as the senior ranking prisoner in the vessel, was given the honor to be the first off the ship, he was not freed. While Imamura had been acquitted by the NEI tribunal, he had been convicted of war crimes by the Australian military tribunal sitting in Rabaul, and punished with a ten-year jail sentence. Consequently, Imamura was transferred to the Australian authorities so that he could serve his sentence on Manus Island.[10]

Fifty U.S. Army trucks, which had been waiting for the *Tjisedane*'s arrival, transported those Japanese with jail sentences directly to Sugamo prison. Included among these men was at least one war criminal who had escaped death: Lieutenant Colonel Masashi KAWABE. While the NEI authorities had carried out the executions by firing squad of almost all Japanese nationals who had been sentenced to death, Kawabe seems to have escaped his death sentence because the colonial authorities ran out of time. Kawabe, who had been sentenced to death in July 1949 for war crimes committed as a member of the *Kempeitai*,[11] had not been shot prior to December 27, 1949—probably because his death sentence was confirmed too late for it to be carried out. As a result, Kawabe's sentence was reduced to a term of imprisonment and he returned to Japan.[12]

Clemency for War Criminals

As the Dutch soon discovered, however, the idea that Japanese war criminals convicted in the NEI actually would serve their entire prison terms in Japan was not to be: Within months, S.C.A.P. took unilateral action—without consulting with the Dutch—and issued Circular No. 5, *Clemency for War Criminals*. This circular, dated March 7, 1950, created a "Board of Parole" that would examine whether a prisoner confined in Sugamo would have his sentence reduced; once a person had served one third of his sentence, he was eligible for parole. As for those serving life sentences, they were eligible for parole after having served fifteen years. Circular No. 5 stated that among the many factors to be considered included: The age of the defendant; his physical and spiritual health; and his family circumstances.

Clemency for War Criminals also created a uniform system of reducing the sentences of all individuals confined in Sugamo. The circular provided that a prisoner who demonstrated "good behavior" and committed no disciplinary infractions, would have between five and ten days subtracted from his sentence. How much was subtracted depended on the length of the prison term. A man with a sentence between five and ten years, for example, would have his sentence reduced by eight

[10] Today, Manus Island is part of Papua New Guinea and is the largest of the Admiralty Islands. As late as December 1952, there were 199 Japanese war criminals imprisoned on the island. See de Groot (n. 8) 398. For more on Imamura see Chapter 10 nn. 26–39, and accompanying text.

[11] *Prosecutor v. Masashi Kawabe*, Vonnis No. 23/1949, Batavia (July 18, 1949).

[12] L. F. de Groot, "De rechtspraak inzake oorlogsmisdrijven in Nederlands-Indië (1947–1949), *Militair Rechtelijk Tijdschrift* (January 1987) 389.

days a month; an individual with a jail sentence of 10 years or more would receive a ten day a month credit.

For the American military authorities, who were the driving force behind this desire to reduce the number of Japanese nationals confined in Sugamo, the provisions of Circular No. 5 were nothing new. On the contrary, they were modeled after the parole and good time provisions that existed in the American Army's court-martial system. Additionally, insisting that Japanese war criminals remain in prison did nothing to promote reconciliation between the Japanese and their American occupiers, and it arguably undermined MacArthur's strategy of creating a demilitarized and democratic Japan. For the Dutch, however, the new rules were alarming and, while Netherlands officials resident in Tokyo were permitted to express their views to the Board of Parole, the Dutch had no authority to prevent the early release of Japanese who had been convicted by temporary courts-martial.

For Dutch nationals, especially those who had been a part of the temporary court-martial process, the parole of Japanese war criminals was a bitter pill to swallow. One celebrated "monster-case" involving thirty members of the *Kempeitai* was particularly egregious. Six of these defendants had been convicted in Batavia in September 1947, and had been sentenced to ten years in jail. But, because of Circular No. 5, all six were paroled between May and December 1951, and sent home to their families, before they had even served one half of their adjudged ten-year sentences.[13]

Before the Allied occupation of Japan formally ended on April 28, 1952, S.C.A.P. had given some form of parole to almost 275 Japanese nationals who had been convicted in the NEI. As a result, only 217 of the 679 who had arrived in the *Tjisedane* in January 1950 remained in the Sugamo prison when Japan's sovereignty as a nation was fully restored.[14]

With the Japanese now having jurisdiction over Sugamo's prison population, pressure from the Japanese public to accelerate the release of prisoners began to build, and included appeals to the government of the Netherlands. A June 1952 "petition" addressed to Mr. P. E. TEPPEMA, the Dutch ambassador to Japan, stated:

Dear Sir,

We, who have experienced the terrible affliction of a defeated nation as the result of the last mistaken war, pledge ourselves to contribute to world peace, rejecting the past mistaken thoughts. The Peace Treaty [Treaty of San Francisco], which we had long been waiting, gave at last the honor to become a member of the peaceful nations of the world, and consequently the remaining dregs of the abominable war are dissolving gradually and we are starting as a new born democratic nation ...

There is, however, one thing which we regret and are sorry for. That is the fact that there are so many [of] our war criminals confined abroad and [in] Sugamo ...

[13] *Prosecutor v. Kinjiro IIZUKA et al*, Vonnis No. 24/1947, Batavia (September 17, 1947); see also de Groot (n. 8) 384.

[14] See de Groot (n. 8) 386.

For all those are still in the custody as war criminals, please give them also sympathetic treatment and by your generosity quickly commute and discharge them, whose returning home is eagerly waited for all by the members of their remaining families. I hereby appeal to you for your help to remove this grieve (sic) and affliction of the remaining families.

I am, dear Sir, etc.[15]

In the meantime, Japanese authorities continued to release prisoners from captivity, either because of "good time" credit or parole. A status report on the Sugamo prison population, dated September 1, 1953, reflected that there was a total of 205 NEI prisoners still in custody, of whom twenty-nine were serving life sentences, twenty-four were serving terms of between twenty and thirty years, and 152 were serving jail sentences of less than twenty years. But the Dutch did not have the most prisoners confined in Sugamo: The U.S. had 340, the U.K. had 104, Australia had 173, France had three, and the Philippines had fifty-three.[16]

The number of NEI prisoners continued to decline in the months that followed: In December 1954, there were only 156 remaining in Sugamo. The beginning of the end of the process came in March 1956, after the Netherlands ambassador to Japan presented a letter to the Japanese in which the Dutch formally agreed to "an acceleration of the release of Japanese war criminals sentenced by Netherlands war tribunals and now detained in Sugamo prison."[17] Not surprisingly, there were only sixty-three NEI prisoners by July 1956. The last NEI inmate was released in 1957 and, with his release, the history of war crimes prosecutions in the NEI from 1946 to 1949 came to an end.[18]

A Postscript

A final postscript on the "aftermath" of Japanese nationals convicted by NEI temporary courts-martial. Kunishige WADA, a member of the *Kempeitai*, had been convicted in October 1946 for war crimes, and had been sentenced to death. But he managed to escape a firing squad, albeit under rather bizarre circumstances. Wada escaped twice from Tjipinang prison. After being recaptured twice, Wada escaped a third time from jail. He remained in Batavia and passed himself off as an Indonesian taxi driver of Japanese descent. Unfortunately for Wada, he was recognized by the police. He was shot and killed while attempting to escape.[19]

[15] ibid 403. [16] ibid 409. [17] ibid 425.

[18] According to the Sugamo prison statistical report of January 1958, only war criminals convicted by the United States remained in the prison. There were 45, of whom 35 were serving life sentences. See de Groot (n. 8) 434.

[19] *Prosecutor v. Kinishige Wada*, Vonnis No. 14/1948, Batavia (September 11, 1948).

Conclusion

The Impact of the Trials on Indonesia and the Netherlands, and on the Development of the Law of International Armed Conflict

The Dutch convened military tribunals, and prosecuted those responsible for war crimes during the occupation of the Netherlands East Indies (NEI), for one reason: To punish those who had murdered, tortured, and otherwise brutally mistreated the Dutch, Eurasian, Chinese, Indian, Malay, and Indonesian citizens of the colony. While some historians suggest that war crimes trials were held for other reasons, *i.e.* to "establish for the legal and historical record that the [Japanese] occupation had been illegal" or to show Indonesians that the Dutch had liberated the NEI from a criminal Japanese occupation, these reasons were peripheral at best in the decision-making process.[1]

The Japanese, and those who had collaborated with them, were tried for the same reason that the Allies in Europe and Asia prosecuted Axis war criminals: because their horrific misdeeds deserved punishment and their victims cried out for justice. This desire for punishment and justice was so important that Dutch colonial authorities continued with temporary courts-martial until the last possible moment—Christmas Eve 1949—and then, fearful that the new Republic of Indonesia would undermine the results achieved by these tribunals, insisted that Japanese war criminals imprisoned in the colony should be transferred to Tokyo to serve out their sentences.

Before discussing the influence of the trials on the law of international armed conflict, it is important to provide some observations on the impact of the trials on Indonesia and the Netherlands.

For Indonesians, who were struggling against the re-establishment of Dutch colonial authority between 1945 and 1949, any memories of the trials of Japanese war criminals quickly faded away and were mostly forgotten. This is not to say that the average Indonesian had not suffered during the occupation, or that he

[1] Robert Cripp, "Avoiding Clemency: The Trial and Transfer of Japanese War Criminals in Indonesia, 1946–1949," 31 *Japanese Studies* (September 2011) 153; Lisette Schouten, "Colonial Justice in the Netherlands Indies War Crimes Trials," *Trials for International Crimes in Asia* (Cambridge University Press 2016) 80.

did not want to see the Japanese punished for their misdeeds. On the contrary, many Indonesians hated the Japanese, especially the *Kempeitai* and *Tokkeitai*. With some exceptions, however, the prosecutions at the temporary courts-martial were focused mostly on bringing justice to Dutch and Eurasian victims—victims who were closely associated with colonial rule and the *status quo ante bellum* and not with the future and a free and independent Indonesia. In any event, those Indonesians who supported the revolution, and therefore looked to the future, were inclined to forget the past.

Certainly, SUKARNO and many of the nationalist leaders who were pushing and pulling their countryman toward a future free from Dutch rule were not particularly interested in war crimes prosecutions, if for no other reason than they had willingly collaborated with the Japanese during the occupation and consequently were uneasy about any illumination of their actions during the war years. Sukarno, for example, had used his talents and influence not only to support the Japanese occupiers, but to inflame anti-Allied sentiment. While his cries of "We'll flatten the Americans! We'll smash the British!" were bad enough, it was Sukarno's enthusiastic recruitment of millions of Indonesians to work as *rōmusha* that meant he was guilty, at least morally, when thousands and thousands of these forced laborers died as a result of Japanese mistreatment.

While a focus on the future and a general reticence on the part of Sukarno and the nationalists provide two reasons for Indonesian disinterest in the war crimes proceedings, a third factor may be even more important: That Dutch soldiers were committing war crimes against Indonesians while the tribunals were ongoing.

During the *Bersiap* or *Bersiaptijd* (loosely translated as a "time of danger") that existed from September 1945 to early 1946, pro-Republic Indonesians murdered thousands of Dutch and Eurasians. Victims were killed (and mutilated) in gruesome ways, including bodies being hacked to pieces and beheadings. As many as 20,000 men, women, and children lost their lives. Many more were wounded. Not all were Dutch and Eurasians; Indonesians who were suspected of collaborating or sympathizing with the colonial authorities also were victims.[2]

With the *Bersiaptijd* as context, Dutch attempts to re-establish the colony after the Second World War, and defeat the Indonesian nationalists, faced unprecedented resistance. In the "dirty war" that consumed the archipelago from 1946 to 1949, Army Chief General Simon SPOOR, the head of the Royal Netherlands Indies Army (Dutch: *Koninklijk Nederlandsch Indisch Leger* (KNIL)), was convinced that Dutch forces must take "extraordinarily vigorous measures" if the guerrillas were to be crushed and colonial rule restored.[3] Special courts-martial

[2] William H. Frederick, "The Killing of Dutch and Eurasians in Indonesia's National Revolution (1945–49): A 'Brief Genocide' Reconsidered," in Bart Luttikhuis and A. Dirk Moses (eds.), *Colonial Counterinsurgency and Mass Violence* (Routledge 2014) 133–54.

[3] Rémy Limpach, "Business as Usual: Dutch Mass Violence in the Indonesian War of Independence 1945–49," in Bart Luttikhuis and A. Dirk Moses (eds.), *Colonial Counterinsurgency and Mass Violence* (Routledge 2014) 69–70. For a fuller treatment of Dutch war crimes committed against Indonesians, see Rémy Limpach, *De brandende kampongs van Generaal Spoor* (Boom 2016).

(Dutch: *Bijzondere Krijgsraden*) were created so that field commanders could quickly try and punish insurgents. When authorized, so-called "summary justice" (Dutch: *standrecht*) sometimes meant that any Indonesian caught with weapons was shot on the spot. But, as often happens when both sides seek to win at any cost, the 45,000-man KNIL and 95,000-man Royal Army (Dutch: *Koninklijke Landmacht* (KL)) soldiers also ended up using physical violence against noncombatants.

As Dutch historian Rémy Limpach and others have shown, hundreds if not thousands of innocent civilians were tortured and killed by KNIL and KL troops, with some of the worst excesses occurring on Java and in the Celebes. All this meant that when Indonesians were the victims of war crimes perpetrated by the Dutch armed forces, they were not inclined to be interested in, much less cooperate with, the on-going prosecutions of Japanese war criminals. In fact, it must have seemed hypocritical to more than a few observers that the colonial authorities were prosecuting the Japanese for the many of same offenses that the Dutch were now committing against Indonesian revolutionaries.

Despite the mass violence perpetrated by both sides, and the end of colonial rule in 1949, the Dutch in the Netherlands could rightly conclude that their war crimes prosecution program in the Indies had been an unqualified success. First, other than the United States, no other country prosecuted more Japanese nationals for war crimes committed in the Pacific: 1038 defendants in 448 separate trials; more than one-third of the accused being prosecuted in Batavia (Jakarta).

Table 1 compares Dutch efforts with other Allied prosecutions in the Pacific from 1945 to 1951:[4]

Table 1 War Crimes Trials in the Far East (1945–1951)

Country	Accused	Trials	Not Guilty	Death	Life	Prison Terms
United States	1453	456	188	143	162	871
NEI	1038	448	55	236	28	705
United Kingdom	978	330	116	223	54	502
Australia	949	294	267	153	38	455
China	883	605	350	149	83	272
France	230	39	31	63	23	112
Philippines	169	72	11	17	87	27

[4] Peter Post *et al.* (eds.), *Encyclopedia of Indonesia in the Pacific War* (Brill 2010) 409. In his authoritative *Military Tribunals and International Crimes* (Bobbs-Merrill 1954), John A. Appleman gives slightly different numbers but statistical data was incomplete when Appleman's book was first published. No reliable data exists on the military war crimes trials conducted by the Soviet Union in the Far East after World War II.

Second, the Dutch in the NEI had succeeded in creating military tribunals, determining the law and designing a judicial process that provided full and fair trials for war criminals. This was a noteworthy achievement, given that more than a few of the judges who served on the temporary courts-martial felt a deep hatred and contempt for the Japanese. This prejudice, which had naturally resulted from their experiences as POWs or internees, certainly affected some trials and, when measured by today's standards of fairness, these men should have been disqualified as judges. Certainly, then Major L. F. de Groot, who had served on the court in Batavia, recognized that some of witnesses (and one has to assume his colleagues) had hard feelings about the Japanese, and that this sort of prejudice probably harmed the process.[5]

Yet a close examination of the records in each case discussed in this book does not disclose any evidence that anti-Japanese prejudice directly affected the determination of guilt or innocence. On the contrary, the court-martial panels were both meticulous and reasonable in considering evidence. There were fifty-five complete acquittals and partial acquittals in more than a few cases. By way of example, in *Prosecutor v. Sone*, examined in Chapter 5, the court determined that the accused was not guilty of withholding food and medicine from either POWs or civilian internees. This was a significant decision since the lack of food and medicine had caused much suffering and death—and it might have been expedient to hold Captain Sone criminally liable. Similarly, in the trial of collaborators Gonda DE HAAN-DE VRIES, and Ferdinand C. M. BANNING, the judges acquitted both defendants after an exhaustive examination of the evidence. But perhaps the best illustration of fairness involved Generals IMAMURA, MARUYAMA, and OKAZAKI. The prosecutor had asked that they be found guilty and put to death on a command responsibility theory. The military court, however, acquitted them and then weathered considerable criticism from the colony's leaders and the Dutch public.

Whether or not any bias or prejudice made the judges more likely to impose a severe sentence is a fair question, especially as the NEI war crimes courts sentenced more Japanese to death than did any other war crimes tribunal in the Pacific. But an analysis of those capital cases reveals that the judges sometimes exercised leniency in those prosecutions where one might expect a death sentence. In *Prosecutor v. Gisaburo YOSHIDA*, the accused was found guilty of multiple unlawful executions yet escaped the death penalty because the court found mitigating facts in his favor. Similarly, although the court-martial sitting in judgment of Shoichi IKEDA was urged by the prosecutor to impose the death penalty for forced prostitution, that court refused to follow the prosecution's recommendation and instead imposed a fifteen-year jail sentence. As explained in Chapter 7, the court found facts that mitigated against imposing a capital sentence.

[5] See Chapter 4 n. 10, and accompanying text.

Table 2 Death Penalty Comparison by Country

Country	Accused	% Convicted	Death	% Receiving Death
NEI	1038	93.4 (969)	236	24.4
United Kingdom	978	88.1	223	32.7
Australia	949	69.5 (644)	153	23.7
United States	1453	84.6 (1229)	143	11.6
China	883	57 (504)	149	29.6
France	230	86.1 (198)	63	31.8
Philippines	169	78.7 (133)	17	12.8

The *Yoshida* and *Ikeda* prosecutions indicate that the death sentence was not necessarily the outcome in an egregious case. Additionally, while NEI war crimes tribunals did impose more death sentences than did any other Allied tribunal, a closer look at the numbers is revealing. Table 2 shows that while the *raw* numbers for capital punishment were highest for the NEI (236 out of 1038 defendants), when this figure is compared against the number of Japanese *convicted* at trial, the percentage of those convicted men being sentenced to be hanged falls into the middle range; the NEI (at 24.4%) was higher than Australia and the Philippines but lower than France, the United Kingdom and China.

A final issue remains for discussion: how did the Dutch war crimes prosecutions in the NEI affect the development of the law of international armed conflict? First, the colonial decision to adopt a radically new legal framework is itself significant. While metropolitan Holland initially used only its domestic penal code to prosecute war crimes, the NEI authorities broke new ground by adopting customary law relating to war crimes. Second, the NEI military tribunals had a number of unique features and "firsts," including:

- the only national tribunal to prosecute a group for war crimes and, if the offenses were committed by the group as an integral part of its day-to-day operations, then the group members were guilty and punished according to their level of involvement;
- the only war crimes courts with a mandatory sentencing framework (death, life, one day to twenty years);
- the first court to prosecute "forced prostitution" as a war crime;
- the only tribunal to prosecute "systematic terrorism" as a war crime;
- the only tribunal to prosecute enemy soldiers for committing hostile acts in violation of an armistice.

As to the influence of the NEI war crimes tribunals on the development of the law of international armed conflict, it seems that only the prosecutions involving "forced prostitution" are well-known, chiefly because *Prosecutor v. Washio* was translated into English and published in the U.N. War Crimes Commission's *Law Reports of Trials of War Criminals*. Given the increasing interest of lawyers in crimes of sexual violence arising out of international and noninternational armed conflicts (including forced prostitution), *Washio* will continue to influence both scholars and practitioners.

In the area of command responsibility, the NEI cases—while important—were overshadowed by the American Army's trial of General Yamashita in Manila. Additionally, as the three senior defendants were found not guilty by the tribunal in Batavia, the influence of their cases has been minimal. This is because trials in which a defendant is found guilty provide the best guidance (and *stare decisis*) for international lawyers. This is unfortunate, since the *Imamura, Maruyama*, and *Okazaki* decisions are important and deserve additional study.

Without question, the trials of the *Kempeitai* and *Tokkeitai* under Article 10 merit more attention than they have received. While it is true that those who study the law of international armed conflict, and those who prosecute war crimes, are uncomfortable with group liability, no innocent person was wrongly convicted in *Prosecutor v. Motomura and 15 Tokkeitai, Prosecutor v. CHOO and 32 Kempeitai Members*, or *Prosecutor v. TANABE, Nakao YAHAGI, Shozo YAMAMOTO, and Tetsuo FUHAJA.*

A final observation. History shows that soldiers in all armed forces are capable of committing war crimes. Soldiers serving in the U.S. Army committed war crimes in World War II, and in Vietnam, and in Iraq and Afghanistan. Other armed forces—British, French, and Italian—likewise have committed war crimes. The war crimes committed by the Japanese in the Indies were different, however, in that they were the manifestation of the race war triggered by the "Asia for Asians" ideology and the code of *Bushido.* The severity, viciousness, and widespread nature of the crimes during the occupation of the Indonesian archipelago reflect these two factors and the records of the war crimes tribunals contain overwhelming evidence supporting this view.

While all those who participated in the temporary courts-martial process from 1946 to 1949 are long gone from the world stage, anyone who reads the pages of this book should gain an appreciation for what they did and their legacy in legal history.

APPENDIX A

NEI Temporary Courts-Martial Cited

Amboina

MAKINO, Prosecutor v. Shujiro, Vonnis No. 30/1948, Amboina, 1948.
SUSUKI, Prosecutor v. Motosuke, Vonnis No. 25/1947, Amboina, 1948.
TANAKA, Prosecutor v. Toru, No. 27/1947, Amboina, 1948.

Balikpapan

IIMA, Prosecutor v. Gakuji, Yoshimitsu OCHI, Shinichi TAKEYAMA, and Yukio NARIKIYO, Vonnis No. 4/1946, Balikpapan, 1947.
WATANABE, Prosecutor v. Shozo, Vonnis No. 3/1947, Balikpapan, 1947.
YAMURA, Prosecutor v. Saburo, Vonnis No. 1/1946, Balikpapan, 1946.
YOSHIDA, Prosecutor v. Gisaburo, Vonnis No. 11/1948, Balikpapan, 1948.

Bandjermasin

FUJIWARA, Prosecutor v. Seitaro, Vonnis No. 40/1947, Bandjermasin, 1948.

Batavia

BANNING, Prosecutor v. Ferdinand Christiaan Marie, Vonnis No. 21/1947, Batavia, 1947.
CHOO, Prosecutor v., Koonosuke, Kiyoshi TANIGUCHI, Kinjiro IIZUKA, Michitaro KATO, Teruo KOBAYASHI, Yoshio TOMITA, Keiji SHIBAO, Masayoshi NAKAGOMI, Nagamoto SUGIYAMA, Tsutomu YAMGUCHI, Buichi FUKUSHIMA, Shigeo GOKA, Shigeru KOBAYASHI, Hajime KOMATSU (alias SATO), Kenji MATSUNAGA, Arata MOIMOTO, Yutaka MIKI, Jitsuryo NAKAHODO, Bunji OGATA, Chuji ONO, Tsumeno TAKANAMI, Masayoshi TSUKAMOTO, Rijuji AIZAWA, Yukio CHIBA, Yoshio DOI, Tatsuyi MAEKAWA, Yoshio NARA, Takuo NISHIMURA, Chiyoki SUZUKI, Sumio TANOUE, Sohei KOBAYASHI, Liong Hone TAN (alias NAGITA) and Nobuzo ADACHI, (33 Kempeitai), Vonnis No. 24/1947, Batavia, 1947.
DIENST, Prosecutor v. William Josias van, Vonnis No. 16/1948, Batavia, 1948.
DUURSMA, Prosecutor v. Douwe, High Military Court of Netherlands East Indies, Batavia, 1948.
ECKHART, Prosecutor v. Franciska Hendrika, Vonnis No. 76/1947, Batavia, 1947.
IKEDA, Prosecutor v. Shoichi Ikeda, Vonnis No. 72 A/1947, Batavia, March 30, 1948.

IMAMURA, Prosecutor v. Hitoshi and Seisaburō OKAZAKI, Vonnis No. 1/1949, Batavia, March 16, 1949.

IIZUKI, Prosecutor v. Kinjiro et al, Vonnis No. 24/1947, Batavia, 1947.

ISHIKAWA, Prosecutor v. Hiroyuki, Vonnis No. 17/1948, Batavia, 1948.

KAWABE, Prosecutor v. Masashi, Vonnis No. 23/1949, Batavia, 1949.

KIMURA, Prosecutor v. Seikon, Vonnis No. 28/1946, Batavia, 1946.

MARUYAMA, Prosecutor v. Masao, Vonnis No. 33/1948, Batavia, 1949.

MASELAND, Prosecutor v. P. H. J. M., High Military Court of Netherlands East Indies, Batavia, March 1949.

MITSUHASHI, Prosecutor v. Hiromu, Keiji OKADA, Chiyomatsu KAWAMURA, Kuizo MURAKAMI, Shiro NAKASHIMA, Eiichi ISHIDA, Taranosuke SAI, Iwao FURUYA, Shinji SHIMODA, Yukio MORIMOTO, and Kenjiro TSUTAKI, Vonnis No. 72/1947, Batavia, 1948.

SHOJI, Prosecutor v. Toshishige, Vonnis No. 28/1948, Batavia, 1949.

SONE, Prosecutor v., Kenichi, Vonnis 24/1946, Batavia, 1946.

TAKAMURA, Prosecutor v. Akio, Vonnis No. 39/1946, Batavia, 1946.

WADA, Prosecutor v. Kunishige, Kinnosuke KAWATAHARA, Katsuya KONNO, Takeshi NOGUCHI, Tarao YAMAMOTO, Isamu HANZAWA, Shoji KAWABATA, Shinichi AMANO, Haruo ISHIKAWA, Kazuyoshi HASHIMOTO, Hiroshi KODAKA, Ryoji MINAMI, Gunjiro ONO, Toshio SASAKI, Tomoyoshi SATO, Yukio UMEMOTO, Hideo OTA (17 *Kempeitai*), Vonnis No. 14/1948, Batavia, 1948.

WASHIO, Prosecutor v. Awochi, Vonnis No. 40/1946, Batavia, 1946.

YAGUCHI, Prosecutor v. Saikuro, Yukiie FUKUI, and Nobuhiro TERUKI, Vonnis No. 9/1948, Batavia.

Hollandia

KOKUBU, Prosecutor v. Shigehiko, Vonnis No. 54/1948, Hollandia, 1948.

Macassar

HATADA, Prosecutor v. Minoru, Kioshi KANAI, Suekichi IKEDA, Vonnis No. 3/1947, Macassar, 1947.

MOTOMURA, Prosecutor v. Shigeki, Chobei SAKAI, Toshimitsu TOMITA, Tooru MINAMI, Shigeo MANABE, Susumu NAKASHIMA, Yoshio ONO, Yoshihiro SHIBA, Tokyo EGUCHI, Isamu SHIMITZU, Tamotsu MASUDA, Masashige OKU, Noboru DOI, Shoichi TERAYAMA, Fusao NAKATA, Shigeichi SENOO, (16 *Tokkeitai)* Vonnis No. 12/1947, Macassar, 1947.

TANABE, Prosecutor v. Koshiro, Vonnis No. 2/1947, Macassar, 1947.

Medan

ICHIJO, Prosecutor v. Minoru, Yoshie GOTO, Taisuke KATO, Miyaji MATSUYAMA, Kiyoshi SATO, Yoshie MORISHIGE, Mitsuru HIRAMATSU, Yoshimitsu SAKATA, Masao NAGATSUKA and Shigeru KAWAKAMA (10 *Kempeitai*), Vonnis No. 119/1947, Medan, 1948.
KATSUNO, Prosecutor v. Mizuo, No. 18/1947, Medan, 1947.
MIYAZAKI, Prosecutor v. Ryohei, Vonnis No. 16/1948, Medan, 1948.
SUGIBAYASHI, Prosecutor v. Takeo, Vonnis No. 94/1947, Medan.
TANABE, Prosecutor v. Moritake, Nakao YAHAGI, Shozo YAMAMOTO, and Tetsuo FUKAJA, Vonnis No. 109/1948, Medan, 1948.

Morotai

OGIHARA, Prosecutor v. Goro, Vonnis No. 26/1947, Morotai, 1947.
SHIMIDZU, Prosecutor v. Katzuaki, Toshiro ISHIGAKI, Sadao NAGASAKI, Kumedjiro FUKUCHI, and Nobuo SAKAMAKI, Vonnis No. 30/1947, Morotai, 1947.

Pontianak

DAIGO, Prosecutor v. Tadashige, Vonnis No. 29/1947, Pontianak, 1947.
KAMADA, Prosecutor v. Michiaki, Vonnis No. 34/1947, Pontianak, 1947.
SANO, Prosecutor v. Satsuki, Vonnis No. 14/1946, Pontianak, 1946.

Tanjung Pinang

YAMAGISHI, Prosecutor v. Toshihide, Vonnis No. 29/1948, Tanjung Pinang, 1948.

Timor Kupang

IWANAGA, Prosecutor v. Satoro, Vonnis No. 14/1948, Timor Kupang, 1948.

APPENDIX B

Judges at Temporary Courts-Martial (1946–1949) (identified in text)

This appendix is a list of all officers who served at temporary courts-martial and are mentioned in this text. Additionally, a short biographical sketch of one of the most important judges, then Major L. F. de Groot, who sat on the tribunal in Batavia, is included.

Amboina (Ceram)

Damen, B.	Lieutenant Colonel
Gaspersz, G. S.	Captain
Haak, E.	First Lieutenant
Loon, H. P. J. M. van	First Lieutenant, later Captain
Ridder, W.	First Lieutenant
Scheddebeurs, C. M.	Captain
Stöcker, F. P.	Major

Balikpapan (East Borneo)

Paardekooper, J. L.	Major
Eyk, B. van	Captain
Meeteren, O. van	First Lieutenant

Bandjermasin (South Borneo)

Bodeman, P.	First Lieutenant
Rijckmans, E.	Major
Wiebols, H. F.	First Lieutenant

Batavia (Java)

Bael, J. C. P.	Captain
Bodeman, P.	First Lieutenant
Campen, C.	Captain
Doornweerd, Th. L.	Captain
Groot, Levinus F. de	Major, later Lieutenant Colonel
Guerts, W.	First Lieutenant
Hartman, J. F.	Major, British Army
Have, J. te	First Lieutenant
Peter, J. H.	Lieutenant Colonel, later Colonel
Rijckmans, E.	Captain, later Major
Rivière, J. la	Lieutenant Colonel
Roosegaarde-Bisschop, R.	First Lieutenant
Schwantje, J. A.	First Lieutenant
Schwaab, M. L.	Lieutenant Colonel
Starp, J. G. H. van der	First Lieutenant, later Captain, Major
Steenbruggen, L. G. R.	Captain
Theys, A. J. A.	Captain
Tiddens, J. P.	Major
Vijver, K. L. H. M.	Lieutenant Colonel
Wiebols, H. F.	First Lieutenant

Hollandia (New Guinea)

Blonk, H. P.	Captain
Bogaard, A. Uyt den	First Lieutenant
Westerndorp, J. H. van	First Lieutenant

Macassar (South Celebes)

Mappoedji, Abdullah daeng	Captain
Claproth, R.	Captain
Struyenkamp, J. A.	Captain
Vellenga, N. M.	Lieutenant Colonel

Medan (Sumatra)

Eskens, J. M. F.	Lieutenant Colonel
Hengel, A. C. van	Captain
Meinesz, J. T.	First Lieutenant
Perdijk Rugebregt, F. E.	Captain
Schrijver, W. P.	Captain
Thomas, W. P.	Major
Vermelen, H. C. A.	Major
Wijk, H. J. C. van	Captain
Zondag, E.	First Lieutenant

Morotai

Bont, F. M. B. de	First Lieutenant
Reemer, F. J.	First Lieutenant
Ridder, W.	First Lieutenant
Schagen, C.	First Lieutenant
Vermeulen, D.	Captain

Pontianak (West Borneo)

Bohm, A. H.	Captain
Essel, C. van	Captain, later Major
Lim, H. O.	First Lieutenant
Martens, C. A.	Captain
Sinnecker, F. M.	Second Lieutenant

Timor Kupang

Bos, F. H.	Ensign, Royal Dutch Navy
Damen, B.	Lieutenant Colonel
Schroder, G. H. H.	Captain

Biographical sketch: Levinus Franciscus de Groot (1903–1991)

Major Levinus Franciscus de Groot (1903–1991) was arguably the most important judge to sit on a war crimes tribunal in the Netherlands East Indies (NEI). He was first a member, and later the president, of the temporary court-martial in Batavia, the most important of the war crimes tribunals. He participated in a number of high profile prosecutions, including the trials of Generals Imamura, Maruyama, and Okazaki. Finally, de Groot wrote a lengthy two-part monograph about the war crimes process that is the only in-depth examination of the event written by a participant.

Born in Santpoort in the Netherlands, on June 26, 1903, de Groot graduated from the Gymnasium in Haarlem, studied law at the University of Leiden, and received his doctorate in 1930. He sailed for the NEI in August and, the following year, received a second doctorate in Indies law.

From 1931 to 1941, de Groot served in a variety of legal positions in the NEI's Department of Justice. On December 10, 1941, after the Japanese attack on Pearl Harbor, he was mobilized as a Reserve Captain (Infantry). After being taken prisoner by the Japanese in March 1942, de Groot was a prisoner of war (POW) on Java until the Japanese capitulation in 1945.

After being demobilized in March 1946, de Groot was appointed as a civilian judge (Dutch: *Landrechter*) in Bandung. In September, however, he returned to the Netherlands for rest and recuperation. De Groot missed the Indies and, in March 1947, returned to the islands, where he took up an appointment as a member of the temporary court-martial sitting in Batavia.

With the birth of the Republic of Indonesia imminent, de Groot returned to the Netherlands in early December 1949. In April 1951, he accepted an appointment as a major in the Military Judicial Service, Royal Dutch Army. He was promoted to lieutenant colonel the following year. After serving in a variety of positions in the Netherlands, Lieutenant Colonel de Groot accepted an appointment as the President, Court of Justice, Netherlands New Guinea, based in Hollandia.

De Groot returned to the Netherlands in October 1962, and resumed working with the Military Judicial Service until retiring in November 1963. In retirement, he worked as an advisor for a Dutch insurance company. De Groot also was an avid waterskier and, in retirement, was the president of the Dutch Waterskiing Organization (Dutch: *Nederlandse Waterski Bond*) for many years.

De Groot's *Berechting Japanse oorlogsmisdadigers in Nederlands Indië, 1946 to 1949: Temporaire Krijgsraden Batavia* (*Judging Japanese War Criminals in the Netherlands East Indies, 1946–1949: Temporary Courts-Martial, Batavia*) was published in 1990, a year before his death on November 14, 1991.

Selected Bibliography

GOVERNMENT DOCUMENTS

Hague Convention No. IV Respecting the Laws and Customs of War on Land, 1907.

Geneva Convention Relative to the Treatment of Prisoners of War, 1929.

Geneva Convention for the Amelioration of the Condition of the Wounded and Sick of Armies in the Field, 1929.

International Military Tribunal, Charter, Trial of the major war criminals before the International Military Tribunal, "The Blue Series," 42 vols. (Nuremberg, International Military Tribunal, 1947–1949) vol. 1.

International Military Tribunal for the Far East, *The Criminal Conspiracy in the Japanese War Crimes Trials* (War Department 1946).

International Military Tribunal for the Far East, *The Tokyo Major War Crimes Trial*, 124 vols. (Edwin Mellen Press 1998).

Netherlands East Indies, *Staatsblad van Nederlandsch-Indië 1946*, No. 44, Definition of War Crimes Decree.

Netherlands East Indies, *Staatsblad van Nederlandsch-Indië 1946*, No. 45, War Crimes Penal Law Decree (Dutch: *Strafrecht Oorlogsmisdrijven*).

Netherlands East Indies, *Staatsblad van Nederlandsch-Indië 1946*, No. 46, Legal Competence in Respect of War Crimes Decree.

Netherlands East Indies, *Staatsblad van Nederlandsch-Indië 1946*, No. 47, War Crimes Penal Procedure Decree (Dutch: *Rechtspleging Oorlogsmisdrijven*).

Rome Statute of the International Criminal Court, treaties.un.org.

United Nations War Crimes Commission, *History of the United Nations War Crimes Commission and the Development of the Laws of War* (His Majesty's Stationery Office 1948).

United Nations War Crimes Commission, *Law Reports of Trials of War Criminals*, vols. I–XVI (His Majesty's Stationery Office 1947–1949).

United States Army, General Headquarters, Supreme Commander for the Allied Powers, Government Section, Memorandum for the Record, *The Case of General Yamashita* (November 22, 1949).

United States War Department, Field Manual 27-10, *Rules of Land Warfare* (War Department, October 1, 1940).

United States War Department, Field Manual 27-10, *Rules of Land Warfare* (Change 1, November 15, 1944).

United States Department of the Army, Field Manual 27-10, *Rules of Land Warfare* (Department of the Army 1956).

Wal, S. L. van der, *Officiële Bescheiden Betreffende De Nederlands-Indonesische Betrekkingen, 1945–1950*, vols. I–XX (Martinus Nijhoff 1971).

Whitney, Courtney, *The Case of General Yamashita: A Memorandum* (War Department 1946).

LAW CASES AND DECISIONS (OTHER THAN NETHERLANDS EAST INDIES TEMPORARY COURTS-MARTIAL (SEE APPENDIX A))

Akayesu, Prosecutor v., International Criminal Tribunal Rwanda-96-4-T (September 2, 1998).

Baba, Prosecutor v. Masao, Australian Military Court, Rabaul, May 28–June 2, 1947, U.N. War Crimes Commission, *Law Reports of Trials of War Criminals*, vol. 11, Case No. 60 (His Majesty's Stationery Office 1949) 56–61.

Bemba, Prosecutor v. Jean-Pierre, Case No. ICC-01/05—1/08 (March 21, 2016).

Delalić (aka Čelebići), Prosecutor v., International Criminal Tribunal for Former Yugoslavia-96-21-T (November 16, 1998).

Hamdan, Salim Ahmed v. Rumsfeld et al., 548 United States 557 (2006).

Halilović, Prosecutor v., IT-01-48-T (November 16, 2005).

Kvočka, Prosecutor v. Miroslav, Case No. IT-98-30/1-T (November 2, 2001).

Kunarac, Prosecutor v., et al., Case No. IT-96-23 & 23/1-A-T (February 22, 2001).

Leeb von, United States v., XI T.W.C. Before the Nuremberg Military Tribunals under Control Council Law No. 10 (Government Printing Office 1950).

Quirin, Ex parte, 317 United States 1 (1942).

Tadić, Prosecutor v., IT-94-1-A Appeals Chamber Judgment (July 15, 1999).

Yamashita, In re, 327 United States 1 (1946).

Yamashita, Trial of General Tomoyuki, Case No. 21, *Law Reports of Trials of War Criminals*, vol. IV (His Majesty's Stationery Office 1948) 1.

BOOKS

Anderson, Benedict R., *Java in a Time of Revolution: Occupation and Resistance* (Cornell University Press 1972).

Appleman, John A., *Military Tribunals and International Crimes* (Greenwood Press 1971).

Aziz, M. A., *Japan's Colonialism and Indonesia* (Martinus Nijhoff 1955).

Baird, J. Kevin and Sangkot Marzuki, *War Crimes in Japan-Occupied Indonesia: A Case of Murder by Medicine* (Potomac Books 2015).

Barenblatt, Daniel, *A Plague upon Humanity: The Hidden History of Japan's Biological Warfare Program* (Harper Perennial 2005).

Benesch, Oleg, *Inventing the Way of the Samurai* (Oxford University Press 2014).

Bergerud, Eric, *Touched with Fire: The Land War in the South Pacific* (Penguin Books 1996).

Berry, William A., *Prisoner of the Rising Sun* (University of Oklahoma Press 1993).

Brackman, Arnold C., *The Other Nuremberg* (William Morrow & Co. 1987).

Chang, Iris, *The Rape of Nanking: The Forgotten Holocaust of World War II* (Basic Books 1997).

Davis, Gavan, *Prisoners of the Japanese* (William Morrow 1994).

Dinstein, Yoram, *The Conduct of Hostilities under the Law of International Armed Conflict* (Cambridge University Press 2004).

Drea, Edward *et al.*, *Researching Japanese War Crimes Records* (National Archives and Records Administration 2006).

Dower, John W., *Embracing Defeat: Japan in the Wake of World War II* (W.W. Norton 1999).

Dower, John W., *War without Mercy: Race and Power in the Pacific War* (Pantheon Books 1986).

Edgerton, Robert, *Warriors of the Rising Son* (W.W. Norton 1997).

Fortier, Malcolm V., *The Life of a P.O.W. Under the Japanese: In Caricature* (C.W. Hill 1946).

Fyans, Peter, *Captivity, Slavery, and Survival as a Far East POW* (Pen & Sword Books 2012).
Friend, Theodore, *The Blue Eyed Enemy: Japan against the West in Java and Luzon, 1942–1945* (Princeton University Press 1988).
Green, Leslie C., *Essays on the Modern Law of War* (2nd edn., Transnational 1999).
Greene, Joshua M., *Justice at Dachau: The Trials of an American Prosecutor* (American Bar Association/Ankerwycke 2017).
Groot, Levinus F. de, *Berechting Japanse Orloogsmisdadigers in Nederlands-Indie, 1946–1949* (Art & Research 1990 (privately published)).
Harries, Meirion and Susie Harries, *Soldiers of the Sun: The Rise and Fall of the Imperial Japanese Army* (Random House 1994).
Heller K. J., *The Nuremberg Military Tribunals and the Origins of International Criminal Law* (Oxford University Press 2011).
Hering, Bob, *Soekarno, Founding Father of Indonesia: A Biography, 1901–1945* (KITLV Press 2002).
Hicks, George, *The Comfort Women* (Norton & Co. 1995).
Higuchi, Wakako, *The Japanese Administration of Guam, 1941–1944* (McFarland & Co., Inc. Publishers 2013).
Hirschfeld, Gerhard, *Nazi Rule and Dutch Collaboration* (Berg 1988).
Holland, Thomas E., *The Law of War on Land* (Clarendon Press 1908).
Hotta, Eri, *Japan 1941: Countdown to Infamy* (Knopf 2013).
Hovinga, Henk, *The Sumatra Railroad: Final Destination Pakan Baroe, 1943–1945* (KITLV Press 2010).
Jansen, L. F., *In Deze Halve Gevangenis: Dagboek* (Van Wijnen 1988).
Jong, Louis de (with an Introduction by Jeroen Kemperman), *The Collapse of a Colonial Society: The Dutch in Indonesia during the Second World War* (KITLV Press 2002).
Keith, Agnes, *Three Came Home* (Hippocrene Books 1948, 1985).
Kemperman, Jeroen, *De Japanse Bezetting in Dagboeken: Tjideng* (Bert Bakker 2002).
Kerr, E. Bartlett, *Surrender and Survival: The Experience of American POWS in the Pacific, 1941–1945* (William Morrow and Co. 1985).
Kushner, Barak, *Men to Devils, Devils to Men: Japanese War Crimes and Chinese Justice* (Harvard University Press 2015).
Kushner, Barak and Sherzod Muminov, *The Dismantling of Japan's Empire in East Asia* (Routledge 2017).
Levie, Howard S., *Terrorism in War: The Law of War Crimes* (Oceana Publications 1993).
Limpach, Rémy, *De brandende kampongs van Generaal Spoor* (Boom 2016).
Linton, Suzannah (ed.), *Hong Kong's War Crimes Trials* (Oxford University Press 2013).
MacArthur, Brian, *Surviving the Sword: Prisoners of the Japanese in the Far East, 1942–1945* (Random House 2005).
McMahon, Robert J., *Colonialism and Cold War: The United States and the Struggle for Indonesian Independence, 1945–1949* (Cornell University Press 1981).
McMillan, R., *The British Occupation of Indonesia 1945–1946: Britain, The Netherlands and the Indonesian Revolution* (Routledge 2005).
Mitter, Rana, *Forgotten Ally: China's World War II, 1937–1945* (Houghton Mifflin Harcourt 2013).
Mullins, Claud, *The Leipzig Trials* (Witherby 1921).
Nederlands Instituut voor Oorlogsdocumentatie (Netherlands Institute for War Documentation), *Kampen in Nederlands-Indië 1942–1948* (NIOD 2010)
Piccigallo, Philip R., *The Japanese on Trial: Allied War Crimes Operations in the East, 1945–1951* (University of Texas Press 1977).

Pictet, Jean S. (ed.), *Commentary on the Geneva Convention relative to the Treatment of Prisoners of War* (International Committee of the Red Cross 1960).

Poelgeest, L. van, *Japanse Besognes: Nederland en Japan, 1945–1975* (SDU 1999).

Post, Peter and Elly Touwen-Bouwsma (eds.), *Japan, Indonesia and the War: Myths and Realities* (KITLV Press 1997).

Post, Peter *et al.* (eds.), *The Encyclopedia of Indonesia in the Pacific War* (Brill 2010).

Reel, A. Frank, *The Case of General Yamashita* (Octagon Books 1971).

Rees, Laurence, *Horror in the East: Japan and the Atrocities of World War II* (Da Capo Press 2002).

Remmelink, W. G. J., (ed. and trans.), *The Invasion of the Dutch East Indies* (Leiden University Press 2015).

Roberts, Adam and Richard Guelff, *Documents on the Laws of War* (3rd edn., Oxford University Press 2002).

Röling, B. V. A. and Antoni Cassese, *The Tokyo Trial and Beyond: Reflections of a Peacemonger* (Cambridge University Press 1993).

Russell, Edward F., *The Knights of Bushido: A Short History of Japanese War Crimes* (Greenhill Books 2002).

Ryan, Allan H., *Yamashita's Ghost* (University Press of Kansas 2012).

Sinninghe Damste, J. S., *Advocaat-Soldaat: Oorlogsherinneringen* (Betaafsche Leeuw 1999).

Sissons, D. C. S., *The Australian War Crimes Trials and Investigations 1942–1951* (Australian War Memorial 2006).

Solis, Gary D., *The Law of Armed Conflict* (2nd edn., Cambridge University Press 2016).

Sunoo, Harold Hakwon, *Japanese Militarism* (Nelson Hall 1975).

Tanaka, Yuki, *Hidden Horrors: Japanese War Crimes in World War II* (Westview Press 1997).

Tanaka, Yuki, *Japan's Comfort Women: Sexual Slavery and Prostitution in World War II and the U.S. Occupation* (Routledge 2002).

Toland, John, *The Rising Sun* (Random House 1970).

Totani, Yuma, *Justice in Asia and the Pacific Region 1945–1952* (Cambridge University Press 2015).

Totani, Yuma, *The Tokyo War Crimes Trial* (Harvard University Press 2008).

Touwen-Bouwsma, Elly and Petra Groen (eds.), *Tussen Banzai en Bersiap: De Afwikkeling van de Tweede Wereldoorlog in Nederlands-Indië* (SDU 1996).

Tromp, Sheri G. (ed.), *Four Years Till Tomorrow: Despair and Hope in Wartime Dutch East Indies* (Vanderheide 1999).

Wigmore, Lionel, *The Japanese Thrust* (Australia in the War of 1939–1945, Vol. IV) (Australian War Memorial 1957).

Wood, James B., *Japanese Military Strategy in the Pacific War* (Rowan & Littlefield 2007).

Yong, Mun C., *H.J. van Mook and Indonesian Independence* (Martinus Nijhoff 1982).

Zwinkels, Esther, *Het Overakker-complot* (Spectrum 2011).

BOOK CHAPTERS

Cryer, Robert, "Then and Now: Command Responsibility, the Tokyo Tribunal and Modern International Criminal Law," in Kristen Sellers (ed.), *Trials for International Crimes in Asia* (Cambridge University Press 2016) 55–74.

Hovinga, Henk, "End of a Drama: The Reception and Repatriation of *Rōmusha* after the Japanese Capitulation," in Paul Kratoska (ed.), *Asian Labor in the Wartime Japanese Empire* (Singapore University Press 2006) 213–34.

La Forte, Robert S., "Resistance in Japanese Prison Camps during World War II," in Vance R. Skarstedt (ed.), *Prisoners of War: The American Experience* (Imprint Publications 2004) 41–52.

Limpach, Rémy, "Business as Usual: Dutch Mass Violence in the Indonesian War of Independence, 1945–49," in Bart Luttikhuis and A. Dirk Moses (eds.), *Colonial Counterinsurgency and Mass Violence* (Routledge 2014) 64–90.

Linton, Suzannah, "War Crimes," in Suzannah Linton (ed.), *Hong Kong's War Crimes Trials* (Oxford University Press 2013) 95–136.

Poelgeest, Bart van, "Figuranten op het Indische toneel: De Japaners in Nederlands-Indië 1946–1949," in Elly Touwen-Bouwsma and Petra Groen (eds.), *Tussen Banzai en Bersiap: De Afwikkeling van de Tweede Wereldoorlog in Nederlands-Indië* (SDU 1996) 95–107.

Schouten, Lisette, "Colonial Justice in the Netherlands Indies," in Kirsten Sellars (ed.), *Trials for International Crimes in Asia* (Cambridge University Press 2016) 75–99.

Zahar, Alexander, "Trial Procedure at the British Military Courts, Hong Kong, 1946–1948," in Suzannah Linton (ed.), *Hong Kong's War Crimes Trials* (Oxford University Press 2013) 13–70.

ARTICLES

Adachi, Sumio, "Unprepared Regrettable Events: A Brief History of Japanese Practices on the Treatment of Allied War Victims during the Second World War," 45 *Japanese National Defense Academy Bulletin* (September 1982) 257–332.

Bassiouni, M. Cherif, "The United Nations Commission of Experts Established Pursuant to Security Council Resolution 780 (1992)," 88-4 *American Journal of International Law* (October 1994) 784–805.

Brants, Chrisje, "Complicated Legacies of Justice: The Netherlands and World War II," 13 *Journal of International Criminal Justice* (September 2015) 763–81.

Brocades-Zaalburg, T., "The Civil and Military Dimensions of Dutch Counter-Insurgency on Java, 1947–49," 1 *British Journal for Military History* (February 2015) 67–83.

Cribb, Robert, "Avoiding Clemency: The Trial and Transfer of Japanese War Criminals in Indonesia, 1946–1949," 31-2 *Japanese Studies* (September 2011) 151–70.

Herik, Larissa van den, "Addressing 'Colonial Crimes' through Reparations?", 10 *Journal of International Criminal Justice* (2012) 693–705.

Levie, Howard S., "Command Responsibility," 8 *Journal of Legal Studies* (1997–1998) 1–18.

Levie, Howard S., "The Employment of Prisoners of War," 57 *American Journal of International Law* (1963) 318–53.

Levie, Howard S., "The Nature and Scope of the Armistice Agreement," 50 *American Journal of International Law* (1956) 880–906.

Linton, Suzannah, "Rediscovering the War Crimes Trials in Hong Kong, 1946–48," 13 *Melbourne Journal of International Law* (2012) 1–65.

Matheson, Michael J., and David Scheffer, "The Creation of the Tribunals," 110 *American Journal of International Law* (April 2016) 173–90.

Meloni, Chantal, "Command Responsibility," 5-3 *Journal of International Criminal Justice* (July 2007) 619, 628.

Mishra, Pankaj, "Land and Blood: The Origins of the Second World War in Asia," *New Yorker* (November 25, 2013) 121–6.

Parks, William H., "Command Responsibility for War Crimes," 62 *Military Law Review* (1973) 1–66.

Pompe, Bas, "The Effects of the Japanese Administration on the Judiciary in Indonesia," 152-4 *Bijdragen tot de Taal-, Land- en Volkenkunde* (1996) 573–85.

Remmelink, W. G. J., "The Emergence of the New Situation: The Japanese Army on Java after the Surrender," *Militarie Spectator: Tijdschrift voor het Nederlandse Leger* (February 1978) 49–66.

Index